SOVIET WOMEN WRITING

Soviet Women Writing

Fifteen Short Stories

Introduction by I. Grekova

Abbeville Press · Publishers
New York · London · Paris

Editor: Jacqueline Decter
Compiler: Elena I. Kalina
Designer: Molly Shields
Copy Chief: Robin James
Production Manager: Dana Cole

First edition
Library of Congress Cataloging-in-Publication Data
Soviet women writing : 15 short stories / introduction by I. Grekova.
    p.   cm.
  English translation of Russian short stories.
  ISBN 0-89659-882-9
  1. Short stories, Russian—Translations into English. 2. Short stories,
Soviet—Translations into English. 3. Short stories, English—Translations
from foreign languages. 4. Women—Soviet Union—Fiction. 5. Soviet
fiction—Women authors. 6. Russian fiction—Women authors.
I. Grekova, I.
PG3286.S6 1990
891.73'01089287—dc20   90-40581
                                          CIP

Contents

LIST OF ILLUSTRATIONS

Three Soviet artists were specially commissioned to illustrate this volume. The stories they have illustrated and the pages on which the illustrations appear are given below.

INTRODUCTION

I. GREKOVA

Before you is a collection of stories by Soviet women writers. Such a volume is by no means uncommon these days; collections of women's writing are published in many countries, and there even are publishers who specialize in "women's literature." In my country, however, we have neither. Why? I'll try to explain.

The main reason, to my mind, is that women in the Soviet Union have long enjoyed equal rights with men. We are not discriminated against economically or socially, so there is no question of any "struggle for equal rights." Equality has, to all intents and purposes, been achieved, and it is all we can do to cope with the rights we already have!

Most able-bodied women in my country work in the manufacturing, service, or cultural spheres. In fact, some professions (schoolteachers, doctors, nurses) have virtually been "feminized," a tendency that is even causing some alarm. There are more women with advanced academic degrees than men. There are no occupations from which women are barred, with the exception, perhaps, of boxing and weight lifting. But even here, the restrictions are on the way out (hardly a welcome development; I, for one, shudder at the thought of a woman superheavyweight). Soviet women receive equal pay for equal work. Every woman is in principle (if not in practice) at liberty to choose any profession and any career. We have gotten used to our equality and have come to take it for granted. There is probably no other country in the world that boasts such a long tradition of women's liberation.

.

9

This is not to say that our lives are free of difficulties and of peculiarly feminine problems. There *are* problems, and they stem from the fact that while we have been granted equal rights with men, we have not been relieved of traditionally feminine duties. Bearing and raising children, running the house, and taking care of a host of time-consuming daily chores are still the woman's responsibility. Much is being done in my country to make things easier for women: The length of paid maternity leave has been increased; mothers can extend their leave without pay but without losing their job; maternity allowances have been raised; and the network of child-care facilities is expanding (though not as rapidly as we would like). And yet the fact remains that the woman has a much harder time than the man who works by her side. The man usually carries one load (his job), while the woman carries three (her job, her children, her home). The Russian language has a special word to describe the daily cares that are such a heavy burden for women. The word is *byt*, and it is variously translated as "everyday life," "daily chores," and "consumer services," but none of these translations conveys the emotional coloring of the Russian. I think that the word *byt* should be adopted into English just like the words "intelligentsia," "sputnik," and, most recently, "glasnost."

For Soviet women, the notion of *byt* encompasses a great many things, including standing in lines, lugging heavy bags of food, riding in overcrowded buses and subways, taking care of children, cooking, doing the dishes, cleaning the house, and doing the laundry. Well-run consumer services would go a long way toward relieving women of many of these chores. But it is no secret that our service sector still leaves a lot to be desired and is unable to free women from a lot of minor, exhausting, and stupefying chores. This burden, combined with work—which alone demands a woman's full output—is almost unendurable (as I know from my own experience, being a mother of three children and a grandmother of four). And yet few Soviet women would give up work and devote themselves entirely to their homes and children. It is not only a matter of earning money (although this is often an important consideration); by giving up work, a woman stands to lose a vital link with society, a sense of her place in life, and the opportunity to take an active part in the life of her country.

Traditionally, the position of a nonworking woman—a housewife—has been looked down upon. I think this is unfair; housework is by no means easier, or less useful to society, than any other kind of work, and it is high time we gave the hardworking housewife and mother her due. But as things now stand, the term *job* refers only to paid employment, not to a housewife's work.

The mentality of our working women is shaped by the fact that they are overloaded and still manage to cope with their many domestic responsibilities. In many families, the wife, not the husband, is head of the household. There is often talk, and not without justification, of a "matriarchal age" in our society. Women tend to get carried away by their leadership roles and begin to acquire the manners and behavior of men; their male partners, in contrast, become feminized. The henpecked husband often rebels and leaves the family.

Everything that I have said about the position of women in the Soviet Union fully applies to women writers. They are not discriminated against in any way. Each works as much and as well as her ability, talent, and free time allow. Free time, however, is a commodity in catastrophically short supply for most women. The favorable changes now taking place in this country will hopefully alleviate the woman's plight.

How many women writers are there in the Soviet Union? There are comparatively few (women account for about one-tenth the membership of the Soviet Writers Union). But the same is true of other creative occupations. Among composers, architects, and stage and film directors, for instance, women are vastly outnumbered by men. Most high administrative posts are also held by men.

I have no statistics handy and, not being a sociologist, it is not for me to explain the reasons for this state of affairs. But that's the way it is, and not only in my country, I suspect. Incidentally, the predominance of men in journalism and literary and art criticism is not as pronounced as it is in literature. A significant portion of newspaper and magazine writing is done by women.

A woman has about the same chance as a man to get her work into print. Men and women alike have to wait an exceedingly long time before they are considered "mature" writers, and they gripe that their work is not being published. We do not have special publishing houses for women, and I don't think there is any need for them. Perhaps my judgment in this instance is influenced by the fact that my main occupation is science. Wouldn't it be strange if science were divided into "male" and "female"?

It seems to me that there are no grounds for dividing literature on a sexual basis either. We can talk of "good" or "bad" literature, but not of "male" and "female" literature. Women writers are just as likely to produce good work as their male colleagues.

Nor do I think there are specifically "feminine" themes in literature. There are just certain areas in which women are more competent than men, and vice versa. Without a doubt, only women can write knowledgeably about the hardships of a woman's daily life and chores, about the gains and losses of "emancipation" (as Natalia Baranskaya did in her highly successful story "A Week Like Any Other"). It seems to me that a woman can write about children, especially young children, with more color, warmth, and insight than men. One of the best books about childhood I know is *Seryozha* by the late Vera Panova. She devoted a good deal of her writing to women—their joys, sorrows, and cares, and the inevitable *byt*. But our women writers do not confine themselves to the subject of family and everyday life. Their experience ranges widely, and so do the themes of their works. Let me mention just a few names.

Natalia Ilina, one of the most notable satirists in the country (a rare gift in a woman), has recently taken to writing autobiographical prose. More than just reminiscences, it is a blend of memoirs, journalism, vignettes, and philosophical writing, and it reflects her unusual life story: She left the country with her parents as a child and experienced all the hardships of life in emigration. She returned to the Soviet Union in 1948 and became a major writer through talent and hard work. Among the people she reminisces about are the poet Anna Akhmatova, the acress Ekaterina Kornakova, the singer Alexander Vertinsky, the linguist Alexander Reformatsky, and the writers Kornei Chukovsky and Yuri Trifonov.

The works of Lidia Ginzburg display a rare artistry, profundity, and incisiveness. A distinguished literary scholar, in recent years she has turned to writing fiction. In my opinion, Lidia Ginzburg is the only Soviet writer who is carrying on the tradition of Alexander Herzen, the eminent nineteenth-century writer and thinker whose book *My Past and Thoughts* is an unsurpassed blend of journalistic, lyrical, and philosophical prose. Of her fiction I would like to single out the autobiographical essay "The Siege of Leningrad: Notes of a Survivor," excerpts of which are included in this collection. Drawing on her own experience, she records the impressions of a person who lived through the unspeakable horrors of the 900-day siege of Leningrad during World War II.

Viktoria Tokareva is known for the imaginative wit and natural humor of her writing. In addition to stories, she writes screenplays, many of which have been made into successful films.

Our women writers do not shy away from the traditionally "male" theme of war. A noteworthy example is Svetlana Aleksievich's *War Is Not a Woman's*

Job. Too young to have experienced the war herself, she painstakingly collected and edited the testimony of women who did live through it and became imbued with the pathos and tragedy of that unforgettable time.

Nina Katerli of Leningrad has an original semifantastic style. Her stories often combine "animated technology" with elements of the fairy tale.

No account of Soviet women's fiction would be complete without mentioning the original, biting talent of Lyudmila Petrushevskaya, a prose writer and playwright, whose plays have been running successfully in many theaters all across the Soviet Union. There was a time when Petrushevskaya was subjected to attack for her works' alleged "earthiness" and "mud-slinging." But new times and mores have had a favorable impact on her career.

A notable figure among our women writers is Tatyana Tolstaya. The bearer of so legendary a literary name, she has a lot to live up to. In addition to the great Leo Tolstoy, there have been two other major writers by that name: the poet and playwright Alexei Konstantinovich Tolstoy and Tatyana's grandfather, the prose writer Alexei Nikolaevich Tolstoy. Tolstaya has certainly been a credit to the name. A relative newcomer to the literary scene, her work immediately attracted attention and has provoked much comment and controversy. Some praise her to the skies, others reject her work, but even the latter cannot deny her vibrant, unique talent. She writes about ordinary, unexceptional, often miserable people, but the drabness of their lives is miraculously transformed through her pen. Her language is highly original, at once elegant and casual, replete with contemporary slang (which is sure to give headaches to her translator).

This cursory survey leaves out a lot of other interesting women writers in the Soviet Union today. Not all of them write in Russian; some come from the non-Russian republics of the U.S.S.R. (Vytautė Žilinskaitė comes from Lithuania, Mari Saat from Estonia, to mention two who are included in this collection).

Typically, many of our women writers have other professions. Nina Katerli, for example, is an engineer (which accounts for the "technological bent" of her fantasies). As I've already mentioned, Lidia Ginzburg is one of the most highly regarded literary historians and theorists in the country, and her prose is marked by scholarly rigor and penetrating x-ray-like analysis.

At the risk of appearing immodest, I'll say a few words about myself. My main calling is science and I am a college professor. I began writing fiction quite early, but was first published rather late. My real name is Elena Sergeyevna Ventsel. This is the name under which I publish my scientific papers, manuals, and books on the theory of probability, operations research, and other areas of applied mathematics. I. Grekova is my pen name. (The "I" does not stand for Irina, as some people believe. *Igrek* is the Russian term for the Latin letter "Y," often used in mathematics to denote an unknown quantity). Naturally, situations and issues involving science figure prominently in my fiction. For example, my story "No Smiles" concerns a woman who is hounded for her unorthodox scientific views (such baiting was not uncommon in the Soviet scientific community fifteen or twenty years ago). It is perhaps significant that the story was written in 1970 but first appeared in print only in 1986 (until that time not a single publishing house would touch it).

In conclusion, I would like to address a few friendly words to the American reader. In spite of all the differences in our political systems, ways of life, and values, the people of the United States and the Soviet Union share much in common. American women, like Soviet women, fall in love, marry, divorce, adore their children, worry about the future, and take part in community life to the best of their abilities. Today, as never before, it is important for us to understand each other, to find common ground, and to learn more about each other. Hopefully, this collection of short stories by Soviet women will attract interest in your country, and American men and women will not only learn something new about our country but will also be able to identify with some of our problems, feelings, cares, and aspirations.

What Are Women Made Of?

Zoya Boguslavskaya

Well, women, what are we made of? How would future generations judge us if they had only literature to go by? How have we been portrayed by writers, filmmakers, and the mass media in the second half of the twentieth century? If we are honest, we must admit that literature and art have pretty well limited the image of today's Soviet woman.

Let's start by overturning the old thinking and see how far representatives of the "weaker sex" have advanced, besides district presidiums, high-level city affairs, peace forums, couture runways, and the service industries. For a moment, let's not concern ourselves with articles celebrating International Woman's Day, which duly note the contributions of women during World War II and in industry and examine their record-breaking achievements in the most diverse fields. Even the first woman in space was our countrywoman. Instead, let's take a closer look at the woman "on the street."

We see that the glorified "mothers of the race" have taken many "privileges" from men that were never their inalienable rights. They wear pants, they smoke, they swear—they even make love by a "bill of fare," as the author of a publication on prostitution and solicitation expressively put it. Our women, alas, have their own "drunk tank," they have abandoned infants, and they have even been known to lead gangs of thieves. Not all that long ago society tried to protect women and children when husbands ran out on their alimony payments; today men are clamoring for protection against women's aggressiveness. Today significant numbers of young women have no desire to marry and cater to the demands of men. These women treat the men in their lives simply as partners in the propagation of the race. Or simply as partners.

This discordant note in women's lives has been only partially reflected in art. A flood of movies has come out in recent decades by such women directors as Larisa Shepitko, Tatyana Liosnova, Lana Gogoberidze, Dinora Asanovoa, Kira Muratova, as have plays by Lyudmila Petrushevskaya, Lyudmila Razumovskaya, Svetlana Aleksievich, Alla Sokolova, and others. These works have revealed some of the destructive processes in women's lives—processes that demand serious sociological and scholarly research.

In the film *Several Interviews on Personal Subjects,* one of the heroines tells a woman correspondent, "I haven't gone crazy cleaning up after him or doing his laundry. I'm free to do what I want. I have a child. I'm happy. Get married? Why should I put a yoke around my neck?"

Where does this way of thinking come from?

One tendency has been defined by the mass media more clearly than by literature or art: Women don't want only the legislated equality of rights in society, they want equality in the family. However, although we have recognized this phenomenon, we have made few changes in the social conditions for spouses. And reality does not let spouses be equals. No one has considered the price women pay for the right to act like men. Is there any way to rectify this situation without destroying the conventional family of the past, in which the husband was usually head of the household? In English-speaking countries women protest that the language itself has perpetuated this situation throughout history: "Man" means both man and human, but makes no reference to women. Isn't this like our joke that woman is man's best friend?

Today newspaper and magazine columnists decry the excessive burdens heaped on our women. According to statistics, each week men have at least ten more hours than women for relaxation, leisure, reading, and so on. What happens to those hours in women's lives? Need we ask? Those same obdurate figures show that women are better educated and more cultured than men today. How do they manage this? At what price?

The psychologist Maya Dukarevich asserts that women lead stressful lives because they do not communicate enough. So the weakest aspect of the weaker sex is not having anyone to talk with! This doesn't mean simply talking at work, in line, or on public transportation, but giving women the chance to talk about their own lives, about their concerns, about themselves; to talk about the daily upsets, humiliations, and frustrations that strain their nerves; to talk about—paradoxically, what they sometimes have the least chance of doing—their good fortune, their success, the recognition of their achievements. Psychologists believe that the dearth of conditions for women to express themselves deforms and distorts their inner world most of all. What price do they pay for giving men the right to reveal their feelings; what price does society pay for women's internalized frustrations, their attempt to be interesting, important, supportive? This is an even more serious topic for sociological and psychological research. And how many more paradoxical secrets, social enigmas, and tragedies of today's women remain unstudied by our scientists, sociologists, and writers?

What do we know about women? About how they think and behave, about their pain, even the state of their health? Don't men too often wrongly interpret women's willingness to take on new responsibilities? The false optimism in the characterization of heroines (in the home and on the job, in predictions of their rosy future) has gradually created a population of art consumers with stereotyped images of women: the gracious hostess, mother of several children, marvelous wife; a woman able to do anything, always rested, well-dressed, smiling. These people do not want the truth. They are disturbed by any unusual, unpleasant situation that shatters their accustomed image of the gentler sex. These are the people who write bales of angry letters to the editors of newspapers, movie studios, and magazines. "Where did you ever see the kind of Soviet schoolchildren that were in *The Scarecrow*? That our girls could put a classmate through that kind of torture! . . ." someone wrote about one movie (directed by Rolan Bykov and written by Vladimir Zheleznikov). She personally had never seen any children like that. People like this don't believe what they haven't seen. Their inability to empathize, to identify with a person of another life experience or another way of thinking, has raised a soundproof wall of misunderstanding that makes it impossible for them to read or to attend the theater or the cinema. But inability is only half the problem; the real problem is "I don't want to know!" and "I don't care to know!" This resolute protection of one's own well-being has engendered profound indifference. We've gotten so accustomed to this indifference that we teach our children: "For God's sake, don't get involved! If someone is getting beaten up, don't butt in! Mind your own business and keep out of it."

Now we see more "tough women," and their numbers are multiplying. These women are ferocious and ruthless. They feel that they have paid a high price for the right to do what they want by not giving in to anyone on anything. Typically, this kind of woman talks back to vendors at the vegetable stand, in her office as head of a textile factory shop, in line at a telephone booth, in the subway. She thinks it demeans her to treat someone like a human being.

The director of a new, privately run couture firm is proud of the firm's unique line and the staff's polite manner with customers. But he complained to me, "The only problem is with the employees. . . ."

"What's the matter? Salaries aren't lower, are they?"

"Are you kidding?! Salaries are one-and-a-half to two times higher!"

"Then what's the problem?"

The director hesitated. "The problem is in their attitude toward the customers. Customers have to try the clothes on, after all. Sometimes several styles. The salespeople have to thank them for their purchase."

"So?!" I said in amazement.

"They say, 'Why should I bow and scrape and say "thank you" and "come again" to every piece of garbage that walks in? I'd rather take a cut in pay—who needs all those thank-yous!'" The director sighed. "I'll never understand why. . . ."

Why don't we know our women? And when we come across something unexpected in their behavior, why do we throw up our hands and then blame them?

There are many reasons. First, Russia has traditionally been a closed society in which any information about women, the family, or relations between the sexes has been regarded as "airing dirty linen." Second, there haven't been any reliable statistics about women (and some of the figures would horrify us today). Third, there's usually a smirk at the mere mention of the "women's question." "Oh, you feminists!" our serious men say dismissively whenever the subject is broached.

And we women support them! How we yearn to exist in that liberated universe where, as some chroniclers would have it, women easily achieved equality in all spheres long ago. This is why so many of our illusions, which are embodied in propagandistic stereotypes, prevent us from seeing reality as it is. And this is why our audiences are so unprepared for realistic depictions of women in all walks of life. The marvelous image of a woman leader created by Vera Maretskaya, or the prominent woman surgeon portrayed by Angelina Stepanova, just doesn't match the women at a dacha in Lyudmila Petrushevskaya's "Three Women in Blue" or the women in Nina Pavlova's "The Little Wagon," or the complicated lives of the heroines in works by Natalia Baranskaya, Irina Velimbovskaya, Maya Ganina, I. Grekova, Tatyana

Tolstaya, and others. Like people who are color-blind, we can't distinguish all the colors in the mosaic of life; we're conditioned to black and white.

When you think of how overburdened women are, you begin to ask a rather complicated question: Don't our women sometimes have too many rights? Do we still need some of them today? And isn't it time to trade some rights for others? After all, a study of the hidden causes for the failings in many aspects of women's lives is essential not just to let them become full participants in economic *perestroika* or to create incentives for new thinking and action, but surely also to bring back the well-balanced women our men and critics dream of so ardently. They are irritated by these unhappy, eternally preoccupied, completely overburdened workhorses, women whose husbands and even children have ceased to regard them as individuals.

But how can we get away from the destructive rhythms of the twentieth century, the dawn of postmodern civilization, the need for men to sacrifice all their time to the Moloch of automated society? We can't. So it is all the more important to change society's attitude toward women, to realize that to inhibit them is to cripple society. But remember: Nothing happens by itself.

Not long ago the American writer Alvin Toffler remarked sadly that when his wife was in school she was the only child in her class whose parents were divorced. Now their daughter is the only one in her class whose parents are not divorced. And this is in America, a country so observant of bourgeois propriety that a senator forfeited his chance to run for the presidency because he was suspected of marital infidelity!

But let's not try to predict the future society of this civilization and instead start to consider the opportunities we have now. For example, does it make sense to encourage so many women to enter traditionally male professions?

Not long ago I. Grekova, author of "Women's Hairdresser," *The Widow's Ship,* and other well-known stories and novels, a woman who successfully combines being a great writer and a mathematician (with a graduate degree in the technical sciences), spoke about "the abundance of women in technical institutes." She believes that "equality in this field would be a catastrophe, and we must not fight for it." Over many years she has observed that when women first pick up a new piece of equipment, they are afraid to take it apart and see how it works, just as someone who is not a surgeon would be afraid to cut into a patient's abdomen. Although I agree with this, I still think that today the main issue is not that it is unproductive for women to work in a number of male professions, but that there must be a qualitative redistribution of women's input into Soviet society. When we see women shoveling icy snowdrifts or pouring asphalt that is then pressed by a steamroller driven by a man, or when we see women unloading sacks of potatoes—it's a national disgrace!

The war's been over for nearly half a century, and there's no longer any need to prove that women are strong enough to lift fifty-kilogram wheelbarrows, or picks, or excavators. It has even been necessary to reconsider having women work on long-distance airplane flights. Studies show that stewardesses over the age of thirty-five often suffer kidney ailments if they don't drink water regularly during flights. Until recently, no one paid any attention to this, like so many other statistics: the growing rate of infant mortality due to the mother's habits, smoking among girls, alcoholism in young women. There is evidence that girls in our country start smoking at age nine or ten, and 60 percent of all high school girls smoke. And what about the high incidence of birth defects among children of mothers who smoke? Doctors believe that the reasons for all this are more social than medical, and that the main reason is the nature of women's jobs combined with too many responsibilities at home.

I think that the redistribution of professions goes both ways: Women have been hired to do physically strenuous male jobs while being pushed out of other professions where they had proved themselves brilliantly. At the same time, many men are taking up traditionally female jobs, becoming tailors, hairstylists, cosmetologists, and waiters.

What if we conduct a serious study of the stronger aspects of woman's nature—her psychology, her physiology, her way of thinking?

Let's take a field such as international journalism or diplomacy. Where are the Alexandra Kollontais and Larisa Reisners of today? For some reason, at the international press conferences that are now so often shown on television, we don't see the attractive faces of Soviet women either among the hosts of these programs or even among the reporters asking questions. Representatives of the weaker sex can be found only on the "other side." Our women writers are rarely a part of the international scene. Their voices are not heard at congresses, forums, symposiums, or round table discussions of artistic problems. How is the world to learn about how our women think, about their way of life, their culture?

The newspaper *L'Humanité* published an interesting article by Gerard Streif called "The Woman Enigma." After stating that Soviet women have undoubtedly surpassed men in many ways and play leading roles in public life, that the working class in the Soviet Union is more than half women, and that the process of feminization is inexorably seeping into the intelligentsia, he concludes that Soviet women live in a society that is entirely run by men, although women make up 73 percent of the teachers, 63 percent of the medical personnel, 40 percent of the scientists and researchers, and even comprise the majority in local government councils.

"We have heard that in your country women spend a lot of time standing in line in stores," Streif said in an interview with the writer Viktoria Tokareva. "They have to do the shopping for clothes and food as well as work, while men spend their free time reading the paper, watching soccer games, and drinking vodka. Is this true?"

Tokareva didn't want to agree, but she didn't want to lie either. She thought for a minute and replied, "Yes, it's all true. But we like it that way, and we want it that way. That's why Russian women are popular in your country. They export well to every country. Your men gladly marry Russian women because they accept any amount of work that can be piled on them, and it's much easier to keep them happy."

We ourselves, journalists and writers in particular, must consider the dense layers of utterly unexamined, unspoken truth about women's lives. Our reality is urban work collectives where there are thirty eligible women to one eligible man. Our reality is young girls moving to the capital on temporary work permits to fill the jobs no one else wants. They usually have no roots and their only goal is to get a permanent residence permit, rent a room, and settle down in the big city no matter what, just to secure the slightest foothold in life. I've had the opportunity to observe some of them at work in a huge laundry. Even there, where the work is fully automated (and there are precious few laundries like that in the country), they stand in front of a conveyor belt and perform one and only one operation: They transfer wrung-out, wet bed sheets from one conveyor belt to the next. The room temperature in the shop is controlled, the humidity is regulated, and the machines do everything, but by the time their shift is over, these women have no desire to do anything anymore. They don't even think about leisure activities, self-improvement, or getting together with friends. They just want to crawl into bed or slip into oblivion some other way.

Until very recently, many areas of study, including women, were closed subjects, but it's a proven fact that an objective analysis of society is possible only when we have a working knowledge of all its component parts.

What if we were simply to elevate the image of women? Trust them, encourage them, involve them in the discussion of questions of the utmost importance? Be unsparing with our "thank-yous" at the highest levels, in local party committees, on the street? Thank them not only for breaking production records, but also for helping abandoned children? Perhaps create more opportunities for them to relax, not only in comfort stations in public places, but during work breaks, in the evenings, on vacation? Find ways to provide them with that rare commodity—communication—in clubs, on dance floors, in cafes? I would like to make one very specific proposal: At least part of women's domestic chores should be classified as work time and their hours on the job reduced as soon as they have children.

A new, very necessary public institution has been created: women's councils. What are they? What are their rights? What is their mandate? They are just getting under way, but we must publicly discuss, widely and candidly, the opportunities and obstacles that lie ahead if we hope to keep the soapbox rhetoric out of them and not let them turn into paper organizations. A tiny cell has appeared in the heart of the Writers Union of the USSR: the Women's Council on International Contacts. I would like international women's organizations in the creative professions—publishing houses, journals, institutes—to be able to study more deeply the phenomena of Soviet women, to get a better understanding of their way of life and thinking.

Society has suffered great losses by dismissing the "woman's question." Whether we provide women with additional free time or not, they'll do half their household chores during working hours anyway. Don't you see how they shop, locate scarce goods, drop their laundry off at the cleaner's, how they take care of their children by telephone several times a day? Of course you do.

In classical Russian literature men were portrayed as indecisive, overly intellectual, incapable of keeping up with women's powerful emotions—the image so brilliantly analyzed by Chernyshevsky in "A Russian at a Rendezvous." There are not many men like Goncharov's Oblomov, Turgenev's Lavretsky, or Pushkin's Onegin today. Man leads today. So men, show us your will and your striving for truth; give serious thought to the question: What are women made of?

1987

Translated from the Russian by Michele A. Berdy

THE SIEGE OF LENINGRAD: NOTES OF A SURVIVOR

LIDIA GINZBURG

During the war people avidly read Tolstoy's *War and Peace* as a means of testing their reactions (not Tolstoy's, because no one doubted that he was equal to life's challenges). And the reader would say to himself, "Yes, now I know that my feelings are accurate. Now I know that this is the way it is." During the siege of Leningrad, anyone with the strength to read avidly read *War and Peace.*

No one can surpass Tolstoy's depiction of courage, of people engaged in the common cause of an all-out war. He also showed once and for all how those caught up in such a common cause actually advance it inadvertently when they seem occupied with solving their daily personal problems. The people of besieged Leningrad worked (as long as they were able) and saved themselves and their loved ones, if they could, from starving to death.

And in the final analysis, that too was a necessary part of the war effort, because in spite of the enemy, a city that the enemy wanted to destroy remained alive.

The following narrative describes a few aspects of that struggle.

I needed to describe not only life in general but also the everyday details of one person's existence during the siege. This person is called simply N. because he is composite and imaginary, an educated person confined to particular circumstances.

Perhaps this narrative will provide our descendants with an insider's view of the siege.

A day in the life of Leningrad, spring 1942. The word *spring,* incidentally, sounded strange. The bread ration had been increased, and streetcars were moving tentatively through the thawed streets. The Germans had stopped the aerial bombing but were bombarding the city every day, several times a day, with artillery shells. The strongest and most vigorous Leningraders had either died by that time or survived. The weak continued to die a slow death. The word *spring* sounded strange.

N., a survivor of the siege whose poor eyesight prevents him from being drafted, wakes up. The previous summer he had woken up differently—he was always roused at 6:00 A.M. by the sound of the loudspeaker that had been installed in the hallway for common use. Later on he got into the habit of waking up ten or fifteen minutes ahead of time and lying in bed, listening. About three minutes before six, unable to restrain himself, he would go out into the hallway in his pajamas. His neighbors would already be standing there half dressed, their faces desperately tense. If the announcer identified the various radio stations in his customary unnatural voice, it would seem to mean that nothing special had happened that day. . . . N. knew that this was an aberration on his part, and that he could not escape it. Incidentally, the broadcast would begin not with the announcer's voice but with short rings and pauses that formed an audible pattern. We had never heard a sadder sound. Then came the station identifications with their fragile illusion of stability. And at last the frighteningly brief information (it seemed to get briefer all the time), which in those days consisted of instructing people where to go. And everyone stood by the loudspeakers with palpitating hearts, receiving the latest instructions. The announcer spoke in an unnaturally deliberate voice, and you could count the seconds separating one word from another, the name of one locality from the next. That's how it had been in the summer of 1941.

People were desperate for information. They would run to the loudspeaker five times a day, interrupting any activity whatsoever. They would pounce on anyone who had been even one step closer than they to the front or to the authorities or to other sources of information. And their incoherent questions would anger the person being interrogated, because the questioners actually wanted to know something entirely different from what they were asking. They wanted to know what it was like when there was a war, what it was going to be like. . . .

The first days were characterized by ignorance strangely mixed with painstaking preparations and with the idea, instilled for many years, that this event was inevitable and shatteringly total.

Everyone who lived through it remembers what he was doing on the first day of the war. Sunday. A short line at the ticket window of the commuter train station. My hand picked up a rectangular cardboard ticket and some change. And at that very moment a seemingly surprised voice (or maybe it wasn't surprise?) said:

"That's Molotov speaking. He's saying something about . . ."

A crowd of people had already formed at the entrance to the station. Words were coming out of the loudspeaker and each of them, independent of its meaning, was a vessel containing the torment that lay ahead, the gigantic torment of the entire nation. The speech ended. I went back home clutching the ticket I'd bought at the station so tightly that my hand hurt. They would wait for me on the railway platform a long time that day and I wouldn't show up. Less than half an hour had elapsed, but we were already being inexorably drawn out of our prewar frame of emotions.

I went back home along seemingly prewar streets, amid objects that were still of prewar vintage but that had already changed their meaning. There was still neither suffering nor mortal anguish nor fear; on the contrary, there was excitement and a feeling, bordering on lightness, that life as we knew it had come to an end.

During the first moments after the event occurred, it seemed that you should rush off somewhere in a terrible hurry and that nothing could ever be the same again. Later it turned out that, for the time being, much remained the same. The streetcars still ran, honorariums were still paid, and stores still sold the usual things. That was amazing. The sense that your former life had ended was so unbearably strong at first that your consciousness, bypassing everything in between, focused entirely on the outcome. Under these unprecedented circumstances, consciousness did not want to flail around; it wanted to be steadfast and stern. Those who were least prepared could find no other way to achieve this than by starting at the end and contriving their own demise. They would say to each other in complete honesty, "What's the use? In all this confusion only one thing is clear—we're done for." For about two weeks they believed that this was the plainest fact of all and that they were dealing with it quite calmly. Then it became apparent that to perish is harder than it seems at first glance. And later on these same people made a great effort and tore their lives from the clutches of malnutrition bit by bit, and many of them, either consciously or unconsciously, contributed to the common cause.

. . . Under siege conditions the closest and most crucial layer of social safe-guards was the family, a cluster of blood ties and daily concerns that invari-ably required sacrifice. Some say that the bonds of love and kinship eased the burden of sacrifice. No, the situation was much more complicated. People found it so painful, so awful to touch each other that, living all cooped up in close proximity, they had a hard time distinguishing love from hatred—hatred of those from whom there was no escape. You could not escape, but you could offend and hurt. And still the bonds did not disintegrate. All pos-sible relationships—formed at work and school, out of friendship and love—fell away like leaves, but families remained intact. Sometimes racked with pity, sometimes cursing, people shared their bread. They shared while curs-ing and died while sharing. Those who were evacuated from the city left these domestic sacrifices behind for those who stayed. There were too few sacrifices (if you survived, it meant you hadn't sacrificed enough), and along with insufficient sacrifice there was repentance.

. . . During periods of maximum exhaustion it became perfectly clear that the mind was consciously carrying the burden of the body. Involuntary ac-tions and reflexes, their primordial correlation with psychic impulses—all these no longer existed. It turned out, for example, that a vertical position was by no means normal for the human body; the conscious will had to take it firmly in hand or else it would slip and plunge as though from a precipice. The will had to make it stand or sit or lead it from one object to another. On the very worst days it was not only hard to climb stairs, but it was also very hard to walk on a level surface. And the will now interfered in matters that never used to be any of its business. "Here I am walking," it said. "That is, my body is actually doing the walking, and I have to keep a sharp eye on it. Let's say I'm trying to move my right leg forward. My left leg moves back, presses down on the ball of my foot, and bends at the knee (and how badly it bends at the knee!). Then it breaks away from the ground, moves forward through the air, and descends, but during that time my right leg has already managed to move back. What the devil! Now I have to track it as it moves backward or else I might still fall down." This was an extremely repulsive dancing lesson.

It was even more humiliating when you suddenly lost your balance. This wasn't weakness, staggering from weakness, but something else entirely. A person wants to put his foot on the edge of a chair to tie his shoe; at that moment he loses his balance, his temples pound, and his heart stops. This means his body has slipped out of control and wants to collapse like an empty sack into an incomprehensible abyss.

A series of vile processes takes place in an alienated body—degeneration, desiccation, swelling—all quite unlike the good old ailments because they seem to be happening to dead matter. The afflicted person would not even notice some of them. "Just look how he's swelling up," others would say about him while he was still unaware of it. People would not know for a long time whether they were swelling up or gaining weight. Suddenly a person would begin to realize that his gums were swelling. He'd touch them with his tongue and probe them with his finger in horror. It would take him a long time, especially at night, to tear his thoughts away from them. He would lie there and concentrate intently on this numb and slimy feeling, which was particularly frightening because it didn't hurt: There was a layer of dead matter in his mouth.

For months on end most people—the majority of the city's inhabitants—would sleep with all their clothes on. They lost sight of their bodies entirely. Their bodies would disappear into an abyss, entombed in clothing, and would change and degenerate down there in the abyss. A person knew that his body was becoming frightful. He wanted to forget that somewhere far away—underneath the quilted jacket, the sweater, the knitted vest, the felt boots, and the leggings—he had an unclean body. But the pain and the itching let him know he had one. The most vigorous people occasionally washed themselves and changed their underwear. Then they could no longer avoid encountering their bodies. A person would stare at himself with a malicious curiosity that overcame his desire not to know. His body would be unfamiliar, spotted and rough, displaying new corners and depressions every time he saw it. His skin was a spotted sack too big for its contents.

. . . A typical [winter] day during the siege began with going out to the kitchen or the dark staircase to split the day's supply of wood chips or small pieces of firewood for the little stove. The night would just be starting to dissipate, and the walls of the apartment houses across the way, seen through the broken glass of the window in the stairwell, would still be dark rather than yellow. A person had to chop by feel, aiming the ax at an angle, carefully sinking it into the wood, and then pounding to split it. People's hands were in very bad shape. Fingers would bend and then stiffen into some accidental position. The hand was losing its ability to grasp. It could now be used only like a paw, like an amputee's stump, or like a stick-shaped instrument. A person would grope around in the dark and scrape together the chips scattered about the stone landing, squeeze a pile of chips between his two stumps, and toss them into a basket.

Then he would still have to carry water up from the frozen basement. The steps leading to the communal laundry room were covered with a layer of ice, and people would descend this incline in a squatting position. And as they climbed back up they would look for indentations in the stairs, using both hands to set their full pails down in front of them. This was a form of mountain climbing.

One had to overcome the resistance of every object by using body and will without the intervention of any technological devices. Going downstairs with his empty pails, a person would look through the broken window and see the narrowing space of the courtyard he would have to get across when his pails were full. The sudden sensation of space, its physical reality, would cause him anguish. How strange that water, which hangs like a rock from his shoulders and arms, presses a person into the ground (and how altogether strange that this colorless, fast-flowing liquid is heavy, like stone). This same water normally has no trouble racing upward through pipes, passing one story after another. The water pipe is a human idea, a connecting link that has overcome chaos, a sacred means of organization and centralization. We normally see only the friendly face of a Janus-like world. But technology, the connecting link, is something we all have in common. The world that gives us technology wants a portion of our lives in exchange for water racing through pipes, for light that obeys the command of a little switch.

When he returned with his pails full, a person could take a rest at the bottom of the stairs. Tipping his head back, he would measure the height he had to climb. In the distant abyss was the ceiling, with some kind of disk-shaped alabaster ornament. The disk was located right in the center of the suspended rectangular zigzag of the stairwell. Staircases, it turns out, indeed hang in midair (peering at them is very frightening); they are held up by an invisible inner connection to the building itself. Tipping his head back, a person would gauge the height of the staircase as it reared on its hind legs, the distance through which his own will and his own body would have to carry water that weighed him down like stone.

During the course of the day, he would have to cross many more spaces of various sorts, the main one being the distance that separated him from dinner. For it was best to have dinner in some institutional cafeteria where the gruel bore some resemblance to real porridge. He would race off to dinner in subfreezing temperatures through a mockingly beautiful city encrusted with frost. Others raced (or crawled—there was nothing in between) alongside him or in the opposite direction with briefcases, string shopping bags, and covered metal containers dangling from the ends of their sticklike arms. People would race through the freezing cold, trying to overcome a space that had taken on substance. The most highly educated thought of Dante, the circle of Dante's inferno ruled by cold. And it would be so cold in the cafeteria that after you came in from the street your fingers would not unbend and you would have to grip your spoon between your thumb (the only digit that worked) and a frozen stump.

Dinner itself was also a matter of conquering spaces, small spaces torturously cramped by lines of people. There would be a line outside the door, a line to the person checking coupon books, a line for a place at a table. Dinner—something momentary and ephemeral (a bowl of soup, so many grams of gruel)—loomed abnormally large and contained many obstacles, all following the classic rules of plot development. People would be asked, "What are you doing these days?" And they would reply, "We have dinner."

There came a period of multiple and consecutive air-raid warnings. On the way to dinner you had to sit them out in basements or plow through a barrage of antiaircraft fire and policemen's whistles. And people would hate the policeman who was trying to save them from a bomb attack; they perceived the bombing as an obstacle in the path to dinner. Some people would leave for dinner around eleven in the morning (this was still usually a quiet time) and sometimes not return from the cafeteria until six or seven in the evening.

Some people would bring food home for their families (if they still had families). The apartment would be pitch-dark. They would build a fire in the stove and by its smoky light pour the cafeteria soup from the jar into a pot and slice about forty grams of bread. Then the person who had come from the outside world where he had eaten dinner would move close to the door of the smoking, flaming stove and warm his hands. And nothing could tear him away from this pleasure until the day's supply of wood chips was used up. Cold would be raging in the dark room behind him. Right by the stove door, and only there, lay a small circle of warmth and light. A circle of life. All you could really warm up was the palms of your hands as you held them out in front of you. Your palms would absorb the firelight racing across them. This provided infinite pleasure, spoiled, however, by the fact that the supply of wood chips was bound to run out.

It was this same anticipation of the end—the realization that the vital forces granted us would inevitably run out—that tainted every joy and the very feeling of being alive. Siege conditions made this formula graphically clear. And they reduced the eternally renewable attainment of eternally destroyed goals to a clearly visible race around a closed circle.

. . . All his life N., too, had dreamed of establishing a daily work routine and even believed that the only reason such a routine never worked was his habit of getting up late (a habit of Leningraders if they aren't bound by jobs that start early). Everything always began with the fact that the morning was already gone, that he had already irreparably ruined the splendid experience of the fullness, the entirety, of the coming day. Everything was already ruined anyway and for that reason N. found relief in letting himself go, and things would happen haphazardly after that. But now the cause-and-effect connection between impulses and actions was crudely exposed and tightened. He would wake up at 6:00 A.M. because, like everyone else in the city (who wasn't on night duty), he went to bed early, and he would get up immediately because he was hungry or because he was afraid of becoming hungry. In the morning he would do the household chores—because not to do them, to put them off, was tantamount to death. He would go to the editorial offices where he worked—extreme nearsightedness prevented him from being taken into the militia or the army. At the prescribed time he would go to the cafeteria at work because there was no way he could allow himself to skip dinner there; they might even serve him without tearing out a coupon (which sometimes happened at that cafeteria). After dinner he'd go back to the office, where there would still be a lot to do. Then he'd go home because he was still supposed to have an evening meal, and besides, there was nowhere else to go. Tanya had left, saying all the right things about how she was going away and leaving him (he had persuaded her to leave, of course), not at all because . . . but, on the contrary, because . . . His friends and colleagues had gone to the front or elsewhere, too. He would have supper and go right to bed, since he had gotten up at 6:00 A.M. and by 10:00 P.M. he was sleepy.

. . . Perhaps it will be possible to think things over in the morning while doing the household chores, carrying out the dirty water or cleaning the stove. Or while walking somewhere, to the bakery or to the cafeteria for dinner. You can't think while standing in line, and you can't think or write after dinner. That's the time when your will falters. Toward evening it gets easier again. But there's generally no point in trying to think during the hours of sharp depression after dinner. It's better to sit in the office and work (those who don't work, who only eat and starve, have a rough time) and listen absentmindedly to the voices of your fellow workers (it's good to have voices around you!).

But then, does a person need to write? Does anyone need to write anything more? Or is being at the front the only thing that matters? Fighting the Germans . . . Everything else springs from the Devil.

Those who saw the things that writers wanted to record will probably never have any need for them to be written down, no matter what they may be. But memory is not willing to retreat; it stands its ground, just as forgetting also stands its ground. Forgetting preserves life by endlessly renewing its powers, desires, and delusions. It will give back to life its essential vanity of vanities after physical and mental torments so excessive that their return seems utterly impossible.

The elastic fabric of life was pulled and stretched to the breaking point; but once the pressure slackened, once the elastic was released, it instantly snapped back to its primordial boundaries and forms. Choices that were open to a person in crisis situations closed up again. Otherwise the people of our generation, for example, would long since have been unfit for life after the siege.

We are continuously amazed both at humanity's unchanging nature (we haven't forgotten anything and haven't learned anything) and at its ability to change. Both principles interact with each other all the while. The system we have set up constantly adapts to changing situations and constantly strives for its original state.

Tolstoy understood how crisis situations can be reversed. He knew that the sky over Austerlitz was clear for only a moment, that in the interval between the French gun barrel and the tsar's casemate, Pierre would revert to being a liberal aristocrat.

But at the time it seemed to us . . . You believed, of course, that after this was over it would never again be possible to babble on about the lyrical hero in literature,* for example. . . . Yes, that's how it seemed . . . but why? Who has ever established that malnutrition is reality while ordinary life

---

*One of Ginzburg's books is *O literaturnom geroe* (The Hero in Literature) (Leningrad: Sovetskii pisatel', 1979). —TRANS.

is an illusion? Is it that once you've taken a peek at reality you don't want any illusions?

And so we obey the law of forgetting, one of the cornerstones of society along with the law of memory—the law of history and art, of guilt and repentance. Alexander Herzen said, "Whoever was able to survive must have had the strength to remember."

. . . At the beginning of the war the city began to acquire unusual details. First of all cross-shaped strips of paper began to appear on windows (to keep the glass from flying out). The authorities had suggested this measure to the citizenry during the very first days of the war. Amid the fluctuating anguish of those first days, when the new mode of life had not yet taken shape, this mechanical activity had a calming effect and distracted people from the emptiness of anticipation. But there was also something agonizing and strange about it, as, for example, in the sparkle of a surgery ward where there were as yet no wounded but undoubtedly would be.

Some people pasted these strips in quite intricate patterns. Somehow or other the rows of glass covered with paper strips created an ornamental design. Seen from a distance on a sunny day, it looked cheerful. Like the gingerbread trim that adorns the cottages of well-to-do peasants. But everything changed if you peered at the strips on the lower windows during bad weather. The yellowness of the damp newspaper, the paste stains, the print showing through like dirt, and the jagged edges formed a symbolism of death and destruction that simply had not yet had time to take hold, to attach itself to the cross-shaped strips.

Later on, people began to board up the windows of homes and stores. Some covered their windows because the glass had already shattered and others so that it wouldn't shatter. Sometimes they used fresh, practically white sheets of plywood for this purpose and sometimes rough, very somber-looking boards. A boarded-up window symbolizes an abandoned building. But in the fall the apartment houses were not yet empty; the population of three million, encircled by the blockade, still filled them to the brim. During those autumn days the symbol of a boarded-up window acquired a horrible reverse meaning—it became the symbol of people cooped up together, buried alive and perishing in darkness. It contained the funereal symbolism of boards, the tomblike feeling of basements, and the weight of a multistory building falling on someone.

The city was filled with a monotonous diversity of details that were expressive and individually different but that blended into one. Dank walls displayed windows covered with fresh plywood, boarded up with rough planks, sealed with paper—blue wrapping paper, colored paper, news-print—and blocked up with bricks. Sometimes one window combined sections of plywood, bricks, glass, and glued-on paper. Symbols varied and became muddled; onerous associations ran together without managing to take shape. Then it no longer made any difference. The windows became covered with ice. People on the street didn't look at buildings anymore. They looked down at their feet because the sidewalks were iced over and they were afraid that the slipperiness and their own weakness would make them fall. They were especially afraid of falling with containers full of soup.

. . . We saw everything in Leningrad during the siege, but we saw fear least of all. People scarcely listened to artillery shells whistling overhead. To wait deliberately until a shell exploded was much more difficult, of course; but everyone knew that you could hear a shell explode only if you weren't hit that time.

The quantitative scale of danger, or, more precisely, the probability of perishing (the degree of probability) holds key psychological significance. The distance between certain death and almost certain death is immense. The danger in Leningrad was constant and relentless, and its relentlessness was designed to wear on people's nerves, but statistically it was not especially great. The danger from bombing and shelling, verified by daily experience, was overshadowed by the enormous number of deaths from malnutrition. This slow kind of death required a completely different sort of inner preparedness. People in Leningrad naturally had a different attitude toward shells and bombs than did front-line soldiers or, later on, the inhabitants of cities that were burned to ashes by aerial attacks.

Few people in Leningrad were afraid of bombings—only those with a special physiological predisposition toward fear. Calmness became the universal and typical standard of behavior, and not to conform to it was more difficult and more frightening than the real dangers. You must be practically a hero to retain your composure in the midst of universal panic. But just try to scream and tear around when everyone else is going about his business—that takes a lot of audacity.

When beauty parlors were still operating normally, I once happened to be stranded at the hairdresser's during an air raid and I observed how ordinary young women continued to give six-month perms amid the noise of antiaircraft fire, exchanging remarks all the while about how terribly frightening it was.

Death can be successfully put out of mind for the simple reason that it is beyond human experience. Death is either the abstract concept of nonexistence or the emotion of fear. In the first instance it belongs to the category of the unimaginable (like eternity and infinity). In order to think concretely about the instantaneous transition from a person in a room to the chaos of brick, metal, meat, and, most importantly, nonexistence, the imagination must work harder than many people's imaginations are capable of working.

. . . From the days of old to the present the word *coward* has had a magical ring. It is all right to be afraid of the common cold, but to fear death is considered shameful. How did such a notion become instilled and ingrained in humankind when the instinct of self-preservation is so strong? Probably because society, the nation-state, could not possibly exist without it and threw all its weight into instilling it.

. . . People from the outside world who ended up in Leningrad would become distressed. "Why aren't any of you afraid?" they would ask. "What do you do to keep from being afraid?" The answer would be: "When you've lived here for a year and a half, starving and freezing . . . well, there's no way to explain it."

Habit alone was not enough. Habit merely weakened the impulses of fear and self-preservation; it helped you suppress them and replace them with others. To avoid being afraid you had to acquire other impulses that were so powerfully primordial as to suppress and consume all the rest.

The siege survivor of the fall of 1941 gave way to the survivor of the winter of 1941–42. He is the person who walks down the street during an artillery barrage. He knows that this is very dangerous and frightening. But he's going to the cafeteria for dinner. And instead of being afraid, he is irritated (they won't even let him have dinner in peace); instead of being afraid of dying, he's afraid of being stopped along the way, of being detained and driven into a shelter so that he won't endanger his life. This person is conscious of the possibility that he might perish, but his immediate sensations are of starvation, more particularly the fear of starvation, and of a hunger-induced haste rushing blindly toward its goal. You can be aware of various things simultaneously, but you can't desire them to the same extent at the same time.

A person wakes up in the night at the sound of an air alert. His hopes for a *quiet* alert are short-lived. The antiaircraft guns are firing closer and closer. What a shrill strike! Or is that actually a bomb? By this time, he no longer thinks about getting up, finding his overshoes, and going to the freezing basement. He's thinking that he shouldn't fall asleep. He doesn't want *that* to happen while he's sleeping. He doesn't want to wake up with the world caving in on him just to witness his own death in one very brief flash that instantly goes out. It's better to be prepared. It's better to lie there listening to the explosions as they come closer and closer. It's better when there's a lead-in to disaster. He is thinking that he shouldn't fall asleep, but in a few minutes he does fall asleep, because he's tired.

What's happening is very frightening. Right now, at any moment—before he can pull up the blanket, before he exhales the air that is expanding his chest—right now reality as he knows it might give way to some other incredible reality that is wailing, ringing, falling from utmost suffering into extinction.

All this could happen, but he doesn't have the strength to be afraid. He wants to sleep. He is amazed at what he was like at the beginning of the siege. Then he would wake up at 1:00 or 2:00 A.M. at the sound of an air-raid warning. That sound was enough to make him instantly forsake his warm bed in favor of the frozen basement. It was a naive wholeness and a fresh instinct of self-preservation not yet eaten away by fatigue and by a constant struggle with suffering. As a result of this struggle, the bed warmed by his body, his body lying peacefully in bed, became a blessing, an object of desire that not even the intellectual stuff of terrible thoughts could overpower.

I know that this is frightening. I want to live. If the worst happens, I will spend my last instant of consciousness cursing myself for being so reckless. I know that I should be afraid and take precautions. But I'm not afraid and can't be afraid, because I want to sleep.

Subtle changes occurred in the reactions of the siege survivor during the summer of 1942. By then he responded only out of habitual nervous tension, which would disappear along with the irritant that had caused it. The moment he heard the all-clear signal, he felt a sort of physical satisfaction, a sense of relief like the sudden cessation of a toothache. This explains people's strange mood swings, strange because of their swiftness. One minute they would be listening for death, while the next they would be chattering away, repeating office gossip; women who were still coming back to life made plans to get hold of stockings or redo a dress.

Stable feelings and imagination no longer played any part in determining nervous reactions, and conscious will did not stand in the way. The powerful impulses of the capacity to resist had managed to reshape everything. People in whom these impulses were not working found themselves in the same position as the sick.

Why was starvation the most powerful enemy of the ability to resist? (The Germans realized this.) Because starvation is continuous and can't be turned off. It persisted and constantly took its toll (though not necessarily through the desire to eat); its most excruciating and depressing effect was felt at mealtime as the food came to an end with frightening speed, bringing no satiety.

The object of the morning excursion outside is the daily trip to the store. A grocery store has now replaced the bakery.* An announcement even hangs on the door: "This store sells bread." Can it possibly be trying to attract customers? At this moment the store is empty and quiet. The clerks are wearing white jackets, sample displays sparkle on the shelves, irritating the customers, that is, those registered to shop here, while the groceries that have not yet been distributed and can't be purchased are laid out on the counter.

. . . During the winter, when bread was apt to run out (this situation was later rectified), lines made sense. But there were also other lines—the result of famine madness. On the day they announced the distribution of fat and "confections," a crowd would already be waiting at the store by 5:00 A.M. People would endure all the agonies of standing in line for hours, knowing that by 10:00 or 11:00 A.M. the store would be empty. It was psychologically impossible to sleep, to become occupied with anything else, or simply to exist without entering the process of drawing near the fat and sweets as soon as they became a possibility.

A line is a collection of people doomed to a communality of enforced idleness and intrinsic divisiveness. Idleness, if not construed as recreation or entertainment, is suffering and punishment (prison, lines, waiting in re-

*In Russia, bread is normally sold in separate shops. —TRANS.

ception rooms). A line is a combination of complete idleness and a heavy expenditure of physical strength. Men are especially poor at enduring lines because they are accustomed to having people appreciate and value their time. It's not even a matter of the objective state of things but, rather, of inherited experience. Working women have inherited from their mothers and grandmothers the notion that their time is worthless. And daily life does not allow this atavism to die out. A man thinks that after work he should amuse himself or relax; when a woman gets home from work, she works at home. During the siege of Leningrad, lines joined the long-standing tradition of distribution and acquistion, the habitual irritability and the habitual patience of women.

In contrast, almost every man who shows up at a store tries to bully his way to the counter without waiting. Men can't explain where they get this feeling that inwardly they are right when outwardly their conduct is clearly wrong. But they know for certain that waiting in line is a woman's job. Perhaps they have some vague notion that their claims are justified because there are so few men in line. But they don't give any reasons; they either behave boorishly or utter the classic phrase: "I'm late for work." "And aren't we late for work?" (Women invariably say *we*. A man standing in line thinks of himself as an isolated individual whereas a woman regards herself as the representative of a group.) "Nowadays everybody's late for work," a woman with a briefcase replies angrily. The man furtively hides the bread he has gotten by this time. There is nothing he can say, but deep down inside he's convinced that even if a woman actually works as much or more than he does, her attitude toward time, toward the value, use, and allocation of time, is different from his. And his attitude gives him the right to receive bread without standing in line. The clerk, a woman with no stake in the outcome, understands this and usually encourages these male claims of privilege.

Extremely few people read books or even newspapers while waiting in line. This comes as a surprise only to those who have never stood in line for hours at a time, day in and day out. The basis of line psychology is a nervous, wearisome yearning for the end, for some inner means of pushing empty time forward; weariness drives out everything that might dissipate it. The psychological state of someone standing in a long line is not usually conducive to other activites. An educated person has naively brought along a book, but he prefers to follow what's happening around him. Pushing up to the counter sideways, he watches the clerk hand out rations to those standing in front of him. If her gestures slow down, he responds by pushing forward with an inner shudder (if the clerk leaves the counter for a moment, the torment is akin to that of a train stopping suddenly). Or he finds satisfaction in closely watching the precise rhythm of her work or rejoices when some time is gained unexpectedly (as, for example, when someone's ration cards are given back to him because he's not assigned to this store).

A person becomes genuinely hysterical when some claimant wedges in ahead of him and then, after receiving his dole, immediately strikes up a conversation with an acquaintance for half an hour, now conversing like a free person, as though he were here on his own initiative. As long as he's in line, he, along with the whole line, is seized by a physical craving for movement, even if it's illusory. The ones behind yell at the ones ahead of them, "Get a move on! What's holding you up?" And then some philosophizer who doesn't understand the mechanics of everyone's mental state will invariably respond, "Where can they possibly go? We won't get there any faster this way."

In the winter the lines of people suffering from malnutrition were morbidly silent. In the spring the habits of those waiting in line gradually changed as the bread ration increased, the weather grew warmer, and greens appeared (people bought beet leaves and boiled them). The lines started to converse.

Humans abhor a vacuum. The immediate filling of a vacuum is one of the basic functions of speech. Meaningless conversations are no less important in our lives than meaningful ones.

The course of every conversation is, in its own way, predetermined, but the springs that propel it are hidden from the participants. Subjectively they are committing an act that is almost independent of any resistance from the objective world that hangs over every *deed*. Conversation is an unrestrained substitute for action, which must always conform to rules. It is a distant prototype of art, which is also a special kind of reality, and people themselves create and destroy the objects that populate it.

Conversation is a replica of passions and emotions; love and vanity, hope and animosity find in it an illusory realization. Conversation is the fulfillment of desires. In conversation over a cup of tea or a glass of wine, insurmountable barriers are broken down and goals are achieved that in the world of actions would cost a great amount of time, failure, and effort.

Conversation is a form of release, and it is also the objectivization of desires, values, ideals, abilities, and possibilities, whether cognitive, aesthetic, or volitional. Above all, conversations with fellow mortals are the most powerful means of self-assertion, a declaration of one's own worth.

Something stated becomes real and acquires a social existence—this is one of the fundamental laws of behavior.

While engaged in dialogue with his neighbor, a person asserts himself both directly and indirectly, by head-on and circuitous routes—from out-and-out bragging and naive talk about himself and his concerns to secret admiration for his own views on science, art, and politics, for his own wittiness and eloquence, for his power over the listener's attention. Self-assertion hides itself in something that is objectively interesting; it buries itself in information or in something aesthetically significant. Sometimes information is only a pretext, and sometimes self-assertion merely accompanies information. One way or another, self-assertion is the imperishable heart and soul of conversation.

There are situations—the existentialists call them borderline situations—when it would seem that everything must change. In reality the eternal motive forces continue their monumental labor (as Tolstoy established once and for all). What was hidden, however, becomes obvious, what was approximate becomes literal, and everything becomes condensed and revealed. This is what happened to conversation during the siege of Leningrad—in editorial offices, in cafeterias, in bomb shelters, and in lines.

A line is an involuntary combination of people who are simultaneously irritated with one another and focused on a single, common circle of interests and goals. This leads to a mixture of rivalry, hostility, and collective sentiment, a constant readiness to close ranks against a common enemy—anyone who breaks the rules. Conversations among people waiting in line unravel because of the enforced idleness and at the same time hang together because of the fixed nature of their content, for they are tied to whatever the line is all about.

Understandably, the business of obtaining food requires statements that have a communicative function ("Who is last? What kind of coupon do we need? How many? Do they have 'Southern' candy today? Is it true that 'Iran' candy comes in wrappers? Then it's not worth it!") and statements devoted to the battle against rule breakers. Formally speaking, the latter are also communicative (they aim for a practical result). But in actual fact the practical element in such statements is just as insignificant as the value of the housewife's time that is expended on the interloper who has wormed his way into line. The sense of justice she appeals to in her usual emotional manner is also insignificant. The practical bent of heckling comments masks a release of irritation, impatience, and all sorts of accumulated passions. Their emotional essence is borne out by the unprovoked rudeness and animosity in replies to perfectly innocent questions like "Do you happen to know how many coupons they take for a worker's ration?" or "How do you cook that?" The answers might be: "What's the matter? Is this the first time you've ever gotten food here?" or "What's your problem? Haven't you ever cooked before?" (Here you begin to suspect that you're dealing with an aristocrat who considers herself above all this.) In the winter you couldn't ask anybody anything: Any question was a longed-for excuse to give a savage reply that would relieve hostility and torment. In better times, along with rude answers one would encounter wordy, substantial replies when the speaker enjoyed playing the role of advisor and guide.

But the soul of a line lies in another kind of conversation, the kind that fills the vacuum of inactivity and is thoroughly predetermined and only ostensibly free. Conversations about food (about life and death) come in the plain brown wrapper of housewives' professional interests.

For intellectuals, for young people, even for men in general this is a fresh topic of conversation from which the ban has just been lifted, and they invent new clumsy and expressive turns of phrase. They are powerless to resist this topic but are ashamed of it as a sign of degradation. For housewives this is simply the continuation of their age-old conversations. For housewives of the immediate prewar period there is nothing new about standing in lines, carrying ration cards, or asking, "What are they handing out?" And so they didn't have to update their terminology in any radical way.

Still, some things did change. First, conversations about food crowded out all other housewifely topics of discussion (school, shopping, domestic help). Second, conversations that were once despised by men and working women (especially young ones), that housewives were forbidden to thrust upon such know-it-alls—these conversations triumphed. They acquired a universal social significance and meaning, the price of which was the terrible experience of winter. A discussion of the best way to cook millet—without salt, because then it *stretches* farther—became a conversation about life and death (for people learned how to increase their millet). Conversations narrowed in scope (to siege cuisine), but they were enriched by the peripeteia of difficulties to be overcome and problems to be solved. And being the most important discussions in the given life-and-death situation, they encompassed all imaginable interests and passions.

When people in line carry on conversations about food, their discussions contain everything: emotional release in reproaches and complaints, cognitive generalization in debates about the best way to obtain, prepare, and divide up food, the recounting of "interesting stories," and all means of self-assertion.

. . . "Oh, dear, I've started eating my bread. Now I'm afraid there won't be any left when I get home."

"You should never start eating here."

A third woman (standing in line for sweets):

"The calmest time is when you've finished it. As long as it's there, it draws you like a magnet. Like a magnet."

"You can't calm down until you've eaten it all. And you can't forget about it."

"It draws you like a magnet."

"Why, I used to clean out the candy bins. I'd buy it a hundred grams at a time."

"And half a kilo of bread and butter is gone in a flash. It's just awful to have to carry it home."

The satisfaction of talking about yourself is duplicated by the satisfaction obtained from intellectual processes. Self-observation turns into generalization based on experience. "You should never start eating it here" is actually a maxim; "It draws you like a magnet" is an artistic image.

"Well, then, my kid and I will eat this right up."

"In one day?"

"What do you mean in one day? In an instant. Before the war we used to go through two hundred grams of butter a day."

"Yes, that was perfect for three people."

"You can't imagine what my kids used to be like. Suddenly they wouldn't want to eat buckwheat porridge. They wanted me to make them oatmeal. Both oatmeal soup and oatmeal porridge. I'd say, 'Pick one or the other, either soup or porridge. . . .' 'No, make both of them.' 'All right, I'll make porridge—'"

"And my boy—he's only seven, but these days kids know everything there is to know about food. Whenever they announce the children's allocation on the radio, he's all ears. 'Children under twelve can get sugar. . . .' He says, 'Mama, that's my sugar. I'm not going to give you any.' And I say to him, 'Then I won't give you any candy.'"

A story about yourself, about your family, specifically about how your family ate in the past, has objective, universal appeal. This is confirmed when a listener responds with a question ("In one day?"). The story about how people used to eat contains a subtext of self-assertion: See how high my family and I could and still can rise above the forces that rule us. The reaction this elicits shows understanding; it indicates that the listener is also above it all and belongs to the same circle, that very circle of people in which a family of three used to go through two hundred grams of butter a day.

The story about buckwheat porridge and oatmeal has an underlying theme: The family lived so well that the children demanded not something better but something a little worse just to be different (out of satiety, the way the gentry used to eat rye bread).

After that would come the eternal female topic of children, now based on new and frightening material. The story of the boy who already knows everything there is to know "about food" has a certain amount of artistic, thematic appeal; but the main point, to be sure, is that this boy is mature for his tender age, that he'll manage to survive, and that he already acts like an adult while still retaining a sweet, childish naivete. But this child who is so well adjusted to life immmediately suffers defeat. For a listener suddenly begins talking about another boy who also behaved like an adult.

"No, my boy, who's dead now, always shared everything. It was amazing. His father and I couldn't take it. But he would hide candy in his pocket. He'd pat his pocket and say, 'That's enough for now.' And he was so unselfish. He would give away his own food. He'd say, 'Mama, you're still hungry. Take some of my bread.'"

. . . Food mania and maniacal conversations about food would intensify greatly whenever there was a breather. People were very quiet during the days of severe starvation. All resources were completely cut off, leaving no room for psychological enrichment with facts, for the use of facts by the eternal human will to affirm one's system of values.

A great amount of suffering leads to a different order of sensations. Thus the critically wounded experience no pain at first and people who are freezing to death fall into a pleasant state at the end. Real starvation, it is well known, does not resemble the desire to eat. It has various guises. It could turn into anguish, indifference, mad haste, and cruelty. It was more like a chronic disease. And, as with any disease, the psyche played a very important role. Those who were doomed were not the darkest, most emaciated and swollen people but the ones whose faces had an alien expression, a wildly concentrated look, who would begin to tremble before a bowl of soup.

A. would come to the cafeteria with swollen, dark red lips, and that wasn't the worst of it. One time the salt disappeared from the tables and the gruel they handed out was undersalted. A. then fell into despair. He rushed from table to table mumbling, "I can't eat unsalted gruel. . . . I can't eat it. . . . Oh, my God, and I didn't bring any along. . . ."

That was definitely a bad sign.

B. came to the cafeteria one day wearing an overcoat with a big patch of cloth torn out of the front. He gave no explanation for this. He just sat at a little table in this overcoat and talked with his neighbors. But then one of the women suddenly dropped a teaspoonful of vegetable oil from her gruel into someone's empty, dirty bowl. "You're extremely wasteful," said B. in a genteel tone of voice and, scooping it out with his own spoon, he ate the oil. He died in the hospital about two weeks later.

During the Russian Civil War* people starved in a different manner, more spontaneously and chaotically (especially in outlying areas). They ate unbelievable things like peelings and rats, varying the ingredients and combining them with something else at the same time. Then suddenly they would get a sack of potatoes. The famine during the siege was not badly organized. People knew that an invisible person would give them a minimum ration on which some would live while others would die—that was up to the body.

Filled with inhibitions, people would monotonously go to the bakery and the cafeteria knowing what to expect. Each of them was given an unvarying daily ration of one hundred twenty-five grams of bread, a bowl of soup, and a helping of gruel that fit on a saucer. Moreover, there was nothing whatsoever to beg, borrow, steal, or buy. Your friend or brother would sit next to you clutching his one hundred twenty-five grams of bread. No matter what torments you suffered, you couldn't ask your best friend for his ration, and if he offered it to you himself, you couldn't take it (if you were in your right mind).

Knut Hamsun[†] described a completely different kind of starvation, the starvation of poverty, which is surrounded by temptations and hope. A person might suddenly find work or be given a loan, he might suddenly steal some food or receive a handout or come up with a decent excuse for dining with friends. . . . The hunger-induced desires of the poor are clouded by miscalculations, envy, and humiliation, but they are not crushed by the invariability of a daily ration.

Private markets opened in the spring and little by little speculators

---

*1918–21. —TRANS.

[†]Knut Hamsun (1859–1952): Norwegian novelist, author of *Hunger.* —TRANS.

crawled out of the woodwork. Beet leaves or even a cup of millet or peas became available—they were unbelievably expensive and hard to find, but available. The rebirth of the money factor caused an emotional upheaval. New possibilities emerged, and with these possibilities passions and vested interests came into play. From precisely that point on, food became the focus of everyone's mental energies (if people had talked at all during the winter, they didn't talk about how so-and-so was eating but about how so-and-so was dying). Food entered the realm of salable goods and quickly acquired various psychological components.

. . . Toward the end of winter the rules of ration-governed existence loosened up. Certain supplemental allocations and purchases like soy milk leaked through, and markets selling beet leaves and nettles appeared later on. The people who withstood winter best were the ones whose sense of self-preservation helped them force the destructive subject of food out of their consciousness. With the appearance of new possibilities, protective taboos fell away, and one's consciousness became open to the beckoning, instinctive desire for food.

Food—in its diverse social forms—has been an object of sublimation from time immemorial. We can recall ceremonial meals timed to coincide with various holidays and events, the ritual of receptions and banquets, the importance of family dinners in the daily lives of the gentry and the middle class, and the undying significance of suppers just for two.

During the siege people did not invite each other over for meals. Food ceased to be a means of social intercourse.

"I'm sorry I've come at such a bad time," X. once said to Y. when he dropped in on business just as Y. was frying oatcakes on his little stove. "I'm disturbing you. Food is such an intimate matter now."

At this, a strange, inhuman expression appeared on X.'s face. Yes, food had become an intimate and cruel matter.

But human affairs never lack psychology. When food lost its psychological properties, it very quickly acquired different ones. Having once been part of the daily routine, it was now transformed into the routine itself; having previously accompanied events, it became an event in itself as well as a realm of social realization and of taste sensations laid bare.

People accustomed to steak and hors d'oeuvres now discovered the taste of gruel, vegetable oil, and oatcakes, not to mention bread. Their fantasies took various directions depending on their cast of mind. Some lapsed into the surrealistic experience of eating roast goose or puff pastry and sardines. Others dreamed of eating huge quantities of whatever they were currently eating. They wanted an endless protraction of those same taste sensations.

A restaurant serving hazel grouse was an abstraction, while this was reality. But such dreams wanted to make this reality enormous. Dreaming of vast quantities of food was not only a hyperbole of satiety but also a struggle against the depression and fear stemming from the momentary, inexorably transient existence of a single helping, even if it were double or triple in size.

People discovered a multitude of new taste sensations, but more revelations were connected with bread than with anything else. This was practically virgin territory because before the war many people in intellectual circles weren't even quite sure how much a kilo of black bread cost.

Some people were seized by a pure passion for bread. They wanted nothing but bread, our daily bread. . . . Others would develop elaborate dreams about bread. For example, they would want to sit before a dark loaf, cut off one thick slice after another, and dip them all into vegetable oil. A. F. said that he wanted only one thing—to drink sweetened tea and eat white bread smeared with butter forever. Still others would vary the bread theme. They would think about hot cereal delightfully stopping up their mouths, about oatmeal with its caressing sliminess, about the heaviness of noodles.

In the spring, people would even toast their bread or let it get slightly dry. Thickly sliced crusts that had dried a little on the outside while retaining their inner freshness were especially good with tea. If you didn't grab the bread out of the frying pan with your hands but ate it with a knife and fork, then it became an actual dish.

Z. told me about an incident that occurred during the siege when he happened to be at a certain house on business. While pouring his tea, the hostess said:

"Now don't be shy about helping yourself to some bread. We have more than enough."

Z. looked at the breadbasket and saw the impossible: the kind of ordinary bread they used to have before the blockade. Uncherished and unshared. Irregular slices of black and white bread lay jumbled among little pieces and crumbs. The white bread, moreover, had been lying there long enough to get hard.

Z. ate without hesitation and without experiencing any desire for that bread; his disappointment depressed him. That unlimited bread would have been appropriate in a dream, but in reality it evidently required a different, prewar apperception.

By springtime the malnourished had gotten back on their feet to such an extent that they felt like asserting themselves and feeling proud again. Some people had a knack for obtaining, preparing, and dividing up food—and they took pride in this as a sign of strength. Others had no such skills whatsoever, for which they, too, felt proud, considering it a sign of superior mental organization. When the markets were revived, some people began to take pride in buying nettles or beet leaves at a particularly low price; others were proud of spending lots of money.

An academic ration,* a dinner without having to surrender a coupon, a package from the outside world became tantamount to a promotion in rank or a medal or an honorable mention in the newspaper. Moreover, an exceptionally clear and crude hierarchy evolved. The Leningrad chapter of the Writers Union would now occasionally receive packages from Moscow. The packages were amazing—chocolate, butter, crackers, canned food, and concentrates. The union's governing body set the distribution quotas. According to their list—kept by the storeroom manager, who weighed out the butter—some of the writers who belonged to the Party cell got 1.8 kilos of butter and others got one kilo (those who were not active in the party generally got nothing whatsoever). Those who received 1.8 kilos were ashamed to brag about it, but they couldn't restrain themselves and bragged anyway. For those who got one kilo, the butter was tainted. Many would have been happier with half a kilo if only this had been proof of their literary and civic merits.

A siege survivor would go back home with his booty. He would carry it in his briefcase, in a covered container, in a string bag—the bread he'd gotten with a first-class ration card, the free soup, two or three turnips that he'd bought, for he could pay whatever price the speculators set. A scholar carried half a loaf of bread that he'd been given for lecturing at a bread factory; an actor cautiously carried a little suitcase in which, after a performance, someone had put a few lumps of sugar that were just as intoxicating as playing to a full house. People carried their social callings with them.

In this scheme of things there was a vital difference between those who lived alone—and there were more and more of them because in every family some members died and others were evacuated to the outside world—and

*Food allocations were based on occupation. Soldiers and defense workers received the most, unemployed dependents the least. People in academic and creative professions fell somewhere in between. —Trans.

those who had dependents, with special ration cards that didn't even go as far as a daily bowl of soup.

Having dependents was a mixed blessing for the breadwinner of a family during the siege. It was a crucial, often fatal, factor because the breadwinner shared his food and, while sharing, lived in a constant fog of rudeness, repentance, cruelty, and pity. At the same time, the members of his household were the last ethical proof, a tangible symbol, of his place in society. One person carries away his booty so that he can swallow it in the silence of his lonely dwelling, while another goes home and spreads his booty out on the table, and someone will respond to it with rapture.

Among the stories of the siege that I collected is the story of O., one of those who received 1.8 kilos of butter now and then, along with crackers and concentrates.

His sister had been stranded in Leningrad (she was many years older than he). For a variety of reasons everyone in her immediate family had perished, and he was obliged to take her in—when her state of malnutrition had become irreversible.

O. is good at streamlining and systematizing. But under siege conditions, with which he was trying to cope by exerting his will in a rational way, his sister was the beginning of a stubborn, countervailing disorder. He became irritated by her ever-increasing uselessness and by the sacrifices he had made and continued to make for her. And he spoke to her about this with a rudeness that surprised even him. But at the same time, on another level of consciousness, it was obvious that without his sister the silence would have been incredible and complete. And it would have been impossible for him to enjoy those dismal forms of relaxation and amusement that he had left behind. The processes of preparing and consuming food were no longer the secret machinations of a maniac; the presence of a second person gave them a semblance of humanness. He looked at the woman stumbling around the stove, with her small, black, tenacious hands so unlike the way they used to be—and he spoke rudely only because rudeness had become a habit by then:

"We're going to eat now. Set out the plates. Wipe off the table so we can sit down to supper like human beings. Clear away this garbage. . . ."

His malnourished sister was an objectifying medium, an audience that appreciated his success in obtaining crackers and concentrates because of his fairly high position in the hierarchy.

Such was O.'s story of the siege, a tale of pity and cruelty.

. . . A person who has eaten his fill cannot comprehend someone who is starving, even if that someone is himself. As he puts on weight, a person gradually loses comprehension of himself, of the way he used to be during the months of severe starvation. The people who survived the siege steadily forgot sensations, but they remembered facts. The facts slowly crawled out of their murky memories into the light of rules of behavior that were already becoming the norm.

"She wanted candy so badly. Why did I eat that piece of candy? I could have chosen not to eat it. And everything would have been just a little better. . . ."

This is a siege survivor thinking about his wife or mother whose death has made the eaten candy irreversible. As the fog of malnutrition disperses, the person who was alienated from himself comes face-to-face with the objects of his shame and repentance. For those who lived through the siege, repentance was just as inevitable as the physical changes caused by malnutrition. Moreover, this variety of repentance—*uncomprehending* repentance—is painful. A person remembers a fact and can't reconstruct the experience, the particular experience involving a piece of bread or candy that incited him to cruel, dishonorable, and degrading acts.

"And that scream because of those millet patties . . . that burned up . . . that scream and then despair, to the point of tears . . ."

Perhaps he will be sitting in a restaurant after dinner one day and become morose from the overabundance of food, which brings on despondency and takes away all desire to work. Perhaps he will be waiting for the check and accidentally fix his gaze on the breadbasket filled with slices of black and white bread. And that practically untouched bread will suddenly convulse his drowsy consciousness with a shudder of recollections.

Pity is the most destructive passion, and, unlike love and hostility, it does not abate.

. . . The circle is the siege's symbol of a consciousness locked within itself. How does one break out of it? People run around the circle and cannot reach reality. They think they are fighting the war, but that's not true—the war is being fought by those at the front. They think that instead of fighting the war, they are merely subsisting, but that's not true either, because they are doing what must be done in a city at war so that the city will not die.

This is what happens to people if their actions are merely responses to events rather than deeds that they initiate. How can an active deed break this circle? A deed is always an acknowledgment of the common bonds (without which one is simply inarticulate) that are obligatory for each person in spite of himself, although egocentric people keep talking and will continue to keep talking in the future (on a worldwide scale) about self-delusion and lack of contact and about absurdity.

Those who write, whether they like it or not, enter into conversation with the world outside themselves. This is because writers die but their writings, without consulting them, remain. Perhaps it would be simpler for the self-contained consciousness to do without any posthumous social existence, with all its compulsory blessings. Perhaps it would secretly prefer to be annihilated completely, along with all its contents. But writers die, and their writings remain.

To write about the circle is to break out of the circle. This is, after all, an active deed, something found in the abyss of lost time.

1942–1962–1983

Translated from the Russian by Gerald Mikkelson and Margaret Winchell

Sleepwalker in a Fog

Tatyana Tolstaya

Having made it halfway through his earthly life, Denisov grew pensive. He started thinking about life, about its meaning, about the fleetingness of his half-spent existence, about his nighttime fears, about the vermin of the earth, about the beautiful Lora and several other women, about the fact that summers were humid nowadays, and about distant countries, in whose existence, truth be told, he found it hard to believe.

Australia aroused special doubt. He was prepared to believe in New Guinea, in the squeaky snap of its fleshy greenery, in the muggy swamps and black crocodiles: a strange place, but, all right. He conceded the existence of the tiny, colorful Philippines, he was ready to grant the light blue stopper of Antarctica—it hung right over his head, threatening to dislodge and shower him with stinging iceberg chips. Stretching out on a sofa with stiff, antediluvian bolsters and worn-out springs, smoking, Denisov glanced at the map of the hemispheres and disapproved of the continents' placement. The top part's not bad, reasonable enough: Landmasses here, water there, it'll do. Another couple of seas in Siberia wouldn't hurt. Africa could be lower. India's all right. But down below everything's badly laid out: The continents narrow down to nothing, islands are strewn about with no rhyme or reason, there are all kinds of troughs and trenches. . . . And Australia is obviously neither here nor there: Anyone can see that logically there should be water in its place, but just look what you've got! Denisov blew smoke at Australia and scanned the water-stained ceiling: On the floor above him lived a seafaring captain, as white, gold, and magnificent as a dream, as ephemeral as smoke, as unreal as the dark blue southern seas. Once or twice a year he materialized, showed up at home, took a bath, and drenched Denisov's apartment along with everything in it, though there wasn't anything in it other than the sofa and Denisov. Well, a refrigerator stood in the kitchen. A tactful man, Denisov couldn't bring himself to ask: What's the matter?—especially since no later than the morning following the cataclysm the splendid captain would ring the doorbell, hand him an envelope with a couple of hundred rubles—for repairs—and depart with a firm stride. He was off on a new voyage.

Denisov reflected on Australia irritatedly; on his fiancée, Lora, distractedly. Everything had already been pretty much decided; sooner or later he intended to become her fourth husband, not because she lit up the world, as the saying goes, but because with her no light was needed. In the light she talked incessantly, saying whatever came into her head.

"An awful lot of women," said Lora, "dream of having a tail. Think about it yourself. First of all, wouldn't it be pretty—a thick fluffy tail, it could be striped, black and white, for example—that would look good on me—and you know, on Pushkin Square I saw a little fur coat that would have been just the thing for that kind of tail. Short, with wide sleeves, and a shawl collar. It would go with a black skirt like the one that Katerina Ivanna made for Ruzanna, but Ruzanna wants to sell, so just imagine—if you had a tail, you could get by in a coat without a collar. Wrap it around your neck—and you're all warm. Then, say you're going to the theater. A simple open dress, and over it—your own fur. Fabulous! Second, it would be convenient. In the metro you could hold on to the straps with it; if it's too hot—you've got a fan; and if someone gets fresh—slap him with your tail! Wouldn't you like me to have a tail? . . . What do you mean, you don't care?"

"Ah, my beauty, I should have your worries," Denisov said gloomily.

But Denisov knew that he himself was no prize—with his smoke-stale jacket, his ponderous thoughts, his nocturnal heart palpitations, his predawn fear of dying and being forgotten, being erased from human memory, vanishing without a trace in the air.

Half of his earthly life was behind him, ahead lay the second half, the bad half. At this rate Denisov would just whir over the earth and depart, and no one would have reason to remember him! Petrovs and Ivanovs die every day, their simple names are carved in marble. Why couldn't Denisov linger on some memorial plaque, why couldn't his profile grace the neighborhood of Orekhovo-Borisovo? "In this house I dwell. . . ." Now he was going to marry Lora and die—she wouldn't have it in her to make an appeal to the place where these things are decided, whether or not to immortalize. . . . "Comrades, immortalize my fourth husband, okay? Comrades, pleeease." "Ho-ho-ho . . ." Who was he anyway, in point of fact? He hadn't composed anything, or sung anything, or shot anyone. He hadn't discovered anything new and named it after himself. And for that matter, everything had already been discovered, enumerated, denominated; everything alive and dead, from cockroaches to comets, from cheese mold to the spiral arms of abstruse nebulae. Take some old virus—swill, worthless rubbish, couldn't make a chicken sneeze, but no, it's already been grabbed, named, and adopted by a couple of your scholarly Germans—just have a look at today's paper. If you think about it—how do they share it? They probably found the useless bit of scum in some unwashed glass and fainted from happiness—then the shoving and shouting started: "Mine!" "No, Mine!" They smashed eyeglasses, ripped suspenders, gave each other a thrashing, puffed and panted, then sat down with the glass on the sofa and embraced: "Hey, pal, let's go fifty-fifty!" "All right, what can I do with you? . . ."

People assert themselves, sink their hooks in, refuse to go—it's only natural! Take the recording of a concert, for example. A hush falls over the hall, the piano thunders, the keys flash like lozenges gone berserk, lickety-split, hand over fist, wilder and wilder; the sweet tornado swirls, the heart can't stand it, it'll pop right out, it quivers on the last strand, and suddenly: ahem. Ahe he kherr hem. Khu khu khu. Someone's coughed. A real solid, throaty cough. And that's that. The concert is branded from birth with a juicy, influenza stamp, multiplied on millions of black suns, dispersed in all possible directions. The heavenly bodies will burn out, the earth will become crusted in ice, and the planet will move along inscrutable stellar paths like a frozen lump for all time, but that smart aleck's cough won't be erased, it won't disappear, it will be forever inscribed on the diamond tablets of immortal music—after all, music is immortal, isn't it?—like a rusty nail hammered into eternity; the resourceful fellow asserted himself, scribbled his name in oil paint on the cupola, splashed sulfuric acid on the divine features.

Hmmm.

Denisov had tried inventing things—nothing got invented. He had tried writing poems—they wouldn't be written. He started a treatise on the impossibility of Australia's existence: He made himself a pot of strong coffee and sat at the table all night. He worked well, with élan, but in the morning he reread what he had written, tore it up, cried without shedding tears, and went to sleep in his socks. It was soon after this that he met Lora and was nourished, listened to, and comforted many a time, both at his place in Orekhovo-Borisovo, where the captain of course drenched them in a golden rain, flushing his Kingston valves again, as well as in her messy little apartment, where something rustled in the hallway all night.

"What is that," asked Denisov, alarmed, "not mice?"

"No, no, go to sleep, Denisov, it's something else. I'll tell you later. Sleep!"

What was there to do? He slept, dreamt nasty dreams, woke up, thought over what he'd dreamt, and dozed off again, and in the morning he drank coffee in the kitchen with the sweet-smelling Lora and her widower father, a retired zoologist, a most gentle old man, blue-eyed, a bit on the strange side—but who isn't a bit strange? Papa's beard was whiter than salt, his eyes clearer than spring; he was quiet, quick to shed tears of joy, a lover of caramels, raisins, rolls with jam; he bore no resemblance to the noisy, excitable Lora, all gold and black. "You know, Denisov, my Papa's wonderful, a real dove of peace, but I've got problems with him, I'll tell you about it later. He's so sensitive, intelligent, knowing, he could go on working and working, but he's retired—some ill-wishers schemed against him. He gave a paper in his institute on the kinship of birds and reptiles or crocodiles or something— you know what I mean, right?—the ones that run and bite. But the research director's last name is Bird, so he took it personally. These zoologists are always on the lookout for ideological rot, because they haven't decided yet whether man is actually a monkey or if it just seems that way. So they sacked poor Papa, bless his heart, now he stays at home, cries, eats, and popularizes. He writes those, you know, notes of a phenologist, for magazines, well, you know what I mean. On the seasons, on toads, why the cock crows, and what it is that makes elephants so cute. He writes really well, none of that wishy-washy puffery, but like an educated person, plus he's lyrical. Poppykins, I tell him, you're my Turgenev—and he cries. Love him, Denisov, he deserves it."

His head lowered, sad and humble, Lora's snow-white Papa listened to her monologues, dabbed the corners of his eyes with a handkerchief, and shuffled off to his study with little steps. "Shhhhh," whispered Lora, "quiet now . . . he's gone to popularize." The study is silent, desolate, the shelves are cracking, the encyclopedias, reference books, yellowed journals, and packets with reprints of someone's articles are all gathering dust—everything is unneeded, disintegrating, grown cold. In a corner of the necropolis, like a solitary grave, stands Papa's desk, a pile of papers, copies of a children's magazine: Papa writes for children; Papa squeezes his many years of knowledge into the undeveloped heads of Young Pioneers; Papa adapts, squats, gets down on all fours; noise, exclamations, sobs, and the crackle of ripping paper issue from the study. Lora sweeps up the scraps, it's all right, he'll calm down now, now everything will work out! Papa's on the wolf today, he's tackling the wolf, he's bending him, breaking, squeezing him into the proper framework. Denisov looked distractedly at the swept-up scraps:

"The Wolf. *Canis lupus.* Diet."

"The wolf's diet is varied."

"The wolf has a varied diet: rodents, domesticated livestock."

"Varied is the diet of the gray one: Here you have both rodents and domesticated livestock."

"How varied is the diet of the wolfling cub—our little gray dumpling tub: You'll find both bitty baby rabbits and curly little lambs. . . ."

Don't worry, don't worry, Papa, my darling, write on; everything will pass! Everything will be fine! Denisov is the one destroyed by doubts, worm-eaten thoughts, cast-iron dreams. Denisov is the one who suffers, as if from heartburn, who kisses Lora on the top of the head, rides home, collapses on the sofa under the map of the hemispheres, his socks toward Tierra del Fuego, his head beneath the Philippines. It's Denisov who sets an ashtray on his chest and envelops the cold mountains of Antarctica in smoke —after all, someone is sitting there right now, digging in the snow in the mighty name of science; here's some smoke for you, guys—warm yourselves up; it's Denisov who denies the existence of Australia, nature's mistake, who feebly dreams of the captain—time for another drenching, the money's run out— and whose thoughts again turn to fame, memory, immortality. . . .

He had a dream. He bought some bread, it seems—the usual: one loaf, round, and a dozen bagels. And he's taking it somewhere. He's in some sort of house. Maybe an office building—there are hallways, staircases. Suddenly three people, a man, a woman, and an old man, who had just been talking with him calmly—one was explaining something, one was giving him advice about how to get somewhere—saw the bread and sort of jerked, as if they were about to attack him and immediately held back. And the woman says: "Excuse me, is that bread you have there?" "Yes, I bought it—" "Won't you give it to us?" He looks and suddenly sees: Why, they're siege victims. They're hungry. Their eyes are very strange. And he immediately understands: Aha, they're victims of the siege of Leningrad, that means I'm one too. That means there's nothing to eat. Greed instantly overwhelms him. Only a minute ago bread was a trifle, nothing special, he bought it like he always does, and now suddenly he begrudges it. And he says: "We-ell, I don't know. I need it myself. I don't know. I don't know." They say nothing

■

and look him straight in the eyes. The woman is trembling. Then he takes one bagel, the one with the fewest poppy seeds, breaks it into pieces, and hands it out; but he takes one piece for himself all the same, he holds it back. He crooks his hand strangely—in real life you couldn't bend it that way—and keeps the piece of bagel. He doesn't know why, well, simply . . . so as not to give everything away at once. . . . And he leaves posthaste, leaves these people with their outstretched hands, and suddenly he's back at home and he understands: What the devil kind of siege? There is no siege. We're living in Moscow anyway, seven hundred kilometers away—what is this all of a sudden? The refrigerator is full, and I'm full, and out the window people are walking around contented, smiling. . . . And he is instantly ashamed, and feels an unpleasant queasiness around his heart, and that plump loaf oppresses him, and the remaining bagels are like the links of a broken chain, and he thinks: So there, I shouldn't have been so greedy! Why was I? What a swine . . . And he rushes back: Where are they, those hungry people? But they aren't anywhere to be found, that's it, too late, my friend, you blew it, go look your heart out, all the doors are locked, time has opened and slammed shut, go on then, live, live, you're allowed! But let me in! . . . Open up! It all happened so fast, I didn't even have time to be horrified, I wasn't prepared! But I simply wasn't prepared! He knocks at a door, bangs on it with his foot, kicks it with his heel. The door opens wide and there is a cafeteria, a cafe of some sort; tranquil diners are coming out, wiping well-fed mouths, macaroni and meat patties lie picked apart on the plates. . . . Those three passed by like shades lost in time; they dissolved, disintegrated, they're gone, gone, and will never come back. The branches of a naked tree sway, reflected in the water, there's a low sky, the burning stripe of the sunset, farewell.

Farewell! And he surfaces on his bed, on the sofa, he's surfaced, the sheets are tangled all around his legs, he doesn't understand anything. What nonsense, really, what is all this? If he would just fall asleep again immediately, everything would pass and by morning it would be forgotten, erased, like words written on sand, on the sea's sonorous shore—but no, unsettled by what he had seen, he got up for some reason, went to the kitchen, and, staring senselessly straight ahead, ate a meat-patty sandwich.

A dark July dawn was just breaking, the birds weren't even singing yet, no one was walking on the street—just the right sort of time for shades, visions, succubi, and phantoms.

How did they put it? "Give it to us"—was that it? The more he thought about them, the clearer the details became. As alive as you and me, honestly. No, worse than alive. The old man's neck, for example, materialized and persisted, stubbornly incarnating itself, a wrinkled, congealed brown neck, as dark as the skin of a smoked salmon. The collar of a whitish, faded blue shirt. And a bone button, broken in half. The face was indistinct—an old man's face, that's all. But the neck, the collar, and the button stayed before his eyes. The woman, metamorphosing, pulsating this way and that, took the shape of a thin, tired blonde. She looked a little like his deceased Aunt Rita.

But the other man was fat.

No, no, they behaved improperly. That woman, how did she ask: "What've you got there, bread?" As if it weren't obvious! Yes, bread! He shouldn't have carried it in his string bag, but in a plastic bag, or at least wrapped in paper. And what was this: "Give it to us"? Now what kind of thing is that to say? What if he had a family, children? Maybe he has ten children? Maybe he was bringing it to his children, how do they know? So what if he doesn't have any children, that's his business, after all. He bought the bread, therefore he needed it. He was walking along minding his own business. And suddenly: "Give it to us!" How's that for a declaration!

Why did they pester him? Yes, he did begrudge the bread, he did have that reflex, it's true, but he gave them a bagel, and a flavorful, expensive, rosy bagel, by the way, is better, more valuable than black bread, if you come right down to it. That's for starters. Second, he immediately came to his senses and rushed back, he wanted to set things right, but everything had moved, changed, become distorted—what could he do? He looked for them—honestly, clearly, with full awareness of his guilt; he banged on doors, what could he do if they decided not to wait and vanished? They should have stayed put, held on to the railings—there were railings—and waited quietly until he ran back to help them. They just couldn't be patient for ten seconds, how do you like that! No, not ten, not seconds, everything's different there, space slips away, and time collapses sideways like a ragged wave, and everything spins, spins like a top: There, one second is huge, slow, and resonant, like an abandoned cathedral, another is tiny, sharp, fast—you strike a match and burn up a thousand millennia; a step to the side—and you're in another universe. . . .

And that man, come to think of it, was the most unpleasant of them all. For one thing, he was very stout, sloppily stout. He held himself a bit apart, and although he was aloof, he looked on with displeasure. And he didn't try to explain the way to Denisov either, he didn't take part in the conversation at all, but he did take the bagel. Ha, he took the bagel, he pushed himself ahead of the others! He even elbowed the old man! And him, fatter than everyone! And his hand was so white, like a child's, stretched taut and covered with freckles like spilt millet, and he had a hook nose and a head like an egg, and those glasses! A nasty sort all round, and you couldn't even figure out what he was doing there, in that company! He obviously wasn't with them, he had simply run up and hung around, saw that something was being given out—so, why not. . . . The woman, Aunt Rita . . . She seemed the hungriest of the three. . . . But I gave her a bagel, after all! It's a real luxury in their situation—a fresh, rosy morsel like that. . . . Oh God, what a situation?! Who am I justifying myself to? They don't exist, they don't! Not here, not there, nowhere! A murky, fleeting, nighttime vision, a trickle of water on glass, a momentary spasm in some deep dead end of the brain; some worthless, useless capillary burst, a hormone gurgled, something skipped a beat in the cerebellum or the hippocampus—what do they call them, those neglected side streets? Neglected side streets, paved thoroughfares, dead houses, night, a street lamp sways, a shadow flits by—was it a bat, a night-flying bird, or simply an autumn leaf falling? Suddenly everything trembles, dampens, floats, and stops again—a short, cold rain had fallen and vanished.

Where was I?

Aunt Rita. Strange traveling companions Aunt Rita had chosen for herself! If, of course, it was her.

No, it wasn't her. No. Aunt Rita was young, she had a different hairdo: a roll of bangs on her forehead, fair, wispy hair. She would whirl in front of the mirror, trying on a sash and singing. What else? Why, nothing else. She just sang!

She must have been planning to get married.

And she disappeared, and Denisov's mother ordered him never to ask about her again. To forget. Denisov obeyed and forgot. Her perfume flacon, all that remained of her, a glass one with an atomizer and a dark blue silk tassel, he traded in the courtyard for a penknife and his mother hit him and cried that night—he heard her. Thirty-five years had passed. Why torment him? . . .

What does the siege have to do with it, I'd like to know. The siege was already long past by then. That's what comes of reading all sorts of things at bedtime. . . .

I wonder who those people are. The old man looks like the farmer-fisherman type. How did he get in there? . . . And the fat guy—what, is he dead too? Oh, how he must have hated dying, his kind are afraid of dying. What squealing there must have been! And his children probably shouted, Papa, Papa! . . . Why did he die?

But comrades, why visit me? What do I have to do with it? What did I do, murder someone? These aren't my dreams, I don't have anything to do with it, it's not my fault! Go away, comrades! Please, go away!

Lord, how sick I make myself!

Better to think about Lora. A pretty woman. And one good thing about her—although she shows all signs of really loving Denisov, she doesn't pester him, doesn't demand uninterrupted attention, doesn't set her sights on changing his way of life, but entertains herself, goes to the theater, to underground art openings, to saunas, while Denisov, thinking arduously, wastes away on his sofa and searches for the path to immortality. What problems could she be having with her father? He's a good, quiet papa, just what the doctor ordered, he keeps himself busy. He sits in his study, doesn't meddle in anything, nibbles on chocolates, writes articles that he puts by for winter: "The master of the woodlands loves a tasty treat of dry, fleshy multicarpels and dry indehiscents. . . . But as soon as the north wind blows, as soon as foul weather begins to sport and play, the Bruin's overall metabolism slows abruptly, the tone of the gastrointestinal tract lowers, and we observe a corresponding growth of the lipid layer. But the minus range doesn't frighten our friend Mikhailo Ivanych: a first-rate scalp and a splendid epidermis. . . ." Oh, to crawl into a cave like a bear, to burrow into the snow, close your eyes tight, grow deaf, depart into sleep, pass through the dead city along the fortress wall from gate to gate, along the paved streets, counting the windows, losing count: This one's dark, that one's dark, and this one too, and that one will never light up—and there are only owls, and the moon, and dust grown cold, and the squeak of a door on rusty hinges . . . but where have they all gone? Aunt Rita, now there's a nice little house, tiny windows, a staircase to the second floor, flowers on the windowsill, an apron and a broom, a candle, a sash, and a round mirror, why don't you live here! Why don't you look out the window in the morning: The old man in the blue shirt is sitting on a bench, resting from his long life, the freckled fat man is bringing greens from the marketplace, he'll smile and wave; here the knife grinder sharpens scissors, and over there they're beating rugs. . . . And there's Lora's Papa riding a bicycle, turning the pedals, dogs are following him, they get in the way of the wheels.

Lora! I'm sick, my thoughts oppress me. Lora, come on over, say something! Lora? Hello!

But Lora doesn't have the strength to come all the way out to Orekhovo-Borisovo, Lora's terribly tired today, I'm sorry, Denisov, Lora went to see Ruzanna, something's wrong with Ruzanna's leg, it's a real nightmare. She showed the doctor, but the doctor doesn't have a clue—as usual—but there's a woman named Viktoria Kirillovna, she took one look and immediately said: You've been *jinxed*, Ruzannochka. And when they put the hex on you, it always affects the legs. And you could probably find out who put this spell on you, Viktoria said, but that is a secondary question because there are thousands of witches in Moscow, and right now the main thing is to try and lift the spell. First off you have to fumigate the apartment with onion stalks, all the corners. So we went and fumigated, and then Viktoria Kirillovna checked out all the potted plants and said: These are all right, you can keep them, but this one—what, are you crazy, keeping this in the house? Throw it out immediately. Ruzanna said that she knows who's out to get her, it's the women at work. She bought herself a third fur coat, went to work, and right away she felt the atmosphere tense up. It's just plain envy, and it's not even clear why they have such base feelings; after all, like Ruzanna says, it's not like she bought the fur coat for herself, she really bought it for others, to raise the aesthetic level of the landscape. Ruzanna herself can't see anything from inside the coat anyway, but it makes things more interesting for everyone on the outside, there's more variety for the soul. And for free, too. I mean, it's almost like an art show, like the *Mona Lisa* or Glazunov; for that they push and shove and wait in humongous lines for five hours and have to pay their own hard-earned rubles to boot. But here Ruzanna spends her own money and presto—art delivered to your door! And then they're unhappy about it. It's just crass ignorance. And Viktoria Kirillovna agreed: That's right, it's crass ignorance, and instructed Ruzanna to lie on the bed with her head to the east. Ruzanna showed her a photo of the dacha that she and Armen have on the Black Sea so that Viktoria could tell her whether everything was all right there, and Viktoria looked at it carefully and said: No, not everything. The house is heavy. A very heavy house. And Ruzanna got upset, because so much money's been put into that dacha, would they really have to redo everything? But Viktoria reassured her; she said she'd find some time and visit the dacha with her husband—he possesses amazing abilities too—she'd stay there awhile and see what could be done to help. She asked Ruzanna whether the beach and the market were nearby, because they are sources of negative energy. It turned out that they're very close, so Ruzanna got even more upset and asked Viktoria to help right away. She begged her to fly to the Caucasus immediately and do everything possible to screen out these sources. So Viktoria—she's really got a heart of gold—is taking a photograph of Ruzanna's leg with her so she can work on healing her down south.

And Viktoria told Lora that her energy core had become completely unfocused, her spinal cord was polluted, and her yin was constantly sparking, which could mean serious trouble. It's because we live near the TV tower and Papa's and my fields are incredibly warped. And as for Papa's case—I'm having some problems with Papa—Viktoria said it's beyond her capabilities, but there's an absolutely amazing guru visiting Moscow now, with some unpronounceable name, Pafnuty Epaminondovich, or something like that; he cures people who believe in him with his spittle. A totally uneducated, wonderful old fellow with a beard to his knees and piercing, piercing eyes. He doesn't believe in blood circulation and has already convinced a lot of people that it doesn't exist—even a woman doctor from the departmental clinic, a big fan of his, is completely convinced that he's basically right. Pafnuty teaches that there's no such thing as blood circulation, only the appearance of it, but juices, on the other hand, do exist, that's certain. If a person's juices have stagnated—he gets sick; if they've coagulated—he'll be disabled; but if they've gone to hell and completely dried up, then it's curtains for the poor guy. Pafnuty won't treat everybody, only those who believe in his teachings. And he demands humility, you have to fall at his feet and beg—"Grandfather, help me, poor, wretched worm that I am"—and if you do it just right, then he spits in your mouth and they say you feel better instantly, it's as if you've seen the light and your soul has been uplifted. The healing takes two weeks, and you can't smoke or drink tea, or even take a drop of milk, God forbid—you can only drink unboiled water through your nose. Well, the academicians are furious, of course. You see, all their scientific work is shot, and their graduate students are beginning to look elsewhere, but they can't touch him because he cured some bigwig. They say that firm from Switzerland came—what's it called, Sandos or something—anyway, they took his saliva to analyze—those guys won't do anything without chemistry, they've got no spirituality, it's just awful—so, well, the results are top secret, but supposedly they found levomycitin, tetracycline, and some sort of psi factor in the old man's saliva. And back in Basel they're building two factories for the production of this factor, and that journalist Postrelov, you know, the famous one, he's writing a very polemical article about how we shouldn't stand for bureaucratic red tape and the squandering of our national saliva, or else we'll end up having to buy back our own resources for foreign currency. Yes, I'm sure of this, and just yesterday I was in that shop called Natasha, waiting in line for Peruvian tops—not bad, only the collars were pretty crude—and I started talking to a woman who knows this Pafnuty and can arrange a meeting with him while he's still in Moscow, or else he'll leave and go back to his Bodaibo in the Far East again. Are you listening to me? . . . Hello!

Silly woman, she, too, ambles along haphazardly, her arms outstretched, groping at ledges and fissures, tripping in the fog; she shudders and twitches in her sleep, reaches for will-o'-the-wisps, her graceless fingers grasp at the reflection of candles; she grabs ripples on the water's surface, lunges after smoke shadows; she leans her head to one side, listens to the swish of wind and dust, smiles a distracted smile, and looks around: Something flickered by just now—where has it gone?

Something bubbled, rippled, tripped, skipped, snapped—pay attention!—behind, up above, upside down, it's vanished, it's gone!

The ocean is empty, the ocean rages, mountains of black water crowned by wedding wreaths of seething foam move with a roar: These watery mountains can run far and free—there are no obstacles, nothing to limit the gale-force turmoil. Denisov abolished Australia, tore it out with a crackling rip like a molar. He dug one foot into Africa—the tip broke off—and then dug in more firmly: good. He pressed the other foot into Antarctica—the cliffs jabbed him and snow got into his boot—steady now. He grasped the erroneous continent more firmly and swayed back and forth. Australia was staunchly moored in its maritime nest; his fingers slipped in the slimy seaweed, coral reefs scratched his knuckles. Come on now! One more time . . . there we go! He ripped it out, broke into a sweat, held it with both hands, wiped his brow on his forearm; Australia was dripping at the root, sand flaked from the top—a regular desert. The sides were cold and slippery, the slime had grown fairly thick. Well, and where to put it now? In the northern hemisphere? Is there any room there? Denisov stood with Australia in his hands, the sun shone on the nape of his neck, evening was coming on, he could see far into the distance. His arm itched under the flannel shirt—yikes, there are bugs or something crawling on it! They're biting! Damn! He flopped the heavy stump back—spray shot up—it gurgled, listed, sank. Ehh . . . That's not the way he wanted to . . . But something had bitten him! He squatted and disappointedly ran his hand through the murky water. To hell with Australia. It doesn't matter. The population there is uninteresting. A bunch of ex-convicts. He only wanted what was best. But he did feel sorry for Aunt Rita. . . . Denisov turned on the sofa, knocking over the ashtray; he bit his pillow and howled.

Deep in the night he nurtured the thought that it would be fine to lead some small, pure movement. For honesty, say. Or against theft, for example. To purify himself and call on others to follow. For starters he'd return all borrowed books. Not filch any more matches and pens. Not steal toilet paper from offices and trains. Then greater and greater things—before you knew it, people would follow. He'd nip evil in the bud, wherever he encountered it. Before you knew it, people would remember you with a kind word.

The very next evening, standing in line for meat, Denisov noticed that the shop assistant was cheating, and he decided to expose him immediately in word and deed. He loudly informed the citizens of his observations and proposed that everyone whose meat had already been weighed and who was waiting in line to pay, return to the counter and demand that it be reweighed and the price recalculated. There are the control scales right over there. How long, O compatriots, will we tolerate falsehood and injury? How long will the greedy beasts, those insatiable leeches, flout the sweat of our labor and mock our dovelike timidity? You, old grandfather, reweigh your brisket. I swear on my honor that there's twenty kopecks' worth of paper there.

The line grew agitated. But the old man to whom Denisov's righteous appeal had been directed cheered up immediately and said that he had cut down counterrevolutionaries like Denisov on the southern and southeastern fronts, that he had fought against Denikin, that as a participant in the Great Patriotic War he now received his bit of caviar on holidays, an iron-shaped tin of ham made in the Federal Republic of Yugoslavia, and even two packets of yeast, which testified to the government's unconditional trust in him, a participant of the GPW, in the sense that he wouldn't use the yeast improperly and make moonshine. He said that now, in response to the government's trust, he was trying to stamp out sexual dissolution in their Black Swan cooperative and he wouldn't allow any lowlifes in Japanese jackets to lead a revolt against our Soviet butchers, that a correctly oriented person should understand that the meat shortage was due to the fact that certain individuals had gotten an expensive breed of dog inaccessible to simple people, and the dogs had eaten all the meat; and so what if there's no butter—that means there won't be any war, because all the money from butter has gone into defense, and those who wear Adidas shoes will betray our motherland. When he had spoken his piece, the old man left contented.

Having listened to the old-timer's speech, a few people grew serious and vigilantly examined Denisov's clothes and feet, but the majority willingly made a fuss, and returned their meat to be weighed. Convinced that they had indeed been variously cheated, they grew joyfully irate and, pleased with their just cause, crowded toward the manager's office in the basement. Denisov led the masses, and it was as though church banners were waving in the air and the unseen sun of Bloody Sunday were rising, and in the back rows some people apparently even began singing. But then the manager's door flew open and out of the dim storeroom, laden with bursting bags—women's bags, quilted ones with flowers—emerged the famous actor, the handsome Rykushin, who just that week had frowned manfully and smoked meaningfully into the face of each and every one of them from the television screen. The rebellion fell apart instantly; the recognition was joyous, if not mutually so. The women formed a ring around Rykushin, the curly-headed manager beamed, fraternization ensued, a few people shed tears, unacquainted people embraced one another, one stout woman who couldn't see what was going on climbed onto a small barrel of herring and delivered such an impassioned speech that it was decided then and there to direct a note of collective gratitude to the central trading organization, and to ask Rykushin to take on the creative leadership of Nursery School No. 238, with an annual appearance as Santa Claus. Rykushin riffled a notebook, tore off pages with autographs, and sent them wafting over the waves of heads; new admirers poured in from the store up above; they led a four-time award-winning schoolteacher who had gone blind with excitement, and Pioneer scouts and schoolchildren slid whistling down the shaky banister, plopping into the cabbage bins. Denisov kept talking hoarsely about truth. No one listened to him. He took a risk, bent down, lifted the edge of Rykushin's bag, and picked at the paper. There were tongues of beef in there. So that's who eats them. Squatting, he glanced up into the cold eyes of the gourmand and received an answering look: yes. That's how it goes. Put it back. The people are with me.

Denisov acknowledged his accuracy, apologized, and took off against the stream.

The view of a serenely existing Australia infuriated him. Take that! He yanked at the map and tore off the fifth continent plus New Zealand. The Philippines cracked in the bargain.

The ceiling oozed during the night. The captain was back. There'd be some money. Why not write a story about the captain? Who he is and where he comes from. Where he sails. Why he drips. Why does he drip, anyway? Can't do without water, is that it?

Maybe his pipes have rusted.

Or he's drunk.

Or maybe he goes into the bathroom, lays his head on the edge of the

Толстой   Сомнамбула Глумах
                и Маркерт

sink and cries, cries like Denisov, cries and mourns his meaningless life, the emptiness of the seas, the deceptive beauty of lilac islands, human vice, feminine silliness, mourns the drowned, the perished, the forgotten, the betrayed, the unneeded; tears overflow the soiled ceramic glaze of the sink, pour onto the floor, they're already up to the ankles, now they've risen to the knees, ripples, circles, wind, storm. After all, isn't there a saying: The heart of the wise is in the house of mourning, but the heart of fools is in the house of mirth.

Aunt Rita, where are you? In what spaces does your weightless spirit wander, is peace known to you? Do you sweep like a wan breeze across the meadows of the dead, where hollyhocks and asphodels grow, do you howl like a winter storm, pushing your way through the cracks of warm human dwellings, is it you singing in the sounds of the piano, living and dying with the music? Maybe you whimper like a homeless dog, run across the night road like a hurrying hedgehog, curl up under a damp stone like an eyeless worm? You must be in a bad way wherever you are now, otherwise why infiltrate our dreams, reach out your hand, ask for alms—bread, or, perhaps, simply memory? And who are these people you've taken up with, you, so pretty, with your fair hair and colored sash? Or are the roads that all of you take so dangerous, the forests where you spend the night so cold and deserted, that you band together, press close to one another, and hold hands as you fly over our lighted houses at night? . . .

Can it really be that this is what lies in store for me as well: to wander, whimper, pound on doors—remember, remember! . . . The predawn clatter of hooves on cobblestone, the dull thud of an apple in an orchard gone to seed, the splash of a wave in the autumn sea—someone is beseeching, scratching, someone wants to return, but the gates are closed, the locks have rusted, the key has been thrown away, the caretaker has died, and no one has come back.

No one, do you hear, no one has come back! Do you hear?! I'm going to scream!!! Aaaaaaaa! No one! No one! And we are all pulled that way, an invincible force pushes at our backs, our legs slip on the crumbling incline, our hands clutch at clumps of grass, at least give me time to collect myself, to catch my breath! What will remain of us? What will remain of us? Don't touch me! Lora! Lora! For heaven's sake, Lora!!!

. . . And she arose from the dark, from the damp fog, arose and moved toward him, unhurried—clip-clop, slip-slop—in some sort of outrageous, slit-open gold boots, in brazen, wantonly short boots; her thin, orphaned ankles creaked, wobbling in the gold leather, higher up a flamboyant raincoat furled and rustled in the black beads of the night fog, buckles clinked and clanked, higher still her smile played, the lunar rainbows of street lamps set her rosy teeth ablaze; above the smile hung her heavy eyes, and all this rustling, all this effrontery and finery, triumph and abomination, the entire living, swirling maelstrom was topped off with a tragic man's hat. Lord almighty, Father in heaven, it was with her that he would share his bed, his table, and his dreams. What dreams? It doesn't matter. All sorts. A beautiful woman, a garrulous woman, a head full of rubbish, but a beautiful woman!

"Well hello there, Denisov, I haven't seen you in ages!"

"What are those puttees you're wearing, my lovely?" Denisov asked disapprovingly as Lora kissed him.

She was surprised and looked down at her boots, at their dead, gold cuffs, rolled inside out like the pale flesh of poisonous mushrooms. What's that supposed to mean?! What's with him? She'd been wearing them for a whole year already, had he forgotten? Of course, it was definitely time to buy new ones, but she wasn't up to it at the moment, because while he had been off keeping himself in seclusion, she'd had a horrific misfortune. She got out to the theater only once in a blue moon, and she wanted to take a little break from Papa and live like a human being, so she sent Papa to the country and asked Zoya Trofimovna to keep an eye on him. Zoya Trofimovna couldn't stand it more than three days—well, no one could, but that's beside the point—so anyway, while she was cooling out in one of those basement theaters—a very fashionable little theater and very hard to get tickets to—where the whole decor is only matting and thumbtacks, where the ceiling drips, but there's a lofty spirit, where there's always a draft on your legs, but as soon as you enter you have this instant catharsis, there's so much enthusiasm and the tears are so divine that you want to burst. So anyway, while she was hanging out there and lapping it all up, hoodlums cleaned out their apartment. They took everything, literally everything: candlesticks, brassieres, an entire subscription set of Molière, a poisonous pink Filimonovsky clay toy in the shape of a man with a book—it was a gift from one of those village writers, a born genius, they won't publish him, but he came on foot from the backwoods, he spends the night with kind people and he doesn't bathe on principle; on principle, because he knows the Fundamental Truth and hates tile with a fierce hatred, he simply turns purple if he sees glazed or brick tile somewhere, he even has a cycle of antitile poems—powerful lines with the strength of timber, all full of "Hail!" this and "Hail!" that, and about magical singing zithers, something really profound—so anyway, his present disappeared and so did that Vietnamese bamboo curtain, and whatever they couldn't carry off they either moved somewhere else or piled up. What kind of people are these, tell me, I just don't know; naturally, she had reported it to the police, but of course nothing would come of it, because they have such awful bulletin boards there—missing children, women they haven't been able to find for years—so how could they be expected to rush out and comb Moscow for a bunch of brassieres? It was good that they didn't throw out Papa's manuscripts, only scattered them. Anyway, she was terribly depressed about all this, and she was also depressed because she went to a reunion of her former classmates—they graduated from school fifteen years ago—and everyone had changed so much that you simply couldn't recognize them, it was a nightmare, total strangers. But that's not the main thing, the main thing is that there were these guys, Makov and Sysoev, they used to sit at a desk in the back row and shoot spitballs, they brought sparrows to school, and on the whole were thick as thieves. So anyway, Makov died in the mountains—and remained there—that was four years ago, and no one knew, just think, a real hero, nothing less, while Sysoev had become fat and happy—he arrived in a black car with a chauffeur and ordered the chauffeur to wait, and the fellow actually slept in the car the whole evening, but when the guys found out that Sysoev was so important and such a big shot, and that Makov was lying somewhere in a crevice under the snow and couldn't come, and that swine Sysoev was too lazy to walk over on his own two feet and rolled up in an official car just to show off—there was a scuffle and a rumble, and instead of warm embraces and beautiful memories they boycotted Sysoev, as if there were nothing else to talk about! As if it were his fault that Makov had climbed those mountains! And everyone became simply beastly, it was all so sad, and one boy—of course, he's completely bald now, Kolya Pishchalsky—picked all the crabs out of the salad and threw them right in Sysoev's face and shouted: Go on, eat them, you're used to it, but we're just simple people! And everyone thought that Sysoev would kill him for it, but no, he got terribly embarrassed and tried to be friendly, but everyone gave him the cold shoulder, and he walked around completely flustered, offering antifog headlights to anyone who wanted to buy them. And then he sort of slipped out, and the girls began to feel sorry for him and started screaming at the others: You aren't human! What did he do to you? So everybody left hostile and angry, and nothing came of the evening. So there you have it, Denisov, why are you being so quiet, I've missed you. Let's go to my place, it's completely ransacked, but I've managed to make everything more or less presentable.

Lora's gold boots squeaked, her raincoat rustled, her eyes shone from beneath the hat, her eyebrows smelled of roses and rain . . . while at home, in the stale smoky room, under the wet ceiling, squeezed between dislocated layers of time, Aunt Rita and her comrades thrash about; she perished, the sash tore, the perfume spilled, and the fair hair rotted; she didn't accomplish anything during her short life, only sang in front of the mirror, and now, lifeless, old, hungry, and frightened, she rushes about in the realm of dreams, begging: Remember me! . . . Denisov tightened his grip on Lora's elbow and turned toward her house, driving away the fog: They shouldn't split up, they should remain together always, united inside one pair of equation brackets, inseparable, indivisible, indissoluble, merged, like Tristan and Isolde, Khor and Kalinych, cigarettes and matches.

The cups had been stolen, so they drank tea from glasses. Snow-white Papa, cozy, like a Siberian tomcat, ate doughnuts, shutting his eyes in contentment. We, too, are like those three—the old man, the woman, the fat man—thought Denisov; we, too, have banded together high above the city; seen from the outside, what unites us? A little family, we need each other, we're weak and confused, robbed by fate: He's out of work, she's out of her mind, I'm out of a future. Perhaps we should huddle even closer, hold hands—if one of us trips, the other two will hold him up—eat doughnuts, and not strive for anything, lock ourselves away from people, live without raising our heads, not expecting fame . . . and at the appointed hour close our eyes a bit tighter, tie up our jaws, cross our hands on our chests . . . and safely dissolve into nonbeing? No, no—not for anything!

"They took all the curtains, the creeps." Lora sighed. "What do they need my curtains for anyway?"

The fog settled, or perhaps it hadn't risen to the sixteenth floor, that light summer fog. Pure blackness and the jeweled lights of distant dwellings looked into the naked windows, and only on the horizon, in the Japanese-lacquer dark, the orange half-circle of the rising moon swelled, looking like a mountaintop that had pushed through, illuminated by fruit-colored morning light. Somewhere in the mountains Lora's classmate Makov, who had risen higher than everyone and remained there forever, slept an eternal sleep.

The rose-colored summit grows lighter, the cliffs are dusted with snow, Makov lies there gazing into the firmament; cold and magnificent, pure and free, he won't decay, won't grow old, won't cry, won't destroy anyone, won't become disillusioned by anything. He is immortal. Could there be a more enviable fate?

"Listen," Denisov said to Lora, impressed, "if those jerks of yours didn't know anything about this Makov, then maybe his coworkers do? . . . Couldn't a museum be organized or something? And why not rename your school in his honor? After all, he made it famous."

Lora was surprised: what museum, good Lord, Denisov, a museum, why? As a student he was nothing to brag about, he dropped out of college, then he went into the army, did this and that, and in recent years worked as a stoker because he liked to read books. He drove his family crazy, it was awful, I know from Ninka Zaitseva, because her mother-in-law works with Makov's mother. There's no way the school can be named after Makov anyway, because it's already named after A. Kolbasiavichius. And his story isn't all that straightforward either, because, you see, there were two Kolbasiavichius brothers, twins, one was killed by Lithuanian partisan rebels in '46, and the second was a rebel himself and died from eating bad mushrooms. And since their initials were the same, and even their own mother couldn't tell them apart, an extremely ambiguous situation arises. You could say that the school is named after the hero-brother, but at one time local hero-trackers came up with the theory that the hero-brother infiltrated the rebel den and was perfidiously killed by the bandits, who saw through the substitution and fed him poisonous soup, while the bandit-brother realized the error of his ways and honorably went to turn himself in, but was accidentally shot. Do you get it, Denisov? One of them is a hero for sure, but which one hasn't been established. Our director was just going crazy, she even filed a petition to have the school's name changed. But there can't even be any question of naming it after Makov, I mean, he's not some steelworker, right?

There you have it, human memory, human gratitude, thought Denisov, and he felt guilty. Who am I? No one. Who is Makov? A forgotten hero. Perhaps fate, shod in gold boots, is giving me a hint: Stop tossing and turning, Denisov—here is your goal in life, Denisov! Extricate this perished youth from nonbeing, save him from oblivion; if they laugh at you—be patient, if they persecute you—stand firm, if they humiliate you—suffer for your idea. Don't betray the forgotten, the forgotten are knocking at our dreams, begging for alms, howling in the night.

Later, as Denisov was falling asleep in the pillaged apartment high above Moscow, and Lora was falling asleep next to him, her dark hair redolent of roses, the blue moon climbed in the sky, deep shadows fell, something creaked in the depths of the apartment, rustled in the foyer, thumped beyond the door, and softly, evenly, slowly—click-clack—moved along the corridor, skipped to the kitchen, made a door squeak, turned around, and—clack-clack-clack—went back again.

"Hey, Lora, what is that?"

"Sleep, Denisov, it's nothing. Later."

"What do you mean, later? Do you hear what's going on?"

"Oh Lord," whispered Lora. "Well, it's Papa, Papa! I told you I had problems with Papa! He's a somnambulist—he walks in his sleep! I told you that they kicked him out of work, well, it started right after that! What can I do? I've been to see the best doctors! Tengiz Georgievich said: He'll run around a bit and stop. But Anna Efimovna said: What do you want, it's his age. And Ivan Kuzmich said: Just thank your lucky stars he's not out chasing devils. And through Ruzanna I found a psychic at the Ministry of Heavy Industry, but after that session it only got worse: He runs around naked. Go to sleep Denisov, we can't do anything to help him anyway."

But how could he possibly sleep, especially since the zoologist, judging by the sound, had skipped back to the kitchen, and something fell with a crash.

"Oh, I'm going to go stark-raving mad," Lora said, growing anxious. "He'll break the last glasses."

Denisov pulled on his pants and Lora ran to her father; shouts could be heard.

"Now what is he doing? Lord almighty, he's put on my boots! Papa, I've told you a thousand times. . . . Papa, for heaven's sake, wake up!"

"Warm-blooded, ha-ha!" shouted the old man, sobbing. "They call themselves warm-blooded! Mere protozoa, I say! Get your pseudopods out of here!"

"Denisov, grab him from the side! Papochka, Papochka, calm down! I'll get some valerian. . . . His hands, hold his hands!"

"Let me go! There they are! I see them!," the sleepwalker broke away, and somehow he mustered incredible strength. His mustache and beard seemed like wintry, woolly things on his naked body.

"Papa, for heaven's sake!"

"Vasily Vasilevich!"

Night flew over the world, in the distant dark the ocean seethed, distraught Australians looked around, distressed by the disappearance of their continent, the captain drenched Denisov's smoke-filled lair with bitter tears, Rykushin, famished with fame, ate cold leftovers straight out of the pot, Ruzanna slept facing east, Makov slept facing nowhere. Each was occupied with his own affairs, and who cared that in the middle of the city, many stories up, in the moon's mother-of-pearl light, real live people were in the throes of struggling, stamping, shouting, and suffering: Lora in her transparent nightshirt—a sight that even tsars would not be loath to gaze upon—the zoologist in gold boots, and Denisov, tormented by visions and doubts.

. . . The countryside around this cluster of dachas was marvelous—oaks everywhere and under the oaks, lawns, and on the lawns people playing volleyball in the reddish evening light. The ball smacked resonantly, a slow wind passed through the oaks, and the oaks slowly answered the wind. And Makov's dacha was also marvelous—old, gray, with little towers. Amid the flower beds, under the damp evening wild cherry tree, his four sisters, mother, stepfather, and aunt sat at a round table drinking tea with raspberries and laughing. The aunt held an infant in her arms, and he waved a plastic parrot; to the side a harmless dog lay endearingly; and some kind of bird walked unhurriedly about its business along the path, not troubling, even out of courtesy, to become alarmed and flutter off at the sight of Denisov. Denisov was a little disappointed by the idyllic scene. It would have been pointless, of course, to expect that the house and garden would be draped in mourning banners, that everyone would walk on tiptoe, that the mother, black with grief, would be lying motionless on the bed, unable to take her eyes off her son's ice ax, and that from time to time first one, then another member of the family would clutch a crumpled handkerchief and bite it to stifle the sobs—but all the same, he had expected something sad. But they had forgotten, they had all forgotten! Then again, who was he to talk, arriving with a bouquet, as if to congratulate them? . . . They turned to Denisov with perplexed, frightened smiles, looked at the bunch of carnations in his hand, crimson like a sunset before foul weather, like clotted, bloody scabs, like memento mori. The infant, the most sensitive, having not yet forgotten that frightening darkness from which he had recently been called, immediately guessed who had sent Denisov; he kicked and screamed, wanted to warn them, but didn't know the words.

No, there was nothing sad to be seen, the only sad thing was that Makov wasn't here: He wasn't playing volleyball under the slow oaks, wasn't drinking tea under the wild cherry tree, he wasn't shooing away unseasonably late mosquitoes. Denisov, having firmly resolved to suffer in the name of the deceased, overcame the awkwardness, presented the flowers, straightened his mourning tie, sat down at the table, and explained himself. He was the envoy of the forgotten. Such was his mission. He wanted to know everything about their son. Perhaps he would write his biography. A museum, but if that weren't feasible, then he could at least arrange a corner of a museum. Display cases. His childhood things. His hobbies. Maybe he collected butterflies, beetles? Tea? Yes, yes, with sugar, thank you, two spoonfuls. He'd have to get in touch with glaciologists. It's possible that Makov's climb was in some way important for science. Immortalization of his memory. Annual Makovian readings. Let us dare to dream: Makov Peak—why not? The Makov Foundation with voluntary donations. The possibilities! . . .

The sisters sighed, the stepfather smoked and raised his gray eyebrows in boredom, the mother, aunt, and infant started crying, but it was a sun shower—all tears dried out here amid the raspberries, oaks, and wild cherry. The slow wind, flying in from distant flowering glades, whispered in his ear: Drop it. Everything's fine. Everything's peaceful. Drop it. . . . The mother squeezed her nose with a handkerchief to stop the tears. Yes, it's sad, sad. . . . But it's all over, thank God, over, forgotten, water under the bridge, it's all covered with yellow water lilies. You know how it is, life goes on! There's Zhannochka's firstborn. He's our little Vasya. Vasya, come on now, where's grandma's nose? That's ri-iiight. Goo goo goo, ga ga ga. Vera, he's wet. This is our garden. Flower beds, do you see? Well, what else. . . . There's our hammock. Comfortable, isn't it? And this is our Irochka, she's getting married. There's a lot to do, you know. You have to get the youngsters settled, you have to take care of everything for them!

Irochka was extremely pretty—young, tanned. The mosquitoes were feasting on her bare back. Denisov couldn't take his eyes off Irochka. A breeze swayed the black berries on the wild cherry.

"Come, let's look at the garden. My tomatoes have really taken off." Makov's mother led Denisov deep into the garden and whispered: "The girls really loved Sasha. Especially Irochka. Well, what can you do. You have a heart, I can tell, you want to help. We have a request to make of you. . . . She's getting married, we're trying to get ahold of furniture for them. . . . And you know, she wants a Sylvia china cabinet. We've tried everything. After all, they're young, you know. . . . They want to live it up a bit. If Sasha were alive, he would have turned Moscow inside out. . . . In Sasha's memory . . . for Irochka . . . a Sylvia, eh? What do you say, young man?"

A Sylvia for the deceased!—cried invisible forces. Eternal memory!

"A Sylvia cabinet, Sylvia . . . Sasha would be so pleased. . . . How happy he would have been. . . . Come on, have some more tea."

And they drank tea with raspberries, and the oaks hurried nowhere, and Makov lay on high in the diamond splendor, baring his unaging teeth to the sky.

Duty is duty. All right then, let it be a cabinet. Why not? From Makov a cabinet will remain. From Aunt Rita—a glass perfume flacon. I traded the flacon. Nothing remained. Sepulchral darkness. The scorched steppe. An icy crust. The mushroom damp of a cellar. The ferrous smell of blood. One sixth of the earth, torn out with flesh. No! I don't want to know anything. I couldn't help. I was little! I am helping only Makov, for all of them, for all, all! And when the polite, heavyset orderlies took away the sobbing captain and he grabbed on to the lintels, the mailboxes, the elevator shaft, spread his legs wide, bent his knees, and shrieked, and then they carried hundreds of little paper boats out of the apartment and gave them to the Pioneer scouts for recycling, as all the neighbors and I stood by and watched—I couldn't help then either, I am helping only Makov!

I don't want to know anything! The cabinet, only the cabinet! The cabinet, a sideboard, a wall unit with bronze inlay—a golden hair's width, no thicker!—with shiny corners, delicate fretwork, and the slight gleam of diamond-shaped panes. Gentle dimples of carving—so soft and light, as though a wild hare had run by—a marvelous, marvelous piece of home!

As though a wild hare had run down the hallway. Lora's Papa. Ping!—he broke something. A flacon? No, a glass. They drink tea with raspberries from glasses. Makov looks at the sky: Get hold of a cabinet in my name! All right. I'll try. I'm prepared to suffer. I'll suffer—and Makov will release me. And so will the captain. And Aunt Rita. And her comrades will lower their unbearable eyes.

Lora breathes evenly in her sleep, her hair smells of roses, the zoologist stirs in the hall, the doors are locked—where will you run away to?—let him run around—he'll wear himself out, get tired, he'll sleep better. "I knew, but I forgot, I knew, but I forgot," he mutters, and his eyes are closed and his legs lithe. Back and forth, back and forth, across the moonlit squares, past the bookshelves, from the front door to the kitchen door. Back and forth, perhaps he's put on Lora's hat or sandals, perhaps he's wound a gauze scarf round his neck or adorned his head with a colander, he likes nocturnal knick-knacks; back and forth, from door to door, with soft skips, lifting his knees high, his hands outstretched as though he were trying to catch something, but hadn't caught it yet—a festive hunt, an innocuous blindman's buff, no harm done. "I knew, but I forgot!"

In the morning the red dawn arrived, the mountain with the black bug of Makov on its peak dissolved, the weary lunatic fell sweetly asleep, degenerate city birds struck up a song, and two sky-blue tears rolled from Denisov's eyes into Denisov's ears.

.

In search of Sylvia, Denisov knocked on all sorts of doors, but everywhere he ran up against rejection. Are you crazy? Imports have been cut back! And Sylvia all the more so! Hah! . . . Even a general couldn't get one! Maybe a marshal, but it depends what kind, what kind of troops. No, comrade Petryukov won't help you. Neither will Kozlov. And don't bother approaching Lyulko—there's no point. Now, comrade Bakhtiyarov . . . Comrade Bakhtiyarov could do it, help that is, but he's a capricious, eccentric fellow, he's got a sort of florid, unpredictable personality, and the devil knows how you can pressure Bakhtiyarov. But you've definitely got to catch him out of his office, in the Woodland Fairy Tale restaurant, for instance, when the comrade is eating and relaxing. You could try going to the baths, the baths would be best of all, and it's an old trick—wait for the moment when the beauty drops her swan feathers to bathe in the spring, so to speak—then you've caught the little bird, you close in and stash the feathers somewhere, and you can ask whatever your heart desires. But Bakhtiyarov is no beauty, as you'll see for yourself, and his feathers and pants and suitcase with underwear and all kinds of tasty goodies are so well guarded, and getting into the bathhouse is so difficult—like Baba Yaga's house, it can turn its face to the forest and rear to people quick as a wink—that you shouldn't even think of getting in there without a magic password. So why don't you try to find him out of town, in the Fairy Tale. Well, what can you do, give it a try. He goes there to relax.

And the Fairy Tale came to pass.

Whew, how warm it was in there, how fancy, and how glorious it smelled! If only Lora were here, and I had a bit more money, yes, over there in that corner under the yellow lamp shade, where the napkins are folded like fans and the armchairs are soft! Peace for a tormented, half-mad soul!

Waiters were passing by and Denisov asked the sweetest and friendliest of them: Comrade Bakhtiyarov isn't here by any chance, is he? And the waiter immediately took to Denisov like a brother and pointed with his little finger, directing him: The comrade's relaxing over there. In a circle of friends and lovely ladies.

Now go on over there—what will be, will be—over there—I'm not asking for myself—over there, where a dome of blue smoke billows, where giggles cavort like gusts of wind, where champagne leaps out onto the tablecloth in a frothy arc, where heavy female backs sit, where someone in a lilac-colored tie, puny, doglike, quickly prances around the Boss, incessantly adoring him. Take a step—and Denisov stepped, he crossed the line and became the envoy of the forgotten, the nameless, those who hover in dreams, who lie covered with snow, whose white bones protrude from the ruts of the steppe.

Comrade Bakhtiyarov turned out to be a round, soft, Chinese-looking person, he even seemed rather a fine fellow, and it was impossible to say how old he was, sixty or two hundred. He saw straight through people, saw everything—the liver, spleen, and heart, but he had no use for your liver or spleen—what good were they?—so he didn't look straight at you lest he pierce right through you, and he wound conversations around somewhere to the side and past you. Comrade Bakhtiyarov was consuming veal of a down-right disgraceful tenderness, as well as criminally young suckling pig; and the salad—a mere three minutes separated it from the garden—was so innocent, it hadn't even had a chance to come to its senses; there it had been, minding its own business, growing, and suddenly—whoosh!—it was picked, and before it had time to cry out, it was being eaten.

"I love to eat young things," said Bakhtiyarov. "But you, my little bunny rabbit, shouldn't—you have an ulcer, I can see it in your face." He was right on target: Denisov had had an ulcer for ages. "So I'll treat you to something that's for your own good," said Bakhtiyarov. "Drink to my health, drink deep to my hospitality."

And at the snap of his fingers they brought Denisov stewed carrots and sweet Buratino soda water.

"I keep thinking, thinking," said Bakhtiyarov, as he ate. "Day and night I keep thinking, and I can't figure out the answer. You look like a scholarly fellow—your eyes are oh so gloomy—come on, tell me. Why is the brewery named after Stenka Razin? After all, my little lovebirds, it's a government organization with plans and quotas to fill, fiscal accountability, socialist competition, Party committees and—oh, goodness, I can't take it—lo-ocal trade union committees! Trade union committees! This is serious business, it's no joke. And then they go and name it after some bandit! No, I don't get it. In my opinion it's funny. Go on, laugh!"

The friends and ladies laughed, the lilac-colored one even shrieked. Denisov also smiled politely and took a sip of his warm Buratino.

"But if you look at it from the other side: Razin, Stepan Timofeevich—he's a folk hero, an inspiration, our national pride and joy:

The wench has seduced him, he's lost all his senses
The cossacks they grumbled—how could he betray?

.

So Stenka took heed and he sent for the princess
And cast Persia's pearl to the swift running wave. . . .

That, you see, is an event with great political resonance—and now we have
some measly little factory with, you get my meaning, a dubious profile. To
my way of thinking, it's funny. Go on, laugh!"

The ladies again opened their mouths and laughed.

"Like grandma's furs stored in the chest . . . he doesn't rot, he doesn't
rust, he doesn't sweat, he gets his rest," the lilac-colored one suddenly
sang, wiggling his shoulders and stamping his heels.

"See what great fun we're having here," said the contented Bakhtiyarov.
"We play around and laugh like innocent children, and it's all within the
bounds of the permissible, we don't go beyond what's allowed, now do
we? . . . And everything's just hunky-dory, but I can see you've got a little
favor to ask of me, so ask away, we'll have a listen. . . ."

"Well, actually, it's very simple, that is, it's very complicated," said Denisov, trying to concentrate. "That is, you see, I'm not really asking for myself—personally, I don't need anything. . . ."

"Oh my willow, green willow, who asks favors for himself? Nowadays
nobody asks for himself. . . . Nowadays you only have to spit—and a bunch
of those inspectoring fellows grab you by your little white arms—did you
spit in the right place, where did you get that spit, and on just what grounds—
but what do we have to do with it, we didn't do anything, we're clean as a
whistle. . . . Can I call you my little chickypoo? 'You're my frost—frost,
don't freeze me out,'" comrade Bakhtiyarov began to sing. "Sing, my little
lovebirds!"

"Don't freeze me out!" they struck up at the table.

"Like grandma's furs stored in a chest . . ." the lilac-colored one tried to
sing against the chorus, but he was drowned out. They sang well.

"Klavdiya's soprano isn't just any old la-de-da," said Bakhtiyarov. "Our
Zykina! Maria, so to speak, Callas, or maybe even better! You sing too,
chickypoo."

Well, they warned me, thought Denisov, opening his mouth in time to the
rhythm. They warned me, and I was prepared—after all, it's not for myself,
and you don't get something for nothing, without suffering you won't get anywhere, I just didn't realize that suffering would be so incredibly unpleasant.

"No sweat, no sweets," affirmed comrade Bakhtiyarov, looking straight
into Denisov's heart, "what did you think, my pretty boy? You need some
kind of article? A ca-a-abinet, is it? Oooh, we're a naughty boy. . . . Why

don't you sing for us personally, eh? Something simple, heartfelt? Give us your best consumer solo, make our spirits rejoice. We're listening. Quiet, my little lovebirds! Be respectful!"

Denisov sang hurriedly, suffering under the gaze of Bakhtiyarov's guests; he sang whatever came to mind, what's sung in courtyards, on camping trips, in trains—an urban ballad about Lenka Sharova, who believed in love and was deceived, and who decided to destroy the fruit of her frivolous lapse from virtue: "She dug a hole, pushed the stones inside, and then wee Zina gave one last cry!" he sang, already realizing that he was in a desert, that there were no people about. He sang of the sentence pronounced by the heartless judges: "To the firing squad with her, to the firing squad it be!" of the sad and unjust end of the girl who'd gone astray: "I walked right up to the prison wall, and there lay Lenka in her death pall," and Bakhtiyarov nodded his soft head sympathetically. No, Bakhtiyarov himself was all right, not bad at all, really, his face even began to reveal some nice cozy nooks and crannies, and if you squinted, it was even possible to believe for a minute that here was a grandfather, an old-timer who loved his grandchildren . . . but of course only if you squinted. The others were much worse: that woman over there, for instance, an awful woman, she resembled a ski—her front was entirely encased in brocade, but her back was completely bare; or that other one, the beauty with the eyes of a cemetery caretaker; but the most horrible of them all was that fidgety giggler, that unstrung Punch with his lilac tie and toadlike mouth and woolly head; if only someone would wipe him out, exterminate him, or burn him with Mercurochrome so that he wouldn't dare look! . . . But then, actually, they're only horrid because they're celebrating my humiliation, my trials and tribulations, otherwise— they're just citizens like anyone else. Nothing special. "There lay Lenka in her death pall!"

"How fine, my sweets!" exclaimed Bakhtiyarov in surprise. "How fine our comrade sang for us! Downright pianissimo and nothing else. No other word for it. Come on now, let's show him our stuff. In reply! Let's give our guest a taste of our D-flat!"

The guests burst into song; the lilac fidget—all attentiveness—conducted with a fork, tears streamed from the beauty's dead eyes; the diners from neighboring tables, wiping their mouths with their napkins, joined the chorus, Klavdiya's soprano entered on a piercing, violinlike note:

Mother, sweet mother, oh mother dear,
Why did you forsake me and leave me behind,

Your son has turned into a thief I do fear,
And my father—that scoundrel—you never did find.

There, in the mountains, the snow began to fall thicker and thicker, sweeping into drifts, burying Makov, his sprawled legs, his face turned toward eternity. He doesn't rot, he doesn't rust, he doesn't sweat, he gets his rest! The snowdrifts rose higher and higher, the mountain creaked under the weight of the snow; it groaned and cracked, and with the roar of a steam engine the avalanche fell, and nothing remained on the peak. A snowy mist smoked a bit and settled on the cliffs.

"Dear visitor! Aren't I your friend—to the bitter end!" cried Bakhtiyarov, grabbing Denisov by the cheeks. "How do you like that! I'm talking in verse! That's me! No stranger to poetry. Eh?! That's just the way I am. Drink your Buratino to my health! Bottoms up, bottoms up! That's the ticket! You know what: Humor an old friend! If you go to town, go all the way! Crawl under the table! For fun! Go on!

"What the . . ." said Denisov, free of Makov. "Who do you think you are, old man? *Arrivederci* to you, I don't need your cabinet. I changed my mind." And he started to get up.

"Under the table! What's going on? What's the matter?!" Bakhtiyarov tore at his coat. "We're asking you! Gentlemen!"

"Go on, go on!" shouted the ladies, friends, guests, waiters, even the cook, who appeared from out of the blue, and the entire room, rising to its feet, moving out from behind the tables, still chewing, made a scene and clapped: "Go on!"

No, for goodness' sake, no, no, no! Why?! I'm a human being, and proud to be one. I won't crawl, go ahead and kill me! . . . Yes, but what about suffering? Hey, remember! Suffering! You're the one who wanted it.

He plunged into despair, as though facing death, he lost heart, he frowned—it didn't help, he wanted to take a deep breath—there was no air left to breathe. And Bakhtiyarov had already thrown back the tablecloth and seated himself sideways so that his legs wouldn't be in the way. He gestured invitingly with his hand: Go ahead, be my guest!

. . . He huddled in the half-light of the darned linen, hugging his knees like an embryo, and gazed dumbly at the women's legs, the silvered tails, and the lacquered hooves; the insidious repast had clouded his hearing and sight; the soprano set his teeth on edge. Here's what I'll do. I know. I'll erect a monument to the forgotten. Even if it's only a flat patch of land in the middle of the steppes, with no fence, no marker—let feather grass or rushes grow there, let the sun scorch the earth till the salt comes out, let gravel or broken glass lie around, let a jackal howl in the evenings or a boisterous crowd feast. Greetings to you, tin cans, and to you, beer caps, glory to spittle, hurrah for squashed tomatoes. A hill of garbage or a salty clearing, the whoosh of feather grass or the whistle of the wind—anything will do, it makes no difference, nothing frightens the forgotten—after all, nothing else can happen to them.

A tearstained, eyeless female face hung under the table and muttered, seeking sympathy:

"Why, tell me why's it allays rile lires, salastically yuffy for some, and others only get lurdle, glud, and droom, why?"

The heart of the wise is in the house of mourning.

The Buratino had made Denisov drowsy, and he fell asleep.

A moonbeam, breaking through a darned patch, stabbed him in the eye. The moonlit tablecloth lay on the parquet floor, a silvery garden stood beyond the window, August ignited stars in the dark. It was as if all the snow from all the mountains were cascading onto the garden, the silence, and the mute paths. Denisov creaked across the floorboards and stood by the window. He hadn't dreamt about anyone today.

The cock crowed, Bakhtiyarov and his warlocks had vanished, the shades were sleeping, the world was at peace.

And what kind of nonsense was this anyway—to be tormented by memories of nothing at all, to ask forgiveness from a dead man for something you weren't guilty of in human reckoning, to clutch handfuls of fog? There isn't any fifth dimension, and no one will keep count of your sins and victories, and there isn't any punishment or reward at the end of the road, there isn't even a road, and fame is smoke, and the soul is vapor, and if you crawled under the table, well, pardon me, my dear, but that was your choice and your personal taste, and humanity will not follow after you in a grateful throng, and unseen forces won't cry out from the everlasting azure: "Good going, Denisov, attaboy! Keep up the good work! We fully approve and support you!"

He walked around the Fairy Tale, pulling on doors, all of which were locked. Well, what a pickle! Now just sit there till morning. Break a window, or what? There's probably an alarm here. It's a small village, everything's out in the open—they'll whistle, lights will blink, the police will move in; if they don't catch you in the garden, then they'll get you on the highway for sure.

"The heavens are wondrous and exultant, earth slumbers in a luminous blue glow," and Denisov is going to rush about among the bushes and watchman's booths, squat behind trash cans, and rustle in the hawthorn to elude the searchlights. There's no point in it. A rampart of darkness encircles the world; incorporeal moon sugar will sift from leaf to leaf, trembling and glinting; sugar, snow, dreams, depths, everything has frozen, everything's dying, growing dull in the senseless beauty, everything's forgotten, forgiven, and anyway nothing happened, and nothing ever will.

Oh, here's the phone. Call Lora. I myself have died—help others to help themselves.

Lora sounded congested.

"Oh, Denisov, take a taxi, come over. A horrific accident happened. What do you mean, you're locked in? In what fairy tale? Have you gone out of your mind, Denisov, I'm in the middle of a nightmare, it's the problem with Papa, I took him to the country, to an old woman, you don't know her, old lady Liza, she's a healer and a wonderful woman. Ruzanna recommended her, to read Papa; how do they do that? Well, they sit you on a stool under an icon, light a candle, the wax drips into a basin, old lady Liza reads prayers, the energy field improves a lot; it's all calculated to last several sessions; so you can imagine, in the meantime I took off for the village store, they have a good selection there, men's shirts from Holland, I wanted to get you some, but they were all gone, and I got held up looking at the goods for shareholders, I don't know what shareholders, some kind of consumer co-op or something. Well, for people who bring in birch sponge mushrooms they have men's moccasins, white ones, Austrian, exactly what you need, you can get jeans for meat and felt pens for carrots, we don't need any of that, but the moccasins would be good; so I said to the salesgirls: Girls, I don't have any birch sponges, maybe you'd sell me a pair anyway? And one of them, really nice, said: Wait for the boss, maybe you can arrange something; I waited and waited, and it was already dark, but no one came, and they said: It's not likely she'll come back—her boyfriend from Severomorsk was supposed to visit her, so I went back, and old lady Liza was in a frightful panic. She said he was just sitting, sitting there and he fell asleep, and when he falls asleep, well, you know what he gets like; he fell asleep, jumped up, threw the door open and started running, and it was dark outside, and the area's completely unfamiliar, and he just ran off, I don't know what to do, Denisov, I've been to the police and they just laugh at me. Anyway, I'm home now, completely wiped out, I mean Papa doesn't have a penny on him, I mean he'll wake up somewhere in the forest, he'll lose his way, he'll freeze, he'll die, he doesn't know where I took him, he's lost, Denisov, what have I gone and done!

. . . So he ran away, he broke out and ran away! He knew, he knew the road all along! The forgotten roused themselves, the shades lifted their heads, transparent apparitions pricked up their ears, listening: he's running, they've released him, go and meet him, go out on patrol, wave flags, light beacons! The sleepwalker is running along impassable paths, his eyelids closed, his arms outstretched, with a quiet smile, as though he sees what the seeing cannot, as though he knows what they have forgotten, as though at night he grasps what is lost during the day. He runs over the dewy grass, through patches of moonlight and deep black shadows, over mushrooms and pale nocturnal bluebells, tiny baby frogs. He flies up hills, he runs down hills, pure and bright and under the bright moon, the heather lashes his fleet legs, night blows in his sleeping face, his white hair flutters in the wind, the forest parts, the maples blossom, the light begins to appear.

How long will he keep running?

1988

Translated from the Russian by Jamey Gambrell

MASTERS OF THEIR OWN LIVES

I. GREKOVA

It was the late 1950s. I was taking a train on one of my long-distance business trips. My heart was burdened by a great sorrow, the nature of which is not worth mentioning, since it has nothing to do with my story. Because of this sorrow, I rather wanted to be alone, so I didn't talk much with the other passengers in my compartment. There were two of them. One was a military man, a formlessly fat colonel with a strand of hair flung across his bald head from ear to ear. He immediately settled in comfortably for the trip and only put on his uniform jacket when he stepped out at station stops; otherwise he traveled in his suspenders and a lilac jersey shirt (ordinary, standard male underclothing). I was irritated by the way he slurped his tea, by the wedding ring grown into his puffy, hairy finger, and by that overall sprawling air of superiority that usually comes from a high salary in conjunction with a low level of culture.

The other one was, in contrast, ascetically thin, stooped, and had a swarthy brownish face scored with wrinkles. When he spoke, his huge Adam's apple bobbed up and down like a float in his long neck. In spite of the wrinkles, the gray hair at his temples, and the thinning hair receding from his forehead, there was something unpleasantly youthful about him.

The second one was harder for me to figure out than the first. At times I almost began to like him; then he would suddenly become unpleasant. He had a good voice—deep, musical, with the elusively refined intonations of a well-bred person. Such a voice was interesting to listen to in and of itself. But then suddenly an offensive, ingratiating note would cut into it like a knife on glass. His eyes were large, blue, and brilliant, but his gaze was indirect, evasive, and the whites were covered with tiny red veins. His exaggerated, unnatural politeness was particularly irritating. All I had to do was walk into the compartment and he would jump up, bow and scrape, and shower me with every imaginable form of courtesy. But when he was silent and gazed pensively out the window, I couldn't tear my eyes away from his sharp profile. He reminded me of someone. Someone I knew very well, from my childhood. It was not until the second day that I figured out whom. It was John the Baptist from *The Appearance of Christ to the People.** That same burning, inspired eye. That same sunken, mournful cheek. It was John the Baptist, only older, balder, and battered by life.

The fourth seat in the compartment was empty. In fact, there were a lot of empty seats in our first-class car. It was usually empty in the corridor, and I spent a lot of time standing at the window alone with my great sorrow. On the evening in question I had also been standing and looking out the window for a long time. The bleak, emaciated, worn-out steppes flew by. It was late autumn—the beginning of winter in these parts. All the furrows in the naked ground were covered with white strips of hoarfrost, like black hair streaked with gray. In places the wind tousled the dry, dead stems of tall weeds, blackened either by the harsh summer sun or by the frost of early winter. A gentle, poignantly pink sunset, stretching halfway up the sky, glowed over the steppes. At one station, next to a water tower, a camel stood, embossed black on pink. What loneliness emanated from that camel! And then—just empty steppes again. Very rarely, human settlements would flash by—two or three clay huts grown into the earth and forgotten amid the steppes. A woman in a quilted jacket with a kerchief pulled down to her eyes stood in front of one such hut, towering over it. Her high rubber boots were covered with mud and the wind tore at her thin calico skirt. The woman stood motionless; only her head slowly followed the passing train. At the very edge of the road a sprawling thistle stretched its black, charred hands and seemed to call out, "Stop! Hear us out! Don't pass us by!" All of this moved me for some reason, and took its place beside my great sorrow in my

---

*A painting by Alexander Ivanov (1806–1858) that he worked on for twenty years (1837–57). John the Baptist figures prominently in profile in the foreground.
—TRANS.

mind. How awful it must be here on an autumn night when the train has already passed, and the sunset has faded, and you are so far from everything: from cities, from people!

The sunset had indeed gradually faded and nothing could be seen out the window. Only darkness—grayer above and blacker below—with an occasional trembling yellow light running through it.

I returned to the compartment. Both of my companions were there. It seemed to me that my arrival had interrupted a conversation that was important to both of them. The thin man didn't even jump up and make a fuss over me. It was obviously just as awkward for them to continue the conversation as it was to stop it suddenly.

"Yes," drawled the colonel, "a lot of water's gone under the bridge! I didn't recognize you at first, you see. Your face seemed familiar, but I couldn't place it. Thanks for reminding me."

"I recognized you immediately," said the thin man in his deep voice. "You've actually changed very little."

"Yes," the colonel repeated, and fell silent. "So Nina Anatolevna's dead. That's a shame, a real shame. What a beautiful woman she was."

The thin man didn't respond to that, only touched his neck and made a nondescript mooing sound. I anxiously stole a glance at him; it seemed to me that he was about to burst into tears. No, I was mistaken; he started speaking in a completely calm voice that even had that ingratiating note in it.

"It's very good to see you again. I'm glad. Very glad."

I began to feel uncomfortable and, besides, I didn't want to bother them, so I set off for the dining car. To get to it, you had to walk quite a distance, practically the length of the train. I kept walking and walking through dimly lit, overheated third-class cars. They were crowded and stuffy and smelled of people. From the top berths men's stocking feet stretched across the aisle; I had to bend down to get by. Women and small children slept and talked in their sleep in the lower berths. In one car, people were playing dominoes, slamming them down on a folding wooden table, and swearing. In another an infant was hysterically and hoarsely crying its heart out while a woman's voice patiently, dolefully chanted, "Aah-ah, aah-ah!" Between the cars the cold, dark connecting platforms swayed and rattled, metal clanged, the buffers hopped and skipped. Here, in the cold and the menacing blackness, the cursed, uninhabited steppe, screaming with loneliness, came into its own. And so they alternated: car and platform, the wretchedness of humanity and of the steppe.

I. GREKOVA

Finally I got to the dining car. I sat down by the window at a table covered with a stained tablecloth and wet cigarette butts on dirty plates. The other tables were no better. There were no other customers in the car except for a dejected, gray-faced drunk in a far corner, who had apparently long since eaten and drunk his fill. He was quietly explaining something to himself in foul language, but he couldn't seem to understand what he was saying and kept asking himself for clarification. Behind the bar dozed a fat, middle-aged barmaid with red hands, wearing a white smock over a quilted jacket and a stiffly starched lace cap. Nobody came up to my table. I walked over to the bar and roused the barmaid. She woke up unwillingly, clearly hating me, but she went and got the waitress (who probably had to be awakened as well). Now this one was gorgeous: a young, stately, heavily made-up blonde with bright purple fingernails. She cleared the table slowly and squeamishly and took my order—just as coldly and with hostility. God, that hatred in restaurants! How well we know it, we single women who don't drink vodka. There were no people in the dining car but I still had to wait more than half an hour before she brought me some slippery meatballs with cold macaroni and bluish cocoa. The tip I left on the tablecloth looked terribly orphaned. The blonde seemed mortally offended, but she took the money.

I was sitting there, unenthusiastically picking at the meatballs with my fork, when I suddenly heard a voice: "May I join you?"

It was the thin man from my compartment. He stood there bowing like a marionette.

I was slow in replying. There were a lot of empty tables around, after all. And I didn't feel like disturbing our solitude. Mine and my great sorrow's. But he couldn't have known that.

"I know what you're thinking," he said. "Why does he have to sit at my table? You're right, of course. But today I . . . in a word, it's difficult for me to be alone today. And our companion, the colonel, has already gone to sleep."

"Not at all, of course," I said hurriedly, "please sit down." He suddenly reminded me of the thistle by the road.

The waitress walked up to us, swaying her hips, and took his order quite animatedly: four hundred grams of vodka and some sandwiches. It was amazing how quickly she brought them.

"Perhaps you will do me the honor?" the thin man asked. "No? Well, no need."

He poured himself a glass and tipped it professionally, even elegantly, into his mouth. He followed this with a bite of his sandwich.

"A thousand pardons," he said, suddenly remembering. "I forgot to introduce myself. Igor Profirevich Galagan."

He stood up again and bowed like a marionette. I had to ask him to sit back down. I rather reluctantly identified myself: name, patronymic, surname, and profession. In our times you always give your profession when introducing yourself. So that it is clear from the start who you are. I mentioned this to him. He listened pensively and smiled after a while.

"Who am I? Why, I don't know that myself. You know what? Let me tell you my story. Then you will see for yourself who I am. You may even be able to explain it to me."

He said this rather charmingly and I liked him for it. I answered with complete sincerity, "It would be a pleasure."

He drank some more vodka and began to speak.

"Well, where should I begin? First of all, I'm a native of Leningrad. Of Petersburg even. All my ancestors lived in Petersburg. I come from an old railroad family. My father was a railroad engineer and so were both my uncles and my grandfather. Everyone on my mother's side also built railroads. A whole clan. But they couldn't make a railroad man out of me. I wanted to be an artist. My father was against it, but I stood my ground. You see, I loved painting with a passion. I literally quivered when I thought about it.

"My parents were very good people, especially my mother. I loved her terribly. If you like, I'll show you her picture."

He rummaged through his wallet with trembling fingers and took out an old photograph on stiff cardboard. The picture had been cut roughly at the edge, probably with scissors; it apparently hadn't fit in his wallet. The picture was of an amazingly charming fair young lady in a high-collared white blouse, with troubled and touching eyes. A pretty, curly-haired boy in a white sailor's shirt and with those same eyes had his cheek pressed against hers.

"Is that you?" I asked.

"Yes, why? Is it that hard to tell? It's not surprising. A lot of years have gone by, and, well . . ."

Yes, life. Who hasn't had occasion to sigh bitterly, observing its cruel trials. But here there was something else. How can I explain it? Here I was struck not by the difference but by the similarity. It's as if someone had said at that moment, "But how weak you are, life! Try as you might, you still couldn't kill the beauty in this face." And indeed, there it was: the genuine, immutable, troubled beauty of these two—the lady and the boy.

"But that's not what I wanted to tell you about, not about my childhood. It was a rather commonplace childhood for a boy from an educated, well-off family. With nursery maids, governesses, and white stockings. With three languages and music. A completely ordinary childhood in our circle, if it hadn't been for my mother. I was her only child. Her love for me was unbounded. And mine for her. We told each other everything and shared our dreams like the closest of friends. I'm not saying this right, it's coming out banal, whereas in fact . . . Anyway, when I wanted to become an artist my father was against it, but she was always on my side, even more than I was myself.

"My father died soon after the revolution, in 1918, leaving just my mother and me. It was a difficult time, what with the famine and all. I was already about seventeen. I attended a fine-arts studio—there were such places then, and each one with a passion for the new. All of life was being built anew—and art, too. Our studio was located in a ruined mansion filled with tattered couches and peeling gilt. The heating didn't work—the pipes had burst. In the room where we worked the floor was covered with ice all winter. To keep warm we burned paper right on the parquet. Such barbarian bonfires! And what a fine crew we were! Hungry, ragged, cheerful, and every one of us a prophet. We worked like madmen. We painted even though there wasn't any paint. We made it ourselves out of whatever we could find—soot, ground brick, slaked lime. . . . It was even interesting to work with paint like that. Every painting was a challenge. Something like solving a problem in geometry when all you have is a compass and a ruler.

"In winter our hands froze and the paint did, too. By the time you rubbed them and warmed them up . . . All this was child's play to me. I was happy, you see. Young, talented—maybe even gifted.

"It was harder for my mother. She kept house, unskilled though she was, and made porridge out of rye, oats, or bran on a tile stove fueled with wood chips. I ate this porridge without even noticing what I was eating. But the grain for it had to be obtained somehow. My mother earned money by giving music lessons to the daughters of profiteers. She also took various things to the bazaar and traded them for food. We didn't have many things left because at the very beginning some detachment or other had confiscated almost everything—most likely illegally. I remember that she once brought me two pieces of sugar the size of bread crumbs. I ate them with hardly a second thought. But while I was eating, she looked at me . . . as if she were praying. She got so thin, she turned a transparent, pale blue. I wasn't very concerned. I was as skinny as a street dog myself, but everything inside me was aflame.

"We had no light in the apartment, of course, so in the evenings it was dark. My mother and I went to bed early, dressed in our felt boots and fur coats, with every scrap of cloth in the house piled on top of us, and then we started to talk. We talked endlessly in the dark. About what? About art, about its prospects, about my projects. About my future. We never talked about everyday life or food or the hardships. This just wasn't done in our house. Even before, we never talked about money, for example. It was simply assumed that decent people didn't talk about such things.

"That's how we lived, and I was happy. Then one day in February 1919, February twenty-fifth—on a lilac-colored evening—I came home from the studio and found her dead."

He stopped and once again made that internal mooing sound, and once again I stole a glance at him: Was he crying? No, he wasn't.

"How I survived after that, how I endured, I can't explain. I was in despair. I was to blame: I had gotten carried away with art (damn it, damn that art!) and in so doing I had killed her, you see. But somehow or other I survived, I even made my way in the world. But that was later. First I served at the front, in a road-working detachment. Then I ran a stable. By the time I went back to Petrograd, life was already getting easier. And once again, I returned to art. I was painting with real paint now in a new studio. Then I managed to get into the Academy of Fine Arts. Just imagine, they accepted me, with my background.* I guess I was lucky. I worked furiously. My work was exhibited when I was still a student. It was well received. I graduated from the academy with honors. But all this, of course, meant nothing. You, for example, probably didn't know that there used to be an artist named Galagan."

"Well, you see, I'm from a different circle and don't know much about art at all. But why do you say 'used to be'?"

"Because he is no more. Look."

He held out his thin brown hands over the table. There was something unnatural about them, not quite human. Maybe it seemed that way because

---

*In the Soviet Union until recently class background was an important consideration in many aspects of life. Middle- and upper-class origins counted against a person, while preference was given to people of working or peasant background.
—TRANS.

his middle finger was much longer than the rest, like an eagle's foot. And these eagle hands were shaking. They literally danced over the dirty table-cloth. To stop them he had to grab the edge of the table. So that's why he's constantly holding on to something, I thought.

"There used to be," he repeated. "There used to be an artist named Galagan. You know, sometimes it seems to me that that person wasn't even me. I was so very happy. I mourned greatly after my mother's death, but I was still happy, you see, in spite of everything. It's as if I were sentenced to that happiness. I kept seeing the paintings I was going to paint, I could feel them—to the point of swooning, of delirium. But the main thing was that I knew I could paint them, that I would paint them, and that life was great. It's hard to believe but, you know, even now I sometimes don't sleep at night and I see those paintings. But now it's very difficult, because of my hands.

"Anyway, what was I just saying? Oh, yes. I was an artist and I lived alone and was happy. Then I fell in love. For the first time in my life. Boy, did I ever fall in love! She was the wife of one of my friends, an engineer. Her name was Nina Anatolevna. A magnificent woman. That's the very word—magnificent. Big, stately, strong. Her hair was ever so pale, almost white. Light hair is usually soft, but hers was wiry, thick, and curly. It stood on her head like Pallas Athena's helmet. And such an improbable color! Everyone thought she dyed it. She was used to that. Somebody would say to her, 'It's true, isn't it, that you dye your hair?' To which she would re-spond, 'No, but I do color my lashes and eyebrows.' Her lashes were long and black, and they stuck together in little spikes from the mascara.

"She was a cheerful woman. She had a voice of unusual strength. I fell in love with her while listening to her sing. I looked into her mouth and saw that her teeth, each and every one of them, were white and strong as a dog's, without a single filling. It was because of her teeth that she had such a good voice. The horn of Jericho. I was simply done for. She had a powerful chest, broad and protuberant. Do you know how many cubic centimeters she could exhale? Six thousand. And what muscles! Just imagine, later on when she and I were married, she would sometimes even beat me. You think it's funny for a woman to beat her man but, honestly, I really loved it. I thought, as the saying goes, if she beats me, she must love me."

"But what did she beat you for? Forgive my asking."

"Not at all! Why shouldn't you, when I took it upon myself to tell you everything. She beat me because of other women. You know, I was always very fond of women. Maybe because I grew up with my mother. I somehow felt more comfortable with them than with men. I liked almost all women.

■

92

Each in her own way. And they liked me, apparently because I knew how to distinguish their unique charms. I even gave in to temptation on occasion. And I always came to Nina afterward and confessed. She never made a scene, like other women—tears and so forth. She would get angry, to be sure, and swear at me. Several times she was even going to leave me for good. But whenever she beat me, I knew that in her heart she had forgiven me. What a woman she was! Words can't describe her."

"If I'm not mistaken, you said she was your friend's wife? And then yours? How did that happen?"

"You know, I fell in love with her immediately and apparently that's how I won her over, by loving her so intensely. But she loved her husband. And she came to love me, too. I know what you're thinking, but she wasn't a flighty woman at all. Except that she and I were married and divorced four times. She would marry me and then she would start thinking that she loved the other one, Lyonya, more. She would leave me and marry Lyonya. Marriage and divorce were easy in those days. To get married the two of you had to appear together; divorce required only the statement of one of the spouses. Now it's hard to believe that such freedom existed. They trusted people. Anyway, my Nina would get married with one of us present, either me or him, but she would get divorced alone. I just couldn't go with her to get the divorces. The third time (I think it was the third) I didn't even want to bother registering the marriage; I said, maybe we should just try it without that. Her eyes flashed at me (she had blue eyes, but they flashed just like black ones) and she started screaming, 'What do you take me for? I've come to you in all earnestness, for the rest of my life!' So we went and got married. I was beginning to feel uncomfortable in front of the girls at the marriage bureau; they all knew us and laughed at us. Very petty of me. But Nina couldn't have cared less. Every time she went to the marriage bureau she was cheerful, proud, happy, and her hair positively shone. But then two or three weeks would go by and she would start thinking. Thinking about Lyonya. She would even cry, feeling sorry for him. You know, she would talk about him in such a touching way that sometimes I would cry along with her—well, not cry exactly, but just go soft out of pity. Once I even said to her myself: go—and I handed her her coat."

"And how did all this end?"

"You know, it ended in the most unexpected way. I felt I couldn't take it anymore and brought my mother-in-law to live with me. I couldn't stand my mother-in-law, Adelaida Filippovna. Probably because she resembled Nina so much, but only in caricature. Nina was big, plump, and strong, while my mother-in-law was corpulent and crass. Nina's voice was loud and clear, like a bugle. My mother-in-law had the voice of a thug. She couldn't stand me, but she loved Lyonya. She lived alone and I didn't even see her much. When Nina left for the third time I went to see Adelaida Filippovna and invited her to move in with me. The old woman simply hated me. But for some reason she agreed and moved into my place. Boy, did she and I go at each other! She could curse like a dockworker, far outdoing me. We lived together for six or eight weeks and then Nina returned. And believe it or not, she returned for good. We got married for the last time and didn't get divorced again. I had played it right with my mother-in-law, it was a brainstorm, as they say. In time I even came to like her and she grew to like me, although we fought no less than before. She died about two years later and I felt very sorry about losing her; that's the way things turn out sometimes.

"Nina and I lived very well. As I already told you, she was a singer, and an excellent one. A huge success. Our place was always full of bouquets, potted flowers, even wreaths. Other singers performed only in concerts or variety shows; they were afraid of straining their voices. Nina was different. She sang everywhere: in the bathroom if she felt like it, or in the kitchen. She would sometimes even burst into song on the street, teasing a policeman. She always sang at home while I was sketching or painting, and it seemed to me that I was painting what she was singing. But I never painted her portrait, I was afraid to.

"Our home was not very tidy. She was not a terribly good housekeeper. And now, since I've brought up housekeeping, I can tell you about Tatyana. Later on she did a lot for us.

"This Tatyana was a large, fat, strong woman, like one of those stone statues from an ancient burial mound. She had a pretty face, though, very Russian. Smooth, wide, and rosy, with languishing eyes and a braid down to her knees. She had been dispossessed as a kulak* and she and her family had to flee their village. Her husband was a nondescript little guy with a runny nose. They had two small children, Nyura and Kolya. The whole family came to Leningrad. Without a residence permit, of course; that was out of the question.† So there they were, living without a permit, holed up in a

---

*A kulak was a well-off peasant. During the Stalinist period, kulaks were considered enemies of the people, were persecuted, sometimes killed, and their farms were confiscated. —TRANS.

†In the Soviet Union, even today, you need a residence permit to live in some of the larger cities. —TRANS.

corner behind a curtain at Tatyana's brother's place. He, too, was a drunk, his line of business vague. Tatyana fed her family and her brother, too. She was bursting with energy. She couldn't get a job, of course; she had no papers. So she began profiteering, as they call it: She would stand in line at a store, buy something, then take it to the market and sell it—for a profit, of course, a modest one, or sometimes for no profit at all if the buyer happened to be to her liking.

That's how she came into our life, through her profiteering. She was recommended to Nina: She can get you anything, Nina was told. And it was true. Nina liked to dress well, although she didn't know how to wear things— she would usually either soil them or burn a hole through them. As far as I was concerned, the simpler she dressed the better. You didn't have to dress Nina up, she was very beautiful as it was. I think I've already told you that. At first Tatyana would come to us on business. And then it just became a habit. She began helping Nina with the housework, she would come by every day. We got used to her and she to us.

"I was always struck by Tatyana's imperturbable composure, I might even say her gaiety. What kind of a life did she have, you might wonder? Struggling alone with the children—her husband didn't count—in a strange city, without a permit. Holed up in a foul basement behind a curtain. Any minute they could have found out that she was living there illegally, and she could have been sent out of the city, or worse—arrested for profiteering. I was constantly amazed: How could she stay so calm? It was completely incomprehensible to me. You know, we damned intelligentsia are born with a love for legality. It's indispensable for us to be registered, recorded, accounted for somewhere, otherwise we're miserable. But Tatyana lived free as a bird. If one of our kind were in her shoes he would worry himself to death with fear; he'd go to the police himself—do whatever you want with me, he'd say, so long as you define my position. But Tatyana's life seemed natural to her, just like anybody else's. She had a wonderful smile. I did a portrait of her with her braid and her smile; it wasn't bad. It vanished later on, like everything else. Nina wasn't overly jealous of her—I got it only once or twice because of Tatyana."

"You mean, you and Tatyana. . . ?"

"Yes." He said this simply, with a kind smile. "I told you I was very fond of women. And Tatyana was even quite beautiful in her own way, for someone of those proportions. The main thing was, she was serene. There was nothing extraneous cluttering up her soul.

"So Nina and I lived well, but we didn't have any children. During that first year, when Nina was leaving me for Lyonya and vice versa, she had two abortions, but we had no luck after that for some reason. We lived that way for five or six years. Then in 1934 Nina got pregnant and we were thrilled. I love children. We were expecting a girl, Lenochka. But it was not meant to be, because soon after that it all started.

"What do I mean by 'it all'? I was a Kirov recruit, you see. You don't? That's right, you're not from Leningrad. We call a Kirov recruit someone who was deported from Leningrad in 1935, after Kirov's murder. Nobody knows for sure how many people were deported at that time. But it must have been a lot. Many thousands. To us it seemed like everybody. Every one of us, after all, lives in a rather closed world, and it seems to us that this world is everything. They didn't deport everybody, of course, mostly the intelligentsia. And above all the old, hereditary intelligentsia, with strong Leningrad roots. They pulled us out by the roots. All of our friends were deported. Nina and I as well. They came one night, took our passports, and gave us two days to leave for Kazakhstan. They even specified the exact village we were to go to. That area wasn't even virgin farmland then, it was an absolute wilderness. Nina was in her eighth month, so I went to see someone—the devil only knows what his position was—who had authority over us, and begged him to let us stay until she gave birth. I remember how he received me. I said to him, 'After all, we're not guilty of anything.' He said, 'You are not being accused of anything. You are being deported as part of a mass sanitation measure. There's nothing I can do for you.' And he laughed, a peculiar kind of laugh, soundless—you know, the way dogs laugh: He opened his mouth and his tongue shook. At that point I realized it was useless to say anything to him. I went home and we started getting our things together.

"Tatyana helped us pack. It was sad for her to part with us, she had become attached to us, after all. Finally she said, 'Don't go.' 'What do you mean?' 'Just what I said, don't go and that's that.' 'But they took our passports.' 'Well, then, live without passports. I do.'

"But how could we! Was it in our power? Legality tormented us. We packed and left.

"The village in Kazakhstan where we were sent wasn't even all that small, but it was awfully far from anywhere, deep in the steppes, about forty kilometers from the railroad. Do you know how lonely it can be in the steppes? I had spent my whole life in Leningrad and was used to feeling the sea close by. But out there—it's terrible even to think about it—there was nothing but dry land for thousands of kilometers in every direction. I was so unaccustomed to it at first that I became very melancholy.

"There were a lot of us deportees in the village, about five hundred, and all of us were from Leningrad. We ran into some of our friends: the Golovins, the Golitsyns, the Gellers. As it turned out, they had sent only the letter *G* to this village. There was nowhere to live, nowhere to work. Nina and I managed to set ourselves up in a hut—more like a clay dugout—together with the owners, and we were thankful they had taken us in. We lived in a corner, behind a calico curtain, like Tatyana at her brother's. The day after we arrived Nina went into premature labor. The hospital was much too far and, besides, there was no way of getting her there. There were camels, but somehow I couldn't bring myself to take her on a camel. A woman doctor, whose name also began with a *G,* assisted at the birth. Nina delivered right there, behind the curtain, and I kept going outside and clenching my fists until my nails dug into my palms. The labor was difficult—it took two days. And the child—a girl—was born dead. Yes.

"Nina was ill for a long time. When she finally got back on her feet, we tried to get on with our lives. It was hard. The main thing was that we had agreed to leave for the sake of legality, but there turned out to be no legality of any kind. Nobody could have cared less about us. Live however you want to and however you can, as long as you register at the regional center every week. A village full of teachers, engineers, and librarians, and not enough work for a dozen people. But we managed somehow. Nina told fortunes in exchange for food. And I tried to paint. Once I even did an oil portrait of a local bigwig and got a leg of lamb for it.

"But all of that wasn't so bad. The worst thing was that they started making real arrests among our population of G's. At night dogs would start barking their heads off. The next morning you'd go out and learn that this one had been taken, that one had been taken. It was terribly unnerving. A man is a coward as long as he is vulnerable and my vulnerability was Nina. I remember going out into the yard at night. The moon would be shining, huge and white. The wattle fence would cast a pitch-black shadow. And you could hear the dogs barking back and forth all over the village. That meant they were coming. And I would be sure that this time they were coming to our place. To get us. You'd become so terrified that you'd think, I wish they'd hurry up and get here. But the barking would grow more distant— that meant they weren't coming for us. In the morning you'd look around— this one's gone, that one. Whispers. Worst of all was the uncertainty: what for, why, whom? The Germans—the Nazis—understood this very well. They had a name for this procedure: *Nacht und Nebel.* Night and fog.

"And then once, on just such a night when the dogs were barking, I felt that I couldn't take it anymore. I'd go crazy. The next day I announced to Nina, 'You and I are going to Leningrad.' 'What do you mean, Leningrad?' 'Just that, plain and simple. We're going to pick up and go.' She agreed at once, even cheered up a little. I myself was more hesitant—the legality issue was stronger in me—but I overcame it and we left. We made our way to the station, sold my suit (it's a good thing Nina had saved it), and bought our tickets. Nina insisted on going first-class. If you're going to live it up, then live it up all the way!

"So there we were, traveling first-class, just like normal people, and no one knew us. We were cut off from everything that lay behind us and ahead of us. It's as if we were flying somewhere. I remember a friend I had in my youth, also an artist. He would say that he wanted to exist without being included on a single list. And there we were—riding along and existing, but not on a single list. That is, there remained, behind us, a list of names beginning with the letter *G,* but we had broken away from that list, and now we had no list. A curious feeling.

"There was a soldier traveling with us in our compartment. A tall, handsome, young fellow. I hardly recognized him today. Yes, that's right—our companion. He's changed, of course—it's been more than twenty years, after all—and his hair has gone gray, but he's still recognizable. He and I reminisced about Nina today. He took a great liking to her then. My Nina was very beautiful, as you know; everyone fell in love with her. And at that time, when we had just broken away from the list and were on the road, she was particularly attractive—as cheerful as during out better times, and a little drunk with freedom. They got a guitar from the conductor and spent whole days singing. His voice was not bad, and Nina, of course, was a professional singer. People from one end of the car to the other gathered in our compartment to listen.

"At one point he went out into the corridor for a cigarette; Nina and I were left alone in the compartment and I said to her, 'I'm envious of him. Some people have all the luck! He goes along and knows where he's going, he has his own place. A master of his own life. But you and I?' Nina didn't respond, she just patted me on the cheek. At that moment he returned and the singing started again.

"That night I retired to the top berth and the two of them remained below. The fourth seat was empty, just as in our compartment today. I lay there on the top berth and kept thinking: What are we going to do in Leningrad? They were talking, and I listened to their conversation. At first they laughed and joked, but then they fell silent. Suddenly I heard him speaking in a completely different voice: 'Do you know what a pleasure it is for me to look at you and your husband, Nina Anatolevna? I look at you and think, there they are, the two of them, young, good-looking—masters of their own lives. And me? I can't even figure out who I am. I want to tell you the whole story: I was on leave and I got a letter from a friend at work that someone had informed on me and I would be arrested as soon as I got back. He didn't spell it out in so many words, of course, but the meaning was clear. So I decided not to return. I bought a ticket and just took off. And now I'm sitting next to you and I appear to be a flesh-and-blood human being, when in fact I don't exist at all. It's something you can't possibly understand.' And then, you see, he burst into tears. And believe it or not, I started crying, too, lying there on the top berth covered with my coat. But Nina was tough, she didn't cry. She just told him, very quietly, 'We are just like you.'"

While he was telling his story, my companion had poured himself several glasses. He wasn't drunk at all, just calmer, and those unpleasant, ingratiating notes completely disappeared from his voice. He sat at the table simply and attractively, like a true master, and I liked him more and more. All the same, when he poured himself another, I asked just in case, "Perhaps that's enough?"

"Oh, you mean the vodka," he said, not having caught on right away. "I thought you meant my story. Don't worry about the vodka. I never get drunk. I need two hundred grams to become normal, otherwise I'm not human. Reverse intoxication, so to speak."

It was completely quiet in the dining car. The stately waitress with the lace crown on her head had come up to us a few times to see if we needed anything else, but we didn't need anything. She finally understood that there was no reason to wait around any longer and she left, throwing a disdainful glance at me over her shoulder. That's how young women look at older ones. The gray-faced drunk at the far table finally calmed down and dropped his head on his arms. My companion briefly placed his jumping hand on mine across the table—a warm, friendly gesture.

"Are you sure you're not bored with my story yet?"

"No, of course not, on the contrary, it's very interesting."

"How nice you are! In that case I'll continue. As a matter of fact, there's not much more to tell. We arrived in Leningrad. Native stones under our feet. We felt like kissing those stones. We had no money, no place to live. And nowhere to go. Most of our friends had been deported, like us. And we were afraid of putting those who remained in jeopardy. And then all of a sudden, without consulting each other about it, we decided: Tatyana's. We went to Tatyana's.

"Her brother the drunk was still living in that same old basement, only he had gone over the deep end by now. We barely managed to rouse him. He told us his sister no longer lived there, her husband had died, her son had been drafted, her daughter had married a worker, and now Tatyana, sensible person that she was, was living with her daughter and even had a residence permit. He gave us her address.

"Just imagine, Tatyana welcomed us like family. She provided us with food, drink, and a bath. We asked her advice about what we should do next. She said, 'We'll see what happens. In the meantime stay with me.' I was even struck by the bold way she had said 'with me,' since the apartment belonged to Nyura's husband. It later became clear that she was in complete charge of the place. The young man, that is, Nyura's husband, hung on her every word. And even in the financial sense she continued to be the head of the household. Where she managed to lay her hands on the money to feed everyone, including us, I don't know. I'm afraid she was profiteering as before.

"I'm probably telling this all wrong. It may seem to you that Tatyana was a bad woman. I'm sure you consider profiteering wrong. In that case I'm doing her an injustice by not telling it right. Tatyana was wonderful, a true human being. Nekrasov could have been describing her when he wrote, 'She'd stop any horse at full gallop, /Go into a burning hut, too!'* She wasn't afraid of anything, she did everything simply and cheerfully. Believe it or not, the whole time Nina and I stayed with her we never once felt that we were living on charity, at her expense.

"In their tiny apartment—a wretched little place in an old wooden building—there was a windowless storeroom and she gave it to Nina and me. And so commenced our life at Tatyana's. Nina and I earned a little money ourselves. She embroidered napkins, I painted little rugs—water nymphs

---

*Nikolai Nekrasov (1821–1878): Russian poet. This line is from his long poem "Red-Nose Frost" (1863). —TRANS.

and swans—and Tatyana sold our handiwork at the market. Not much, but it helped a little.

"I soon learned to paint in a pretty way. You know, in essence our taste is spoiled, because what is truly pretty is what everyone likes: huge eyes, heart-shaped lips, a swan against the setting sun. Tatyana could have sold more of these rugs—there was a demand for them—but she was afraid it would be found out where she got them.

"We lived like that for two years, hidden away from everyone. We didn't go out on the street, since we might have been noticed. If we saw that someone was coming to see Tatyana, Nina and I went off to our storeroom and sat there very quietly. When the visitor left, we came back out. Once, even, a policeman stopped by. He hadn't come for us but in connection with Tatyana's dealings at the market. She took care of him in short order, charming him, even treating him to some vodka, and he left eating out of the palm of her hand.

"All in all, life wasn't bad, but it was tedious without books (Tatyana didn't have any, and I had already read her almanacs many times) and without fresh air. I even thought occasionally: Did we really do the right thing in leaving? There one could at least manage to breathe from time to time.

"The most difficult thing for Nina was not being able to sing. She couldn't sing because the neighbors would hear. Sometimes she'd forget herself and burst into song and I would have to say to her, 'Nina, don't sing.' Once she gave me a look that frightened me. I immediately understood what she was thinking: It's fine for you, you can paint, nobody hears that. But I couldn't paint anything anymore except swans and water nymphs. I even dreamed about them at night.

"We had been living like that for about two years when I began to notice that something was wrong with Nina. First of all the look in her eyes changed. Before they had been so blue and open, but now they became gray, suspicious. Once, as I was coming into the storeroom, she hid something from me. I saw it anyway: It was a tiny little shirt, what do they call it . . . a smock. Only very tiny, smaller than for an infant. I almost started rejoicing, although I was frightened at the same time, but then it turned out that Nina wasn't pregnant at all, this was just the beginning of her mental illness. And all because of the baby.

"When Lenochka died, Nina didn't grieve very much. No, don't misunderstand me, she cried like any mother would, but grief didn't break her. She didn't lose the sparkle in her eyes, or her voice, or her bearing. But the two years in the storeroom had broken her. I soon realized what was going on. It was enough to see her sitting in a corner rocking a bundle of rags, calling it Lenochka. . . . I understood everything at once. And she would sometimes burst out laughing. 'Keep it down, Nina,' I would say. She would fall silent and start to tear her hair. I would find clumps of it every day on the cot in the storeroom—such beautiful, shining locks—she would tear whole strands out. I . . . ."

Once again he mooed a little with his mouth closed. I knew by now that this was nothing, you just had to wait it out and he would start speaking calmly again. He still didn't speak, so I urged him on in my mind: Go on, go on. . . . He continued:

"Tatyana and I had to put Nina in a hospital. She understood very little by then. We agreed that Tatyana would take her and say she had found the sick woman on the street. I wouldn't go with them so as not to give myself away. It was all the same to me whether I gave myself away or not, but Tatyana was worried about Nina; she wanted her to have somewhere to return to when she got better. I agreed. I accompanied Nina only as far as the corner. It was the first time I had been outside in two years. The sky was so blue it hurt my eyes. At the corner I kissed Nina. She looked at me—and, I swear, it was a completely lucid look. I watched them walk away in the sun, she and Tatyana, and her hair stood straight up on her head and shone. I will remember it for the rest of my life. I never saw Nina again. That is, I saw her once more—in her coffin."

We sat silently. He didn't speak, I didn't ask any questions. Two or three minutes passed. By the way, what had become of my great sorrow? It didn't seem to exist anymore.

"My Nina died in the hospital. I won't bother telling you about it. I went completely numb then. I was totally indifferent. I sat in the storeroom and didn't say a word. And when I finally spoke, it turned out that my hands had begun to shake and I couldn't even paint swans.

"Tatyana literally nursed me back to health. And do you know what she did? She bought me a passport and a new name, she found me a job. I became a bookkeeper in a workers' guild. My name was Ivan Matveevich Sidorkin. Nobody pried into my life. And right before the war I even got a better job: I became a proofreader in a scientific research institute. A friend of mine from my old life found the job for me. He knew who I was but that didn't scare him. Not everyone's a coward, after all. I didn't know a damn thing about science, but I knew three languages and somehow managed. I lived at Tatyana's as before, but I had a residence permit by then, and was almost legal.

■

And that's how I lived until the very beginning of the war. But in the winter of 1941 I was arrested. And what's interesting is that they arrested me under my new name, for the crimes of Ivan Matveevich Sidorkin. And, if you can imagine, when they arrested me I was glad in some sense. It gave me solid ground of some kind under my feet. I immediately told the investigator my real name. He didn't believe me, he thought I was covering my tracks. I told him, 'I'm Galagan.' To which he responded, 'Don't try to fool me, you're Sidorkin.' He said this, then opened his mouth and laughed soundlessly, like a dog. That's when I recognized him. He was the same guy with the dog's laugh who had deported Nina and me. I recognized him, but he didn't recognize me. There were thousands like us, after all. Then I lost control of myself and told him, 'You swine, you! You think you're the master of life. But you're just a mangy cur.' And I belted him in the snout. After that I was severely beaten in prison.

"I was sentenced to twenty-five years—a life sentence, in effect. The charge was something straight out of a melodrama. There was supposedly a secret organization in Leningrad that was waiting for the arrival of the Germans and was forming a government in advance. And I supposedly had been assigned the portfolio of minister of trade. That's what they said, 'portfolio.' I couldn't have cared less, I signed everything, but I was adamant about one point. I confessed to being a minister, but not minister of trade. I demanded the portfolio of minister of art. They told me: There's no such ministry. And I said to them: But we had one. I participated in the conspiracy, not you. I'll bet some of them even believed that the conspiracy they had made up really existed! People often tend to believe in obvious phantoms. I was no longer afraid of anything—I laughed at them, thinking, even if you beat me I will still not agree to be minister of trade. But they didn't beat me anymore. True, they didn't let me sleep—they'd wake me up in the middle of the night and shove statements under my nose for me to sign, but I wouldn't sign them. And, believe it or not, I convinced them. They gave me the portfolio of minister of art! That made me feel good. Later on, when I was already imprisoned in the camp, I would often remember that I had managed to break them, and I felt like a human being.

"Being imprisoned was not all that bad. Or else the camp I was in was a relatively benign one. Other people tell horror stories. The camp was in Siberia, far from the war, and we were hardly aware of it. Except that the food got worse, but it was still tolerable, you could get by on it. It was cold, of course. The winters were hard. But generally speaking, none of this was terrible. Terror is the only thing that is truly terrible—those hellish nights when I was still vulnerable. We prisoners—all of us doing time under the fifty-eighth*—got on well together, and the authorities didn't oppress us much. When we were being led out to work, our escorts were amazed that among all of us men you didn't hear a single four-letter word.

"What was really hard to take was the 'believers.' That's what we called the people who believed that some of us were guilty. This is how they reasoned: It's impossible that all of this is completely senseless, that the whole country has gone mad. Therefore there must be some who are guilty. Not everyone, far from everyone, there are innocent people, too (I'm innocent, after all!), but where there's smoke there's fire (you may have heard this banal saying). Yes, there's smoke, but there must be a fire somewhere, too. When in fact we were all smoke and there was no fire at all. At least I never ran into a single instance. There were those who grumbled and criticized, but not a single one was really against the state. On the contrary, all were 'pro.' I never even came across people who were embittered, not excessively so, anyway. I guess it's saintly, that Russian intelligentsia of ours.

"Well, what else should I tell you? I've pretty much finished. I was released in 1954, rehabilitated in 1956. I was given a permit to live in Leningrad and even monetary compensation for a time.

"I saw that guy, the one with the dog's laugh, one more time. I was summoned to give evidence against him. I was, you see, the one and only member of our council of ministers still living. Yes, I saw him. He had changed a lot and wasn't laughing. I wasn't about to destroy him; I didn't mention that they'd beaten me. In all fairness, after all, I had hit him first.

"So, I think I've told you everything. You asked me before who I am. Well, I don't know myself. I settled in Leningrad at Nyura's place—Tatyana's daughter, remember? Tatyana herself died during the siege of Leningrad, Nyura's husband died at the front. She took up with someone else, but he walked out on her. She was left with a little boy. Sashenka's his name. I really fell for the boy. Nyura works and I take care of Sashenka. Such a fine little kid, with blue eyes. When I take him for a walk everyone thinks he's mine—some think he's my son, others, my grandson. So I live at Nyura's as a nanny. And I'm not ashamed of it in the least. You asked me who I am. If I had told you earlier that I was a nanny, you wouldn't have believed me.

"And where am I going now? Well, it's just silliness, I guess. I still have some money left from my compensation, and I wanted to go visit Lenochka's

---

*A catch-all statute against "anti-Soviet behavior" used frequently during the Stalinist period. Most political prisoners were sentenced under this statute. —TRANS.

grave. To see how she's doing there, whether they've dug it up. The grave was so very small."

He finished speaking and then added, "Yes, masters of their own lives. I've never, in fact, met anyone who's a master of his own life. Except perhaps for Tatyana. But she doesn't count. What kind of master is that—a profiteer? What do you think, do they exist anywhere—real masters of their own lives?"

"They must," I answered.

1960; first published in 1988.

Translated from the Russian by Dobrochna Dyrcz-Freeman

THE MONSTER

NINA KATERLI

"If only things were the way they used to be," said Aunt Angelina, and wiped her eyes.

"The way they used to be? Thanks very much! That's all I need. 'The way they used to be.'" Anna Lvovna could be seen choking back her tears and sniffling. "All my life I've lived in this apartment and cooked soup on a single burner in my own room, and I scarcely use any gas at all. And until very recently I had to go to the public baths, even though we have a bathtub right here. I was afraid to go to the toilet too often, not to mention the way my personal life . . ."

"No, if only things were the way they used to be," Aunt Angelina repeated obstinately. "I simply can't look at him the way he is now."

I myself had gotten used to the Monster, and even as a child had not been very much afraid of him. I was born after he moved into our apartment, so for me there was nothing unusual about coming across a shaggy creature with a single crimson eye in the middle of its forehead and a long scaly tail, whether in the hall near the bathroom or in the kitchen. But why go in for descriptions? One monster's very much like another, and ours was no more monstrous than the next.

They say that before I was born the other tenants in our apartment had filed an application with some agency, requesting that the Monster be evicted and housed someplace else, even that he be given an apartment all to himself. But the application was rejected on the grounds that if all monsters were given individual housing, there would be nothing left for large families. The argument ran that there were too many monsters and too few apartments, and when our application was turned down, the reason given was: "Yours is not the most serious case: There has not been a single fatality or instance of grievous bodily harm."

The fact that Anna Lvovna's husband had been turned into an aluminum saucepan for a whole month did not constitute grievous bodily harm, apparently. They say that as soon as her husband had returned to normal after having had borscht boiled in him and meat stewed in him for a month, he immediately abandoned her for another woman. Anna Lvovna was left on her own and since then has never forgiven the Monster for ruining her life. But the Monster claimed, on his honor, that he had turned Anna Lvovna's husband into a saucepan only because the man had been sweet-talking his mistress every evening from the phone in the hall, and he would have left home in any case. That way, at least he stayed home one more month, even if he spent the time as a saucepan.

I don't know how the story would have ended—Anna Lvovna, they say, was threatening to drop a burned-out light bulb in the Monster's feeding dish—but at that very time the Monster set off to work as an exhibit in a long traveling exposition organized by the museum of ethnography and anthropology.

In time, the tale about Anna Lvovna's husband came to be forgotten, but as the Monster grew older, he began to turn nasty, and gave us no peace at all.

You'd go into the bathroom and the sink and bathtub would be full of frogs and newts; or suddenly all the refrigerators would begin to howl horribly and heat up, the milk inside them would boil and the meat would roast; or else poor Anna Lvovna's nose would erupt in a boil of amazing size that changed color with each passing day: One day it would be blue, the next day lilac, and the day after that a poisonous green color.

It should be mentioned that Aunt Angelina and the Monster were on somewhat more equable terms. If she found a tortoise in her cupboard instead of bread, she would exclaim with pleasure, "Look, a reptile! I'll take it straight to the kindergarten for their pet corner!"

I now realize that when I was little the Monster simply couldn't stand me because I annoyed him so much. Everything I did annoyed him: I clattered up and down the hall and I laughed too loudly and I loved peeking into his room at him. So he kept giving me tonsillitis. Not serious cases, but the kind that if you so much as laugh you lose your voice, and if you run you get sent to bed.

When I grew up, the Monster did me great harm for a time; whenever anyone called me up, he would always get to the phone before the others and hiss, "She's not in. She's gone out with someone else."

I live alone now. My parents are no longer alive, I have never had a family of my own, and Aunt Angelina, with whom I share the apartment, takes care of me after a fashion, but as for the Monster . . . At least he's stopped tormenting me. Of course, if I come back late from the theater or from visiting friends, I'm bound to trip over the cat in the hall even though we've never had a cat. Or I'll tear my new dress on barbed wire. But that's nothing— mere trivialities. And recently even that kind of thing has stopped happening. Something's gone wrong with the Monster. You wouldn't recognize him: his eye has turned from red to a kind of dirty ginger color and his fur has gone gray; to put it in a nutshell, our Monster is getting old. He's stopped going to work and sits for days on end in his room, just hissing occasionally and sometimes sighing. And it was only today that Aunt Angelina said she'd prefer things the way they used to be because it broke her heart to look at the Monster, and she didn't have the energy to sweep up his scales after him.

"About those dreadful scales I totally agree with you, Angelina Nikolayevna," declared Anna Lvovna. "It's disgraceful! He must be made to do an additional week of cleaning duty. Nobody should have to wipe his dirt up after him!"

At this point the conversation came to a sudden halt because the Monster's door squeaked loudly, and a minute later there he was in the kitchen.

"Picking on me behind my back, eh?" he asked, and his eye reddened slightly. "Well, now I'm going to make you all freeze. You've never felt such cold!"

And the Monster began to blow so hard that his cheeks turned blue and his head started to tremble.

He blew and blew and suddenly I noticed Aunt Angelina shivering and jumping in place and knocking her legs against each other and rubbing her nose as if it had been frostbitten.

"It's so cold, oh, it's freezing!" she moaned dolefully, for some reason winking at me. Then she suddenly screeched, "What are you standing around like that for? Keep moving! Keep moving! Or else you'll catch your death of cold! Hands on your waist! Bend your knees! One, two, three!"

I wasn't that cold; in fact, I was even rather warm, all the more so because we were in the kitchen and all the gas burners were lit. But Aunt Angelina was winking and shouting so that I, too, put my hands on my hips and started doing knee bends.

"There you go! There you go!" shouted the Monster gleefully. "Now you're going to dance for me!"

I scarcely had time to think before Aunt Angelina grabbed me by the hand and began leaping about in a frenzied dance. I followed her lead.

"This is a nuthouse!" declared Anna Lvovna angrily and left the kitchen.

The Monster stared after her with a frightened look, then turned to Aunt Angelina as she danced and asked quietly, "Why isn't she dancing? Why did she go away?"

"She's stiff with cold!" shouted Aunt Angelina, gasping for breath but continuing to dance. "Can't you see?"

But the Monster had already forgotten what he had been asking. Dragging his tail and leaving a trail of scales across the floor, he went over to his refrigerator and opened the door.

"Where's my bone?" he said in perplexity, "I remember it was here yesterday, I bought it at the store!"

"Your bone? There it is, you made soup out of it this morning, don't you remember?" shouted Aunt Angelina, stamping away, but at the same time managing to pass the Monster her own white enamel saucepan with soup in it.

"I did? Oh . . ." and the Monster looked uncertainly into the saucepan, "I never had a pot like this."

"But it really is your pot, I just cleaned it up a bit, that's all."

"Aaargh!" he roared, "You dare touch my pot?! I forbid you to! For that both of you will . . . you will both . . . turn to stone for thirty-five minutes!"

Aunt Angelina suddenly froze the way children do when they play Statues. As fate would have it, my nose started itching and I was about to rub it with my hand when she inconspicuously but painfully jabbed me in the side, so I froze, too.

The Monster glared at us triumphantly, then grabbed the boiled chicken out of Aunt Angelina's saucepan and ate it whole.

"A delicious bone!" he rumbled, licking his lips, and then took pity on us.

"You can go now," he said dismissively, and strode imperiously out of the kitchen, slurping soup from the top of the saucepan.

"Why did you give him your entire dinner?" I asked, when the door closed behind the Monster. "And where is his bone, anyway?"

TISHCOV

"He didn't have a bone!" said Aunt Angelina, "He hasn't been to the store for a week."

"Then what's he looking for?"

"God knows! Maybe he forgot. Or maybe he's just being that way to show us that everything's all right. But he doesn't have any money, not a single kopeck, and he's going hungry."

"What about his pension?"

"He doesn't have a pension! He's an exhibition object, and . . . he's been written off, dropped from the show." Aunt Angelina lowered her voice. "It's as if he doesn't exist. And now I'm afraid about his room. I'm afraid he'll be evicted. Just make sure you don't tell Anna Lvovna."

"I won't breathe a word," I said, also in a whisper.

Aunt Angelina and I began taking turns buying bones and chopped meat from the butcher and leaving them in the Monster's refrigerator. On one occasion she left two apples and a small carton of kefir.

"All this meat's very bad for him! It can ruin his digestion," she said. "I wanted to buy him a big bottle of kefir but he always immediately bolts any food he has, so I bought a carton instead."

"He's bound to throw out the apples," I said.

"We'll see. Maybe he won't realize. Lately his eyesight's been getting poor," and at that moment Aunt Angelina looked around at the door; Anna Lvovna was just coming into the kitchen.

"It makes me laugh just to look at the two of you," she declared. "All this undercover charity—do you think I'm blind? Such pretense—what a show! And for whom! If he was human, it would be one thing, but he's not, he's just vermin."

"You should feel sorry for him; after all, he's old," I said.

"My dear, pity's not a feeling you should brag about, pity's humiliating. And in this case," she said as she put her coffeepot on the stove, "in this case, pity doesn't enter into it. It was one thing when he was making himself useful in his . . . in his freak show; we could put up with him then, but not now. Animals should live in the wild."

The Monster had crept into the kitchen so softly that we didn't even know he was there. He now stood in the doorway and his eye was as ruddy as it had been in the first flush of youth.

"So, I'm an animal, am I?" he said slowly and slumped onto a stool. "I'll show you."

His breathing was heavy and irregular, the sparse gray fur on his head and neck stood on end.

"I'll show you. . . . Your . . . legs . . . will . . . give way . . . beneath you! . . . Yeah! . . . You will . . . all . . . fall . . . on the floor . . . and then . . . One, two, three . . . All fall down!"

Aunt Angelina and I collapsed simultaneously. Anna Lvovna remained standing, leaning against the edge of the stove, and grinned, staring the Monster straight in the eye.

"And you?" said the Monster. "What about you? This doesn't mean you, I suppose? Fall down, I tell you!"

"Give me one good reason why I should," she said, scowling.

"Because I've put a spell on you, that's why."

"Oh, you slay me," said Anna Lvovna, going right up to him. "What have we here, a magician? All you know how to do is leave your scales all over the floor and help yourself to everyone else's food! You're just trash and you're due for the dump! Just garbage. You've been written off!"

"Written off?" repeated the Monster in a whisper. "Who's been written off? Me? Written off? Not true, not true! I can do anything! Look at them! They fell down!"

"Ha! Ha! Ha!" Anna Lvovna burst out laughing. "They're just pretending. They're sorry for you, see. You've been written off. You've lost your job. I've been to the museum myself and I've seen the directive with my own eyes."

"No!" The Monster leapt up from the stool and rushed from the door to the stove, thrashing his mangy tail across the floor. "I'll show you. I'll turn you into a rat! A rat! Now!"

"Ha! Ha! Ha!" was Anna Lvovna's only reply, and suddenly she stamped on the Monster's tail with all her might.

The Monster screamed. One after another great tears streamed from his eye, which immediately turned pale blue and dimmed. Aunt Angelina and I jumped up from the floor.

"You ought to be ashamed of yourself! Let him go! An old man. Don't be so cruel to him!"

"A rat! a rat!" hissed the Monster, forgetting himself, and he poked Anna Lvovna in the shoulder with a dark and crooked finger. "One! Two! Three!"

"Ha! Ha! Ha!" sniggered Anna Lvovna.

But now Aunt Angelina and I began to shout. "A rat! A rat!" we screamed. "You're a rotten rat! Vermin! One! Two! Three!"

Suddenly Anna Lvovna was gone.

She had just been laughing in our faces, her shoulders shaking in her white blouse, when suddenly she was no more. She had totally disappeared, as if she had never existed.

The kitchen suddenly fell silent. Something live jabbed against my foot and immediately leapt away to the wall. I screeched and jumped onto the stool.

A large gray rat shot across the kitchen and scuttled under Anna Lvovna's table. The Monster was whimpering softly, his face turned toward the wall.

"See," said Aunt Angelina, "you did it. Don't cry. Now let's go and have some soup."

"It's you who did it, not me. And it's true, you know; I have been written off. There has been a directive."

"What do we care about directives," said Aunt Angelina, carefully stroking the Monster's fur. "Don't you be afraid of anybody. And if anybody touches you I'll give him . . . I'll give him ants."

"And so will I," I said. "Okay?"

The Monster didn't reply. Slumped against the wall, he dozed off, shutting his eye and wrapping his thin hairless tail around his legs.

1987

Translated from the Russian by Bernard Meares

In Memoriam

Tatyana Nabatnikova

October 9. My son is an exact replica of his father, even though he grew up almost entirely without him. Environment never supersedes nature.

Just like his father he raises his eyebrows high up on his forehead, averts his eyes, and sits that way in vacant silence, feigning pensiveness in order to wait out the boredom of his visit.

"Go, Serezha, go," I say.

"Well, Mom, I've got to run, you feel better now," he says, quickly coming back to life, and only when he's already at the door does he suddenly remember. "By the way, Mom . . . I can't come tomorrow."

And his face screws up in a grimace of false sympathy just like his father's: brows like a little bird with its wings hanging down.

"You don't have to, son, you don't have to. The doctor says you shouldn't visit me too often."

He left, and my grim neighbor Ekaterina Ilinichna sighed bitterly, saying nothing. I'm not bitter. I understand. All I have to do is remember myself at twenty. At that age it's difficult to come to grips with death.

I have a good idea why he can't come tomorrow: It's Friday evening—friends . . . or a girl. Our crowded apartment free at last, a festival of independence. . . .

I hear Nurse Olya (her station is right outside the door to our ward) calling my doctor.

He has eyes you sink into, there is more hidden behind his face than ap-

.

pears to view. He leaned over and sat on the edge of my bed. Without wasting time, he took my wrist in his left hand, affectionately touched my cheek with his right, and, drawing back my lower lid slightly, peered into my eye; only then did he ask solicitously, "What's the matter?"

I caught my breath. "Doctor, tell my son that he can't come to see me—often."

The doctor didn't say a word, he simply answered with a look of understanding. At the end fate has sent—just to tease me—someone who understands without explanations.

October 10. He noticed the notebook on my night table and the ballpoint pen that lay on top of it. "I'll bring you a pencil, Magdalina Yurevna. It's hard to write with a ballpoint while lying on your back."

He's right: The ink doesn't flow, and I turn over on my side with difficulty, lay the notebook at the head of the bed next to me, and write almost by touch, without seeing.

He returned ten minutes later, planting firm steps on the floor, and once again caught me unawares (I hadn't had time to focus my attention) with his ravaging walk. How small the ward is: five steps from the door to my bed. What can I do in the span of those five steps? I am like a starving man who lifts a morsel of food to his mouth—his nostrils have just begun to twitch from the enticing smell, he has just managed to open his mouth—and the steps have already ceased. My avid, starving eyes did not have time to bite off even a crumb of his procession, let alone sate themselves—and he was already at my bedside. And only the teasing memory, like the lingering aroma in the nostrils of a starving man, of those insufficient five steps, and no matter how I strain myself to absorb them, I always run out of time—it's agonizing!

If I were to get up out of my bed, check myself out of the hospital, and go on living—I would lie in wait for him in the morning at the entrance, stealthily keeping watch from the building next door (I'm forty, Lord, forgive me!), and I would follow him unnoticed right up to the door of the hospital, solemnly, desperately devouring his every step, trying to fill up my empty, famine-stricken granaries with his steps. . . . I didn't even have time to finish this sentence: Ten minutes later he came into the ward—five steps—and brought me a soft automatic pencil. "Thank you, Doctor." He nodded to me with his firm gray eyes and abruptly walked out, and for a long time afterward I could still feel the traces of his fingers on the warm edges of the pencil. Now I can write comfortably in my "working" position with a large book propped under my notebook.

October 11. Why am I suffocating, unable to draw a proper breath? They put me into pre-op, ran tests, yet say nothing about an operation. Is it too late? I'm afraid to ask; I don't want to make him lie to me.

October 12. You know that you're dying in the most pitiful and helpless fashion. You're aware of it all the time, you forget only when you're asleep, and when you wake up the first thing you remember is: I'm dying. Every morning is a return to dying. And the constant thoughts: Stop this humiliating, submissive waiting. There are a lot of ways out—for instance, don't breathe, and that's it. Or . . . in general, there are a lot of ways out, I think them through in detail, but only in the hope that none of them will be necessary, that all of this has nothing to do with me. Constant cowardice: Hide—and they won't find you. Or at least drag it out. As if a postponement would change anything.

October 13. I say, "Doctor, afterward, give my notebook" (and I myself still don't know to whom. A secret, momentary fantasy: to him. Let him find out. Oh, the shame!) ". . . under no circumstances to my son, but only . . . only to my mother, if she . . ."

"You'll give it to her yourself when you check out."

So he's lied at last. He's succumbed to lying.

How about a trade, Doctor? I'll tell you ruthlessly about love, and you in retaliation, point-blank—about my death. Well, Doctor, what do you say?

"You'll give it to her yourself when you check out." "From your lips to God's ears, Doctor." And he hurriedly went on to the next bed: The rounds continued.

And say I fell in love—and it saved me? Is that possible?

There was a flood or perhaps simply a storm in the dead of night. I waded up to my waist in the sea, the darkness of the water and the sky merged behind me and wisps of lights on the shore glowed feebly in the darkness. I walked toward the light, but remnants of the storm—waves—washed over me one after another; strange waves—coming from the direction of the shore. I sensed that I was stepping on the corpses of people who had drowned, I even had an urge to bend down and lift one of them up out of the water: What if it turned out to be someone I knew? But I remembered that it was dark, I wouldn't be able to recognize anyone. Besides, I wanted to make it to shore, to the living, as fast as possible.

And far away on the shore, people were running along the edge of the water distressed and worried, each searching for loved ones who had survived the flood.

I thought about the people who had drowned: How absurd—to perish right near the shore. And I hurried out of the darkness toward the people and the lights, although I was still up to my waist in water. But the waves that came rolling in from shore were growing higher and higher, they were cresting and breaking and there was no way I could get through them. Suddenly I realized: These apparently calm waves were in fact dragging me back out to sea. I was not getting closer, but farther and farther from shore, and the people on the shore had become very tiny, and the darkness was about to merge with the water not only behind me, but also in front of me, and I couldn't do anything about it.

And I no longer thought of the people who had drowned as "they," I was already thinking "we."

On the shore the distant, helpless people were still running back and forth, there was no one among them looking for me. And all the people were "they." And we were the ones who had drowned. And the waves, the waves . . .

That was the dream I had. Now it's all clear. In my dream I had already crossed the divide between "we" and "they." Now I have to get used to the idea while awake.

October 14. "Well, Ekaterina Ilinichna, what's the matter with you? Hurry up and get well, otherwise there'll be no one to feed us," said the head doctor with that rehearsed confidence that deceives only those who very much want to be deceived, knowing full well that Ekaterina Ilinichna would never budge from here on her own two feet.

She worked as a cook for the doctors. Our doctor, she said, sometimes brought his little girl to lunch when his wife was away on a business trip. . . . I'll never, never get to see his little girl. I'll never know which of his treasures she inherited: He has a certain way of turning his head. . . . If only it were possible to grasp that mannerism and render it in words. . . . He also has a certain glance: a flick of the eyelids that is not quite questioning, but more like calm attentiveness. And now all this . . .

Ekaterina Ilinichna underwent an operation two months ago (for a stomach ulcer, she said) and checked out of the hospital. Now she's back in again and sinking very fast, but she is trying not to understand what is happening. I can see from our doctor's eyes, by the haste with which he leaves her on his rounds, how heavy a burden it is for him.

She is dying, and he, like a god, has granted her immortality for her remaining days, while he lugs her around in his own soul. Like a mountain climber on the ascent, he's carrying her knapsack for her.

He doesn't have to carry mine, I'll do it myself. He seems to understand that.

The dingy ebb and flow of hospital life, the feeble shuffling of slippers along the corridor, the tinkling of syringes in sterilizers, metastases of pain through the quiet of the wards—those are the last sounds my ears will hear.

It's hard for me, terribly hard. . . .

Beyond the door at the nurses' station two nurses are chattering and exchanging smiles: sounds from beyond the hospital, from beyond death, indecent sounds of life in the middle of a crypt, an insolent, tactless reminder. . . .

An attack of despair and malice. But it has passed.

October 16. What has life yielded to me of love's luxury but deathly losses— one betrayal after another.

I suddenly remembered the heated marital quarrels I used to start with my now-forgotten husband. Their secret purpose was to test his love. To frighten him with the idea that I didn't love him and could live without him. And suddenly I realized with horror that he wasn't frightened! He would go to bed and sleep peacefully, without suffering, having the advantage of indifference on his side. After this the quarrels ended and so did the love.

At last there will be no betrayal, because I expect nothing.

The structure of my son's soul is exactly the same as his father's: four

poles, four crossbeams. No matter how I've tried to fill this empty paral-
lelepiped, everything helplessly tumbles out; there is nothing for it to hold
on to.

Now, before the final reckoning, I am not ashamed nor do I find it terrible
to admit to myself at last what was concealed beneath the deeply embedded
greasepaint of my role as loving mother: I do not love my son.

October 17. Ekaterina Ilinichna said that the doctor's daughter is not his
own—she's adopted. That means she has inherited neither the turn of his
head, nor his glance, nor his straight, needlelike eyebrows. It means that I
am leaving less undone in life than I thought.

It hurts so much. . . . I'm afraid to sleep. I'm afraid of the relentless
dreams—they terrify me. I'm tired and I want to forget, at least for a little
while.

October 18. Sveta came to visit, from work. She exclaimed: Magdalina, when
are you getting out of here and coming back to work—things are a mess
there!

My voice breaking, gasping for breath, I told her that in the lower right-
hand drawer of my desk, on little sheets of paper ("Make sure they don't get
thrown out by accident, they look like rough drafts"), are the results of an
experiment that I have been running for half a year, they are already worked
up, let Nikolai Sergeyevich deal with them himself. But at that moment—a
salvo of five rapid-fire steps, which dissolved immediately, like the trail of a
star—he came in, my gray-eyed doctor.

His firm gaze, like a king's herald, clears the way for him and muffles
voices. In the cleared silence he allowed me to finish what I was saying. With
a glance he dismissed Sveta, who immediately took her leave, and then he
said in a tone of slightly derisive reproach, "Is it so important that the experiment not go to waste?"

When he speaks, I expend more effort in trying to memorize and preserve his voice than in trying to understand the meaning. "One has to work
in life, Doctor. And take that work seriously," I said. He realized that he had
offended me and smiled. "But what about people who make bombs? Or take
another profession—spying. Intelligence officers are respected. But they're
professional liars. Aren't they?"

And here I caught him. "Doctor! Doesn't your profession sometimes require you to lie?" And I looked at him. He kept silent, but looked back at me fearlessly, as if he were asking: Will you keep a grip on yourself? I'll manage, my eyes said to him in reply. And he to me: Well, bear up, old girl, you're on the right track. We're no cowards.

And so we held our peace. Well, that's it, it means that there's no doubt about it anymore: It will be over soon.

October 19. "Did you sleep today, Magdalina Yurevna?" he asked, palpating my protruding stomach with his fingers, listening there to something I didn't understand.

I didn't answer immediately; in my mind I hastily ran through my nightly dreams in the darkness—through the pain—incredible dreams about him that are awful to repeat even to myself: he, I. . . .

I answered: "No."

He stopped moving his fingers.

"They told me you have been refusing injections. That's foolish, listen to me: Pain distracts us from what is most important. And you have to live fully now."

He looked at me persuasively, and I recalled something he once said to a sick little boy: "Well, friend, if you can't have what you want, you have to learn how to want what you have." Fine, I'll take the shots, which you don't admit are morphine.

Submitting to him is my final joy. He said I have to live fully. I understand: I have to think over all my unexpended thoughts and come to terms.

October 20. When I was a child we had a neighbor with a singsong voice. She would come to visit my mother and speak in such soft, downy tones. I would half drowse at the table, not letting a word of this tender lullaby escape me. Then for two or three days afterward I could re-create the experience: I'd rest my head on my hands and float in the remembered sounds that rocked me to sleep. . . . But after three days the memory would fade away.

Why did I think of that? What could be the reason? Oh yes, that's it. Ekaterina Ilinichna had the same voice when she was still able to talk. Now Ekaterina Ilinichna is no longer among the living.

After they carried her out and I was left alone in the ward, I summoned him and asked him to be taken there, to that other shore, today, right now—I didn't want to go on anymore.

He took my hand, which has become loathsome to me (since I've been ill, my whole body has become repulsive to my soul; isn't death just the soul forsaking the body that has become repulsive to it?), he looked into my eyes, which were bursting from a surfeit of pain and said, "You aren't ready for what you are requesting. And the pain—I'll think of something right away."

"You don't have to anesthetize me. If I'm no longer able to endure life on my own, I don't need it anymore, take it away from me."

I said this at the height of despair, but some insatiable part of me still untouched by death once again managed to marvel at the straightness of his nose and brows, at the clarity of his gaze—O Lord, his gray eyes, the darkness of those light eyes—and at something else that baffled me, that words could not convey.

"I don't want to live to see tomorrow," I whispered bitterly.

"See, there is still some bitterness left in you. People who have exhausted all their reserves don't talk like that. Stop it. Now I'll take away your pain—not with medicine," he said, palpating my stomach with his fingers.

He walked out and soon returned. By what he began to do, I finally understood (roughly) the nature of my illness: The passage from my stomach is blocked up by a tumor, and although I am not eating and drink almost nothing, my life juices cannot free themselves, my stomach has swelled up, it is crushing my lungs, I am suffocating.

He pushed a rubber tube into my mouth to let my torment pass out of my stomach through it. I choked and coughed, a convulsion constricted my throat, tears welled up in my eyes, we caused each other suffering—and it was the only interaction with him I was capable of.

He wiped my lips with a napkin himself, and I felt no shame.

As if I were his child.

I no longer have enough strength left to be amazed.

In all likelihood, my soul, having suddenly come to its senses, has decided to live its last hours on this earth in the most beautiful way possible.

October 22. He is sick. Who is taking care of him? His wife? Does she place compresses on his forehead and bring him tea with lemon from the kitchen?

He is lying there helpless, feverish. If only I could take him in my arms and carry him, carry him around the room. Just as I would carry my son in my arms all night long when he was small.

Another doctor, with a shrill voice, made the rounds; he looked around the ward. "What's going on, why are there two empty beds? We have patients with no place to lay, but here!"

"Lay"—that's the word he used.

"The doctor in charge won't let us put anyone else in here," Olya answered.

He sat on my bed, took my pulse without looking at me, and sniffed, "That dandy of ours is putting on airs. What do you mean he won't let you? What makes his patients better than ours? Why should conditions in his ward be better than in ours?"

Olya didn't answer; he stood up, still without having looked at me.

Oh, you monsters! "Dandy." That was the foulest thing anyone could say about him. The most exacting sculptor could have found nothing to alter in his harmoniously irregular face.

At times I close my eyes and on my eyelids I see a negative of something that I've never seen before and haven't even thought about. Myself, for example: a white silhouette against a dark background, face turned toward my thrown-back arm. It seems my soul is no longer firmly attached to my body. As in a dream, it has half separated itself from me, soars above me, and I am looking at my half-abandoned body.

Love is quiet. It keeps silent, because when it is there, it becomes clear that there are no words or gestures or images that could even come close to expressing it.

Is it possible that he won't get well before I die? Then again, what difference would it make?

October 23. The head doctor came by with his entourage.

"So. We really must fill up the ward. There have been complaints about your arbitrariness," he said, and I could see whom he was speaking to. So he's not sick. Thank God, he's all right.

"We'll talk about it," he answered.

With a kindly grimace studied to perfection, the head doctor sat on my bed and with forced attentiveness, also studied, inquired, "Well, how are we feeling, my dear Magdalina Yurevna?" He had to glance at my chart first in order to call me by name. He had sweet-talked Ekaterina Ilinichna the same way. I wanted to answer according to the rules of polite behavior, "Thank you, not bad," but I thought: The hell with it, I have very little time left to live and I would be going against the promptings of my soul to observe the rules of polite behavior in response to his official charity. He even has the gall to call me "my dear." He doesn't even use his own words—God didn't give him any words of his own—he simply comes to work, loads dozens of official words onto his tongue, innumerable "my dears," and distributes them, without even drawing on his own stashes.

I turned away and said nothing.

And then the entourage moved on, but my doctor lingered for a second, touched my hand—gratefully!—and said, "Hatred is a valuable substance. It shouldn't be squandered on trifles."

He sees everything.

October 26. When I was only twenty-five I felt as if my life had already been lived to the full. As if I had sat down at a table, sampled all the dishes, satisfied my first hunger, and continued to eat with sated indifference, at peace with the fact that I wouldn't regret tearing myself away from the food, standing up, and walking off at any moment.

So what is there for me to be afraid of?

They give me injections—and I sleep. He comes in the morning, feels the outline of my liver, marks it in ballpoint pen on my stomach with little crosses. My little grave markers. He looks at me long and strangely, almost with envy—as if we were standing in line for watermelons and, even though there would be enough for everyone, I was already close to the head of the line while he still had a while to wait, shifting from one foot to the other.

October 28. Do you remember, Magdalina, do you remember how after sleepless fatigue, he dozed off, curled up on the ground, and his numbed legs flinched convulsively? I extricated myself from sleep, put his head on my knees, and smoothed his hair with weightless fingers so that he would sleep more easily. I cleared the brown earth of stones so that it would not be painful for his legs to lie on. The closeness of the airport, the oppressive air lay heavy on my head, flights were delayed for two days, and I soundlessly smoothed his light hair so that at least in his sleep he might forget how tired he was. In the evenings Linda sat on a bench near the house, holding her monster on her knees and slowly concealing herself from the persistent sun in the shade of the planet. And you survived to my time. How foolishly we cram ourselves into the procrustean bed of convention, but we don't fit in and think that this is our misfortune, while it is really our luck. You are the realization. On the shore amid the grass and the trees a soldier is playing a bugle and dancing under the September sun. And that was a premonition of you.

Most probably I'm lying. Everyone did broad jumps. But he said it anyway. And that was also a premonition of you. Oh well, he won't come, but what's so terrible about that? But inside of me something is ripping apart, ripping apart, and the last thread of hope has snapped. I was grieving not for you, but for myself, as I never came to be. How could I have held on to this into my forties?

God, what gibberish I've written. What are these injections doing to me?

My son came again. The look of a sated animal, devoid of expression and meaning. A two-legged animal, the result of my sex life, which was as untalented and monotonous as a cheap pendulum.

Blasphemy? No. What an unrestrainedly audacious honesty has come to life in me. I would like to carry on just as boldly and not die. As it is, I've always hidden behind proprieties: the procrustean bed packed with coffins of decorum.

November 1. Landscapes inaccessible to the artist.

Water fills the darkness and a torrent of moonlight pours down through the clear gaps in the clouds. And the moon water quivers in the dark space. Inaccessibility.

And the vision renews itself as often as I want to see it. In the ultramarine twilight the splash of oars, the sound of unbearable happiness, the sky grows beyond the bounds of my eyesight, and a soundless echo from the sky, I die out, I dissolve in the incorporeal darkness, I no longer exist, and the vision renews itself.

What is this? My first practice flights to the beyond?

November 3. I have the freedom of choice conferred by death: I can choose between death and everything else at any moment, whenever I want to. After all that has already been, death is the best of all the remaining pleasures.

I now look down upon life. The way an adult looks down on the games of childhood. I have already surpassed life.

November 5. I feel nauseated from an aversion not to any imminently approaching moment, but to the present moment: It's repulsion toward the very sequentiality of time itself. I don't want to and can no longer live in time, I resent the very notion of time.

I don't want to get up, but it is unbearable to remain lying down. All things are equally bad, the distinction between better and worse has vanished. I have lost all desire, and the movement of life in time has become impossible and intolerable.

November 6. With my strangely sharpened sense of hearing I overheard a conversation today at the post beyond the door. Olya was anxiously saying to someone, "We have to warn the coroner that he might be called in tomorrow. The postmortem will have to be performed immediately, because the body will spoil over the holiday, and she has to be transported to Latvia, to her homeland."

"What about the zinc coffin?" a woman asked in response.

"Her son has already ordered it."

What foolishness—to transport me to my homeland—did I really want that? Perhaps I said something when I was delirious? It's unnecessary, pointless. All that will remain of me will be a heap of rotten flesh—what's the point of moving it? I mustn't forget to call this off as soon as someone comes in.

It is as if I am moving out of the zone of temporal activity. My years will stop growing, and everything that is subordinate to sequentiality will come to an end: the beating of the heart, metabolism, movement through space.

There will be some new quality—yes, but what? I dimly picture a soft darkness, prickly flashes of lightning, but it is beyond my imagination.

Only one thing remains: to wait and see. Fear has been replaced by curiosity.

It doesn't hurt to die. And for a long time now life has been nothing but boring repetition. I imagine the road home from work in the twilight of winter, silent crowds of dark pedestrians walking past the illuminated stores, my son, the weather. . . . I've seen and imagined it all before and so I can let it go without stopping.

I already see my doctor at a distance, like the edge of a forest on the horizon. I already look at him as though out of distant memory. He sat down and I took his hand. A small palm, filled with life; inside something pulses, beats, lives with much to spare.

I said to him, "I'm going to remain silent: Words are repugnant to me. But I want you to know: I feel very good now."

He nodded to me from far away, from the blue haze of the horizon: He believed me.

"Don't give me any more shots: I want to see with my own eyes: After all, it's only once . . . it's too important. . . ."

He looked at me, and his gaze was one of tender solemnity. No, I couldn't say what his gaze was. Then something snapped, and he quickly, quickly turned away. . . .

He did this not for me, because I was leaving, but for himself, because he was staying.

Many people never find the time their whole life long to notice how lonely they are.

I squeezed his fingers and released him completely.

November 7. Today's the day. I now know for certain: today.

I must not forget to tell the doctor not to leave the hospital today before five o'clock.

And I have to hold out until evening—to give Mama my notebook.

I lived badly: I was afraid of death, and so I lived at half strength. It should be the other way round: If death is not frightening during life, then life won't be frightening either. . . .

The doctor did not want to be present at the autopsy.

He carefully closed the notebook. He wanted to put it in the drawer of the night table, but changed his mind. He held it hesitantly over the wastepaper basket: shouldn't he throw it away? He could take it home—well, and then what? It would lie among the eternally preserved pile of paper rubbish and several years from now he'd come across it—he'd reread it and feel sad for a few minutes until his wife called him to supper. And at supper he would find out that Lenka had gotten a D and that she'd missed gym class—and all that would seem more important than empty memories.

There was no one to give the notebook to: Magdalina's mother hadn't come after all—he'd been told that she had died at the same time, at five o'clock.

To die at the same time—that's the most one person can do in memory of another.

But how can a living person preserve the memory if it will soon be buried by domestic cares, by his wife's cold; today he performed a stomach resection on Kharitonov—and not altogether successfully, and how is he now—have to go and see, think—so it would be better to throw this notebook in the wastepaper basket than leave it lying pitifully in a dusty pile of old letters.

But his hand refused to move. The doctor rolled the notebook into a tube and slipped it into the inside pocket of his topcoat. Then he stepped up to the mirror, took off his cap, looked at himself as if he were a disinterested observer, grinned: and that was all.

Sighing, he left the interns' room and wandered down the long corridor in the direction of ward seven, where Kharitonov was slowly coming to after the operation.

1984

Translated from the Russian by Catharine Theimer Nepomnyashchy

THE OSTRABRAMSKY GATE

GALINA KORNILOVA

I am not beginning my story just yet. First I am going to the square next to the train station to catch the number eight bus, which will take me along the edge of town, then across a flat plain covered with sparse shrubs; after that it will turn off the road, and finally stop at the corner of a quiet street in a suburban village.

Now I would like to propose the following: Let's suppose that a completely different person were to get off the bus at this stop instead of me. Someone who knows absolutely nothing about the place to which he has come. What, in that case, would be the first thing to catch his eye? What feelings and thoughts would come to him as he walks toward the railroad tracks past the steep-roofed houses? In all likelihood, none. Without any particular interest or emotion he would examine the facades of buildings behind the already thinning crowns of trees, a glass booth where they sell lemonade and sandwiches with shriveled slices of cheese, a newspaper kiosk, blue-and-green-striped, like a zebra. He would come to the railroad tracks and climb up a shaky, creaking staircase to a wooden bridge, above which the wind carries the smell of burning, of coal smoke and fuel oil. From the bridge the traveler would look out over the environs of the village and once again he would find nothing remarkable in them. "How ordinary everything is here . . ." he would probably think, seeing the square on the other side of the street covered with puddles after the recent rains; a standard department store building off to one side; a "Beer and Beverages" stall closed for lunch; a white dog sniffing a pile of reddish slag by the water tower. He might even yawn out of boredom, glancing to the right where a narrow road stretches along the tracks and identical cinder-block houses stand behind a stockade fence. . . .

I myself, however, unlike the bored traveler I have invented, knew exactly where I was going and what village I would encounter beyond the railroad crossing. For that reason, as I stood on the wooden bridge, I peered out at the surrounding landscape with anguish and fear and tried to find something remarkable in it, something out of the ordinary. But I could not find anything of the sort. The reflection of a telegraph pole cut across a puddle in the square. The white dog leapt over the pile of slag and trotted off toward the beer stall. A slight breeze fluffed up the dirty-gray broom of the dog's tail and fanned it off to the side. From behind the stockade that fenced off the plots of land with their cinder-block houses a calm, questioning male voice was answered immediately by female laughter.

By now I was walking on the road alongside the stockade, looking over the low fence at children playing with a cat by a porch, at wooden tables and benches under the trees, at stacks of firewood, barrels of rainwater, a variety of sheds. A brand-new, bright-red motor scooter stood by the door of one of these sheds, next to another an old woman wrapped in a warm shawl was throwing grain from a bowl to some fluttering chickens. On the almost leafless apple trees pink balls of apples still shone, and heavy lengths of sheets and blanket covers waved to me from ropes hung in the yards.

Then the even line of the wooden fence came to an abrupt end and was replaced on the left side of the road by a stretch of low-growing evergreens. Forests of this kind are especially prevalent around the Baltic: slender-trunked little pines that have not yet grown strong, on low, gently sloping hills. Walking barefoot would be unpleasant in such a forest: It has a thick undergrowth of thyme, bilberries, and heather. Grayish, swirling thickets of heather tumble out of the forest onto the side of the road like foaming surf. From them, and from the sun-warmed pines, the honey smell of flowers, evergreen needles, and resin wafts onto the road. It is possible that our bored traveler, drawn by this woodland aroma as I am, would walk down the embankment, crunching the heather underfoot, and dive under the low evergreen curtain. And then something would inevitably happen to him that would force him to see everything around him in a completely different light. . . .

I ran down the embankment, catching my hair on the low branches, and slipped behind the first row of pines. At that very second the forest came to life. It started rustling, flapping heavy wings, and howling savagely, as hundreds of black birds, shrieking hoarsely, swept up through the trees. Their dark mass eclipsed the yellow disk of the sun for a moment, and their frenzied cries, filled with unrelenting malice, drowned out the sound of a freight train that was passing by on the other side of the road. Shuddering from an incomprehensible dread, I jumped back onto the road. But even here they raced by in hedge-skimming flight right over my head, not stopping their screaming for a minute, those sharp-beaked, sharp-clawed creatures that looked like winged rats—the true masters of this place.

No, something is not quite right about this quiet copse and the unruly flock of crows above it. Something is not quite right about these sickly pines whose crooked trunks are reminiscent of the spines of tubercular children, nor about this excessively dry, seemingly lifeless grass underfoot. For that matter, the entire village beyond the forest is also strange. Its carefully emphasized ordinariness, its mediocrity, suggests a kind of falsification, something like a skillfully erected stage set designed to hide something dreadful from the human eye, something that is not at all ordinary. Or am I imagining all this simply because the name of this village—Paneriai—wails in my brain like a siren, compelling me to look around at every step, and gaze with distrust into the faces of passersby, whose tranquillity astounds me. Did they forget? Did they tire of remembering?

The local birds, however, have forgotten nothing. And believe me, it is by no means my imagination that is at work here: It's enough to take one look at those flocks to understand what's going on. Generation after generation of crows have lived with the genetic memory of the abundant repast that was once consumed by their ancestors in the pine copse. That's why even to this day they circle these very same pines, land on these same heather-covered hills, blindly hoping for an imminent feast. Fledglings invariably inherit the habits of their carrion-crow parents, and when they leave the nest they in no way resemble our reserved and alienated gray urban crows. With piercing cries they fly low over the forest, over the railroad tracks, over the rooftops of the houses, peering down vigilantly: Will a steaming bounty be spread out for them down below once again?

Say what you like, but in my opinion it would be difficult to live here, next to that winged gang circling over the forest and the little museum on the edge of the copse that outwardly appears so cozy. But inside, illuminated by white lamplight, the trifles of human life are laid out behind the glass of display cases: a pince-nez with cracked lenses in a metal frame, an aluminum spoon, tailor's scissors with long blades, a plastic comb with missing teeth, a bunch of keys on a rusted ring, a child's knitted mitten with a hole in the thumb. . . . Things that belonged to people whose lives came to an abrupt end over thirty years ago in the pine copse overgrown with heather.

A sandy path leads from the door of the museum to these pines and the hills beyond, climbs the gentle slope to the top, and only then is that which was at first concealed from view by the curtain of evergreens and the thicket of shrubs revealed: gigantic sheer-faced reservoir pits. Empty black eye sockets staring blindly at the sky, into which withered leaves and colorless dead pine needles are tossed by the wind. Next to each of these pits is a neat little plaque on a peg with a figure: "10,000," "7,500," or "5,200"—the number of people shot by the Nazis and buried in the pits. So what if the foliage now rustles peacefully all around and the smell of wilting grass and flowers fills the air? There are things in this world that cannot be veiled by any fragrance, that do not disappear with the passage of years or the change of seasons.

That's why you head back almost at a run and now, in your haste, you don't pay much attention to the houses, the yards, or the people. It is only in the bus, looking out the window at the gloomy plain, dotted here and there with patches of shrubs, that you realize that on their journey *they* saw this very same landscape, the details of which drifted past them in reverse order. For the end of their journey was the forest I had left behind, while its beginning may be considered a square in the city toward which our bus was now speeding. The story I am about to tell concerns that beginning.

I heard this story thirdhand, you might say. The eyewitness to the events— an old woman who had lived through the occupation—related it to her mistress, a well-known Lithuanian actress. She, in turn, told it to me one warm Sunday afternoon as she and I were wandering around the city. But first about the city itself.*

A person who comes here for the first time should do the following: Go up to the top floor of any building in the center of town, on Lenin Prospect, for example, or on Chernyakhovsky Street, and look out the window. What

---

*The city described here is Vilnius, the ancient—and current—capital of Lithuania. Before World War II it was part of Poland. —TRANS.

would you see from there? The distinctive silhouettes that constitute something of a graphic symbol of the city, and then it will become easier for you to make sense of the rest. From this height an amazing panorama opens up before you: something like a sea that is simultaneously rippling and frozen. A wave, shooting straight up at its crest, descends along the inclines, twisting into rings and spirals as it falls, and, in so doing, forming multistepped graded fantastical semicircles. All of this together is known as the baroque style. Here and there the soft, rhythmically flowing waves are pierced by the sharp lines of Gothic spires. But only here and there. The sharpness and frenzy of the Gothic buildings are instantly softened by the feminine silhouettes of the baroque structures flanking them; they dissolve against the background of curved planes and ovals.

Charming softness is a feature that can come to define not only a person's character, but also a city's. And here one finds it in the architecture, in the climate, in the unhurried movements of passersby on the street, in the weeping willows streaming like green fountains at intersections, in the silence of the tiny medieval courtyards.

But for this very reason it is difficult to visualize the events that took place on these streets more than thirty years ago. They seem improbable precisely because they are so out of keeping with the city's soft and joyous look today.

The events I am about to relate took place in the southern part of town, on a square that opens out from the famous Ostrabramsky, or Medininksky, Gate. The first name comes from the sharply pointed shape of the gate's Gothic arch during the Middle Ages.* The road from the gate led to the Medininksky Castle, whence its second name. But there is even a third—"Aušros"—which in Lithuanian means "dawn." Above the gate, which had been cut into the ancient fortress wall, is a Catholic chapel containing the miracle-working icon of the Ostrabramsky Madonna. You can still see the icon today: a young, dark-complexioned, fine-featured face filled with secret dread and prophetic sorrow. During important holidays the large shutters of the window in the church above are opened and then the miracle-working Madonna can be seen from afar, from the street. Dozens of people drop to their knees at that moment and as a result the street comes to resemble an open-air temple of sorts. On the other side of the gate, beyond the fortress

---

Ostra means sharp or pointed in both Polish (the language of the original name of the gate) and the Russian of the text. —TRANS.

wall, there used to be a town. It has long since become part of the city, and only certain houses there, smaller and more modest than those in the center of the city, testify to the former provinciality of the area.

. . . We passed under the arches of the gate and found ourselves in a rather small square paved with stone. Looking around it my companion said, "You know, during the war there was a market here."

I was not at all surprised. Closed in by the sides of houses, the space behind the ancient wall indeed seemed to be a perfectly suitable place for a market. It could, for example, have been located in the area now occupied by a small garden, over there, where three narrow streets descending toward the square from the hills converged.

"It was over there, where the garden is," my companion continued, confirming my guess. "An ordinary bazaar, where local peasants brought their wares from neighboring villages. And here, next to the gate, ran a road. . . ."

That's how she started the story that she had heard from an elderly Polish woman, whom we shall call pani Stanislawa.*

On that autumn day—more precisely, on that October morning—the then-still-young pani Stanislawa set off for the market. Now, of course, it is not important what she had intended to buy there; she herself would probably not be able to recall. All that matters is that on that particular day and at that particular hour she found herself in the square in front of the Ostrabramsky Gate. It is not at all difficult to imagine what the square looked like then, since bazaars in all parts of the world and throughout history have looked more or less alike. In the middle of the square long tables made of wide planks nailed together stood in a row beneath wooden canopies of the same construction. To one side of them, in an open space near some tethering posts, a dozen or so varicolored horses hitched to carts stood munching hay. And behind the row of tables, closer to the road, clustered a group of women, offering customers skeins of undyed wool, finished knitted items, woven baskets, homespun rugs, and clay utensils. In other words, the kind of handmade odds and ends that one can find at any market.

But at the same time the bazaar we are talking about must have been significantly different from all other bazaars, for it was operating during wartime in a city occupied by the Germans. It is obvious that on the counters of this market there were no items such as butter, sour cream, or eggs, nor

*"Pani" is Polish for Miss or Mrs. —TRANS.

Г. Карнилов. Остабрамские борота.
л. Макар

could there have been. A wartime market was, of course, both poor and expensive. It was also taciturn, wary, and poorly dressed. The residents of the city, as well as the peasants who came to town to buy, sell, get the news, and see their relatives, had all grown threadbare over the months of war; moreover, they tried to dress as simply as possible. The times were such that it was better not to be conspicuous. The only thing the women could allow themselves on a Sunday was to tie flowered kerchiefs around their heads, and even these were not especially colorful.

As we all know, market trading always begins at the crack of dawn. And that's why the square in front of the city gate had been bustling since early morning. Rumbling along the cobblestone pavement, carts drove up one after another, vendors noisily hawked their wares, customers bartered. They poured into the aisles between the rows of stalls in an ever-thickening stream, stopping in places to ask about prices, then moving on.

As the sun rose over the horizon, it drenched the city in a bright chilly light. The ancient walls were touched with pink, the spires of the cathedrals blazed gold, the winding little Vilnele River flashed silver. On the square, the horses' backs shimmered in the rays of the sun, the faded flowers on the women's kerchiefs came to life, the sad young face of the Madonna over the Ostrabramsky Gate radiated its wondrous colors.

Bathed in the light of the autumn sun, the city with its towers and fortress walls, churches and tiled-roof houses resembled a floodlit theatrical stage on which a medieval mystery play was about to begin. And indeed, there was not long to wait. . . .

Midday had already passed when the people milling about the bazaar suddenly heard strange sounds in the distance. Something like a protracted rumble, or a rustling, was coming from far-off streets, drowned out periodically by the harsh bellowing of German commands. Conversations and arguments ceased of their own accord. Vendors and customers alike forgot for an instant about the wares on the counters; they raised their heads and looked around in alarm. The marketplace gradually fell silent and became all ears.

The shouts of the Germans kept growing louder and more distinct, the people in the square looked with increasing alarm in the direction from which they were coming. Almost everyone in the city knew the sound of Germans shouting out their commands; they had had occasion to hear it before. But that did not make the piercing cries any less terrifying—quite the opposite. It is even possible that German SS officers were specially trained to bellow like animals at people in order to scare them to death in advance.

■

But now the screams seemed all the more frightening because it was impossible to figure out what was going on in the city. One could only guess that both the commands and the vague muffled rumbling were gradually moving in the direction of the bazaar. So, after a brief period of confusion, some of the people who had gathered in the square hastened to return home. The market women bustled about, quickly gathering their wares; the carts rolled off with a clatter. But those who did not want, or were unable, to leave the market immediately, crowded together at the very edge of the road and stared in the direction from which the disturbing noise was coming.

The Germans bellowed louder and louder and it was no longer difficult to recognize the shuffle of thousands of human feet in the monotonous, protracted rustle that accompanied the shouting. The heavy living mass was by now very close by, flowing into the streets nearest to the square. Suddenly, in the crowd of people rooted to the spot in the square, words ignited like a spark and passed along the rows:

"They're taking the Jews!"

"They're taking the Jews from the ghetto!"

The already terror-stricken crowd shuddered with a foreboding of something horrible. Hundreds of eyes stared at the yellow section of wall that blocked their view of the street leading to the center of the city. But a row of people in dark, ragged clothing was already emerging from it, swaying on the cobblestones like a boat in shallow water, and behind that row yet another and another. Like a dark, slow-moving river, a gray heaving mass, they poured into the square.

Pani Stanislawa had told her mistress, "To this day I can't get that picture out of my mind."

There is nothing surprising about that. All the others who were there on the square that day must also remember it still. Human memory is such that certain events are never erased from it, whether the person likes it or not. Just what each of them was feeling at that moment, however, that I cannot say. I can only guess. Especially since the eyewitness herself did not touch upon this aspect of it; she described only what she saw.

They saw rows of exhausted, pale people in dark, tattered clothing move past, surrounded by SS soldiers. There were extremely old men who could barely move their feet when they walked and leaned on the shoulders of younger men; there were youths, almost boys, whose stern, very unchildlike gaze seared the faces of the people thronging by the road. There were women, old and young, with wisps of hair straying out from under their black kerchiefs, with lifeless eyes and deadened faces. Some of these women pressed children to their breasts. Yes, there were children in this sorrowful, slow-moving procession. They minced along, gripping their mothers' hands or skirts, while others, the younger ones, were carried. But the quiet, barely audible cry that was periodically heard above the rows was not coming from them. It was the adults who sobbed, mourning over the fate of their children.

The one and only cart, hitched to an undersized, light-chestnut horse, moved along in the middle of the procession. In the carriage, with his back to the driver, sat an old rabbi, stooped and wizened, resembling more than anything an incorporeal shadow. A few days before (some well-informed person again reported to the whole bazaar) he had lost the use of his legs. Stretching his dry, shaking hands over the heads of the moving crowd, he continuously mumbled something, while his head, covered with a striped tallith, fell feebly onto his chest.

From the first days of the occupation the city had forgotten how to speak loudly. On its streets only German speech was used with full force. The city fell mute during those minutes when the sad procession stretched from one end of it to the other. Not a single sound could be heard except for the quiet crying of the women, the clatter of the wheels of the lone cart carrying the rabbi, the heavy breathing of the marching people, and the shouts, sharp as the lashes of a shepherd's whip, of the German escorts.

It was utterly incomprehensible why they were shouting like that. The people in the column, after all, were obediently going where they were being led. Not a single one of them made any attempt to lag behind, stop, or break out of line and throw himself at his executioners. One might even suppose that the soldiers were nervous. After all, even for trained SS soldiers this task could not have been particularly pleasant or easy. In any event, they spared no strength in bellowing. And after every one of these shouts the women in the crowd at the bazaar hastily crossed themselves.

But the others, the ones now walking past them in slow, irregular rows, did not seem to hear the shouts at all. To an onlooker it might have seemed that they neither heard nor saw anything around them. Even when they raised their lowered heads for a moment, one could tell that they saw before them not a city square filled with a silent crowd, not their raving escorts, but something completely different.

Then, suddenly and unexpectedly, the involuntary spectators in the square saw the rhythmical movement of the column come to a halt. It was as if those who were walking in front had suddenly run up against an invisible barrier that stopped them. Row after row caught up to the ones in front, slowed their pace, and stopped. Their view of what was happening up front was blocked by the heads and backs of the others. They could only hear a discordant chorus of excited women's voices. But the petrified spectators by the side of the road could see every detail of what was happening.

The Germans had put mostly women and children in the first rows of the column. One of these women, a tall, heavyset, aging Jewess, was particularly conspicuous. Her tight gray curls bristled against the light kerchief thrown over her head. Her face was puffy and an unhealthy, waxy yellow; her regular, once-beautiful features had hardened in lifeless detachment. But the flame of a bonfire still blazed intensely on this scorched, barren earth. For in her ravaged face, grown wan and hard from grief, huge eyes burned like stars, and anyone who took one look into the dark depths of those eyes could no longer tear his gaze away from them.

". . . Thou hast doves' eyes within thy locks; thy hair is as a flock of goats, that appear from mount Gilead."*

The moment the first row reached the Ostrabramsky Gate, the woman with the gray curls thrust her head back and stopped dead in her tracks. The others glanced at her in confusion and immediately began to stop. As one they all looked in the direction of the dark-complexioned Virgin Mary grieving in her church tower above the gate.

The elderly woman suddenly fell heavily to her knees and raised her swollen hands over her head.

"Mary!" she called out, hoarse and frenzied. "Look over here, Mary! Look at us!"

Huddled together and shuddering in fear, the remaining captives looked at the kneeling woman.

"Mary!" the old woman continued to shout, and for an instant her voice drowned out all the other sounds in the square. "Remember who you were, Mary! You lived among our people! Save our children! Don't let them perish, Mary! Save them!"

And next to her, one after another the darkly clad women dropped onto the dusty cobblestones. It was as if the trees of a large forest were toppling one by one, felled by the saw of a lumberjack.

"Mary! Mary! Mary!" the women repeated, sobbing, prostrate on the ground. Raised in prayer, their convulsively trembling hands were like still-living branches.

Now the hushed crying of the peasant women at the side of the road

*Song of Solomon 4:1, King James Version. —TRANS.

joined the sobs of the Jewish women fallen on the pavement. And such moaning, such wailing hung over the square in those moments that it was no longer possible to tell whether it was rising up from the earth to the sky or whether the heavens themselves were crying over the wretched earth.

Even the German escorts became visibly distraught. Their shouts were drowned out by the wails and sobs of the crowd and they looked around as if beset, obviously not knowing what to do next.

And it was then that the Jewess with the blazing eyes got up off her knees, tore from her skirt the tiny girl who was clinging to it, and forcefully pushed her out of the column. She simply tossed the child into the crowd by the road. And the crowd parted for an instant, then swallowed the girl up, hiding her behind people's backs. Immediately something inconceivable began to take place in the square. Mothers, sobbing out loud, pushed one child after another out of the column. They loosened their embrace on their children and pushed them to the side of the road, threw them to where arms were already outstretched to catch them as they flew out of the column. The peasant women quickly tore the flowered kerchiefs from their heads, threw them on the dark little heads of the children, and ran off to the nearest streets with the children in their arms.

A living storm raged in the square until the escorts regained their senses and jumped into action. Once again they started running up and down the column, bellowing and clicking the bolts of their rifles, driving the people forward. It was not a short journey to the place where the inhabitants of the ghetto were being taken that day.

The sobbing women got up off their knees and plodded on, constantly looking back at the crowd in which their children had disappeared. The Germans were now using the butts of their rifles to shove and prod the stragglers, so the people in the column were no longer walking slowly, but almost running. Just past the square, the street along which their route lay dropped sharply down, as befits roads that lead to the kingdom of the dead.

". . . We must needs die, and are as water spilt on the ground, which cannot be gathered up again. . . ."*

Concluding her story, my companion added the following: Many of the children who were saved that day survived the war and the occupation. She herself, for example, knew a woman who was still rather young and worked in the post office in the city of Anikščiai. The woman's name is Mariam. In Lithuanian she is called Marite, which in Russian, of course, would be Mary.

---

*2 Samuel 14:14, King James Version. —TRANS.

Her last name is Lithuanian, naturally, since she grew up on a farm with a Lithuanian peasant family. These people had children of their own as well, so Mariam now has several brothers and sisters. Mariam says that she has no recollection of that awful day, because she was only two years old at the time. But later, when she came of age, her adoptive parents told her the whole story and explained who she was. They did not want to keep the truth from her; after all, her natural mother was in that procession, perhaps her father as well. It is also possible that other relatives of the girl were there, her older brothers or sisters.

On that day the Nazis led them all down the road that heads southwest out of the city, in order to shoot them, along with thousands of Russians, Lithuanians, and Poles, on the wooded hills of the totally unremarkable village of Paneriai.*

1987

Translated from the Russian by Dobrochna Dyrcz-Freeman

*Known to the Jews of Vilnius as Ponar. —TRANS.

REPAIRING OUR CAR

BY NATALIA ILINA

First let me tell you what happened to me. A red light went on in my Zhiguli and wouldn't go out. That meant the battery was not recharging and something was obviously wrong. No way around it, I had to go to the service station. Every car buff knows what's in store for him at the service station. I knew, too, and acted accordingly: I got up early, put some sandwiches in a bag, bade a fond farewell to the family, and headed out. I waited in line until the station opened and I managed to get inside the gate, but they didn't let me into the shop. They told me that it was a new station and wasn't yet equipped with some of the instruments needed for certain tests. Calmly I headed for another station. Again a line, and this and that, but finally I made it into the shop. I ran around for about twenty minutes trying to find out who the electrician was here. Twice I told the whole story of the light burning on my dashboard, but to the wrong people: first to a motor mechanic and then to a body repairman. They both heard me out, but said they couldn't help me. Finally I managed to establish who the electrician was. A stern, aging man, he was doing something, bent over the open hood of a Zhiguli, surrounded by a crowd of people in their coats. I joined the group, trying to figure out what was going on. I got it. The electrician's name was "Uncle Zhenya" and his every word was met with cries of approval and fawning smiles. When Uncle Zhenya said to a gray-bearded car buff, "Get out of the way, you're blocking the light!" everybody pounced on the gray-bearded man and even started dragging him out of the way. It seemed that I, too, pulled him back, trying to catch Uncle Zhenya's eye. I didn't catch his eye, though. And then Uncle Zhenya, raising his morose eyes, suddenly said, "Eh, Pavel Pavlovich! Hi!" How this Pavel Pavlovich beamed, how proud he was that Uncle Zhenya had recognized him, and how we envied Pavel Pavlovich. A few people implored him in a whisper to put in a word for them with Uncle Zhenya. Realizing that they'd never get around to me, I left for a third station. . . . There, after various attempts, I managed to persuade one of the electricians to come over to the car. The electrician, a skinny guy with blond hair and sideburns, said that the generator was dead and had to be replaced, but apparently they didn't have any generators. I ran over to the warehouse, where it was confirmed: no generators. But a shipment of them was supposed to be delivered that day—it just might come in. I waited. I met other people waiting for parts. I told them about the light burning on my dashboard and they told me their stories. We grabbed a bite together and the hours flew by unnoticed. Suddenly I saw the second electrician walk by. He was a blond with sideburns too, but fat, and several clients ran alongside him, looking into his face and smiling imploringly. . . . All of them begged him to take a look at their cars, but the electrician stopped by mine. What a stroke of luck! He asked, "What's wrong with it?" And since everybody here knew what the problem was, they all answered in unison. The electrician told me to open the hood and start the engine. He stuck his hand under the hood, turned something, and, presto, the light went out. Turns out it wasn't the generator at all, but some simple little adjustment. The first electrician had been wrong! Everybody had a good laugh. And I laughed louder than anyone. Boy, was I lucky!

I drove home that evening in a blizzard. The light on the dash didn't come back on and I was happy. The generators weren't delivered that day, after all, and, shuddering, I thought about what I had been spared. I would have spent at least a month hunting around for a new generator, which, as it turned out, I didn't need at all. I felt so lighthearted, so good.

At home there was a package waiting for me with a postmark on it and a manuscript inside. A strange manuscript. No return address and no signature. It started like this: "A concussion, two broken ribs, a dislocated arm, bruises—these are nothing compared with the torment that . . ." What followed was crossed out. Then: "No, I can't just sit down and write a final draft. I'll simply jot down everything that happened and that will be my rough draft. . . ." But the author never got around to cleaning up his rough draft. What was going on? Maybe he was no longer alive and his relatives found this envelope while sorting through the deceased's papers and mailed it? If the author is still alive, and I hope he is, he can hardly be in good health. . . . Having familiarized myself with the manuscript, I decided to offer it to the reader.

"I was tormented by a recurring dream. It's night. I'm driving in my Volga, which is still in one piece, with its former blue seats (does somebody else have them today?), the windshield wipers are squeaking, cleaning the windshield, when suddenly a hand reaches out of the darkness and plucks off the windshield wipers. The windshield becomes covered with snow and I try to stop—the brake pedal gives way; I try to pull over to the side of the road—the steering wheel is gone. The car tilts to one side and I surmise that one of the wheels is gone—that same hand had unscrewed it while the car was in motion and would now turn me over and throw me in the ditch. I'm awakened by the sound of my own screaming. . . .

"A snowstorm was in fact raging in the courtyard that day. It was the end of December, evening came early. . . . No. I have to tell everything in order.

"You can repair a person, but a car—never. After getting out of the hospital, I started towing the Volga on a rope to all the service stations, one by one, pleading with them to replace the wrecked body with a new one. They refused point-blank. And then suddenly I remembered Sasha. He's a former student of mine who graduated ten years ago and now holds an important post. I called Sasha. A kind person, he recognized his former professor's voice right off, and I brought the Volga up to the gate of the X repair shop two days later. . . ."

(NOTE: The shop is named in the manuscript, but I prefer not to name anybody or anything. The manuscript is, after all, anonymous.)

"The director, a middle-aged man with blond hair, was nice and promised to replace the body. Oh, happy day! 'I'll call you in about a week, you'll bring the car in, and we'll have everything ready by then. We'll take off the old body and put on a new one. How does that suit you?' I answered with a joyous smile. The director smiled too. Such a nice guy, blond, with lively gray eyes. Once in a while the left one wanders. It up and rolls to the side. . . .

"A week later nobody called. Two weeks later, still no call. I started calling myself. I had been at the shop at the end of September; I remember the yellow leaves of the linden trees peering in the window. It wasn't until the middle of November that they told me to bring the car in. There were a lot of cars crowded in the alley near the gates to the shop and some people scurrying about. Three of them ran up to me: 'Sell me the seats! Fifty rubles!' I said that I wasn't selling anything, but they didn't listen to me. 'Seventy-five!' 'One hundred!' And they pulled dirty ten-ruble notes out of their breast pockets. Fortunately, the Volga was taken into the shop, and the excited voices could be heard shouting in its wake: 'Two hundred!'

"I was taken aback by what the director had to say: He wouldn't be able to do the job in one day. He explained why at length, but I don't remember his explanation, I remember his wandering eye and the strange words uttered in a whisper: 'Take everything out of the car and take it away with you.' 'Why?' 'Anything can happen!' whispered the director; his left eye returned to its normal position and looked straight at me.

"This conversation took place in the shop. There were cars standing on the tile floor and people milling about, not buying and selling or talking idly, but working; it's always pleasing to see people working, and I found it pleasing, too, even if my dream of taking my car home today had collapsed. . . . What was it I wanted to say? Oh, yes. The director's advice upset me. I opened the trunk. What should I take out? What should I take away? The pump? The jack? The bag of tools? The spare tire? What was I going to do, roll it all home in front of me? I grinned and looked askance at the director, but he didn't look at me. The others, however, did look at me. Several pairs of shining eyes stared at my open trunk and silence reigned in the shop. I slammed the trunk shut. And right away voices could be heard again, engines hummed and tools clanked. A car that had come to a halt on its way up on a lift resumed its ascent. The queer stupor came to an end, or had I merely imagined it?

"Then what happened? I remember. I told the director that I wasn't going to take anything out of the car, because I had nothing to put it in and no way to take it home. 'And there's no need to,' said the director loudly, 'everything will be fine. I'll call you in about a week.'

"A week later nobody called. Two weeks later, still no call. And I started calling myself.

"Finally the day came when I heard the words I'd been waiting for: 'Everything's ready, come and get your car!' I decided to go the next morning. I slept badly that night and heard the moaning of the December wind. My brother-in-law Petya showed up in the morning: 'I'm going with you!' And I understood the meaning of the words I had accidentally overheard my wife saying into the phone: 'Petya, I beg you! Try to understand, he's still not well!' We went in Petya's Zhiguli.

"It was snowing hard. . . . In the alley people were scurrying about and in the shop motors clanked, hummed, and roared. . . . Smiling, the director said, 'Feast your eyes on your car!' There were two other men with the director. I don't remember their names or their positions. . . . One was bright-eyed and friendly, the other sullen. . . . Both of them pretended to be admiring the car's new body. But it was old and looked as though this was not the first time it had undergone rejuvenation. . . . But Petya and I noticed that later. At the time we saw only the seats—they were gray, dirty, and burnt in two places. . . . 'These aren't my seats!' 'They're yours, they're yours!' said Friendly gently. 'Who else's could they be?' the director asked sweetly. Sullen wasn't listening; at that moment he was looking under the back fender for some reason. 'They're not his seats!' said Petya. The director and Friendly didn't persist for long. The seats could have been switched; it's an oversight, what can you do! At this point Sullen emerged from under the fender and, unaware of what had transpired, bellowed: 'What do you mean they're not yours? They're you—' He suddenly fell silent—Friendly, it seems had stepped on his foot. . . . I asked them to put my seats back and they answered that it would be impossible, where could they find them now? They promised to install other seats, but for a price. . . . That's when I happened to notice the steering wheel and I froze. It was a black, scratched-up relic that looked as though it had been taken off a truck. God save us! And then I heard Petya's voice (he had opened the hood): 'Where's the battery?' Three voices responded: 'There was no battery!' 'What do you mean there was no battery?' I screamed, feeling my heart begin to beat wildly. 'Easy,' Petya said to me, and to them, 'How are we supposed to drive it?' 'Run over to Bakunin Street and buy a new battery,' Friendly advised. 'Right,' said Sullen, 'you'd be better off with a new one anyway, yours was only so-so, if I remember—' And he suddenly fell silent; apparently, his foot had been stepped on again. But what had they done with my steering wheel? It had been the color of ivory and smooth. 'You mean this isn't your steering wheel?' the director asked softly, his left eye rolling to the side. 'It really isn't yours?' Friendly asked, surprised. And Sullen barked, 'There was no steering wheel when he brou—' Again they didn't let him finish. I ran to the door and opened it. The snowstorm was still raging and I took a deep breath, which made me feel a little better. . . .

"Petya went to buy a new battery. Somebody brought me a chair and I sat down. Engines roared and lifts whirred around me. The backs of the men working on my car blocked it from view; they were removing the steering wheel and taking the seats out. At the same time I saw that they were taking the seats out of one of the Volgas standing nearby. I kept looking at the door leading to the warehouse, waiting to see what kind of seats they would bring in. Perhaps they would even be the original ones. But they didn't take anything out of the warehouse and when I looked over at my car again I saw that seats were already being installed. I walked over to the car. These seats were gray, too, but they were clean and much better than the other ones; still, where had they come from? How could I have missed seeing them being brought in from the warehouse? Apparently, there were moments when I blanked out.

"The store didn't have any batteries. Friendly appeared and said with a kind smile that they were going to put in a battery so that we could get as far as the exit. 'And then what?' 'We'll think of something.' But Sullen, appearing out of nowhere, yelled, 'What's there to think about? We'll give 'em the one that's been lyin—' But, as usual, they didn't let him finish his thought.

"I ran to pay the bill. The cashier said that she couldn't accept such a large sum, that it had to be transferred by mail. I rushed over to the post office and got in line. They wanted thirty-five rubles for the transfer. It was downright offensive. I ran back through the wind and blinding snow. The cashier said that she would try to accept the money if someone would take her home to get her knit jacket: There was a strong draft from the window. Petya took the cashier home and I stayed at the shop. Suddenly the thought hit me: What about the serial number? The car registration had the serial number of the old body on it; the new one had to be written in! Friendly said that the sales department would take care of that. I waited until Petya got back, dashed outside, forgot where I was going, and stopped. It was dark. The streetlights shone and the snow swirled under them. I rushed over to the cashier again. She was wearing her knit jacket and felt warm, so she took my money. In the sales department, however, I was told that they didn't have the right to put the serial number of the new body on the registration, but that they would put the invoice number down instead. . . . I listened to them blankly, nodded, and then, running back to the shop, grabbed my head in my hands. How can this be? The invoice number on the registration, but the serial number on the body of the car. Why can't they put the serial number on the registration? Sullen's voice: 'The body isn't registered anywhere, it's been a long time since—' Again, he wasn't allowed to finish, and Friendly appeared next to him saying, 'Don't worry, we'll hammer in the invoice number on the body and hammer out the old number.' They brought over a tall young man in a greasy beret and he started hammering—a wondrous business, the point of which I didn't understand. Petya dismissed the whole thing, and no one would explain anything to me. Sullen tried, but they led him away the minute he opened his mouth.

"Friendly himself drove the car as far as the exit, went just past it, stepped on the brakes, and yelled, "Vasya!' Sullen emerged out of the dark, hugging a battery to his chest. They took out the one that had gotten the car as far as the exit and put in the other one. 'You can keep this one until you buy a new one,' said Friendly. I gratefully shook his hand, but I was concerned: Why had they changed the battery while the motor was running? 'Ha!' said Sullen, 'if we had shut off the—' But Friendly interrupted him, loudly wishing us a pleasant trip.

"We stalled after about three hundred meters, just as we turned onto a wide, busy street. It was impossible to get the car started again or even to get it over to the curb. A policeman and about ten passersby tried to help Petya and me, but the car wouldn't budge; the wheels wouldn't turn. The cries of "One, two, three, go!' the advice being given by the crowd on the sidewalk, the car horns honking, and the police whistles blowing all merged in a tormenting din in my head. We managed to get the car over to the curb only with the help of a tow truck that had been summoned by the police. We got back home that night in Petya's Zhiguli and in the morning, while I lay with a cold compress on my forehead, Petya went to get the Volga that we had left on the street. It was brought home on a truck: The brake shoes had been stretched so tight that they had jammed. On top of that it turned out that the hand brake was gone (the lever was there, but the "works" had disappeared), the battery was dead, and the radiator was leaking. . . . Petya tried to tell me something else, but my wife ran in and said, 'Leave him be, can't you see he's had enough?'"

With this the professor's manuscript came to an end. . . .

This was a man who, by his very nature, should not have owned a car! The professor was as trusting as a child. "In a week," they told him, and he believed them. They promised to take care of everything in one day and again he believed them. He saw somebody else's seats and was astonished. He saw a steering wheel that wasn't his and was stunned. He took the disappearance of the battery as a tragedy, and one day spent in the shop drove the professor into a catatonic state. Really now, can a person with such weak nerves have anything to do with automobiles?

What, tell me, was the cashier guilty of? It was snowing hard, there was a draft, the woman had forgotten her knit jacket, and what did she see? An absent-minded professor running around. The professor had his brother-in-law with him and the brother-in-law had a car, so why not take advantage of the situation?

Or the story with the serial number . . . It was right there in plain Russian: The number can't be entered on the registration. It can't, and that's all there is to it! Any normal car owner would have kept his mouth shut and would not have asked any questions. But the professor had to know the whys and wherefores. It was plain silly.

A friend of mine had to have his car painted. For three months he tried to get one of the service stations to take his car. No moaning, no groaning. My friend understood: More and more people have cars, and even if there are going to be more service stations, there will still be far from enough of them, which means there will be fewer and fewer of them. . . . Understanding this, my friend did not demand, but pleaded and even begged. His entreaties were rewarded. They took his car in. They kept it two months, but they did paint it. Then my friend wanted to drive the car home. He looked—no battery. He took a taxi to get a new one and when he came back he saw that the taillights were gone. He bought new taillights but when he returned something else was missing. And so on. Did he get upset? Not a bit. He said with a smile: "I'm lucky. Others have it worse!"

Indeed they do! A certain Ivan Ivanovich (a friend of a friend) went to pick up his car from the repair shop and found that two wheels were missing, the front left and the back right. He asked what had happened to them and was told that they had never been there, that that was the way he had brought the car in. Did Ivan Ivanovich quarrel or get upset or scream? Nothing of the sort. He managed to find two other wheels, paid for them, and set out for home, but halfway there the car stalled: Something in the car hadn't been fully repaired. . . . Ivan Ivanovich didn't have nightmares afterward, nor did he lie about with cold compresses on his forehead. He's happy and healthy, he laughs and plays cards. I heard that he's even planning to get married. . . . It makes sense only for people of such endurance to have anything to do with automobiles.

1973

Translated from the Russian by Steven W. Nielsen

FIVE FIGURES ON A PEDESTAL

VIKTORIA TOKAREVA

Tamara Kruglova, a staffer in the letters-to-the-editor department of a Moscow newspaper, saw her husband start drinking again after a five-year hiatus. In those five years, he and everyone around him had completely forgotten the troubled times when he had hardly ever been seen sober. It was all so long ago, it seemed it had never happened and would never recur. But alcoholism has the nasty habit of rearing its ugly head as if five years are nothing. Same set, same characters, same lines—and on with the same old show. Hovering above it all is the same penetrating odor. Tamara called it the odor of lost hopes.

Five years back, her husband had been a regular in the hospital; whenever he started on a binge, he would give himself up to the care of the State. Old Fenya, the ward nurse, would say as she emptied the trash out of his nightstand, "Messy people, these painters."

Tamara's husband was not a painter but a sculptor, and a fairly successful one at that. Now and then his sculptures were sold in foreign countries and mounted in town squares. He was thought to have talent.

In the early days of their love, the fact that he had talent, that he was gifted, had meant something. But with time he had taken his gifts off to the studio and left only his illness and sour disposition at home.

In the studio he soared on the wings of artistic inspiration, or whatever they call it. People came to see him there, young women included, and there was a nonstop round of wild parties. The discussion was on a high intellectual plane. They ate and drank, nibbling on the little mushrooms and cucumbers that Tamara's mother pickled for the winter and sealed up in glass jars.

Tamara was sorry to lose these precious foods and regretted the waste of her mother's hard work, but she put up with it. Sure, it would be nice to have a husband who wasn't a celebrity or a man of the world, who didn't belong to the entire world, but was yours, only yours, someone you could take by the arm and go off to the supermarket with to bring home sacks of potatoes together. But husbands like that were few and far between. . . . Besides, somebody had to live with the talented ones.

The sculptures sometimes sold, sometimes didn't, but eating and raising a son were daily necessities. So Tamara ran around like a chicken with its head cut off, staggering under the weight of her shopping bags. She had varicose veins in one leg and had gotten used to limping. Imagining herself as she looked to others, she saw a woman listing to one side, heavy bags in both hands, rear thrust back and chest jutting forward, gazing into the distance.

She couldn't unload anything onto her husband: He had talent. Her son coughed, her mother gave orders. So Tamara consoled herself with the thought that she wasn't the first and she certainly wouldn't be the last. Nowadays, in the 1980s, it was the woman who kept the family afloat. Women toiled like Volga boatmen, giving men the opportunity to be true to themselves, to be creative, and not to bring home any money.

And so her husband started drinking again after a five-year hiatus. The hiatus had been prompted by fear. A doctor they knew had frightened him, saying that if her husband kept on living the way he was, softening of the brain would occur in half a year. Tamara's husband, imagining his unique brain turning to mush, stopped drinking on the spot. But in five years the fear had gradually worn off and everything was starting all over again.

Tamara threatened to hang herself unless he gave himself up to the care of the State then and there. He didn't quite believe her, but at least it got his attention, and he picked up the phone, while Tamara went off to the paper where she worked in the letters department.

At one time, before her difficult love match, she had been in love with letters. She had been nicknamed Tamka the Prospector because she was always digging for golden nuggets of fates, stories, and problems. Then her own fate, story, and problem had grown to unmanageable proportions, overshadowing everything else.

They could have divorced, but then he'd fall apart, or so she thought. They could stay together, but then she would fall apart. Life with an alcoholic is like being in a war zone: constant maneuvers through the line of fire. You run a few yards and hit the dirt. You pick yourself up, run a little farther, and hit the dirt again. And you never know what's in store for you tomorrow—or even tonight.

A psychiatrist and physician they knew—the same one who'd frightened her husband so effectively—had earned his doctorate with a dissertation entitled "Wives of Alcoholics." So wives of alcoholics were a separate social subunit, capable of being studied as an individual group or species.

Tamara was engaged in these and similar meditations when she was called into the office of the head of the department, Vladimir Alekseyevich—Vlad for short.

"How about taking a little trip for us?" he asked. "We've got a very interesting letter here—a soldier who hit his mother-in-law over the head with an ax."

"No, thanks," Tamara replied.

"May I ask why?"

"I have a family, that's why."

As a rule, it was the disgruntled and the discontented who wrote letters to the editor. Sighs, tears, and perplexed inquiries poured into the editorial office in an unending stream. People were seeking the ultimate justice, and they saw the editorial office as the ultimate arbiter. In her early youth and for ten years thereafter, Tamara too had striven for this higher scale of justice, and to attain it she had been ready to sacrifice an arm, a leg, an eye, or any other organ she had two of. But now all she really wanted was a pair of jingly Turkish pants—and off to the harem! So what if her husband had upward of forty other wives? The main thing was to be provided for and saved from constant harassment.

"Don't you have any professional pride?" asked Vlad in growing frustration. His irritation gathered over Tamara's head like a thickening cloud.

Tamara said nothing. Time and life had devoured her pride. She really couldn't have cared less who had hit whom and why. She herself was being hit over the head—by life—but she wasn't writing any letters or complaining. Everything looked picture-perfect from the outside: She was the contented wife, not of some lowly clerk, but of a talented man who was known throughout Europe, if not worldwide; the mother of a darling nine-year-old boy; the daughter of a loving mother. But that was all from the outside. Inside, there was the daily struggle for survival, and the lonely bed at night. Tamara had even forgotten her gender. Probably neuter.

Her friends chattered on and on about their intimate lives, but she had neither the time nor the energy for intimacy, and even if she had, she couldn't have shared it with anyone. That would have tarnished her husband's reputation; he was, after all, a national figure. It would amount to an attack on government property to disgrace him. So she had to go on holding their life together single-handedly, the veins bulging out of her legs, a hernia on the verge of erupting, but a confident, May Day–parade smile always on her face.

People often asked her, "Why don't you just quit working?" They assumed that Tamara was rich and famous, that the 150 rubles a month she got from the editorial department would not make or break the family budget. But those 150 rubles, plus her mother's pension, were the only real income she could count on. The occasional fee her husband received went toward paying off their debts, of which they had far too many to admit. The money that appeared out of the blue went straight back into the blue so fast it seemed they had simply lost it.

In addition to the money it brought in, the editorial department was a social club for Tamara. Here she could breathe a sigh of relief and get away from the storms that were always threatening to break at home. Tamara's mother hated her son-in-law. She thought he didn't do enough to help her daughter, didn't appreciate her fine qualities, and had simply climbed onto their shoulders for a free ride.

The son-in-law, for his part, felt that since he was making a contribution to the spiritual development of the entire world, humanity as a whole was indebted to him, and his wife and mother-in-law, as concrete representatives of humanity, should be happy that their shoulders and no one else's had ended up under his backside.

Tamara's husband had a fantasy: He'd come home one day to find his mother-in-law gone. Where to? No one would know. Maybe she'd have kicked the bucket or wound up in the poorhouse or gotten married. The main thing was, she would be gone. But Tamara, who guessed her husband's secret wishes, was ready to blow up his entire studio, with all his sculptures, if he dared to touch one hair on her mother's head. Her mother was the only person who really loved Tamara and helped her—although for all her deep daughterly love, Tamara had grown tired of her mother's despotism and stupidity. Even in her younger days, her mother had never been big in the brains department, and in old age she'd turned completely asinine. She harped on the same old things day after day. It was like a constant drizzle. The editorial department seemed like Monte Carlo in comparison, nothing but fun and games. There, Tamara was in touch with herself, with her standing in society, and, ultimately, with her boss.

■

"So you won't go?" Vlad asked again.

"No."

"All right, I'll send Koval," decided Vlad. "Koval will be delighted to go. But I'm sorry for your sake—you started off so well."

The train for Dnepropetrovsk left at ten in the evening.

Tamara climbed into the railroad car, which smelled of coal and combustion, and of something else resembling gunpowder. The car was empty and lacked illumination, like Tamara herself.

In her purse she had the letter from the soldier who'd hit his mother-in-law over the head with an ax. A Raskolnikov, no less. He was already in prison when he wrote the letter.

"Dear editors. I would like to know if the courts have scales, and if they're accurate. I studied hard in school, reaching for knowledge like a sunflower reaches for the sun, got all the way through eighth grade and went to work tending pigs at the kolkhoz pig farm. I served in the ranks of the Soviet Army, and it was when I was serving in those ranks that an article called 'A Soldier's Joy' was in the local paper. It said I won a Moskvich car that I didn't win. They reprinted it in a Moscow paper and my wife and mother-in-law read about that car. So when I get home to my native kolkhoz, my mother-in-law asks, 'So, where is car?' My wife tried to poison me, but it was the dog and not me that got poisoned. And now I'm in prison doing eleven years of hard labor, and my wife's running around with the guy she was cheating on me with when I was serving in the ranks of the Soviet Army. There's a soldier's joy for you."

Not a word about his mother-in-law or the ax. Tamara checked the files of the Moscow papers. Yes, there had been an article, written by a local correspondent. She would have a lot to investigate down there. Eleven years might well be a fair term, but more than one person was guilty: The sentence should have been spread out among three, not dumped all on one.

Tamara went into her compartment. It was already occupied by an individual of the male sex—from all indications, a man on a business trip. He looked like a dependent person: dependent on his salary, his superiors, his wife, Soviet light industry. And this dependency suited him, for by his horoscope he was a Capricorn, and by his very nature he was a goat. Goats can manage quite well on a string tied to a stake. The most they will do is try to stretch the string as far as it will go; they would never dream of snapping it and heading off to all four corners of the earth.

Seeing Tamara, the goat perked right up. There were only the two of them in the compartment, and that created enticing prospects. Tamara had once been attractive—it was not for nothing that a sculptor had given her a second look and then made her his wife. She would still be pretty were it not for her harried expression and general frenzied air. The doctor's dissertation stated that all wives of alcoholics—exactly 100 percent—suffered from neuroses. In every single case, the constant irritant of the drunken husband shattered the nervous system. Tamara's attractiveness was hidden by neurosis—only the toil and travail showed through. But the compartment was poorly lit and the goat didn't notice Tamara's travail; he took in only her stateliness, relative youth, striking clothing, and unusual perfume.

Tamara sat down opposite him and turned to look out the window. She was thinking, Here's my life in a nutshell: traveling in an antediluvian railroad car with a goat to an unknown town on account of a letter from a former pig tender who's now in jail.

The goat had been rummaging around in the meantime, and he produced a bottle of wine.

"Do you have a corkscrew, by any chance?" he asked insinuatingly.

"No!" screeched Tamara so loudly that he jumped, and the empty glasses clattered on the table. That "no" was an outcry against her entire life.

The businessman stared at Tamara in astonishment and asked, "What are you, crazy?"

At that very moment the conductor, a woman, came in and demanded, "Tickets and money for bedding."

"I'm not going anywhere with him!" Tamara declared.

"Well, I wouldn't go anywhere with you, either," he replied, offended. "Who needs you, anyway . . . mangy feline."

"All the other berths are taken," the conductor intoned as if by rote.

"That's not true, the whole car is empty!" Tamara protested.

"The whole car is sold out."

The conductor took the money for the bedding and left.

Tamara said nothing as she dragged the mattress and pillow down from the top berth and covered them with the dampish, worn bed linens. She lay down without undressing, turned her face to the wall, and fell still. She tried to hide her despair, but it emanated from her like radiation from uranium ore. As the compartment was narrow and the radiation was powerful, the businessman couldn't help but sense it.

"Do you want me to leave?" he asked softly.

"No, it's all right," Tamara answered. "I've got a headache, that's all."

He got up and left the compartment quietly, closing the door behind him.

The train traveled on into the night. In her mind's eye, Tamara saw the studio: cigarette butts and ashes all over the floor, empty bottles, grime, the narrow cot in the corner, and five figures on a pedestal—an unfinished sculpture. Five sorrowing female figures shedding tears over a fallen soldier. And the sculptor himself huddled on a cot in an alcoholic stupor. He wakes up, reaches down, picks up a bottle and takes a swig, then goes back to sleep. He eats nothing, his liver is rebelling, and his brain refuses to work for such an idiot. He won't remember anything of these days—as if he'd been lying in a dark sack the whole time. In two weeks he'll slowly begin to come out of it. His graying stubble will be half an inch long, like a convict's, and he won't be able to face people in his postalcoholic depression. His body will be like a dog that has taken a beating, like a car after a crash.

Next will come the period of remission, during which he'll get on with his work. This is the time when whatever is going to be created will be. He'll go on a working binge and resent time spent eating and sleeping. Like Lermontov's Mtsiri, in his head "a single thought doth reign, a single, burning passion." But after a while his soul will begin to toss and turn restlessly. Prealcoholic ennui will slowly creep up on him.

That will signal the onset of another binge. He has a lovely way of putting it: "the pathology of the gifted." Similarly pathologically gifted friends, or simply smart bums, will come around—people who are just as degenerate as the husband of old Dusya the yardkeeper, only they've read more. And so it will start all over again: two more weeks in a dark sack.

It hadn't happened for five years—five years on the wagon. But a reformed alcoholic and a healthy nondrinker are not at all the same thing. A reformed alcoholic is someone who's taken a heavy loss: It's as if a light has gone out in him. People who leave their homeland probably feel the same way: Nothing's missing, but nothing's satisfying. The psyche of a reformed alcoholic is distorted. Everything that was hidden now surfaces: greed, egoism, misanthropy. A reformed alcoholic is boring. Tamara sometimes even caught herself thinking, If only he'd start drinking again! In his drinking bouts, especially at the very beginning, there were spectacular moments. Words of love, exalted sentiments, ardent vows. She believed them every time. Afterward he'd forget all about them.

A treadmill situation, and Tamara was the squirrel. How could she get off? The treadmill was solidly built. . . .

The businessman came back, lay down, and fell still. Maybe he, too, was crying. Maybe he had his own treadmill. And the conductor and the whole crew, too, perhaps. And the train, like a time capsule, was hurtling them through life. A trainful of tears rushing through the universe.

There were plenty of taxis in the square outside the station, with drivers sitting around just waiting for passengers.

Sending Tamara off on this assignment, Rozita the bookkeeper had said, "If you need a car, hire one. Same thing for a plane. Just so long as you give me a receipt—something in writing."

Taxis and planes were within Tamara's rights. Receipts were her duty.

Tamara approached all the taxis, telling the drivers where she wanted to go: a village called Solnechny. Nobody wanted to take her there. These days, drivers pick their own itineraries and clientele.

Not far from the taxis, she noticed a car of a make that was new to the world. She guessed it was a do-it-yourself job, but that was easy enough to figure: The car's haphazard shape and coloring proclaimed it loud and clear.

A young man with a face that was fine-featured, pure, and sad sat behind the wheel: He looked like a fallen angel.

Tamara went up to the car. The angel looked at her. His eyes were large and dark gray, like puffs of smoke or bits of storm cloud. In either case—ethereal.

"Are you free?" asked Tamara.

"Where do you want to go?"

"Solnechny, about forty kilometers from here."

"I know it. Get in."

There goes my receipt, thought Tamara.

The angel started the engine. The car snorted, jerked, then settled down, and its wheels began to spin. They were off.

"What's this contraption called?" asked Tamara.

"Dzhorik."

"What?"

"A *dzhori* is a donkey, and *dzhorik* means little donkey. I built him myself, and he adores me for that. It's a long way from being a heap of scrap metal to becoming a moving vehicle. He may look horrible, but don't let that bother you; he's got a heart of gold."

"What's your name?" asked Tamara.

"Georgii."

"There are too many notes to sing there. What do they call you for short?"

"Whatever they want—Zhora, Gera, Gosha, Yura, Egor."

"Which do you prefer?"

"I answer to them all."

"Then I'll call you Yura."

Yura. . . . The angel didn't look much like Yura Kharlamov, but the two of them had the same way of speaking, of smoking. Yura Kharlamov also held his cigarette stiffly, screwing up one eye from the smoke. He had the same way of talking, too—inwardly laughing, outwardly cool.

Once she and Yura had been strolling around town and had stumbled across a strange-looking dog near a garbage dump. When they got a better look, they saw that it must have been a domestic pet once, but had gotten lost and was now showing signs of neglect. From a pedigreed animal it had turned into a stray, yet its slim muzzle and long, collielike body attested to its aristocratic past.

Yura Kharlamov was like that dog, only in reverse: A mongrel exterior hid a fine, noble interior, a refined sensibility beneath a drab covering. But when he looked at Tamara, the drabness disappeared, his soul shone through, and he was wonderful. . . .

Dzhorik was a low-slung vehicle, descended from a race car. Tamara was seated comfortably but had the impression she was riding only inches above the road. And when massive trucks from the MAZ or KrAZ automobile works came up alongside, she felt like Gulliver in the land of the giants.

The town and its stone buildings soon gave way to the orchards and farmhouses of the Ukraine.

Tamara's mother had been born in a Ukrainian village. Sometime before the war, her father had been studying in a polytechnical institute and had gone to the mines to get work experience. He caught sight of Tamara's mother, young and full-figured as she was then. Being a short man, he was attracted to tall, solid women, and simply went crazy over her. He brought her to Leningrad and introduced her to his large, very proper, musically oriented family. They all fell silent at first sight of her. When they recovered the power of speech, they asked in horror, "Lyova, wherever did you find this girl?"

Then Lyova, too, looked at Tamara's mother and saw he'd gone overboard, but there was no getting out of it. Tamara's mother didn't like either Leningrad or her husband, and often dreamed of the six-foot-tall Panko, whom she had left behind in her Ukrainian mining town. Tamara's father and

■

mother fought sometimes, but even then, her father remained refined: He was simply defending his masculine dignity. The upshot of it was that he died right after the war, leaving her mother a widow. She used her widowed status to send Tamara away for the whole summer to the Ukrainian village where two of her sisters still lived. The third sister had been driven off to Germany by the Nazis during the war, had married there, and now sent packages from Munich.

Tamara remembered arriving at her aunts' place when she was a little girl, settling in, and speaking Ukrainian the very next day without a trace of an accent, even though she'd never used the language before. Her genes had obviously been hard at work and, together with her excellent musical ear, had enabled her to capture the cadence of Ukrainian speech. She had taken to the language like a duckling that approaches a river for the first time and, without the slightest foreknowledge of its capabilities, dives straight in and swims off.

Looking around her, Tamara started to think, Maybe I should go find Yura Kharlamov and settle down here, far away from Moscow. In Moscow, you had to go out of town for every gulp of fresh air, every blade of green grass had to be purchased at the market, and you knew in advance what each day would bring. In five years, her husband would produce another sculptural composition, her son would be not going on ten but almost fifteen years old, and she would be not thirty-eight, but forty-three. And that was all.

"You're from Moscow?" asked Yura.

"Yes."

"What are you doing here?"

"I'm on assignment. A soldier hit his mother-in-law over the head with an ax."

"So you're an investigator?"

"No, a journalist."

"Journalists are involved in things like this, too?"

"Sure. The walls in my department are dripping with blood and tears."

"I used to think about going into journalism, but I ended up studying auto mechanics."

"What happened? Did you get thrown out?"

"Not at all—I'm an engineer."

"Then what were you doing at the station?"

"Waiting for you. Before and after work I take Dzhorik out to scare up business. I want to build a new car, and for that I need money."

Tamara thought of her husband, who hadn't earned a ruble for years.

He'd been trying to find himself, using vodka, and the money for the vodka came from her. So she had to support both the family and his search, all by herself. You can't tell your son to just wait. He has to eat every day, three times a day. Her husband had remained untouched by these things: They were beneath him. Then, finally, he had found himself. His work was accepted, and he was told, "Hey, man, you're a genius." Tamara counted for nothing: The sculptures were his, not hers. Her life went on, resembling the fertilizer you put into the ground to make rosebushes grow. Who thinks about fertilizer—cow manure—when looking at roses?

"Do you have a family?" asked Tamara, envying his wife in advance.

"Not anymore. We're divorced."

"Why did you get divorced?"

"I was always working on this car, and she got bored and left me for the neighbor. He rents the other half of our house. Now I've got the car but no wife."

"Are you sorry?"

"Well, if I had a wife, I wouldn't have the car."

"Which is more important?"

"You can't always show your wife off, but a car is a real eye-catcher."

Tamara knew he was joking, but "in every joke there's an element of a joke," as her friend Nelka would say. An element of a joke, and all the rest is truth.

"What does your neighbor do for a living?" asked Tamara.

"He's got a finger in every pie and a hand in the till."

"You mean he steals?"

"He takes chances," Yura preferred to say.

"Why on earth did she leave somebody like you, a craftsman, for a thief?" Tamara asked indignantly.

"He has something special . . . a kind of magnetism. All the birds in the place flock to him. My wife included."

"He probably feeds them," Tamara surmised.

The angel turned toward Tamara. Such an idea had never entered his head. But it was true, the birds did flock to the neighbor because he threw out feed for them, and he had thrown out money stolen from the government for the angel's wife. It was all very simple. Nothing mystical, purely material.

"Keep your eyes on the road," Tamara ordered.

The angel turned back to the road, an astonished expression still on his face.

.

Yura Kharlamov had worn exactly the same expression when he saw his name on the list of students accepted to study journalism at the university.

They had started the course together. Tamara was a Muscovite; Yura, from the provinces. She would bring lunch from home and they would spread it out on a windowsill and eat it together. Once Tamara bit into a tomato and it splattered unexpectedly, leaving dark red splotches all over her imported white suit. For some reason that scene had stuck in her memory. She also remembered the time, just after they had enrolled in the university, that Yura had invited her to a restaurant and treated her to crabs with mayonnaise. They had eaten four helpings of crabs apiece. All that year he saw her home on the streetcar. They would get on at the first stop. The whole car would be empty. They would sit very close together, Tamara by the window. The streetcar would gradually fill up, but they wouldn't notice. They were fenced off from the rest of the passengers by his love. For Yura loved her, and she basked in his love. She would say, "If you become famous, I'll marry you."

She wanted to be a famous person's wife, no matter what. She craved exalted sentiments and the good things that went with them. But most of all, she craved prestige: She wanted everyone to be filled with admiration, slightly envious, and longing to take her place. And that was indeed how it was. At banquets everyone drank to their health. The sculptor drank, too. And then all the others would go home, but he would fall asleep with his nose in his plate, and she would have to cart him away. A drunkard is as heavy as a corpse, impossible to lift. She would have to run for a taxi and make the driver carry the body to the car, like a sack of paving stones. And unload it at the house, too, dragging it right up to the elevator. That's prestige for you.

"I will definitely become famous," Yura had promised in the streetcar.

He wanted to be a writer, an international journalist, anything at all, so long as he won the tall, striking Tamara, her hair as blond as a northerner's.

Once, in the middle of July, they went out to a favorite professor's dacha. Walking through the forest, they kissed. Tamara leaned her back against a pine tree and got tar on her blouse. And they couldn't stem the rush of emotion and desire and lay down in the nearest hollow; it was carpeted with pine needles and shaped like a grave. They embraced in a frenzy. Tamara couldn't hold back and wanted to go all the way, but Yura loved her so much that nothing came of it. She couldn't forget that. And then, toward the end of the summer, she met her sculptor and got married in a hurry. Her classmates at the university were horrified at her betrayal. Everyone could see that Yura loved her with an intensity that comes only once in a lifetime, and they were outraged for him. They declared a boycott. Yura didn't take part in it; he was utterly prostrate. Later he gave up his studies and left Moscow. Where was he now?

He had stopped seeing her home, but once, when she came down with a fever, she went up to him and said, "I don't feel well—take me home."

Yura wanted to go with her, but a silent herd of students closed in around him. Somebody even grabbed his sleeve as if to say: Don't stoop so low, don't go. He stayed with the group; it would have been awkward to reject their solidarity, even though it was the last thing he needed.

Tamara was waiting and couldn't understand why he didn't react. But he just stood there, his eyes blinded by grief, looking nowhere. Tamara headed home alone, and she really was ill. The earth swayed beneath her feet and an icy band gripped her forehead. She'd been going through life like that ever since, alone and unsteady. And somewhere there was Yura, the exact same expression still on his face.

"Here we are," said the angel.

Tamara took out the letter and read the address: 8 Khlebodarnaya Street.

A group of children came running out onto the street and raced alongside Dzhorik, whooping with delight. It was obvious that cars were rarely seen in the village, and this one was a real first. It was like a mythical beast with five legs—a mutant.

A leggy girl with windblown blond hair was running at the front of the pack. She resembled Tamara as a child.

The soldier's mother came out of number 8. She wasn't old, maybe forty-five, but she seemed tough and sinewy, like a well-worked cart horse. One sensed that she had pulled many loads, and was still pulling.

"Lyonchik! Hey, Lyonchik! You come see, for Petko they come!" she cried, darting into the house.

Tamara turned to look at the angel.

"Go on in," he advised.

"But what about you?" Tamara asked. She was afraid to be left there without him.

"I'm off to work," the angel replied, smiling guiltily.

"How much do I owe you?"

"Not a thing." His smoky eyes caressed hers. "You had the pretty face, I had the gasoline. All the best!"

He turned and, holding himself very straight, walked away without looking back.

The soldier's mother poked her head out of the house. "So come in already, Gossakes!"

Timidly, Tamara went in.

The house consisted of an open entryway and one large room. In the middle of the room was a table covered with melon rinds and bread crumbs. And flies: Tamara thought the house must be the site of a fly congress; they seemed to have flown in from all points of the globe. She had never seen so many flies in one place.

Lyonchik lay on top of a blanket on a broad couch by the door. When he saw them come in he rose, but he was still groggy, and it took him a while to figure out what was going on. Was he just waking up? But then why was he wearing pants and lying on top of the blanket? He must have gotten up, eaten some melon and bread, and then lain down again. He was healthy-looking and smooth-featured, obviously younger than his wife. Apparently she pulled the load while he snapped the reins.

"For Petko they come!" she pronounced ingratiatingly.

Lyonchik stood up, assumed an air of importance, and went over to the table.

"So is like this," he began imposingly. Tamara noticed that his eyes were unmatched: One was blue, the other brown. Nature sometimes indulges in such whims—or defects.

Lyonchik launched into his narration, speaking in a mixture of Russian and Ukrainian. Petko's mother watched his face intently, bobbing her head as she listened. Lyonchik was obviously considered the brains of the family—indeed, of the whole village. Later it turned out he was a watchman at a warehouse.

The story went like this: Petko reached for knowledge like a sunflower reaches for the sun, got all the way through eighth grade, and went to work on the kolkhoz. Tamara knew all this from the letter. Then he married Lidka, a neighbor and classmate of his. He moved in with Lidka's family—became a "seddler," as Lyonchik put it. But Lyonchik was more than ready to help the new family out. "I will build little shed, I think, dig well for them." He was constantly emphasizing the interest he took in Petko's fate, and that seemed slightly suspicious to Tamara.

"Are you his father or his stepfather?" she asked.

"Not real father," the mother put in. "Real father die from cow."

"Gored?" asked Tamara, horrified.

"No, no—we selled cow, buyed vodka. Two case. Well, and then he die."

"Aha!" Tamara exclaimed. "So it was vodka, and not the cow, that killed him?"

"What is difference?" broke in Lyonchik irritably. "Is no more—this is all."

"All right, so you dug the well. Then what?"

"Then child is born. Girl child. And Lidka say to Petko, 'Go home, I don't need you.' Petko come to us, and I say, 'When you have child, together you must live.' So he go back to Lidka, and she say, 'You stink. Get out of my sight.' And he come home to us. And so he is going always back and forth. Until called up for Soviet Army. And everything else, you know."

But why Petko had ended up in prison was something Tamara still didn't understand. She was about to ask when the door opened and the angel walked in. He took a chair and sat down next to Tamara as if it were the most natural thing in the world to do.

"What about your job?" she asked.

"I thought you might need help getting back," answered the angel.

"But your job?" Tamara asked again.

Yura raised his eyebrows and spread his hands in complete resignation, and his face even managed to convey genuine regret about taking a holiday.

"Repeat to comrade?" queried Lyonchik.

"Yes," Yura replied.

Lyonchik repeated his story word for word, with all the same pauses. Tamara realized he had told it many times before and knew it all by heart. With every retelling, he polished his image by showing indefatigable concern for his stepson's fate. But it still wasn't clear how Petko had ended up in prison.

"What about the car?" asked Tamara.

"What car? Where is this car?" asked the soldier's mother in agitation. "This car he never see. And mother of Lidka say, 'You blow money for car on good times. Give back money for half.' Where he will get this money? So he hit her."

"With an ax?" Tamara asked.

"She is healthy as horse—you go see for yourself!"

"Where does she live?"

A girl came in—the same one who had been running after the car. She cuddled up to Lyonchik.

"I have seen them already," she said.

Tamara realized that this was Lyonchik's daughter.

"Take to Lidka," her mother told her, adding, for their benefit, "She will show you."

The girl flushed with joy and left the house. Tamara and Yura followed her out.

"I can't understand any of this," admitted Tamara.

"Why not? It's very simple. Nobody needed him."

"You are bringing Petko home?" asked the girl.

"Who is he to you?"

"He is brother."

"Do you miss him?"

"He balakaled with me."

"Talked," Yura translated, and strode off toward the car with a basketball player's springy step. His gait exuded the confidence of youth: It seemed to say that everything would work out, for Tamara as well as for Petko.

Tamara was grateful to Yura for sticking with her—defending her, fencing her off from the whole streetcar. She had forgotten what it was like to feel protected. The sculptor, by his very nature, was a second son, and a difficult, sickly one at that. And of late her mother had been forgetting everything and reverting to childhood. So Tamara was essentially alone with three small children. But here was somebody walking ahead of her, opening car doors for her, translating unfamiliar words. It was almost as if she had gone back to her youth, when there were no neuroses, only boundless, untapped energy, a feeling of lightness, and the expectation of happiness from one minute to the next.

Petko's wife was named Lidka. She had small black eyes like watermelon seeds and was shaped like a figure eight, one round ball on top of another—the bottom one larger.

She was standing outside her house, looking suspiciously at the approaching vehicle.

The girl jumped out of Dzhorik first.

"Ha, Lidka!" she cried. "Now you will pay for sending me away."

"When I send you away?" Lidka asked in real astonishment.

"When I come to play with Tonechka, and you say, 'Go to devil.'"

"When I send you away?" Lidka repeated.

The girl had decided that Lidka was her enemy and believed she was now bringing just retribution down upon her head. Petko would be freed and Lidka locked up in his place. She was out to settle her own accounts.

"I'm from the paper." Tamara took out her credentials.

It was just pro forma—normally, people took her at her word. But Lidka held out her hand, took the document, and studied it carefully, checking Tamara's face against the picture as if she were a customs official. Having satisfied herself that the document was in order, she said tightly, "Come into house."

The house was tidy: lace curtains, embroidered pillows. Lidka was obviously a decent housekeeper.

A five-year-old girl—Petko's daughter—was sitting at the table drawing pictures with colored pencils. She looked at the new arrivals with total indifference.

"Go play outside, girls," Lidka told them.

The elder scooped up the younger one and carried her out of the house. As the little one wriggled in her arms like a captured beetle, she said, "You must listen to me, I am aunt to you."

Tamara realized the two girls were in fact aunt and niece, although the aunt was just three years older than the niece.

Lidka gave Tamara and Yura chairs but remained standing, as if to say that the interview had to be kept short, she did not intend to shoot the breeze. Lidka was a woman without charm and with no desire to be liked. She might also have resented the intrusion of outsiders into her home and her life.

"Excuse me," Tamara began guiltily, "but could you explain how it all happened?"

"All what?"

"Why was your husband sent to prison?"

"Not me that send him—it was court."

"I understand. But what happened on the day of the crime?"

"Well, we begin watching television in evening—'Four Tankmen with Dog'—and then Slavik comes in with plyashka."

"What's a plyashka?" Tamara asked Yura.

"Is bottle," Lidka answered quickly. "Petko says, 'We want to eat.' I say, 'Is not restaurant here.' So, they drink. Slavik says, "I sleep here tonight." But I say, 'Is not hotel here.' Then they leave, but Petko comes back and hacks mother."

"With an ax?" asked Yura.

"Well, yes, with hatchet."

The girls began to screech outside, quarreling about something, and a dog began to bark. Suddenly, a stentorian command drowned out the children's voices and the dog's barking. A formidable old lady, broad as an oak, strode purposefully into the house. It was Lidka's mother.

"From newspaper," Lidka told her tersely.

Her mother immediately cocked her head to one side, fixing a look of beatitude on her face.

"I am Christina," she intoned on a single note, like a Russian liturgical chant.

"Excuse me, but was it you whom Petko hit with an ax?" asked Yura incredulously.

"I don't remember nothing." Christina continued her recitative. "He hit me, and I don't remember nothing."

She stared blankly into the distance, the very personification of a martyr who has lost her memory, but Tamara caught the sharp, birdlike, penetrating look in her eyes. Under the right circumstances, she would have made a fine character actress. Tamara had a few more questions to ask, but she realized it was no use. Christina was not about to step out of character.

Tamara turned to Lidka.

"Here in the letter it says you tried to poison your husband, but he gave the food to the dog, and the dog was poisoned instead."

"Where is this dog?" asked Lidka, staring at Tamara with unfeigned amazement.

"I don't know," Tamara answered. "I'm asking you."

"Where is this dog?" asked Lidka again with the same intonation.

It was clear that nothing more could be accomplished in that house. Tamara stood up.

"And what part did the car play in all this?" asked Yura. As an automobile expert he was mostly concerned about the car. "Did he win it?"

"Well, naturally! In newspaper they write it. In newspapers no lies. It is press."

"He sell car, then blow it all on good times," Christina spoke up, unable to remain silent. This was her sore spot.

"Do you want him to be released?" asked Tamara.

The women were silent. They seemed to fear that if Petko were released he would come back and finish off both of them.

"I do not know," said Lidka. "As judge decides, so it will be."

The head of the kolkhoz was at his desk. He was surprised that a journalist had come all the way from Moscow for so trivial and clear-cut a case.

"In your opinion, was his sentence justified?" asked Tamara.

"Absolutely!" His Russian wasn't bad. "His wife drove him to it, of course, but it's a big country. Go someplace else and get down to work, I say. Because if everybody starts grabbing an ax, there won't be enough of them to go around."

"What about this business with the car?" asked Yura.

"He never won it. A correspondent turns up at his unit and asks, 'What's the latest on your military and political training?' So Petko pipes up and says he's won a Moskvich, but that's the farthest thing from the truth."

"So he was lying?" asked Yura in astonishment.

"You bet."

"Why?"

"He's an idiot," said the kolkhoz head. "Now he's doing time for his stupidity."

"Why didn't the correspondent check it out?" asked Tamara in surprise.

"It didn't occur to him that Petko might be lying. What would be the point of lying? He believed him, that's all."

"How do you know?"

"It was an open trial, meant to be edifying. Everyone from the village went. The correspondent was there, too, as a witness."

"Was Petko a good worker?" asked Tamara.

"When he first got out of the army, his work was good. Later he let himself go, stopped shaving, slept in the pigsty with the pigs. I asked him, 'What's wrong with you?' He answered, 'I can't live this way anymore—help me.' So I called Lidka in and said to the two of them, 'You're both young, not bad-looking, why can't you live together?' She says, 'I'll live with him when he gives me half the money for the car, which he blew on good times.' So I sent her out and said to him, 'Don't let me hear another word about your wife or by God I'll give you what for.' But why are we sitting here, talking about them? Come, I will show you what hothouses we have, what milkmaids, and our Vadim—"

"Who's Vadim?" asked Tamara.

"He's a bull—the likes of which you've never seen, even in Spain. Put him in the ring and he'll send all the toreadors to kingdom come in no time flat."

"Some other time," Tamara replied with a smile. "We still have to see the judge in town and look through the case file."

"What for?" asked the kolkhoz head in surprise. "It's an open-and-shut case."

"We have to print a reply to a letter," explained Tamara.

"Who wrote the letter?"

"Petko."

"That figures. He would have to get all of Moscow into an uproar. He's in prison for his stupidity—let him stay there and not drag people away from their business."

A truth seeker, or perhaps a mere gossipmonger, was hanging around outside the kolkhoz's administrative offices. He might actually have been both—it's often hard to draw the line between truth and gossip. He was wearing black cloth pants and a sports jacket.

He approached Tamara, jabbed his long, sinewy fingers into her ribs and, speaking rapidly, as if afraid he wouldn't get to finish what he had to say, informed her that Lidka was a rotten bitch who had never loved Petko. Everyone in the village knew that. She had married Petko to spite Vasko, whom she had been seeing "for ages."

"And how long is 'ages'?" asked Tamara.

He didn't reply, as he was in a hurry to speak his piece. He was obviously used to not being heard out and had learned not to let up.

Vasko had promised to marry Lidka, but had changed his mind and gone off to live in town, where the girls curled their hair and painted their nails. What did he need Lidka for? So Lidka married Petko to spite Vasko, who had turned out to be a real bastard. But after the wedding, Vasko had shown up again. The old love had not grown cold. Petko went off to the army, where he led the correspondent into oman.

"Error," Yura translated.

"Why?" asked Tamara.

The gossipmonger hastily explained that both the Samusenkos, Lidka and Christina, were so greedy they'd outrun a hare for a single kopeck, but here there was a whole "car" at stake. Petko had been counting on buying back Lidka's love. Petko with a car—that was a different thing altogether from plain old Petko. But when he returned from the army without the Moskvich, his mother-in-law asked, "Where is car?" Their dream had already become so much a part of their lives it was as if Petko had robbed them. They persecuted him, and he took an ax to his mother-in-law. Vasko got scared and took off. But now that Petko was behind bars, Vasko was living with Lidka. Openly.

"How come we didn't see him?" Tamara asked in amazement.

"He is there. . . . Petko should have hit him, not his mother-in-law. Why hit her? But this is how it happened. She is alive and kicking, Lidka is with Vasko, and Petko is in jail."

"Do you feel sorry for him?" asked Tamara.

"Sure I do! Eleven best years of his life down the drain. And all because of that bitch, please to pardon my language."

A woman in a brightly colored cotton dress came up to the gossipmonger, grabbed him by the scruff of the neck, and led him away like a naughty boy. He obediently shuffled off after her: He was obviously used to such treatment.

Tamara guessed that, apart from advancing the cause of truth, the gossipmonger had been hoping to make a few rubles. But he'd been foiled.

They returned to Dnepropetrovsk in silence. Tamara was tired and hungry, Yura stared pensively straight ahead of him. They had rubbed up against someone else's misfortune. It clung to their skin, to their clothes, and refused to come off. The picture was clearer now. As Tamara saw it, Vasko was a real bastard; the girl next door had been head over heels in love with him since she was sixteen, maybe even fifteen, and he had played it for all it was worth. Yet all the while he'd been counting on marrying the daughter of an Onassis. After all, another Russian boy had snagged that millionaire's daughter, and Vasko was no worse than him! But Dnepropetrovsk was not exactly crawling with millionairesses, so Vasko had gone back to the village. It was also possible that his old love had not grown cold, as the truth seeker put it. Lidka was trapped on a treadmill. She tried to get off by dumping Petko, but Petko proved difficult to dump. He played his trump card, an imaginary car. And one untruth led to another. Petko, too, found himself on a treadmill. He tried to jump off with a swing of an ax—and landed right in prison.

"There's always a love affair in these things," said Tamara. "*Cherchez la femme . . .*"

"*Cherchez la* vodka," Yura corrected her.

"What do you mean?"

"Lidka refused to give them anything to eat. She said, 'Is not restaurant here.' So he and Slavik were drinking on an empty stomach. He got loaded and grabbed an ax. Don't forget, his background isn't the greatest. His father died from vodka—they sold the cow to buy two cases. The sons of alcoholics become drunkards themselves. What else could you expect?"

"That's not the point," protested Tamara.

"Sure it is. Ninety-five percent of all crimes are committed under the influence."

Yura stopped Dzhorik by a little store, got out, and quickly returned carrying bread, sheep's-milk cheese, or *brynza,* and two cartons of cream.

They began eating in silence. Never in her life had Tamara tasted such delicious dark bread or such fresh, fragrant brynza. It was one of her favorite foods: She crumbled it into soups and onto vegetables and macaroni. How on earth had Yura guessed? And yet it made sense. He was not indifferent. He had taken the time to figure Tamara out, was attentive to her, anticipated her needs. If only someone had been attentive to Petko, none of this would have happened. But plain old Petko was of no good to anyone. First, Lidka got even with Vasko using Petko. Then there was Petko's uncaring stepfather, who had his own family to worry about. Or maybe the stepfather had been first. Next, there was the blasé correspondent, who couldn't have cared less about his work or the newspaper: At the very least he should have asked to see the winning lottery ticket. But he didn't. There was also the head of the kolkhoz, who didn't want to get involved with the greedy Samusenkos—he had enough problems as it was. The only person who loved Petko was his mother, but she didn't get to vote. Petko was caught on a treadmill of indifference. How many unseen accomplices in the crime there were. Yet they were never tried, never sentenced. They didn't even realize they were accomplices.

"He's gotten himself into a real mess," said Yura, who obviously couldn't get Petko out of his head.

"He was dumped into a real mess," Tamara corrected him. "He would never have gotten there on his own."

"You intellectuals."

"What?" Tamara didn't get it.

"You try to understand these people. But I hate them," Yura said quietly but clearly. "A while back I was crossing a bridge and ran into a band of these Petkos and Slaviks. I walked toward them, wondering, 'Will they push me over the side or not?' I don't know how to swim."

Tamara imagined the fragile fallen angel on a narrow bridge. Far below, as at the bottom of a precipice, the water glinted. And coming toward him was a rowdy, disheveled, crazed mob. It wouldn't take much for them to push him over the side: They only had to keep on walking straight ahead. Just one little nudge, and a man could be written off.

They arrived at the municipal court building.

"I'll wait for you in the car," said Yura. "I've had it with your soldier."

"He's more yours than mine," retorted Tamara as she got out of Dzhorik.

The judge stared fixedly at his desk. Having a representative of the press check up on his work was nerve-racking and humiliating. It meant he wasn't trusted.

Tamara was leafing through the fat case file. It contained the article entitled "A Soldier's Joy." Not a word about the poisoned dog, though. Obviously, it was a detail that mattered only to Petko. And where was that dog, anyway? There was nothing about Vasko either. Tamara read the sentence: The soldier had been convicted under the intentional homicide statute. He had acted not in the heat of passion but with malice aforethought. He left Lidka's place, walked home, picked up the ax, and went back, clutching the ax under his jacket. His destination was clear across the village, giving him plenty of time to sober up and change his plans. But he was bound and determined to kill Lidka. When he got to the house, however, she was sitting on the toilet; his mother-in-law barged into view instead, and it was her head, not Lidka's, that stopped the blow. Her head turned out to be tough, and she survived. Fate had stepped in—it was not Petko, but fate, that had spared his mother-in-law. The criminal acts occurred in the presence of his daughter, who was able to attest to the accused's actions. She had screeched in horror; Petko shoved her into a closet. The fact that the crime had been committed in the presence of a minor, and a fully cognizant one at that, had been an aggravating circumstance.

Tamara pushed the legal document away. Everything was clear now. In his letter, Petko had depicted himself as the victim of a misunderstanding: By printing false information, the press had landed him in prison. Now it should get him out. There he was, an unfortunate slave of love, locked up for no good reason, with a huge barrel of potatoes in freezing cold water to peel.

"Do you remember him?" Tamara asked.

"I do," replied the judge shortly.

"What sort of impression did he make on you?"

"Not great."

"Which means?"

"Nothing special about him."

"He didn't impress you as a soul in torment?"

"Everyone who comes in here is a soul in torment." The judge, like Lidka, was not disposed to chat.

"But don't you think eleven years is a pretty stiff sentence? After all, his mother-in-law survived."

"Of course it's stiff. It's no picnic out there in the camps. But people like him are weeds—they have to be rooted out."

"What do you mean, 'rooted out'?" Tamara asked in astonishment.

"What good are they?"

"They're human beings, like everyone else. People are people."

"He's not a person. And they're not human beings."

"I wouldn't want to end up in your court," Tamara confessed.

"See that you don't." He smiled. He had good teeth and fairly good manners. With his thin face, pallid complexion, and squeaky-clean air, he looked like a German. A Nazi, thought Tamara, and suddenly she wanted to be outside, with Dzhorik, to whom she'd become very attached. The time she had spent in the judge's office seemed interminable and pointless.

Tamara said good-bye and went out, running down the stairs like a college applicant who's just seen her name on the list of accepted students. She was carried along by youth, unaccountable joy, and hope. Very soon, it seemed, she would find the way to get off the treadmill. She was running toward her way out.

Petko's story had become clear, and clarity was a kind of liberation. She could put him and all the people in his village behind her now.

The angel was standing by Dzhorik talking with a girl. She had a cascade of blond, curly hair, like a finely fleeced sheep.

Tamara stopped short. Her unaccountable joy stepped lightly aside, giving way to fatigue. She suddenly realized that her angel Yura had lived a whole life before that day, and this girl was part of his yesterdays. Tamara had somehow gotten the idea that he hadn't really existed before she came along, but as it turned out, he had. He had been loved, and he was loved now by this little sheep, who was just right for him: bright, carefree, without a burdensome past. As for Tamara—what had she been thinking of?—wife of an alcoholic, squirrel on a treadmill.

The angel saw Tamara. He said good-bye to the sheep and off she went in her short little dress, hooves clattering across the road, legs smooth and straight as spaghetti.

Tamara felt like a rubber toy whose stopper has been pulled, letting all the air escape. She suddenly had the urge to sit down on the pavement.

"What's wrong?" Yura came up and asked anxiously.

"Nothing. Everything's fine."

"I don't believe you."

"Take me to a hotel," she requested.

They got into the car. Tamara felt alienated and more—no, worse—than alienated. She felt hostile.

"What's with you?" Yura asked, taking her hand.

"Nothing. I'm tired."

"That's all?"

"Yes."

"Is being tired a good enough reason for . . ."

"For what?"

"Forget it. I'll take you to a hotel."

Now it was his turn to be offended. They drove off, two alienated people.

Dnepropetrovsk was celebrating the anniversary of the All-Union Leninist Communist Youth League, and all the hotels were filled to overflowing with Komsomols of the 1920s, 1930s, and so on, down to the 1970s. There were no rooms anywhere, no place to stay. It was also impossible to leave town, as Tamara had scheduled a meeting for the following day with the correspondent who had written "A Soldier's Joy." She didn't know a soul in Dnepropetrovsk. Her only option was to go to the train station and sit in the waiting room until morning.

"I can offer you accommodations," Yura said rather formally. "I have a fold-out bed."

Tamara was silent.

"Come on, what's going on?" Yura asked softly, searching her face with his smoky eyes.

What could she tell him? To her, he was both himself and the other Yura, the first one. She couldn't imagine the other Yura replacing her with someone else. Not while she was still alive. It was like seeing herself in the grave. How could she explain it?

Yura lived on the edge of town in a wooden house. It was a long building, actually two houses placed end to end. The whole of this privately owned dwelling had once belonged to his parents. Hard times had obviously forced them to sell off the second half, which was now inhabited by the neighbor to whom all the birds flocked, including Yura's wife. Each half had its own entrance, but Yura must have run into his wife from time to time on the dwelling's private plot.

They went into Yura's part of the house, which consisted of two rooms and a kitchen. He went straight to the kitchen to put some water on to boil. Tamara investigated the other rooms, in one of which stood a table and a chair, in the other, a fold-out bed.

"You've got lots of space here," Tamara remarked.

"My wife took all the furniture, and the dishes," Yura explained simply.

"What do you eat on? Newspapers?"

"Of course not. I have a plate and a fork. Supper will be ready in a minute."

He took some homemade sausages, pickles the length of a small finger, and fat, melon-sized tomatoes from a small, suspended refrigerator. He also produced a bottle of wine.

"Where'd you get that?" Tamara exclaimed.

"My mother brought it yesterday."

"Where is she?"

"She lives in the center of town. She remarried about a year ago and moved in with her husband."

"How old is she?"

"Fifty. Seventeen years older than me. It's so nice to see that she's happy."

So Yura was thirty-three, Tamara figured. Five years younger.

"They were in college together. It was first love for both of them. Then they went their separate ways, but now they're back together," Yura continued, telling his mother's story.

It occurred to Tamara that there weren't many variations on the theme of love; that was why they repeated themselves over and over, only with different sets of characters.

The water was boiling now. Yura poured it into a basin and added cold water.

Tamara was sitting on a stool, silently following his movements. He brought the basin over, kneeled down, took her shoes off, and put her feet into the basin. The water was lukewarm.

"What are you going to do, wash my feet and then drink the water?" asked Tamara, referring to an Eastern rite of humility.

"No, I'm not going to drink the water. But this will wake you up in no time, you'll see. Tomorrow I'll bring you cold water straight from the well."

"You can't, I've got lumbago."

"Cold is used to treat lumbago."

He began massaging the soles of her feet with his strong, gentle hands. Tamara sat looking at the hair, dark as a gypsy's, at the nape of his neck, and at the black vicuna sweater stretched across his back. She was older than he, but she felt like his daughter. Nobody had ever taken such good care of her—it was always she who cared for others. Her heart melted with gratitude.

"Off you go!" commanded Yura.

She went off barefoot across the kitchen, leaving dark, wet footprints behind. She felt a lightness in her step, as if she would remain suspended in the air if she were only to jump. It was probably the way cosmonauts felt when they experienced weightlessness.

Yura poured two glasses of wine, and they drank. The feeling of lightness traveled from her feet right up to her head and set it spinning pleasantly. The sausages were fresh and redolent of garlic. They tore the tomatoes apart instead of cutting them, and the edges sparkled, like watermelons.

Petko had floated far off into unreality, as if it had all never happened. Like the dog that had first been poisoned, then hadn't been. All there had ever been was this clarity, this purity, the wooden house, tomatoes the size of melons, and the solicitous, fine-featured face of the angel.

"Who were you talking to?" Tamara asked.

"Where?" Yura asked with his mouth full.

"By the car."

"When?"

"When we were at the courthouse."

"Oh," Yura recalled. "That was Rimka, Rudik's wife."

"Who's Rudik?"

"He studied auto mechanics with me, but he's a bartender now."

"How come?" asked Tamara, although she couldn't have cared less about Rudik's life story.

"He has to support a wife and three children."

"That girl has three children?" Tamara asked in amazement.

"Yes. What's so surprising about that? She's thirty-five."

"Do you think she's attractive?"

"Who?"

"Rimka."

■

"She's my friend's wife," Yura said again, and Tamara realized that he didn't consider his friends' wives fair game. He didn't even notice them: They were appendages to his friends and had no importance individually.

Tamara felt as though she were rising from her own grave. Before her stretched an entire life to be crossed on clean, light feet. It was as though the soft spot at the top of her head hadn't closed up in infancy. Hope poured right in, and it was too much. She dropped her head and started to cry.

Yura didn't stop her. He stayed where he was, sitting on the windowsill.

"Go ahead and cry if you want to," he said, switching to the familiar form of address. "But don't forget: Whoever dreamed life up was no deadbeat—he did a damn good job of it. We're the ones who spoil it. We take it and spoil it, with these very hands." He held out his lovely, intelligent hands so Tamara could see.

"But can we fix it?" asked Tamara.

"With these very hands."

"And what about you . . . is everything the way you want it to be?"

"Not yet. But it will be."

Tamara rummaged in her pocketbook for a handkerchief. It smelled of home.

Tamara dreamed she was thirsty, and she woke up thirsty. The moon was peering in the window, and that upset her. Somewhere she had heard that the moon was inhabited by departed souls who saw everything that was happening on earth—it wasn't all that far away. She got up from the fold-out bed and went to the kitchen. Yura wasn't to be found in any of the rooms. Where had he gone? To sleep in the other half of the house, with his wife?

The door leading outside was partly open. The moon lit up the doorway, where a wisp of cigarette smoke curled slowly upward.

Tamara went out onto the porch. Yura was sitting there, smoking. His prominent shoulder blades showed through his black sweater like underdeveloped wings. A black angel.

Tamara sat down beside him.

"Why aren't you sleeping?"

"Don't feel like it."

"You don't have any place to sleep," she deduced. "There's only one bed."

He was silent.

"This isn't fair—go get some sleep, and I'll sit here for a while."

"We're not on guard duty, you know."

"Then let's lie down together. We'll put the mattress on the floor and lie on it. Just get another blanket."

Again he was silent. The wisp of smoke formed some sort of sign in the air.

"You don't have another blanket," she deduced again. "What did she do, leave you with nothing? She's just plain greedy, like Lidka Samusenko."

"Let's not talk about it. Look, there's a hedgehog."

"Where?"

"Over there . . ."

Tamara peered into the dark. She was afraid the hedgehog would run up and take a chunk out of her foot. She moved closer to Yura, felt his shoulder next to hers. Yura didn't stir. They sat in silence, like Br'er Fox and Br'er Rabbit. They were united, not by the quest for truth about Petko, but by the same thing that had brought Robinson Crusoe and Friday together on their island: the need to survive. Tamara and Yura were linked by something else, too, though: a shoulder. That was exactly what Tamara needed—a shoulder, in the literal as well as the figurative sense.

"It's nice here," Tamara admitted. "I could just stay like this."

"So why don't you?"

"I am."

"Not just for now, but for good."

"I have a son, a mother. And a husband."

"You're married?"

"Sort of."

"Sort of doesn't count. And you can bring your son and mother with you."

"What would we do here?"

"Grow cucumbers."

Tamara grinned in the darkness.

"As a matter of fact, it's very interesting; you just don't know enough about it. You grow a cucumber, pick it when it's still small and pimply, and it's like your own kid."

"So I'd be in the vegetable garden. And where will you be?"

"Working during the day, and building the car at night."

"In the shed?"

"That's right. And you'll bring me my dinner."

The hedgehog made rustling noises in the grass. Tamara was chilly, but she didn't want to move away from Yura's shoulder. They got up soon anyway and went inside.

They put the mattress on the floor and lay down under the blanket. They

■

stayed that way for a while, looking up at the ceiling. A tension grew in them and kept building. There's a term in physics: critical mass. The slightest impetus, even a loud noise, is enough to set off an explosion. An apple fell from a tree outside the window, conforming to the law of universal gravity. Tamara imagined the hedgehog sticking its needles into the apple and carrying it off to its young. She shivered. Yura drew her to him with a powerful gesture, and everything went haywire.

The moon was shining in just as before, but Tamara was no longer afraid of it. She had found shelter in the soft rain of Yura's tenderness. He kissed her gently, steadily, placing his kisses side by side, leaving not an inch uncovered. What was he building? Happiness. For the first time, Tamara realized that happiness meant being part of the whole, part of the universal harmony: trees and leaves, sky and earth, earth and galaxy. Tamara was a part of all that; it couldn't do without her.

The sculptor's loving was uninspired, as if he had lost touch with life. All he knew was his work; he was incapable of truly caring, belonging to another person, opening up to another person. He belonged to his great idea alone and was concerned only with the spiritual fetus that was maturing within him. The rest he couldn't give a damn about. The rest was unimportant.

But the rest was Tamara, the whole of her unique life—God's great idea. Whoever thought her up was no deadbeat. And since he had let her loose in life, she must be there for something.

"Breathe on me," Tamara begged Yura. She liked his breath. It smelled like breast-fed babies: milky, reminiscent of meadows and grasses.

She fell asleep happy.

When she opened her eyes the sun was shining. Yura was talking to someone, but soon he came back in, wrapped in a sheet like an ancient Roman emerging from the baths.

"Who was that?" asked Tamara.

"My wife. I didn't let her in."

"What did she want?"

"Who knows, she always wants something or other."

"When I'm gone, you'll go back to her," Tamara said. She knew how hard it was to leave a Yura.

"I'm never going back to her. And you're not going anywhere. We're going to be happy, like the one who dreamed it all up had it planned. It's going to work out for us. I know. Believe me. Just believe—that's all you have to do."

He lay down beside her and took her in his arms.

"You're going to be late for work again," Tamara reminded him.

"I'm not going anywhere. And neither are you."

"And neither am I."

"We're going to be together all day."

"Won't you get in trouble?"

"No," Yura reassured her. "I've got some days off coming: I gave blood."

"What for?"

"To have days off."

"But how did you know you would meet me?"

"I didn't know, but I was waiting. And when you wait faithfully enough, you get what you want."

"I don't believe that for a minute. My friend Nelka waited faithfully for years and even fought for what she wanted. Finally she got it, but he died."

"So she was using the wrong ammunition. She created mental monsters, and they ganged up on her and let her have it."

"Let him have it," Tamara corrected him.

"Take your soldier—he was using the wrong ammunition, too. He lied, bowed and scraped, and finally committed a crime. The monsters and baby monsters he created closed in on him and dragged him off to jail."

"Don't give blood anymore," Tamara begged. "You're see-through enough as it is."

She kissed him, closing her eyes so that nothing could distract her. And they floated off, like the couple in the Chagall painting who fly over houses and rooftops. Over Petkos and judges. Over case histories and fates. All alone, just the two of them.

Tamara was like Eve once she'd bitten into the apple. Somebody was bound to come along and expel her from paradise.

The train picked up speed as it pulled out of the station. Yura was running after it, like in the movies. Or maybe the movies resembled real life at times. Some business trip! Some "Soldier's Joy." Everything thrown together in one basket: Petko's grief, Tamara's "unexpected good fortune on a long journey." And now, Moscow awaited her. In the past two days she had completely forgotten she had a home, a husband, and all the hassle that went with them. Now all that was rushing toward her at the speed of a hundred kilometers an hour. She was still in paradise, but hell awaited her. How could she ever fuse the two places, the two Tamaras?

An Old Man, a Komsomol from the twenties, was sitting in her compart-

■

185

ment. You couldn't call him an "oldster" or a "granddaddy"; he was an Old Man, pure and simple. Like Hemingway's Old Man, the one who snagged that huge fish—or was it the other way around?

Tamara didn't feel like getting involved in a conversation. Yura had promised to come to Moscow, and there they would work it all out. She was daydreaming, fenced off by Yura from the Old Man, who unfortunately insisted on sharing his impressions. He began to tell her all about the old friends he had met at the Komsomol celebration. Nearly all of his buddies were dead—more were *there* than here. Still, he had run into two, one of whom had done time with him.

"Where?" Tamara asked, coming back down to earth.

"What do you mean, where? In the camps."

"What for?"

"Don't you know anything about the history of our country? I'm a part of that history."

"Tell me, does prison break you?" Tamara asked naively.

"As you can see, I'm still in one piece."

"What kept you going?"

"Three very simple things: Faith, Hope, and Love."

"Love for women?" Tamara questioned him.

"For one woman—my wife. Surviving for yourself alone isn't really worth it. But for your wife . . ."

"Did you have children?"

"Why 'did'? I still do. My grandson is married already. They're good kids—went off to work in Angola. I asked why they'd decided to live in a climate like that, and they told me they had to make money. They want a car, an apartment, furniture, and they want it all right away. When I was young we didn't need such things—we lived for the common good. Nowadays it's every man for himself."

"Times have changed," suggested Tamara.

"The time of hope was ours. Yours is the time when hope has past. But maybe I'm just too old, and it's time for me to head on home."

"Home—where's that?" Tamara wasn't sure what he meant.

"Where we all end up."

"What about Love?" Tamara reminded him. "Faith and Hope may have grown old, but Love is eternally youthful, the years don't change her."

"Ah, to be seventy-five again . . ." lamented the Old Man.

"How old are you now?"

"Seventy-six."

Tamara laughed. The compartment was small, and it instantly filled up with happiness.

The conductor came in and sternly demanded their tickets and money for bedding. She was the same one as before, but she didn't recognize Tamara, even though only two days had passed. Maybe she was just pretending not to recognize her. She must have had her own difficulties. And what did she care whether one person jumped off the treadmill into prison, and another into love?

Absolutely nothing had changed at home. Two days is a long time, and yet a short time. A person's life can be turned upside down in two days and the world won't take any notice. And thank goodness for that; otherwise, it would be all you could do to keep up with the upsets in people's lives.

Tamara's husband wasn't there, he was off drinking in his studio. Her mother walked around in belligerent, glowering silence. She didn't trouble to avoid objects but plowed straight into them, sending everything in her wake flying, crashing, and all but bursting into flame. She couldn't accept the fact that her son-in-law drank and there was nothing she could do about it. She felt as if she were living in a cesspool and had no way out.

When she caught sight of Tamara, her eyes blazed and hurled invisible spheres of lightning, which simply bounced off Tamara, in her blissful mood, like plastic balls. Tamara hugged her mother, kissed her soft cheek, and suddenly thought, She must have loved once, too, and been loved in return.

Tamara now recalled that sometime after her father's death, two Yashas, a fat one and a thin one, had turned up by her mother's side in quick succession. The housekeeper didn't approve of the Yashas and called them "Pudgy Yasha" and "Puny Yasha." Puny Yasha had a son, and that had prevented Tamara's mother from taking the decisive step. Pudgy Yasha was in charge of a furniture store. He got furniture for Tamara's mother, but jacked up the prices. Not by much, but Tamara's mother was still deeply hurt that her knight in shining armor should be so materialistic. With one hand he proposed marriage, while with the other he was already making a profit off his beloved. Neither of the Yashas was destined to share her life.

"Mama, do you remember the Yashas?" asked Tamara.

"Tyu!" her mother snorted in surprise. "What a thing to remember!"

Ukrainianisms like *tyu* tended to pop up in her speech.

"What makes you say that?" Tamara objected. "Why should you be ashamed of your past?"

"If I had a husband, I wouldn't be getting underfoot here," her mother said with a sadness that took Tamara by surprise. "It's only when you're past fifty that you really need a husband. So you won't be all alone."

Tamara never knew her mother had such thoughts. She thought her mother was content with her old age—if old age was something you could be content about.

"But Mama, you have us," Tamara reminded her.

"Yes, I have you. But you don't have me."

"Stop talking nonsense," said Tamara in confusion and went off to her son's room.

She ran away from her mother and the conversation because there was a good deal of truth in her mother's remarks. They all took advantage of the work she did but ignored her personal experience. They weren't interested in her as an individual. When her mother started moralizing and preaching, Tamara wished deep down inside that she were deaf and dumb, that she would just do her work and keep quiet.

Her son-in-law and grandson weren't even aware of how much Tamara's mother did. They believed that the spotless house, the borscht, apple turnovers, and clean shirts materialized all by themselves, without human intervention. In revenge, Tamara's mother called them "exploitators." Tamara often saw those little old American ladies with blue curls who traveled around the world in wheelchairs, and nobody seemed to think it was odd. On the contrary, it showed great respect for life. But as for Tamara's mother . . . she wasn't so old, only sixty, and yet she was living without hope—as the Old Man had said, "when hope has past." Her nerves were shattered by the monotony of her life. The days went by identically, like carbon copies, against a generally dreary background. Maybe someday someone would reflect on it all and write a dissertation on "Mothers-in-Law of Alcoholics." But mothers-in-law weren't a subject of scientific inquiry. Mothers-in-Law and Old Men were things of the past, of what was over and done with.

"Mama, would you like to travel abroad?" Tamara asked her loudly.

"Tyu!" her mother responded. She was incapable of living only for herself. She hadn't learned how.

Tamara's son, Alyosha, had been in the third grade for two weeks now, but he was still having a hard time waking up after summer vacation. He had a hard time waking up under the best of circumstances—you could even throw cold water on him. Tamara woke him not with cold water but with cuddles and kisses from head to toe. He needed affection like he needed oxygen, and he himself was as affectionate as a little girl. When they were with other people, he didn't leave his mother for a second, and would lay his head on her shoulder as if to fasten her to him and proclaim that she was his. Sometimes that kind of sculptural composition was out of place—at the theater or the doctor's office, for example. Tamara would say sheepishly, "How can I discourage him?" She couldn't imagine Alyosha getting married and laying his head on another woman's shoulder, and she was prepared even now, years in advance, to tear the other to shreds. She already had the makings of a mother-in-law.

Alyosha opened his eyes and sat up in bed. He had missed his mother terribly in the two days they'd been apart.

"What did you bring me?" he asked eagerly. He had gotten used to his mother's generosity with presents, but this time she'd come all the way back from another town empty-handed. She'd completely forgotten. Thank God she'd at least brought herself back.

Alyosha dove back under the covers. He always had difficulty with changes in his physical surroundings, and getting out of a warm bed was just as hard as plunging into cold water. Tamara was afraid he might be deficient in thermal adaptability, and beyond that, she was concerned about the genes he had inherited. He was the son of an alcoholic, after all. Still, the genes on his mother's side were strong, vigorous, and fortified with fresh peasant blood. Tamara was counting heavily on them.

In the second grade, when he was eight years old, Alyosha had plucked *The Iliad* off a crowded shelf and started to read Homer with the same enthusiasm as "Mukha-Tsokhotukha."* Tamara had begun to fear he might be pathologically gifted, but her doctor had told her, "There's nothing pathological, just giftedness. He's a very bright little boy, but that usually passes with age. He'll grow up to be a perfectly normal young man."

Still, the effects of bad genes could crop up at any age, in myriad and sundry ways. Tamara was always gazing anxiously at her son, hoping to ward off trouble in time, to ambush and defeat the invisible enemy before it attacked. Her constant anxiety only intensified her love for Alyosha, who returned it in kind. It was as if their circulatory systems were still one, the way they were when he was inside of her.

*A classic Russian children's story in verse by Kornei Chukovsky. —TRANS.

Her friend Nelka asked, "What's going to happen if at the age of forty he announces he'd like to ride the elevator all by himself?"

But he was a long way from forty. And today, Indian summer glowed outside the window, and his grandmother was setting the table for breakfast: cottage cheese and oatmeal.

Tamara's mother placed a great deal of faith in oats. Horses fed on oats alone, and they worked . . . well, like horses. It followed, therefore, that oatmeal provided both body mass and energy reserves. The staff of life was not some strange Chinese ginseng, but those good old oats, and they should be eaten every day. That way, you never had to worry about genes, ulcers, or something even worse.

In his short life, Alyosha had learned to detest four things: coercion, indifference, oatmeal, and black caviar. He hated too much attention, he hated no attention at all, he hated oatmeal, and caviar—the food that stank of fish oil—simply made him throw up.

They sat down at the table, each with a different mission. The grandmother's was to cram the staff of life down Alyosha's throat. Alyosha's was not to cave in to pressure. Tamara's was to neutralize both sides, thereby averting armed conflict.

Alyosha's grandmother loved him to distraction, with all the strength in her mutinous soul, and her love was expressed in the form of oatmeal. Insofar as dialectics dictate life's patterns, love sometimes assumes the most indigestible forms and formulations.

They sat in silence around the table, piously remembering their missions.

"In my opinion, he will die an early death," began the grandmother, speaking of Alyosha.

This was the first move, the opening gambit. If her grandson did not eat his oatmeal, he would not survive. Perhaps Tamara would be frightened into taking her mother's side and then, between the two of them, they would break Alyosha's resistance. He would start eating oatmeal every morning and grow up healthy as a colt, immune to all diseases.

Tamara could see her mother's strategy, but the word "die," used in such close association with Alyosha, completely rattled her composure.

"Mama, how can you throw words around like that?" Tamara demanded, her eyes glinting coldly. "What is this verbal incontinence?"

Alyosha sensed that he had won a point. With an eagle's defiant glare, he shot a look at his grandmother.

"He doesn't eat, this son of yours, he only nibbles." Alyosha's grandmother refused to admit defeat. "Just sandwiches and appetizers."

This was a transparent reference to the fact that only drinkers nibbled. Tamara's mother was rubbing salt in the wound, hinting at Alyosha's dubious heredity.

"Just two spoonfuls, Alyosha," Tamara begged him. "Pinch your nose and swallow, like medicine."

"Mama, it's slimy, it's icky." As Alyosha looked his mother straight in the eyes, his own clear glance expressed only martyrdom in the cause of truth.

Tamara instantly melted. She could not argue with martyrdom in the cause of truth. Besides, time was running out; Alyosha had to leave for school soon, and Tamara could not allow her child to go off on an empty stomach.

"Will you eat some sandwiches if I make them?"

"Okay, if there's no brynza," Alyosha agreed.

Tamara hurriedly made the sandwiches. Her mother sat staring with the burning intensity of a fanatic. The same expression had marked the faces of those who had gone to the stake for their faith—and of those who had sent them there.

Tamara set the plate of sandwiches and a pickle before her son: He loved spicy food. Cottage cheese, like his grandmother, had no hold over him.

"You might as well set him up with a shot glass," his grandmother suggested.

"What for?" Alyosha wanted to know.

"Grandma's joking."

Tamara couldn't get mad at her mother—she felt guilty toward her, and toward Alyosha. She had wanted to be happy without them, apart from them. But what about them?

Everything was still the same at work, too. What could possibly have changed in two days?

Tamara sat in her office waiting for Yura to call. They had agreed that he would phone her at work. But the telephone remained silent, and that was strange. Incomprehensible, even. She had already been at work for an hour, and still there was no sign of life from him. If she'd been in Yura's place, she would have called six times by now. Maybe that was the difference between men and women.

The phone rang, but it was just an internal call. Tamara picked up the receiver. It was Vlad.

"Could you possibly come to my office?" asked Tamara. "I have to stay by the phone."

Vlad thought about it. On the one hand, such a procedure was a threat to his authority: Once you started trotting around to see your subordinates, they'd run you off your feet. On the other hand, even though he was a Soviet, he was still a man—and Tamara, even though she was his subordinate, was still a woman.

Vlad strode into Tamara's office and settled comfortably into a leatherette armchair. He was heavyset and balding, with sleepy eyes and a thick nose. A drowsy mule. It suddenly occurred to Tamara that even Vlad must have someone who embraced him and kissed his sleepy eyes, after which he would wake up, open his eyes wide, and become handsome.

"What are you staring at?" asked Vlad.

Tamara was afraid he might read her thoughts and hastily handed him a copy of the court sentence. He read it over carefully, then looked up.

"What's worth writing about in this? What's going to interest the reader?"

"A man was of no use to anybody and went berserk," proposed Tamara.

"He should have made himself useful instead," Vlad retorted. "If you're useless, you're worthless—a nonentity."

"Maybe he was driven to it."

"What could drive a man to become a nonentity?"

"Love."

The soldier was in love with the girl next door, fondled her figure-eight curves, had a child with her, and didn't ask for anything more. She was a part of him and he was dragging her by force into his life. But she was pulling away. He tried to kill her, but it didn't work. Just like in *Carmen*, except that it had worked for José. Why should one soldier get away with something, and not another? Why was José a full-fledged human being, and Petko a nonentity?

"Prosper Mérimée wrote about it and it was interesting for the reader," Tamara reminded Vlad.

"Prosper Mérimée was not the head of a newspaper department. He was simply Mérimée. I, however, have a role function."

"You have a what?" asked Tamara.

"A role function. We're supposed to educate the reader with positive examples, acts of heroism, so he'll think, 'I could do that, too.' We must elevate man's opinion of himself. But after reading this story, you feel like putting a noose around your neck. Why should we be rummaging through all this garbage?"

"For the soldier. Maybe we'll be able to get his sentence reduced. Even if it's only by a year, that would still be something: ten years instead of eleven."

"Where did he work?"

"What difference does it make?"

"Tell me anyway."

"In a pigsty tending pigs."

Vlad was silent.

"I know what you're thinking," Tamara said. "You think he went from one pigsty to another, and society won't even notice he's gone."

"That's right." Vlad nodded in agreement.

"But society isn't just an abstraction—it's you, me, him. . . . Yes, him too. He didn't live in a vacuum, but in society, and society should help him. That's where being humane comes in."

"What if being humane means doing precisely nothing?"

"That's your role function talking. What do you really think?"

"I think that life is rough, and we have to help people pull through. We have to light a lamp of hope, not dunk them back into the garbage pit."

The phone jangled, the rings tripping over one another in their haste. Tamara snatched up the receiver and shot Vlad a supplicating look.

"Okay, I'm leaving." Vlad got the message and headed out.

Tamara thought he took a very long time—an eternity—to get out of her office. He walked like a man who has forgotten to put on his pants and is embarassed about showing his bare behind. He obviously needed his role function as much as he needed his pants—to give him self-confidence. Role functions should be conferred only upon people without hang-ups.

Finally Vlad got out and shut the door firmly behind him.

"HELLO!" Tamara yelled into the phone.

"It's me."

"Why did you take so long to call?"

"I didn't know what to say. Now I do."

"Tell me!"

"Car number eleven, seat number thirteen. I'll be in Moscow tomorrow. See you tomorrow."

"Wait!"

"We'll talk tomorrow."

"Wait!"

"All right, I'm waiting."

Tamara was silent, but it was a clamorous, exultant silence. People keep trying to invent a perpetual motion machine, but the most perpetual motion of all is love, and its fuel never runs out—it's self-charging.

Suddenly Tamara sensed that the silence had become empty, that the line had gone dead and there was nothing there.

"Hey!" she called out fearfully.

"I'm here." Yura spoke quietly from the void. "I'm here. I'm not going to disappear."

The train was due in the next morning. It seemed as if morning would never come, but it did—and the train even arrived on time. It stood there, massive and grimy, as if it hadn't been cleaned since 1913. Tamara realized that the moment her dream was to materialize had come. The dream was already taking on details, features, even odors.

Yura was standing stock-still by his railway car. People streamed slowly by him. Tamara stopped short as if someone had grabbed her by the shoulder. She saw him, but he didn't see her. He was looking around anxiously. A fallen provincial angel. His hair was cut too short in the back and his fake leather jacket hung on him awkwardly. But that wasn't the real problem—it was the general air of stiffness, unadaptedness. He was not at home here.

Tamara's friend Nelka said, "All vacation acquaintances should be checked out under Moscow skies." Yura didn't check out under Moscow skies. In the Ukrainian village of Solnechny, among poor Petko's relatives, and in his own wooden house, Yura was special, even super. Here, all that had disappeared. His fine features were so expressionless he seemed to have no face at all. The Yura she had known before was gone, leaving only a cipher in his place. And what was to be done with him? Tamara suspected that if she went up to him, he would see how dismayed she was. She would have to fake a joy she did not feel, play a role. And then what? Where could she take him? The hotel situation in Moscow wasn't much better than in Dnepropetrovsk. So she'd have to bring him home. Her mother would see straight through her and ask, in a stage whisper, "Where on earth did you find this boy?" She didn't like her son-in-law, but at least he belonged to her, was part of her life, like a chronic disease. This other fellow was a foreign body, and Tamara's mother rejected anything foreign with her characteristic bluntness, bordering on rudeness.

She could take him to Nelka's. Nelka would keep quiet about it—she was a regular Swiss bank—but then something would break down in their relations. Tamara would stop being the Tamara of before: She'd become more like Nelka, in a way. But their friendship needed distance. Nelka would look at Yura and give her diagnosis: "You two have different mentalities."

Nelka believed, or maybe she had read it somewhere, that surrounding the physical body is another one, a mental body. Your physical body is a given, whereas your mental body is what you've acquired in the course of your life. It sort of encases the physical body but can't be seen with the naked eye—a kind of spiritual frame.

The train, grimy and antediluvian, stood right beside Yura, and he was part of that train, not of Moscow. Tamara was part of Moscow, the biggest city in the country. The women of the Renaissance might have been after pure love, without a thought for mentality, but Tamara, a representative of the 1980s, had to have, in addition to love, the city, the newspaper, telephone calls, Nelka. She had to be among people, among letters, always among something. . . . She could handle living in a wooden house growing cucumbers, but only in the summertime, and only for a month, maybe two. The remaining ten would have to be spent on the treadmill—and she hoped to God it never stopped turning.

Their physical bodies matched, but their mental ones didn't. They had different mentalities.

Tamara drew back from this difference, leading with her heels. It wasn't easy to walk that way, so she turned and began walking normally, facing forward. She was heading out of the train station, and she was afraid Yura would see her and catch up with her. It seemed that all the people coming toward her knew she was running away, and disapproved.

The unfinished monument to the fallen warrior stood in the center of the workshop: five female forms with their heads bowed in sorrow. The warrior himself lay in a corner of the studio, and his place on the pedestal was occupied by the sculptor, who was asleep with his hands cupped under his cheek. The studio was filled with the heavy, lingering odor of lost hopes.

Tamara walked up to the monument. The women's faces had merely been roughed out, not finished, but Tamara recognized herself in the central figure. There she stood, tall and stately, with her head bowed. Her hair was formed by a single heavy swatch that nearly covered her face, but it was she, all right. Next to her was her mother, a sorrowful old lady with her complexes about oatmeal and growing old alone. The other three also seemed familiar. Looking closer, Tamara recognized Lidka, with her round face and figure-eight figure, and next to her, Petko's mother, hefty, big-boned and meekly grieving. Last in the row was Petko's mother-in-law, who was crying, her hand held to her face.

The sculptor had never seen the women from Solnechny in his life: He was simply portraying women in mourning. Perhaps all grieving people really did look alike. Or maybe he, with an artist's raw sensibility, had intuited the pain of the times, and everyone who looked at the monument would recognize people they knew. So everything that hurt people hurt him. That was why he was an artist. And why Tamara was an artist's wife.

As her friend Nelka would say, "You've got to pay the piper." Tamara was paying, and she knew what she was paying for.

She stood staring at the monument. The sorrowing women were arresting; they drew you in, invited you to shed tears with them.

The sculptor awoke and sat up. His eyes were red-veined, but he was lucid.

"Is that you?" He was checking to make sure.

"It's me. I'm back."

"Were you away?" he asked in surprise.

"Yes, for two days, on business."

"What day is this?"

"Wednesday."

"Goddamn drunkard!" he reproached himself.

"But you're coming out of it now, aren't you?" Tamara questioned discreetly, referring to his sobering up.

"Yes—but what for?"

"To work."

"Naw, it's no use, I'm no good."

He was torn apart by doubt, and his creative suffering was exacerbated by postalcoholic depression. He was going round and round, painfully, on his own treadmill.

"My brain's already turned to mush, it'll be dripping out my nostrils soon." He was making fun of himself, but self-irony always contains an element of self-pity. He pitied and hated himself.

"That's not true! All your work is good," Tamara said with conviction. "And this is one of your best."

"It's been done before, in the fifteenth century. Korovkin called it a rip-off of the *Pietà*."

"It's not a rip-off. It's a reworking of the theme, and you've added something of your own."

"You really think so?"

"I know so."

"But why rehash what's been done before?"

"People have suffered in the twentieth century just as they did in the fifteenth. And the fallen soldier is also a sort of a god—he died for others, didn't he?"

"My support comes only from you. You're the only one who understands me."

"You poor little orphan. . . . Everyone understands you!"

"Really?"

"Really. And Korovkin's an idiot."

He went up to her, hid his face in her hair, and clung to her, like a child in the dark.

"I bet I stink like a brewery," he said guiltily.

"Nonsense . . . Let's go home and get some hot food into you: Mama's made some nice bean soup."

Tamara led her husband out of the studio. He held her hand tightly, as if afraid he might get lost.

"It's for you," Tamara's mother said, laying the receiver down by the phone. "Who is this person?" She always had to know everything.

Tamara went to the phone. She knew it was Yura calling even before she heard his voice.

"Hello," Tamara said.

"I'm leaving today," Yura said matter-of-factly. "I called to say good-bye."

Tamara was silent. She was waiting for questions. But none came. "Isn't there anything you want to ask me?"

"No. I understand everything."

"What do you understand?"

"Everything. You need to know I'm not in Moscow anymore. You need to be at peace. That's why I'm calling."

"When are you leaving?"

"In an hour."

"You don't want to see me before you go?"

"No."

"Are you mad at me?"

"No, that's not it. I smashed up my face and I don't want you to see it."

"How did you do that?"

"I borrowed a friend's motorcycle and drove it into a tree."

"Did it hurt?"

"When it's head-on, it always hurts."

"What's your car number?" Tamara asked.

"There's no point."

"What's the number?"

"Five, if you really have to know. But I don't want you to see me, and I'd rather not see you."

"You know—"

"Hang up," he said.

Her mother was standing right behind her. Tamara put down the receiver.

"Who was that?" her mother inquired suspiciously.

Tamara didn't answer. She went to Alyosha's room to help him with his music homework. Her husband was asleep in his room behind a tightly closed door. He was sleeping it off, restoring himself. Things were falling back into place.

Alyosha stared dully at his music notebook.

"Fa—ti," began Tamara.

"A fourth."

"Keep going."

"Two whole tones, one semitone."

"Think . . ."

Alyosha frowned.

"Try to remember how the keyboard looks. How many black keys are there between fa and ti?"

Alyosha's eyebrows wriggled as he tried to figure it out.

Tamara stood up abruptly and left the room. Alyosha thought his mother had just gone out for a few minutes and would be right back. While he was waiting, he completely forgot about piano keys. He generally forgot about sixths, fifths, and fourths the very instant it was possible to put them out of his mind. He thought whole tones and semitones were excruciatingly boring, and he couldn't understand why he needed to know about such things. Why did he have to study music when he could put on a record and listen to any piece he wanted, and in the best rendition, too? Before there was musical technology, people had to know how to play music in order to hear it. But nowadays . . . Why waste so much time on something he would never need? Alyosha went on thinking these thoughts, but still his mother didn't return.

Finally he picked up a felt pen, opened his solfeggio textbook, and started adding arms and legs to the quarter notes, making little people out of them. He drew ears on the whole notes, and they turned into Mickey Mouses.

Tamara raced along the platform. There were only eight minutes to go until the train left, and she still had to get past five whole cars and into the compartment. It's amazing how speed and strength come out of nowhere when you really need them.

Yura was sitting on the lower berth, reading a paper. A wide purple bruise stretched from his right eye downward, and his cheek still had marks, as if someone had scored it with a cheese grater. He was already back on his own turf in the train, and had again become uncommon and severe, a proud angel. An angel roughed up by people.

When he saw Tamara he stood up. She went to him silently. There was no time left for words. She lightly touched his bruises and scratches. She wanted to ask if they hurt, but there was no time for that either. She pressed her face close to his and then, cutting through the distance between them, she kissed him. Once again she became part of the whole, knowing all the while that this whole was about to be torn asunder into two useless halves.

The conductor looked in and said, "All visitors are kindly asked to leave."

"Go . . ." Yura started disengaging her hands.

Tamara clung to his shoulders as if she were being thrown off the train at top speed and had to hang on for dear life.

He gently but firmly began to loosen her fingers one by one. Tamara sobbed in despair.

He took her by the hand and led her along the corridor. She followed him obediently, crying bitterly and making no attempt to hide her tears. Her face was crumpled; she looked anguished and old. People were dashing along the corridor in both directions, but Tamara wasn't ashamed. She just didn't care.

He led her out onto the platform and started to say something, but the train jolted. He stepped back into it.

"What'll you do now?" Tamara shouted through her tears. She wanted to cry out, "Stay, become invisible and follow me like a shadow, sleep with me, eat with me, breathe on me. I'll live my life, and you'll live it too. . . ." But nobody could become invisible. He was going away, taking with him the pure love you cannot do without, once you've known it.

"I'm going to build a car!" he called back. "And I'll name it Tamara!"

■

Tamara burst into wild sobs, as if he had said something hurtful.

The train left, the platform emptied. The rails converged, diverged, crossed, and then ran parallel. Tamara stood rooted to the spot as if the train had left her behind in midjourney and she didn't know what to do, where to go.

A large cloud floated across the sky, leading a flock of cloudlets behind it.

Half a year later Tamara was on a flight to the north, to a place not so distant, yet distant enough, where Petko Dovgan, formerly a soldier and now a prisoner, forger of his own misfortune, was serving time.

The rule of the *zek,* or prison inmate, was: Don't believe in anything, don't fear anything, don't ask for anything. Petko had been asking for help, so he obviously believed. Therefore, he was not a fully formed zek. Tamara would see him, he would see her. In the crowd of unseeing eyes he would find those of a person willing to help. And then the treadmill of bestialization would be broken.

As always, it had been hard to leave home. Her husband's heart was giving him trouble: The "motor" was out of order. It was understandable— even cars, made of metal, got their tune-ups once a year, and this was a human heart. Alyosha had eaten a cockroach for a ruble on a bet. Tamara's mother had for some reason taken the side of the cockroach instead of being concerned for her grandson. She had started calling Alyosha a storm trooper and stopped talking to him, stopped paying attention to him. Alyosha couldn't stand it and spent a lot of time crying in the bathroom.

Yura didn't phone and gave no signs of life. It was as if he'd been swallowed up by the earth. Or had soared away, like the angel he was. Tamara wasn't even sure now whether he had really existed or had simply been her interplay with her own dreams. Dreams were often likened to birds, and with good reason: They were meant to fly away.

Everyone is dependent on everyone else. Tamara herself was dependent on Yuras and the sculptor. But one has a life of one's own as well, and like a musical theme in the universal orchestra, it has to be played out.

And no matter how much life puts you through the meat grinder, no matter what kind of mincemeat it makes of you, other people aren't supposed to be affected, to suffer. As they used to say in Chekhov's time, one must fulfill one's duty.

The plane flew over Moscow and Dnepropetrovsk, over Yuras and sculptors, over clouds and cloudlets. The earth turned slowly, majestically, on its axis.

Even the earth had its treadmill.

1987

Translated from the Russian by Debra Irving

LAINE'S HOUSE

NATALIA BARANSKAYA

The house was over a hundred years old. Laine's grandfather had bought it, along with the lot. The property was located near a small town, just beyond the mill. The town grew and expanded, and in about twenty years it had gone past the mill, her grandfather's property, and a little lake overgrown with sedge. Then it began to move upward, taking over yet another hill.

In time the lake turned into a marsh. They tried to drain it by digging ditches around it, but the low land remained damp and uninhabited. And Laine's house, now situated within the city limits, still stood on open ground.

There were only a few old houses left in the town. People became affluent and began building their own homes, wanting a modern look. Little light-colored brick houses with attics under slate roofs and two small round windows, one on either side of the entrance, completely crowded out the traditional one-story Estonian structures that had sprawled along the street.

Laine loved her old house—she was born there and had lived in it for half a century. She was pleased with the house: good hands had built it out of seasoned hardwood. The walls rested on a foundation of fieldstone. Over time the stone had nearly sunk into the ground, and the house seemed to sprawl even more, stooping under the weight of the steep tiled roof.

It was a big and roomy house—thirty paces long and fourteen paces wide, with tall, blue-and-white-tiled Dutch stoves, four bedrooms, a spacious entryway and kitchen, and a lot of storerooms and cubbyholes for various household needs. A narrow, winding stairway with creaky steps led up to the attic and a summer bedroom called "the garret." The house had been remodeled more than once, spruced up and changed here and there, but no major renovation was ever done. Shortly after the war, Laine's mother, Helve, filled in the cellar under the entryway; to compensate, they enlarged the one beneath the shed. Even earlier, before the war, her parents had built a heated indoor privy with a cast-iron toilet. Her mother was proud of it and used to say that such conveniences were found only in the best houses in big cities. This is nothing unusual nowadays. And quite recently, Laine and her husband widened the narrow old windows and inserted modern frames with three-part shutters; this made the house brighter inside and gave it a less gloomy appearance from the street.

Most of the changes were made in the kitchen. Her grandfather's hearth was replaced by a large cast-iron stove with circular burners and heavy iron doors. Later on they added a white enameled beauty, a gas stove on slender legs. They didn't tear down the old stove, however—they needed it for heat in winter when the weather was freezing cold and for cooking during the major holidays.

A great many things in and around the house were of recent vintage: the colored linoleum in the kitchen and entryway, the sofa beds and easy chairs, the floor lamps and wall lamps, the glassed-in greenhouse in the garden, the motorcycle garage, and the electric motor that pumped water out of the well.

But the house itself—its walls and floors—retained the smell of olden times, the subtle aroma of dry, healthy wood. And a few trees still survived from her grandfather's day—four big lindens along the street in front of the house and a decrepit alder with diseased bark and withered limbs in the backyard.

The town where Laine lived did not appear on the map of Estonia as a resort, but so many people poured in during the summer that it functioned as one. It had its attractions. Five wooded hills and five lakes in the immediate vicinity, the ruins of a medieval fortress, sandy soil, and a mild climate, as well as a park, a beach, and a restaurant on the shore of the largest lake—these features maintained its fame as an unofficial resort.

The largest number of visitors came during the swimming season—July and August. Local residents rented out every available space to the vacationers to earn as much as they could during the short summer.

Laine also rented out part of her house, crowding herself, her husband, and three children into one room, or sometimes into the garret under the roof or into the little bathhouse they had built in a corner of the shed.

This July, Laine had rented out three rooms. They were still waiting for some elderly lodgers to occupy the fourth room. In the meantime, Laine slept in the garret, leaving her family downstairs. She liked to sleep alone. The nights were short and she wanted quiet, solitude, and complete rest.

She would go downstairs early in the morning, a little after five o'clock, lowering her big flat feet carefully to keep the steps from creaking so much. She would pause for a moment by the two rows of shoes standing in the entryway and straighten them up.

Today, too, she lined up one of the four wedgies that belonged to the old ladies from Moscow (either sisters or friends), evened up the pointed shoes leaning against a pair of men's brown oxfords (a middle-aged Leningrad couple), and glanced angrily at the tennis shoes of various sizes scattered about—the sand hadn't been shaken off on the porch, which wasn't the fault of the husband or children but of the curly-haired mommy (a family from Kalinin). Then Laine picked up the white sandals belonging to her sixteen-year-old daughter, Piiret, and looked at the heels—to see if the girl had gone for a walk with anyone after the dance.

Laine washed her face and turned on the stove to make coffee. A cup of coffee and a piece of bread were her breakfast before she left for work. Food wasn't all that important to Laine. Cooking took up too much time. She had enough to do without that, especially in the summer. She made only one meal a day, dinner.

By six o'clock Laine was already at the artel, working. She wove rugs and runners on a hand loom, making native Estonian designs with wool thread on a cotton warp. After two o'clock there was the housework: the cleaning, the laundry, the garden, the orchard—berries and apples—the chickens in the pen behind the shed, and the muskrats in the wire mesh cage at the edge of the marsh. There was plenty of work to fill the whole long day and even part of the bright northern night.

Laine was amazed at her lodgers' passion for food. She felt that Russians ate too much. The big refrigerator and one of the pantries were always filled with their groceries.

Overeating was not Laine's main complaint about her renters. It troubled her that people could actually leave their own homes and go off to live in someone else's. They said that city air was bad in the summer. But didn't they mind paying sixty rubles a month, or ninety—like the couple with children—for air?

She would have minded—she didn't spend money on trifles, on things you couldn't see. She also minded expenditures for things that people ruined and that became nothing but—God forgive her—shit. She was perfectly willing to spend money on solid, durable, well-made things. Her house contained many necessities: a washing machine, sewing and knitting machines, a motorcycle with a sidecar, two bicycles, a TV set, a big radio in a console, and two transistor radios. One belonged to Ensen—that's what she called her husband—and the other to their daughter Piiret. She herself had plenty of appliances: a juice maker, a pressure cooker, a coffee grinder, and an electric meat grinder. Music, movies, TV programs—these were wintertime diversions. So was good food. When the tomatoes, cucumbers, stewed fruit, and fruit juices were all bottled and canned, when the cold weather set in, when the lodgers departed and the family occupied the whole house, then she could finally relax. She could knit, sew, play records, watch TV, play the *kantele*,* and sing with her husband and children.

Even though Laine secretly found fault with her renters, who seemed odd and incomprehensible, she was attentive to them and always courteous. They were her second job, after all. Not as important as the art of weaving but more lucrative and for that reason just as dear. At times Laine thought that when she reached retirement age she might abandon her loom in order to devote all her time and energy to the house. It was not easy for her to keep up, though she did get help from her children and from her husband after he came home from work. Her legs would get especially tired. Toward evening Laine, dead on her feet, would hobble around like an old goose.

But in the morning she was as energetic as ever. When she was through with breakfast, Laine would lock up the sleeping house and stride down the street without pausing as she greeted and replied to her neighbors, who were also on their way to work: *"Tere, tere, terviste!"*†

After finishing her household chores one evening, Laine went outside to sit in the yard for a little while. The sun had not yet set even though it was almost 10:00 P.M.; its rays, slanting at a low angle, were cold and pale. The marsh gave off dampness and the smell of plowed earth and cut sedge—the muskrats were digging new passageways, trying to get under the wire fencing. The middle-aged Leningrad couple and the sisters/friends from Moscow were sitting on a long, narrow bench facing the flower bed. A big gray tom-

Kantele: a Finnish psaltery used in folk music. —TRANS.
† *Tere, tere, terviste:* Hi, hi, hello. —TRANS.

cat, named Mikki, was rubbing against the women's legs. Laine sat down on a corner of the bench after saying "*Tere*"—she knew her lodgers liked to answer her in Estonian. They began a strained conversation (Laine had trouble speaking Russian) about the weather, about waiting in line at the restaurant, about the cat, who was too lazy to catch mice in the house but went hunting for rats and moles at night.

The young couple came out of the house and stood nearby. She was wearing a short, low-cut sundress; he had his arm around her dark shoulders. Someone asked if the children were sleeping. Yes, the children were asleep. Since this was their first visit, did they like the town? Yes, they liked it very much. They had already roamed around two hills, stopped at two lakes, climbed the ruins of the fortress—what a shame that so little remained of the old walls. . . .

"They say there's a very old house around here where a father buried his disobedient son in the cellar," said the young woman, pressing closer to her husband.

"There's more than one very old house around here," the middle-aged man from Leningrad began to reply, eyeing the young woman's shapely figure and tan legs with pleasure. "There are several houses like that around here, but no one knows which one the story is about—"

"That is talk," Laine interrupted. "That is folk tale. Scare disobedient childrens. Each place has own folk tale—"

"Has its own legends," one of the women from Moscow corrected her.

"Tell us this legend," asked the young woman.

"Oh, so we like horror stories, do we?" The Leningrad man smiled at the woman. "The young folks want to send chills up and down their spines—"

"That is folk tale," Laine repeated, getting up. "But the truth is completely something else. Truth is to get up much early in morning. . . ."

And she spread her lips, smiling at her own joke, but her expression remained cold and her small, light eyes looked at them angrily, disapproving of the empty chatter and idle life of the people gathered in her house. But softening her voice and look, Laine immediately added:

"Good night until get up. Don't hook door, please. Piiret to come home late from dances."

The door in the entryway clicked shut, and the stairs leading to the garret began to creak. The rest of them also began wishing each other pleasant dreams as they went their separate ways.

And soon the house grew quiet.

.

Laine lay on a couch by a wall papered with colored pictures from magazines and advertising brochures and looked out the window. A withered branch from one of the linden trees traced lines across the pale sky, making it seem cut into pieces. Sleep wouldn't come, and her thoughts began to whirl. Pushing aside the thick layer of peaceful, prosperous years, her agitated memory went straight to the heart of distant, terrifying days.

The war was drawing near. Her father had been taken to a training camp. Her older brother, Tiit, had reached draft age and gone into the army. Laine, her mother, and her younger siblings—her little brother and sister— remained at home.

Her older sister lived on a farm. Sirja's husband was in an army camp, too. She was afraid to stay on the farm by herself and planned to move back home with her daughter.

Alarming rumors were spreading around town about spies hiding in the forests, about bands of armed men—either outlaws or insurgents—visiting farms at night. Everyone was afraid, including Laine.

The women had seen their men—their sons and husbands—off to the front. They felt lonely and defenseless. The war was getting closer, though it hadn't touched their town yet. Battles were raging somewhere nearby, but they were still out of earshot.

The surrounding silence was filled with apprehension. People tried not to leave their dwellings. They would go out only for the bare essentials, busying themselves in their yards and sheds—they were hiding things. Whenever they met, the neighbor women would swap the latest rumors: The Germans were very close, their own troops were in retreat, farms were burning. . . .

One night, while Laine lay sleeping, she heard movement in the house. People were speaking in muffled voices. Something was being dragged across the floor with a rustle. Then it sounded as if feet were stamping, and a male voice said loudly and clearly, "Quiet!" Laine wanted to find out what was going on, but she was sleeping soundly, the way adolescents do, and she couldn't wake up. Sleep was stronger than curiosity. Several times she thought she'd already gotten up and gone to have a look. But she couldn't break the grip of sleep to get up and go. For the life of her she couldn't tell what she was dreaming and what she was actually hearing.

Someone seemed to be moaning or crying; someone else was swearing under his breath. Someone was shuffling his feet and banging something on the floor. Apparently they had brought firewood into the kitchen and lit the stove. There was the sound of buckets clinking, but maybe it was something else metallic—the bolts in the shutters. The wood crackled loudly in the firebox, but maybe it was the crackling of gunfire somewhere close by. Maybe it was the weather acting up: rain was falling, the wind was howling, and the branches of the linden trees were sweeping across the roof. Something tapped and rustled along the walls and shutters; stones were rolling somewhere, rumbling. Maybe it was thunder pealing, or cannons firing, or just some empty wagons driving by.

Laine couldn't wake up all the way, get out of bed, and go see what was happening. Then she fell into a very deep, dreamless sleep. And when she awoke it was morning and quiet all around.

Everything was the same as always: The shutters were open, and breakfast—pans of porridge and milk and a pot of coffee—stood on the warm stove.

Towels, rags, and laundry were drying on the clothesline above the stove. Her mother had already done the wash, apparently, and was now busy in the shed, wearing her husband's warm jacket—Laine saw her through the window. The younger children were still asleep.

Laine ran out into the yard toward the water pump to wash up. Her mother said sternly, "Don't any of you go anywhere. The Germans came into town last night." Laine gasped—where in the world were Sirja and her little girl? But she didn't dare ask a lot of questions. Her mother was frowning, and there were dark circles under her eyes—she must have slept poorly, worried about her oldest daughter.

Her mother brought a freshly butchered chicken into the house and told Laine to pluck it. Then she lit the stove again. She got some of the dried herbs she'd gathered during the summer and simmered them in a blackened pan. She strained the liquid and let it cool. Then she made a dough with the herb water. Laine had never seen this before and asked, "What are you doing?" Her mother answered, "I know exactly what I'm doing, but you seem to have nothing better to do than ask questions."

Laine set to work cleaning the house. Then they ate dinner, but all they got of the chicken was soup, giblets, wings, and the neck. The rest her mother had stashed away in the cool pantry where they kept various supplies. Maybe she was saving it for when Sirja and her little girl arrived?

Her mother was acting rather strange: She would suddenly start to sing, then freeze in the middle of the kitchen with a pan or dish in her hands and stand there in silence, looking as though she were listening to something deep down inside. Listening anxiously. But to what? Laine, always a bit timid around her mother, didn't dare ask any questions.

She wouldn't let them go out, but she sent Laine on lots of errands: first to the henhouse to see if there were any eggs, then into the yard to clean pans with sand, then to the shed to pick through the potatoes one more time. And no sooner had Laine sat down after finishing one task than her mother was already thinking up a new job for her. But she hardly ever let the younger ones out of the big room. If they raised a ruckus and made noise, she would hiss at them, "Sh-h, sh-h." When they quieted down and went to sit in the kitchen, she would yell at them with uncharacteristic rudeness, "What are you lounging around for? Don't you have anything to do? Get the hell out of here!"

They spent two days that way. On the third day her mother got ready to go out. She took a basket and a can. She told Laine to bolt the door and not let anyone in. Or answer if anyone knocked. They had never locked the door during the day before unless they planned to be gone for a long time, but now they were bolting it.

Laine asked if they could play in the yard. No, they couldn't. Maybe when she got home. "You've got to realize that the war has come into our house. . . . You'd all better just sit still. And you might say a prayer together. . . ."

Her mother's voice shook. And after locking the door, Laine stood in the entryway for a long time, confused. Her mother sounded strange somehow. She had never asked them to pray before.

Then Laine glanced into the big room. The younger ones were busy drawing. Laine closed the door softly and stood by the stove for a moment. There was something she was supposed to do after her mother left. She tried to remember what it was and for some reason couldn't. It was quiet in the house, so quiet that the stillness rang in her ears. And in that stillness she heard a faint groan. A moaning voice, barely audible, called out, "Sirja, Sirja." Then another groan, and again, "Sirja, Sirja, Laine." Her heart began to pound, and her mouth went dry. She couldn't tell at first where the voice was coming from. Then she realized that it came from the storeroom where clothes were kept. That storeroom, a small, dark room, was located between the kitchen and her parents' bedroom, and the door to it opened into a tiny hallway. When Laine slid the catch aside, the door wouldn't open. She ran her hand from top to bottom until she felt a big bent nail. It hadn't been there before. She turned it and went in.

It was dark in the storeroom and the air, dense and sticky, was filled with an animal odor. Someone was lying on the floor on a mattress, breathing heavily. Laine peered into the thin, unshaven face a long time before her eyes adjusted to the semidarkness and she recognized her older brother. She cried out in fright:

"Tiit, is that you? What's wrong?"

She sat down and leaned over him. Bloodshot eyes looked at her without recognition. Moving his dry tongue with difficulty, he said:

"Sirja . . . tell them . . . I need . . . a doctor . . . tell them . . . I'll die."

He closed his eyes so she wouldn't see him cry, but tears rolled out from under his eyelids. Laine left, shut the door softly, and turned the nail back into place. She wasn't supposed to have seen a man cry. She slumped down in a corner of the kitchen and, pressing her hands to her mouth so the younger ones wouldn't hear, she began to cry bitterly and painfully.

Her mother came home, her basket full of packages, small sacks, and vials with pharmacy labels. Laine helped her mother get the stove going, brought in some water, and made supper by herself. Her mother was brewing herbs again and straining them through a sieve. Laine went into the room where the children were so she wouldn't be in the way while her mother attended to Tiit.

But when the younger ones had gone to bed, Laine went to her. Helve was sitting in the kitchen with her big hands on her knees, looking straight ahead with a fixed gaze. Laine asked:

"Why didn't you get a doctor for Tiit?"

Her mother was not surprised that Laine knew. She didn't answer right away, and when she did, she spoke slowly. It was obviously hard for her to utter these words.

"I can't get a doctor. I'm afraid. I'm afraid of everybody. I'm treating him with herbs. And powders, too. He's got a fever. Of course he's got a fever. He's feverish and delirious. And such a tiny wound. In his right side. Their truck was shot up with submachine guns . . . everybody, everybody. The owners of the Maivoli farm found Tiit. . . ." Her mother sighed deeply and shuddered. "Don't go in to see him. And keep quiet, keep quiet, or we're all done for: Tiit, the children, you, and I. And our house. The house, too. Nobody knows. Nobody must know."

She pressed her apron to her lips to stifle her sobs and waved Laine away.

They didn't talk about it anymore. Her mother didn't leave the house, and Laine didn't look in on Tiit. But her mother would go into the storeroom in her presence and hid it only from the younger children. Without consulting her mother, Laine would often find something for her little brother and sister to do in the orchard, the shed, or the yard.

Three more days went by that way. Suddenly it turned cold, rain mixed with wet snow started falling, the trees stopped blooming, and the herbs stopped growing.

Despite the bad weather, women and adolescents bundled up and kept busy in their yards and sheds in the twilight, dragging things out and hiding them, covering them with firewood and trash. The age-old fear for one's possessions, fear in the face of deprivation and ruin, drove everyone.

A few days earlier Laine had also helped her mother hide some of their belongings. After dragging part of the firewood away from the wall in the shed, they buried a trunk filled with clothing, silver candlesticks, and tableware—Helve's dowry, which had once belonged to her grandmother. "Everybody is burying things," her mother had said then. "And we must do what everybody else does."

There came a night when Laine remembered these words.

For some strange reason she woke up in the middle of the night. All was quiet in the house, and it was quiet outside, too. She awoke suddenly, in surprise and alarm. Her heart began to pound; there was a thundering in her ears. She began to listen to her heart and realized that its pounding was echoed by some kind of noise in the house. There were occasional muffled thumps somewhere near her head. When she rose up to listen, the noise stopped. When she lay down, the thumping began again. The noise was coming up through the floor into the head of her bed. Laine got up, threw on some clothes, and went into the kitchen. It was unusually cold there, but quiet. Laine stood still for a moment, wanting to go back to bed, and then headed for the bathroom. Darting into the entryway, she came to a stop—she'd almost tumbled into the cellar. the trapdoor was open. A faint light from below barely lit up the opening. Something clinked in the depths of the cellar and immediately fell silent. Laine lay down almost flat and, grabbing the floorboard at the edge of the opening, lowered her head. Her mother was kneeling by the back wall of the cellar. She had a spade in her hands. A candle burned in a bottle, illuminating an oblong pit, the bent figure of her mother, freshly dug earth, and a long, dark bundle beside it.

Her mother asked, "Is that you?"

Laine answered, "Yes, Mama."

She became frightened even though she still had the childhood habit of fearing nothing as long as her mother was near. Her mother repeated in confusion:

"Is that you, child? Yes, of course it's you."

"What are you doing, Mama?" Laine's voice shook.

She desperately wanted her mother to answer rudely, "Can't you see I'm burying our things?" But her mother said softly:

"Go to bed, child. If I'd wanted your advice, I'd have called you myself."

Laine went back to her room, lay down, and shivered for a long time, unable to get warm. She listened anxiously with a keen nocturnal ear. Her mother went out into the yard, and the spade clinked in the shed. She came back in and bolted the door. She stood in the kitchen. Stood for a long time without moving. Took off her jacket. Threw it on the floor. Sat down on a stool. Quiet. Stillness. And suddenly a mournful howl, as though a dog had started to whine in the kitchen. The howl broke off abruptly. Quiet again.

It was quiet in the house for several days. Her mother was silent. She tied a black scarf around her head; her darkened face and lifeless eyes were barely visible. Laine was silent, too.

Only at the very end of the war, a year after her father was killed, did Laine ask, when she and her mother were sitting alone at the table:

"Mama, who killed Tiit?"

Looking at her plate, her mother said:

"I don't know where Tiit is."

They never talked about him again.

Tiit was listed as missing in action.

Thirty-five years had passed since then. Time was covering the experience with cares, joys, sorrows, aggravations, pursuits. But she could not forget. It had happened, and not only in the past—it was still going on. Maybe it couldn't be forgotten because it was still there. It lay at the bottom of every-thing, at the bottom of their lives. Except that no one knew—she was the only one. It was painful. But nothing could be remedied, nothing changed. Nothing could be done now.

And the story they told about the disobedient son was simply a folk tale. When Laine heard it for the first time, her heart stopped. She was seized with fright. But later she found out that it was an old folk tale. Very old. Ancient.

The house stands as it stood before. As it will still stand for a long time to come. Some have left the house, and others have moved in. Her mother died soon after her father was killed. Her sisters moved away. The older one, Sirja, lives with her daughter in Rakvere and takes care of her grand-children. Marjam, the younger one, became a singer, a soloist with a choir in Tallinn. Her brother, Mikkel, left Estonia altogether—he's a captain in the merchant marine.

Laine brought her husband, Ensen, into the house. She gave birth to her oldest daughter while her mother was still alive and named her Helve in her mother's honor. Then Piiret was born, followed by Tomas and Maili. The house was full again. The oldest girl, Helve, had married recently and moved to Kohtla-Järve. She would come back when she was ready to have children.

The house now belongs to Laine. To her and her children. Laine paid Sirja for her share; Marjam and Mikkel didn't want either the house or any money.

The house is her house. Hers and Tiit's. Only she musn't think about that. It's painful to think about it.

"Get dressed up, my darling brother, kas-ke, kas-ke, quick, get ready, dearest brother, kas-ke, kas-ke. Don your handsomest apparel, kas-ke, kas-ke . . ."

This is what they'd sung as children. Their mother had taught them vari-ous songs. They all had good voices.

No, she wouldn't fall asleep tonight. It was already 4:00 A.M.

Laine got up, made the bed, and, after glancing at the rose-colored sky, left the garret and carefully went down the stairs.

It was quiet in the house. Two rows of shoes stood in the entryway. Laine picked up Piiret's sandals and shook her head—the girl had been walk-ing through the grass. She must have a talk with her today. Dances are one thing, but late-night strolls are quite another.

And Laine went into the kitchen to make herself a cup of strong coffee.

1981

Translated from the Russian by Gerald Mikkelson and Margaret Winchell

THE CAVE

MARI SAAT

The boy wanted to become a cyclist just like Ants Väravas.* He dreamed of seeing far-off cities, many-tiered highways; he dreamed of winning the Peace Marathon.† With the coming of spring young cyclists raced onto the highways in droves and he was among them.

His team often trained on a highway that ran along the seashore. About fifteen kilometers out of town this road turned left, away from the sea, and rose sharply up a hill. This was where the summer homes began. Sandy roads meandered toward this vacation spot through a pine forest and then on toward the shore and a steep sandstone bluff. In two or three places rickety wooden steps led down the bluff to the beach. The boys usually stopped there, left their bicycles at the top, and wandered along the rock-strewn shore.

The bluff had crumbled in places. There, a raspberry thicket climbed upward and alder shoots reached down to meet it. Every year, with the melting of the snow, a few stout old alders fell down the embankment; the rain and the sea lapped away at these fallen trees, gradually turning them into

*Estonian cyclist Ants Väravas (b. 1937) was Estonian champion on many occasions, Soviet national champion three times, and a member of the Soviet Olympic team. —TRANS.

†The Peace Marathon, initiated in 1948, is a major bicycle race in Eastern Europe. —TRANS.

naked, horned logs, but some still clung to the shore by their roots and grew verdant.

The bluff was full of caves, shallow depressions for the most part, but one of them was the real thing—a large, hollow expanse behind a rather narrow opening. The boys often stopped at this cave and called out to each other or cursed—the resonance was especially good here.

On one occasion there were three of them in the cave—the boy himself and two others. It was shadowy and dank inside. The boy glanced at the mouth of the cave—it looked almost round, bright blue and glistening. Suddenly the opening drew into a narrow slit, seemed to undulate for a moment, and then sprang open again. The boy screamed and jumped back a step, stumbling into one of his companions.

"Why are you so jumpy, stupid!" the other boy shouted angrily.

Seems they haven't noticed a thing, thought the boy and quickly exited, following on the others' heels. But on the way back to town, he couldn't stop thinking about what he had just seen. A thought flashed through his mind: Hadn't he left his watch back there on the rocks when they took a dip in the water? And that was exactly what he called out to the others as he headed back alone, although he could feel the watch in his pants pocket.

The sun was setting. A deep blue evening was moving in from the east— sea and sky merged into one, the waves were tinged with green. The craggy sandstone bluff was immersed in orange light; its rocky face cast sharp shadows. The mouth of the cave loomed black and from it coldness radiated out toward the boy. It seemed even smaller now than in the daytime. Perhaps the opening always closed for the night, like a buttercup or a tulip blossom, and the earlier contraction had been a kind of forewarning. The boy stood on a low rock a few meters from the mouth of the cave. His naked thighs were covered with goose bumps. He took a faltering step toward the cave, then turned around and dashed up the steps.

"I'll take a closer look at it next time, in the daylight," he told himself.

The following day was Saturday. He didn't have to study. He ate quickly, as soon as he got home from school, then he took his bicycle and rode to the sandy bluff alone.

He skipped from rock to rock far out into the sea, squatted, and felt the water with his hand. He longed for the time when he would be able to swim in the water, not just dip into it—the water was searingly cold. The vast sea lapped and glistened between the rocks; rolling yellow sand and pebbles were visible on the bottom, and green algae undulated gently. The sky was bright blue. A sea gull cried. On the bank up above, a green haze already covered the trees and birds clamored in the branches.

The shoreline was still in shadow; the sun had not yet reached it. The mouth of the cave, a deep, dark cavity in the bluff, promised cool shade and today it didn't seem the least bit frightening. The boy hopped along the rocks back to shore and entered the cave as he had done so many times before, and yet today he was a bit more anxious than usual.

The boy's eyes were unaccustomed to the darkness. He involuntarily extended his arms out before him, took a few steps forward to the middle of the cave. And suddenly he was seized with fear. As he turned to rush out he happened to notice that the mouth of the cave was jagged, almost wrinkled; its slimy walls clung to him—the cave was trying to suck him into itself like a terrible man-eating flower! Then a bright blue disk flashed before him and the ground beneath his feet sank into an abyss. The cave contracted a few more times and the boy was flung out onto the shore.

He landed in the sand among the rocks. He was weak, thoroughly shaken, terrified, but above all he felt insulted and ashamed, and he burst out crying.

The boy awoke to the soft touch of the evening breeze coming from the sea. He raised his head. The sun was sinking into the water. Its last pink rays slid across the surface of the water at a slant and smoldered in the sky. The mouth of the cave now lay at his back; it seemed to him that the wind wasn't coming from the sea, but that the cave was sucking air into itself. Horror welled up in him again. The wind stroked him; it seemed to the boy that he was growing light as a feather and that the air was carrying him along with it. Once again fear seized him; he leapt to his feet and flew up the stairs.

He pedaled as fast as he could the whole way, not daring to cast a glance behind him, and it wasn't until he reached the vestibule of his own building that he felt his strength wane. His apartment was on the first floor—he had only to drag the bicycle up ten steps, but he sat down on the very first one. A light burned in the vestibule and warmth radiated onto his back from the apartments above. Gradually he began to sense that it was already late, unacceptably late; they were waiting for him—his mother was anxious and his grandfather was angry. He no longer felt his weariness now, but his heart was so heavy he couldn't get moving.

When he finally snuck into the vestibule, bumping doors with his bicycle, his mother and grandfather were standing there waiting for him. His mother loved order and precision—she taught statistics at the institute.

"So, are you saying good-bye to bicycle riding now?" Mother asked.

The boy shrugged his shoulders and looked down, not daring to raise his eyes; he could feel his grandfather's bushy eyebrows and his mother's flashing glasses upon him. He had always been a little afraid of them. Suddenly he glanced up—those shiny glasses and bushy eyebrows were staring at him, but they didn't frighten him; on the contrary, thanks to them, he felt completely out of danger now. How peaceful and secure it felt to be under their protection! After all, they only wanted to protect him from the evil that lurked inside him and constantly set up snares and lures for him; they wanted to protect him from the cave! They had been worried about him.

Mother's beloved round cheeks had sunk and it seemed to the boy that her glasses were glistening with moisture. The boy wanted to shout that he loved them both, that he didn't want to go anywhere away from home, no matter what punishment they came up with for him; from the bottom of his heart, he wanted exactly the same thing they wanted for him—to be a good boy! He would become a famous cyclist yet, he would win the Grand Prix and then they would be proud of him! But he merely gulped and began to blink his eyes; looking down, he furtively rubbed and rubbed the chrome frame of his bicycle with his finger. His grandfather's slippers paced the corridor rhythmically—back and forth, back and forth—and from the kitchen, the delicious aroma of meatballs forced itself upon his nostrils—Grandmother was warming up supper for him.

For several days in a row, the cyclists trained on another road, making it easy for the boy to avoid the cave. After all, he did want to keep his distance from it. Yet every time another route was chosen, he felt a twinge in his heart, a slight letdown. It's true that the feeling wasn't very strong, but it wouldn't let go and didn't subside, as if a small magnet were pulling him toward the cave. And one day, when he and Mihkel were simply out for a ride after school, the boy himself suggested that they go to the bluff.

Why not, he thought. Me, afraid? What's there for me to be afraid of? And if I don't want to—well, the cave can't move from the bluff, can it? Besides, I'm really going there only for some of those good flat stones to skip!

Mihkel was large and powerful. His lower lip drooped a bit, he cursed and swore heartily—purely out of habit. During their workouts he was faster, bolder, and stronger than any of the others; and yet the coach said he held no promise: he already smoked cigarettes and knew the taste of liquor. And he quickly grew bored with everything. Now, too, he soon gave up skipping stones and stalked off in the direction of the cave. The boy followed him out of the corner of his eye, holding his breath.

Mihkel disappeared into the cave, but there was no movement at all—the mouth of the cave remained wide open as before.

"Oh-ho-ho!" Mihkel shouted and his voice boomed.

The boy gave a start.

"Oh-ho-ho!" Mihkel shrieked at the top of his lungs and it seemed to the boy that the bluff began to quiver.

But it was only pieces of clay crumbling down the bank and that might have happened even without the shout. Perhaps a mouse running along the edge had dislodged a stone.

The boy followed his friend. He sauntered into the cave as if there were nothing special about it—somehow he knew at once that it would remain motionless today. As he stood there in the middle of the cave now, that knowledge was in fact a disappointment to him; he wanted the cave to give at least some sign of life, even a flinch—its motionlessness made him indignant. His eyes grew accustomed to the darkness and he surveyed the large space around him: water trickled and dripped from the walls. The floor of the cave had been trampled in the center but at the edges it was soft, loamy; an empty tin can lay on the ground along with piles of brush and scraps of paper; there was excrement in one corner. Scorn welled up in him. He looked—the mouth of the cave was covered with raspberry shoots and tufts of grass resembling tangled hair. To think he had been afraid of this filthy clay hole! He had cried and kept his mother waiting—all because of this?

A fat black spider slid past his feet.

"Give me a cigarette!" he said to Mihkel.

"Hah, you don't know how to smoke, all you do is puff!" said Mihkel.

It was true he didn't know how, but that wasn't the point. He took only two or three puffs and then extended the cigarette butt toward the wall of the cave. He watched as the smoldering end of the cigarette, quivering slightly, neared the wall of the cave and it seemed to him that the wall tried to draw away. No, he wouldn't urinate in the corner of the cave or make a pile there, his scorn had to make itself felt more profoundly than that. The cigarette went out with a hiss. And suddenly the boy felt a painful twinge inside him—as if he had extinguished the cigarette in the flesh of a living human being; droplets of water welled up around the burnt spot on the cave wall like tears.

He tossed in bed throughout the night, unable to fall asleep. Something was weighing heavily on him. He turned onto his back, stared wide-eyed at the luminous ceiling, curled into a ball on his side, squeezed his eyes so tight that black spots immediately began to dance before them and his temples pounded.

"I'm a traitor!" he whispered and threw himself down again, his eyes wide open.

Gradually his eyelids began to close.

"The cave trusted me, it was meant for me alone," he whispered plaintively, his eyes half-closed.

"I hurt it!"

"I hurt it! Traitor!" The pounding in his temples would not cease and continued throughout the night.

When the alarm clock clamored in the morning, he jumped out of bed, not knowing whether he had dozed off during the night or had lain there with his eyes open. But he wasn't sleepy, quite the opposite in fact. His temples throbbed as if a taut metal wire were twanging inside them; everything irritated him, made him angry—the blare of the alarm clock; his toothbrush, which dropped out of his hand in the bathroom as he brushed his teeth and bounced along the stone floor with a clatter; his grandmother, who, as if to mock him, asked whether he had slept well. . . . At school he was summoned to the blackboard to answer a question about free-fall acceleration. He knew the answer, of course, but suddenly an indifference of sorts overcame him. A fusty old man now moldering in the gray dust of history had once tossed some stones off a slanting tower. It seemed so idiotic, senseless, for him to give an account of that now; he thought it best not even to open his mouth. The teacher tried to hammer an answer out of him; the girls in the first row tittered. He felt hatred for those girls and pressed his lips together tight.

That night he grew even more irritated when he noticed his grandmother furtively keeping an anxious, compassionate eye on him, as if he were ill or condemned to death.

His mother paced back and forth across the room in agitation.

"I forbid you to ride that bicycle," she said, "for two weeks."

Old sourdough! thought the boy and his eyes filled with bitter tears. No, not tears of remorse—this was just so much hot air to him! All their punishments and prohibitions, even bicycle riding! Oh, how he hated them! He was especially infuriated by the fact that his mother had said "for two weeks," by

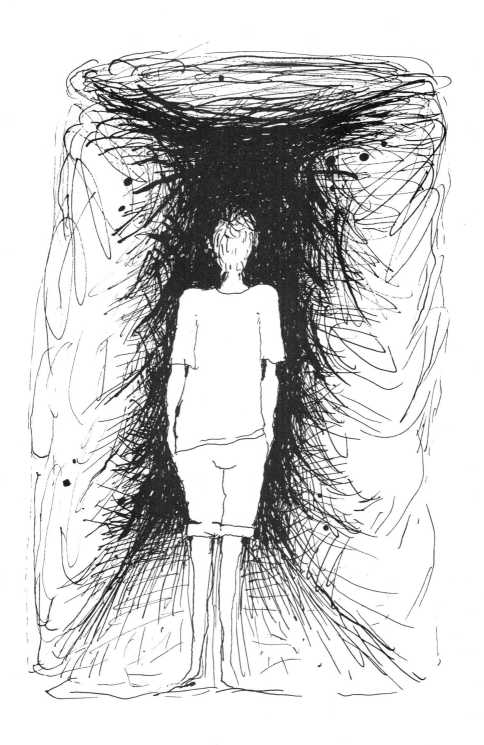

the way she had pressed her fingers together, adjusting her glasses—her pinkie primly erect—and by the soft padding of fat undulating on her hips.

Now Grandfather took him in hand and began to explain free-fall acceleration. Grandfather brandished his finger at the boy's nose, pursed his lips self-importantly, spattering saliva, as if his knowledge of free-fall acceleration gave him some sort of supremacy over the boy, the right to bear down on him. The boy glared at him antagonistically, scowling: his mother, who couldn't curb her appetite; his teacher; his grandfather; some old man who had had nothing better to do than toss stones off a tower—they were all trying to make him buckle under, force him onto the same path their slippered feet shuffled down, so his would shuffle down it too.

"Where is my father?" he wanted to hurl in their faces. "What have you done with my father?" He wanted to watch his mother blanch, turn red, his grandfather lose the power of speech for once. . . .

He looked at his grandfather almost victoriously. And suddenly his hostility turned to astonishment—he saw his grandfather for the first time: so many wrinkles! Like a wilted white cabbage leaf. What a thin, veiny neck! How small and withered he was, nothing but a big, flabby stomach, like a half-deflated ball—but wasn't that his grandmother? They were two of a kind! And he had thought his grandfather was a big, strong man?

When he was finally left in peace in his own room late that evening, the discovery continued to jar him. He felt that something had gone deeply awry.

"Father!" he whispered softly.

Where might his father be now? His father existed somewhere, of course. Perhaps his ship was sailing the Pacific Ocean at that moment and he was sitting in a cabin drinking rum; he felt sad because he knew he was supposed to have a son somewhere, but had no idea how to find him.

The boy got his flashlight, snuck into the bathroom, took off his clothes. There, in the dusky glow of the flashlight, he wanted to summon an image of his father in the mirror for a moment.

"Come on, come on!" he whispered very softly and everything grew cloudy before his eyes: his father, big and strong as the trunk of an oak, with a broad, hairy chest, very hairy, muscular arms, and a thick black beard; Father would take him along and they would sail all the seas, scrap their way through waterfront bars, hurl knives. . . . The cave—they would go there together! Yes, Father would know what to do!

His eyes cleared and there was nothing in the mirror but a lanky boy's naked body, light, tousled hair, a child's round cheeks. . . .

The boy's house was filled with alarm: Despite the strict ban, he had taken his bicycle and disappeared. He had taken advantage of a moment when his mother and grandfather were at work and his grandmother had gone to the store. It was all the more alarming because the boy had never gone against their will before—he had been obedient, a good student, in fact it had seldom been necessary to punish him; he himself had always known when he had done something wrong and he hadn't dickered over his punishment. Something must have happened to him now.

They phoned the coach, the boy's friends, but there was no training session and not a single one of his friends was out biking—Hans was at home studying, Jaak was at a meeting of the school radio club. . . .

Mother paced the room in her high-heeled street shoes. She had just come back from Mihkel's, who didn't have a telephone. But Mihkel himself was at home under house arrest and didn't know a thing. Now mother was too distracted to notice that she had forgotten to take off her shoes.

She leaned her hands against the windowsill: It was such a beautiful, clear evening; couples walked back and forth along the boulevard, doddering old folks and callow young people alike; children ran along the walk in front of the building shrieking. . . .

Letting their children run around outside so late at night, what kind of people are they! Mother thought automatically and at that moment her heart contracted painfully, her own boy was out there, completely alone; she turned away from the window, adjusted her glasses.

"We have to call the police," she said, kneading one hand, then the other.

"Well . . ." muttered Grandfather—he was very much against having the police meddle in his family's affairs.

"We'll wait until a quarter past ten," Mother said. "Not a minute longer."

And just then the boy walked in. He didn't sneak in furtively, like a child who had done wrong; rather, he placed his bicycle properly against the vestibule wall and stood before them, as if anticipating a cheerful surprise. Mother rushed over to him.

"Where in the world have you been so long!" she cried, bursting into tears. The boy hugged her, pressed his face into her hair—he was half a head taller than his mother.

"I'll never do it again, honest, I'll never ever do anything like that again!" he said comforting his mother, caressing her. And his assurance was not the tearful one of a child; he gently gave her his word as a gift.

My mother! he was still thinking tenderly in bed. His family seemed extraordinarily precious to him. His mother crinkled her nose in such a funny way when she was worried or upset or when she scolded him, like a rabbit, a soft white rabbit. So what that they had again forbidden him to ride his bicycle, they were all the more dear to him because of it. They loved him and that's why they worried about him.

But he didn't regret what he had done, he had had no other choice. He himself was at fault. He had been cowardly and cruel, he had fled the cave and, ashamed of his own cowardice, he had wanted to take vengeance on the cave when it stood there wide open, helpless, before him. That's why he had gone back to the cave, and stood there with his feet apart, his heels firmly planted on the ground.

"Flatten me if you want!" he had whispered, ready for anything. The cave began to sink down on him. For a second everything went black before his eyes, a hot spurt shot through him, sweat poured down his face and back, as cold and bracing as well water, and suddenly he felt that the cave was giving way to him, to his rhythm, to the rhythm of his breathing, as he willed. The cave was playing a game with him!

The boy's eyelids slowly began to close. The luminous ceiling of his room sank into blackness, swaying gently. It was as if he were again surrounded by that soft, dusky space. As if pumps of some kind had started up beneath his bed, jerking it up and down. The jerking grew stronger and stronger, it made him queasy, in fact, and then he began rising into the air, quaking and quivering like an old airplane. Suddenly he was flying. It was amazingly easy! He floated up to the ceiling. Rowing with his hands, he circled about, navigated around the chandelier. It was so easy, so much more pleasant than riding a bicycle. And he, fool that he was, had preferred his bicycle until now!

At the beginning of summer, the boy was once again on his way to the cave. Happily, the school year was over, he would soon be going to bicycle training camp, and now he had gotten his mother's permission to take a two-day trip with Jaak. She wouldn't have allowed him to go with Mihkel, but Jaak had always been held up as an example in his house, as he had been at Jaak's.

To allay any suspicion at home, he gave Jaak another call the morning of the trip, but neglected to dial the last digit and, with a voice loud enough to be heard through the entire apartment, cheerily shouted into the mute telephone: "Jaak, is that you? Are you ready? Okay, then, let's meet in front of your house, I'm on my way!"

Who would have suspected that Jaak was actually on a trip to Kiev with the radio club?

Before, the boy had often wished that the cave were located closer to the city, somewhere near his home so that he could stop there on the way to school. Now he wanted exactly the opposite—to be able to ride a long, long time, all day in the hot sun, and then, exhausted, sweaty, weak-kneed, come to the cool shade of the cave as if he had arrived at Mecca. He pedaled as slowly as he could, yet it took him only an hour and a half to get there.

He set up his tent among the hazel trees on the bank and lay in front of it the whole day, counting the infrequent clumps of white clouds as they scudded by. The water was still cold; swimming was out of the question, and there were very few people on the beach—it was unlikely that even during the day anyone would have bothered him, forcing their way into the cave. But he was deliberately waiting for evening. He had always had to pass through here in a rush and sometimes the cave undulated, sometimes not— undoubtedly this was because, in his great haste, the boy could not concentrate every time, could not truly desire. But today he could forget himself there at the bottom of the cave, abandon himself completely to that undulation—the abrupt, jolting surge followed by the fading, waning undulation; he could rule it, guide it. . . . When the sun sank beneath the shoreline and the air grew cool, the boy stood up and walked slowly, as slowly and confidently as possible, down the stairs, savoring each step that brought him nearer the experience he so desired.

He turned toward the shore. In the rays of the setting sun on the fiery red, sandy bluff, the black hole was rhythmically closing and opening. The boy gave a start, as if he had been boxed on the ears—the cave contracted; someone else was there playing the game meant solely for him!

He turned and stormed into the sea; a large rock stood in his path; he began to climb over it, stubbornly wanting to go straight forward; he reached the top—far down below, other jagged rocks could be seen. A gentle wave rolled over them.

Fall down there headfirst and you're done for! thought the boy.

The sun painted the surface of the water red; for a second he imagined he saw something white on the seafloor with red spewing out of it. Seized with self-pity, he threw himself down on the rock, bit his lip, and licked the rock's salty surface with his tongue.

The sand crunched. The boy listened and raised his head. Two border guards were making their way along the shore. The boy pressed himself tightly against the rock. The border guards passed by without noticing him—the rock was far from shore and slanted toward the open sea. The boy watched them go. They stepped in unison and as each footstep sank into the sand, there seemed to be a pause, a moment of reflection.

The boy pushed himself onto his elbows. He breathed wearily, slowly. The rock still retained the day's warmth and seemed, itself, to rise and fall under the boy's stomach. The sea rolled in to shore and back out again with a sigh. The trees rustled on the bank high above—the rustling swelled and died away in rhythm with the waves. The mouth of the cave expanded and narrowed slowly, languidly—the entire shore, the sea, and the land breathed and somewhere, on the opposite side of the bay, his grandfather and grandmother slept, snoring gently. His mother breathed softly. His father slept, head lowered on a table, and an empty rum bottle rolled back and forth in a corner of his cabin. High in the sky a sea gull glided and lazily flapped its wings.

1972

Translated from the Estonian by Ritva Poom

MITIGATING
CIRCUMSTANCES

IRINA POLYANSKAYA

1

And suddenly the March wind sprang up on schedule, whipping the city trees
to the ground, so that even the crows couldn't hold on to the branches but
were blown off and sucked into the current of air—just like the shreds of the
Latvian Philharmonic poster from the advertisement kiosk; the wind toppled
the dilapidated fence around the old Latvian cemetery, and it seemed that at
any moment the ancient tombstones would break loose from the slabs and
scatter every which way through the city, and the stone angels atop the
gravestones would flap their cracked wings and fly off like doves onto the
city square, where there was a clear need for a messenger from the splendid
past, where everything was new and four stories high, while the old part of
the town was submerged in spring mud, more the town outskirts with every
passing year. Spring rang all the bells, summoning everyone to meetings, to
picnics, to something reckless and gay, and that's why the pupils in the city
high school opened the windows wide, jumped right into the melting snow,
and charged like mad to the nearby cemetery. . . . Noisily and joyfully, like
baby grackles, they gathered around the familiar graves that were too old to
frighten them or evoke thoughts of death, and then sat down to tell ghost
stories on the very spot under the shining white trunk of a birch tree where
three days later two gravediggers, despondently poking their shovels into
the still-frozen ground, would dig a hole for the pupils' singing and music
teacher.

■

And so, skirting a massive tombstone crowned by Niobe, whose stone folds the wind tried vainly to fan open, they sat on damp benches and decided that the singing teacher wouldn't dare complain to the school principal about them; he wasn't that sort of person. At that very moment the teacher walked into the empty classroom and said, "Hello, children"—only to be answered by a gust of wind outside the window. The schoolchildren took turns sitting on the knees of an eyeless statue that looked the wind in the face unblinkingly, and by that time the teacher had already made his way through the school corridor and set off wherever his eyes led him, driven by the children and the wind. The children noticed that the clouds over the city were flying madly toward the river. "But, my God, the sky is so disarmingly splendid even at the hour of death!" the distraught teacher suddenly thought as he crossed a road down which a car was racing like the wind of death. The instantaneous death of the man mingled with the moaning of the trees, with the clouds flying over the chilly world, and with the shreds of the day-before-yesterday's posters from the kiosk near the Polytechnical Institute, where in less than one month, when spring had come to its shores and the Daugava had turned from a gray foaming avalanche of water into a meek, lowlands river, a fresh notice appeared about the sale of the teacher's piano.

Of course, you and I were not to blame, either directly or indirectly, for the death of that quiet man, who, while idolizing Chopin to distraction, had to teach his pupils the kindergarten songs "Along the Road a Lapwing" and "A Little Bird under My Window," although we were learning the same songs in another school. You were little then, however, and in kindergarten you were taught: "The sparrow jumped to the road from the tree, there's no more frost, cheep-cheep, cheep-cheep." The couplet was sung by a soloist, but you never did learn how to be a soloist, and when the chorus came in on "cheep-cheep" you joined everyone else in awkwardly flapping your still-weak wings in imitation of a sparrow.

It was a Sunday morning in April 1957, the last Sunday of that rapidly and irrevocably departing April, reflected in clean windows, puddles, store windows, and the black lacquered boxes of two upright pianos that had been delivered to the store the previous evening. In our city at that time few residents could afford to buy a piano, but we could because our father gave his all to serve science and in so doing earned money for us, so that neither you nor I wanted for anything. The cuckoo clock showed exactly seven o'clock on that April Sunday, and at the very moment when the bird convulsively thrust its birch body out of the clock, Father shouted loudly, "Time to get up!"

In our room we had a children's corner, where a toy table and chairs stood neatly and tidily, the table set with toy dishes. Father himself had made a doll's bed out of four supports and some kind of netting and Mama had sewn the mattress and blanket, under which my plastic Nadya and your grubby rag doll Mercedes slept; Father woke us up, and we, in turn, woke up our daughters. That I remember perfectly. But which reproductions hung in the nursery I can't recall, although I suppose that they were by Shishkin and Savrasov, who were Father's particular favorites. Everything in our room was permeated with light, sun, patches of sunlight. When we opened the wardrobe and turned its hidden mirror to the light, the room was endlessly reflected in it. That's not important, however. Soon they brought the grand piano, and both Nadya and Mercedes were put on the shelf, because the piano took up not only the entire room but also all of our free time. Think back: The days until they brought it were numbered. Why don't we return for a little longer to that morning, when Father came up to the door and knocked. . . .

No sooner had the knuckles of his dry and expressive hands knocked on our door than you tore out of your bed and flung your arms around his neck. You were very thin, and your nightgown hung around you like a bell. Father distractedly patted you on the back and put you on the floor, but he was looking at me.

"Did my children sleep well?" he asked me, but you shouted, "Yes, yes!"

"Oh, don't make so much noise, Taya," he said and, after stroking your hair, walked up to me. "Well, come on, get up, child. I can see that one eye is already awake."

"What about the second one?" I asked sleepily.

"Now we'll wake up the second one too."

"And the third?" I persisted.

"Our Gelya has only a pair of eyes," Father patiently retorted. "And both of them are already open and looking at this marvelous day."

"Girls, do your exercises," Grandmother ordered from behind Papa.

"But I don't want to do my exercises," I said. "I'd rather dream about doing my exercises instead."

"Then, my daughter, you'd better dream about delicious cheese pastries too."

"No, I'd rather eat cheese pastries."

"Then get up, child. The rooster has already crowed."

"Will fat Tsilda be coming soon?"

"Fat Tsilda, too."

"And will Gosha quietly bite his nails?"

"Gosha is a hard worker, child, in contrast to some people who are sleepyheads."

"Is Tsilda a sleepyhead?"

"How would I know?"

He picked me out of bed and lifted me over his head. Everyone told him that we were as alike as two drops of water. I hung over him like a raindrop and saw that tears of jealousy were welling up in your eyes, even though you were still smiling. Father lowered me onto the bed again, swatted me lightly—get dressed!—and after stroking your hair once more, went to wake up Mama.

Grandmother, humming something, was tidying up her tiny room. Her bedroom was the storeroom, because Grandmother was in the habit of reading late and didn't want to disturb anyone. So she lived in the storeroom, like Mouse-the-Burrower, but none of the neighbors or Father's guests were deceived by that storeroom or by the folding bed covered with a dingy blanket or by the table lamp with its burnt shade—there, incognito, lived a queen—no Mouse and no Burrower at all. It was her weak but commanding voice that would wrench Father away from the paper he was writing for the Mendeleyev Congress in Moscow: "Sasha, Sasha, come here!" The girls, hearing their grandmother's summons, would grab on to him, and Alexander Nikolaevich, wresting himself from his labors, would go out into the corridor and lean against the door of Grandmother's bedchamber. "Sasha, listen to this divine thought," Grandmother would say and musically declaim some passage from *Peer Gynt* or *Faust* to her son. Father, closing his eyes, would absorb what she read and ask her to repeat it. Mama, who didn't dare pry Father away from his work, thought this was a demonstration of the spiritual unity between her mother-in-law and her husband. She saw absolutely nothing urgent in the excerpts Grandmother read, and Father's pose seemed unnatural to her; after the divine thought had been read and repeated, Mama would stick her head into the storeroom and ingenuously inquire if she should fry or boil potatoes or bake eggplant to go with the cutlets. Hanging above Grandmother's bed was a reproduction of Rembrandt's *The Anatomy Lesson of Dr. Nicolaes Tulp*. This painting frightened us a bit; there was far more warmth, for example, in *Venus Sleeping* and *St. Inessa,* which Grandmother had torn out of the magazine *Ogonyok,* but Father thought that both Venus and Inessa would do irreparable damage to the atmosphere of chastity in the family, so Grandmother kept both beauties in a folder marked, "The Application of Organic Reagents in Inorganic Analysis." Here Grandmother also kept her diary, the cover of which bore the inscription "Dum spiro spero"; in the evenings Grandmother wrote denunciations of our pranks addressed to posterity. We thought that this notebook contained unthinkable revelations, great secrets, and profound thoughts winnowed from her readings of Ibsen and Goethe. We suspected that Grandmother encoded her notes; moreover, they were undoubtedly written in German, which she knew fluently; at one time we dreamed of penetrating the mystery of her diary, but we thought that if we tried to do so, something terrible would happen— either an evil wind would grab us and carry us away, or we'd each turn into little goats, like Ivanushka and Alyonushka in the fairy tale, who drank water from a goat's hoofprint, so we only tugged on the braid around the blue folder and didn't dare go any further. Many years later, when we understood perfectly well that to read someone else's diary was blasphemy and sacrilege, even though we were not threatened by an evil wind or transformation into goats, the diary was gone, and so was Grandmother. Mama once told us that there was really nothing special or profound in it; she had read the diary on the sly when no one was at home; there were old-fashioned recipes interspersed with expansive criticism of her, Mama, and besides, girls, Grandmother loved you very much, especially you, Taya, which was reflected in the pages of her notebook between descriptions of how to make puff pastry stuffed with meat and eastern sweets called "chak-chak," which were devoured with great appetite by Papa's graduate student Gosha and his laboratory assistant, Tsilda, while Natasha only praised and admired them, since she didn't want eastern sweets, Gelya, my child, she wanted your father, who on that memorable morning, surveying his domain, woke us up with a loud voice while Grandmother announced that she would make breakfast herself, so Mama Marina needn't trouble herself. . . . Remember how displeased Father was by that and his remark that there was no reason to spoil Marina? Grandmother countered that today was Sunday and Tsilda, Gosha, and Natasha were coming to breakfast, and she would bake cheese sticks for their visit.

Actually, Grandmother didn't like Gosha or Tsilda and had even less affection for gray little Natasha; she called them freeloaders, not, of course, because they breakfasted on her cheese pastries every Sunday, but because the students Gosha, Natasha, and Tsilda weren't worth the little finger of their teacher Alexander Nikolaevich, her son. They were all insufferable mediocrities before whom her Sasha cast pearls. But Father, on the contrary, believed that the important thing in science wasn't talent or intelligence, but human decency; for him, Gosha's and Natasha's mediocrity was a guarantee of their honesty and conscientiousness. Our father often erred, seeing a virtue in its opposite.

He was in general a man of such bizarre oddities that you and I, who suffered his disappearance painfully and spent long and exhausting hours trying to understand his character, still don't concur with the one-sided views of him or the versions promoted by his many ill-wishers who sympathized with our family. But we didn't need their sympathy, which reeked of the carnal pleasure of kitchen gossip; we wanted to know the truth, but, just as in the fairy tale, no sooner had we climbed an oak to catch the duck than the duck flew away; once we finally caught the duck and took its egg, the egg wouldn't break, but, thank heavens, a mouse ran by, shook its tail, and the egg dropped and broke—and we held the needle that spelled death to the evil Koshchei; but the needle couldn't be broken or burnt or sunk—it only pricked our fingers. We know the following about him: He was indissolvable in time and in place, like a drop of oil on water. Yes, our father could not be devoured by the epoch he grew up in, when he was vulnerable from all sides, being the son of a rural schoolteacher who had retreated with Denikin's army; nor could he be devoured by the epoch when, disdaining his deferment and going off to the front as a volunteer, he was taken prisoner, was moved from a concentration camp outside Vitebsk to Germany, returned to his homeland only in '45, successfully passed the security check, and began to work again. It seemed that Cronus, listlessly working his jaws as he chewed his children, had spit out this inedible one in bewilderment, and fate, like an ancient old woman, was thus compelled to rewrite his testament twice and favor Alexander Nikolaevich with a long, full life of scientific inquiry. Indeed, death came right up to him several times, chilling him with penetrating blue eyes that could see the horizon clearly but couldn't discern anything close up and so left empty-handed. On the outskirts of Moscow his entire battalion laid down their lives, and only he, seriously wounded, survived. After the war Father was once several minutes late—and he was never late for anything, with the exception of this one time—for a plane that had an accident on takeoff and crashed right before his eyes. If death itself couldn't do anything to him, what could people do? And if he, protected solely by his belief that his path was correct and righteous, didn't wish to adapt to time and never sullied his conscience in the process, then people had no choice but to adapt to him.

He headed a laboratory at a branch of a scientific research institute in our city; he was permitted to select his own group of graduate students, and four of his students, who had graduated with honors from institutes in Riga, put up with the ordeal of working with him. He set up a special course covering a number of subjects, which the graduate students had to pass in a fantastically short period. He insisted that they study English; they sat down with their textbooks. Father didn't adhere to a schedule of any kind but demanded that they work as much as they had to, for the sake of the cause, as he would say—and they submitted. For all that, Father gave them ideas and proposed experiments—and his students thoughtfully and laboriously wrote their dissertations. He wanted to train comrades-in-arms, martyrs to science, true scholars—but the majority of his students cherished only the dream of getting their master's degrees and finding decent jobs. Needless to say, the difference in intellectual and spiritual levels and ultimate goals sooner or later had to creep into his relationship with his students, but for the time being, through the efforts of the latter, everything went smoothly and calmly, and Father didn't suspect that the joint breakfasts to deepen their friendship on Sundays were only a fiction, a feast of Lilliputians at the home of the Giant, whose eyes had the strange capacity to see far and overlook the obvious. Perhaps he judged everyone by his own measure, and, detesting outright, innocent lies, he didn't sense the basic deformity and falsity in anyone's character. He regarded everything around him as if it were at his own command: The sea was smooth and calm, and there were no floating islands, underwater reefs, treacherous cliffs, or unseen icebergs. Father piloted his ship with a sure hand and didn't perceive the true intent of his crew, who were planning a mutiny at the final port of call. And indeed, if he had been able to notice so-called trifles, he wouldn't have stuffed poor Gosha with cheese sticks, because Gosha found them so revolting he literally sacrificed himself as he swallowed them down bite by bite.

As God is my witness, we even felt sorry for Father, to whom almost everyone lied. Even seemingly independent Grandmother, as she consolidated her influence over her son, was in no hurry to open his eyes to his students, preferring to be contemptuous of their servility secretly and congratulate Natasha derisively on the publication in a scientific journal of a paper Natasha had coauthored with Father, thereby demonstrating that she knew perfectly well who was the "co" and who was the "author," so to speak. That's how they lived, Father and his students, two of whom, it's true, rarely visited our house; one of them was genuinely engrossed in the study of ion-exchanging resins and Father, who respected the creative process, didn't bother him, and the other had a small child. They weren't with us on the last Sunday morning that we spent without the piano, and, when Grandmother asked Father not to trouble our mother since she would be making breakfast herself, Mama—Marina—had just opened her eyes and was listening in horror to her own inner voice—only the night before she had firmly resolved to study German in the morning, as Father insisted. But now all of her strength had dissipated; she was such a poor weak little thing. It was just a pity.

. . . Father's best student, who loved science with the same purity and integrity as his teacher, was Albert Krauchis. Father treated Albert as an equal, and, however strange it may seem, he gained more in stature next to Albert than next to those who might have provided a flattering background for him. He respected Albert for the same thing that he respected in himself: Albert, like Father, had achieved everything on his own; he was a self-made man. He, like our father, had fought in the war, and although he had been called up at the very end of the war, he had been wounded and had spent time in one hospital after another until 1947. After he recuperated he studied on his own to enter the Polytechnic Institute. At the institute he studied chemistry very seriously and landed in Father's laboratory several years after graduation. He was superior to all of Father's other students in age and intelligence. Father never raised his voice to Albert, and Albert never winked behind Father's back or made caustic remarks about him. He believed Father was a great scientist. Albert regarded his colleagues with impatience, I would say: It was clear their spiritual and intellectual obtuseness was torture to him. Memory has preserved his image intact, for he was worthy of it. As a rule, every member of our family had a completely different opinion of the same people; those whom Father liked were secretly disdained by Grandmother and Mama; those who impressed Mama were disliked by Grandmother for being uncultured. Loafers and idlers, whom Father detested with a passion, found a defender in Mama. But everyone agreed about Albert: Mama, not indifferent to good looks, forgave him his flat African nose with its big nostrils and his protruding lips; Grandmother closed her eyes to Albert's scant knowledge of art; Father didn't notice that

Albert smoked like a chimney; and we didn't understand very well that he was a grown-up and spoke to him in a familiar tone, despite the fact that he didn't try to win us over with either his tone of voice or chocolates. When you and I began to think for ourselves, we understood that Albert was the first harbinger of love, a love that appears for no reason, and we realized that that was exactly the way love should be: One doesn't love for beauty, or for intelligence, or for refinement of character, but for the image as a whole, and an unmistakable sign of this feeling is your freedom, verve, and comfort in the presence of that person. Yes, comfort, in our strict home, where everything was strict, even though the rafters of our house were not supported by marble columns and Father walked around in his slippers. You and I recognized Albert's knock at the door. It didn't require great wisdom to recognize it; actually, the door had a bell that everyone rang with varying degrees of aggression, depending on the person. But Albert would always knock first and only then remember the doorbell. And we would fly to his knock, sweeping aside all obstacles and impediments. Instead of a welcome, you, Albert, and I would say in unison, "Forgot about the bell again—well, what can you do?" "Albert's here, Albert's here!" Our house was filled with this springtime shout, and from everywhere—from study, from burrow, from underground lair—we all rallied to that battle cry, all of us transformed into a family through Albert's wizardry. Albert slowly took off his skimpy gray gabardine coat, and Grandmother, with the smile of a grandmother and not a lady of class, checked it to see if a buttonhole was torn or a button dangling. She was delighted! A button was dangling! "Well, what can you do?" Albert lamented as he said hello. "Hello, hello," said Father, who had imperceptibly appeared among us, "Hello, hello." They shook hands like equals. "Hello, Marina Yakovlevna!" "Hello, Albert." Mama looked him over from head to toe with an affectionate grin: After all, she knew that he liked her, she knew she could be happier with him than with Father, as could you and I.

"They say New Year's is almost here," Albert said, exuberantly rubbing his hands together from the cold. "And, imagine, in just a few days! The entire city smells of pine pitch and oranges. Tell me, is there room in your house for a big, green-boughed fir?"

"We don't have a stand for it," Mama reported regretfully.

"Yes, such bad luck," Father said, chuckling. "You know, I made a special trip to the store and even went to the market—there wasn't a single one anywhere, so we'll have to settle for fir boughs in a vase."

"Do you have hands?" Albert persisted cheerfully and then asserted, "You do have hands. That means that you'll have a stand. Now we'll commandeer everyone ages six to ten to look for small boards to make it."

"It's too late," Grandmother said. "Where will we find a tree the day before New Year's Eve? They've all been sold."

"We're not going to buy one," Albert said, shrugging his shoulders, "Ha-ha—*buy one!* The tree will come to us itself, right, kids?"

You and I, seized by a premonition that sent shivers down our spine and arms, cried, "No, no!"

"What do you mean, no?" Albert responded calmly. "Now move out of the way, give me some room. Angelina, Taya, give me your hands. Now let's shout: 'Come to us, Little Fir Tree!'"

"Come to us, Little Fir Tree! Come to us!" we began to squeal, and no one scolded us.

"Tap, tap." Albert said, "I can hear one-legged tapping along the asphalt of August 5 Street. Tap-tap. It's getting closer, someone big and fluffy is going into house Number Three."

Father looked at him with interest, we with adoration, already knowing that something was about to happen.

"What's the matter, can't you hear it?" Albert said casually. "She's here, your guest, she's already here, but she can't get up the stairs on one leg—go get her." We finally guessed, took off like the swiftest of birds, and flew coatless down the stairs: There she stood, our guest, the tree, on the first-floor landing! And our smiling father hurried down to us, while Mama and Grandmother, who were touched and holding hands like schoolgirls, stood frozen in place: Everything just as promised—a young, green-boughed tree!

"Good Lord, Albert," Mama finally said. "Where did you get it? How splendid!"

"Yes, what a lovely tree," Grandmother chimed in.

"Thank you, Albert," Father said. "And I thought we'd have to make do without a tree this year."

You and I had no words. We just took turns hanging around Mama's neck, and then Father's, and then Albert's, until one of the grown-ups noticed that we didn't have our coats on. "Now march inside and put on your coats," Albert shouted after us. "Then out you go to find small boards, this size"—he showed us with his hands—"and not tiny ones like this, got it? We're going to make a stand. Alexander Nikolaevich, do you have a saw?"

"We'll look around," Father said, pleased.

We didn't have the piano yet then—and our first New Year's tree had pride of place in the nursery. Grandmother circled the tree with a broom and dustpan, sweeping up needles, and you and I rode around it—me on Albert's shoulders and you on Father's—and suddenly we shouted together, "What about a star? And ornaments?" Albert put me down, took hold of my ear, leaned over, and said to me in a venomous whisper, "Do you have hands?"

And even now sometimes, when you and I are thinking hard, trying to figure out some problem, our cheeks resting on our fists, we suddenly burst out laughing at the same time, shaking our heads: "Do you have hands?"

And I remember a deep blue evening, blue snow outside the window, blue twilight, full of peace and warmth, in our room by the tree. Albert and Father had already retired to the study. We were sitting amid a mountain of cut paper, candy wrappers, cotton, and rags, and Grandmother was going through one egg after another. The holes were too big, the shells split open, so once again we called Albert for help. "You can't do anything for yourselves," he griped, and, puncturing three eggs with a needle, he sucked them dry one after the other. Just think: Those fragile clowns with Chinese eyes painted in indelible ink are still among our tree ornaments to this day, while Albert hasn't been with us for a long time, nor Father, and Grandmother is no longer in this world, our strength is sapped, years have passed, and the cumbersome furniture is gone along with the silk lamp shades—only eggshells survived the shipwreck, and this circumstance suggests that to survive, you don't need to be as big as a cupboard, as sturdy as a stool, or have the endurance of a camel—here is this shell of incredible fragility and durability, not ground to bits by the press of time and events; we look at it and sunbeams of memory continue to jump from one object to the next. And then we were put to bed, and Albert left, and after that we didn't see him for a long time, even on the last Sunday morning that we spent without the piano. Father's other students came, but Albert wasn't there.

That morning Mama got out of bed and went up to her reflection in the looking glass, and sleepy Marinas rushed toward her from all sides. The mirror was three-sided, and Mama could see herself in three dimensions all at once. She appeared in it as a wife and mother of a family; pressing against this image and supporting it from the side panels were the profiles of a lovely woman and an intelligent woman—a teacher of nineteenth-century Russian literature at the Pedagogical Institute. Our father also appeared to us as a trinity: head of the family, teacher, and scientist. The two side images, which to us were incidental, have survived him. We recently acquired a serious chemistry book he coauthored with Natasha, who could reflect his every thought and facial expression with the faithfulness of our looking glass, before which Mama combed her long hair, gilded by the morning sun.

She was pretty, but unfortunately we no longer remember her beauty. When we were forced to wake up from the long, flowing dream of childhood and folly, we found her suddenly gray and eternally exhausted, but back then, as photographs reveal, she was exceptionally pretty, resembling Turgenev's heroines, whom she described with passion and rare eloquence in her classes at the Pedagogical Institute. There was always a record player in the hall where she taught her Russian literature course, and when Mama discussed Dostoevsky's *White Nights,* for example, she would put on the overture from *The Barber of Seville* by Rossini. I think that her classes, accompanied by music, must have been imprinted on the memory of her students forever. Violetta and Alfredo's impetuous duet accompanied the analysis of Turgenev's *On the Eve*—yes, I'm certain that even now when any of Mama's former students hears *"Addio, del passato bei sogni ridenti,"* * he unplugs the electric razor, rubs his chin with his palm, and begins to recall the past and Mama. But she couldn't master German, which was a barrier separating her from Father and Grandmother, even though she was obliged to study it, otherwise Father would have excommunicated her as the holy church expelled a heretic—that was his little joke. For us they were united and indivisible—our parents, father and mother—but they themselves discovered they were eminently separable. We didn't know anything about those bloodless battles played out in whispers behind locked doors, while Grandmother stood in the corner of the kitchen like a scorekeeper, tallying up points in her son's favor.

That morning Grandmother looked in on us again—you were wiping away your tears—"Come on, girls, hurry up and finish your exercises"—and went into the kitchen. You and I immediately stopped doing our waist bends to the right and left. Without stopping our loud counting—"And one! And two!"—we started making "sun bunnies" on the wall using the mirror in Mama's compact. To this day whenever we wish we can still see the compact and the sun bunnies; some things have remained faithful to us.

The cuckoo again squawked out its call, time was pulling us by the hair into the unknown, but we didn't feel its tug then; we went our way and it went its way. In those days—remember?—people had only begun to hone their taste and acquire things, appreciate the taste of things. Our father said

---

*"Adieu, sweet, happy dreams of the past." From Verdi's *La Traviata.* —TRANS.

that in his youth people just didn't think about things, they thought about other matters, that is, about nonthings, which, thank heaven, have never been fully rejected. Then people started acquiring things, demanding that they be brand-spanking new, as life around them should be; they cleared away the now unwanted cacti from the windowsill and threw out curtains and cushions; they rid themselves of the carriers of the Philistine virus—those sets of ceramic elephants (remember how wonderful it was to chew on a chalky trunk?)—the world was renewed by things and played this game as zealously as the previous generation had rejected it. Televisions and refrigerators began to appear in apartments, little potbellied objects of luxury and signs of prosperity; furniture was bought piece by piece, since no one had even heard of wall units or living room sets. Fashion became very important. Marina made herself dresses, each more fashionable than the last, and the third—the most fashionable—was from the magazine *Sew It Yourself* that Father brought from Moscow: piqué inserts were stitched to the top of the bodice, a piqué-lined yoke was sewn to the shoulder seams, its ends passed through a loop and tied in a bow. The skirt was generously flared and billowed in the wind, it was tightly cinched at the waist, especially if the waist was tiny, like Marina's. No one except our father, who didn't want to waste a minute, read on public transportation yet—the distances weren't as great as they are now. In those days the buses had female conductors, older, good-natured women with rolls of tickets slung across their chests. Girls cut off their braids, and whether their new hairdos changed the way they acted or their new life-style changed their hairdos it was impossible to tell. No one yet wore narrow pants, which Father condemned with the fervor of a Savonarola. Many documentary films and newsreels appeared—interest in them was enormous; everyone was reading memoirs. Tuberculosis was successfully being treated with streptomycin, there wasn't a word about coronary disease or cancer, the moon goddess Selene was still out of reach, the space dogs Belka and Strelka were still ordinary dogs barking at passersby, tailors were suddenly mobbed by clients, lines appeared at the beauty salons, Marina curled her hair, and we hadn't yet gotten sick and tired of the words *connections* and *strings*. The sets changed; entirely new conflicts appeared, which literature embraced with some delay; the scale of false values became completely different; a multitude of hobbies and pastimes appeared; later, people even began to collect icons, which our father, at one point in his Pioneer youth, had put in a sack and thrown off a pontoon bridge into the river, having decided to put an end to the dark legacy of the past in one fell swoop. These icons eventually resurfaced—Grandmother's and many others—but from that memorable Sunday morning until this moment our cuckoo has popped out to remind us of the hour more than one hundred thousand times. By the way, lovers of antiques also took to hunting down cuckoos like ours. In those years people began to vie with each other to send their children to music school. That fate didn't bypass you or me either. How did we live then—was it good or bad? If we say "good," we'd be lying to some extent; if we say "bad," we would be deviating from the truth, and our father had no tolerance for deception or deceivers, which apparently explains why he didn't love you enough: After all, he very much wanted a boy, a son, an heir, a student, but nature *deceived* him, foisting you on him instead of a son. He was so wounded by your birth that he didn't want any part in choosing a name for you, and you were christened with the first name that they came across, because you, still nameless, were melting away before their eyes, and Taya sounded like the Russian word for "melt." Yes, you were sickly, you started walking late, you held your head to the side as if listening to the earth, which was calling you, weak one; your speech was scarcely audible. When Grandmother sang her favorite romantic song, "So Give Her Charity!" you inevitably began to sob so copiously and with such heartfelt sorrow that you made our mother blanch. Now it seems as if you and I traded lives at one point, for if you take your childhood and attach it to my adolescence, you get one biography, a logical development of character: Your life took my course. You, so puny, quiet, barely alive in your childhood years, grew up into a strapping girl with a firm will and unbending character—your father would have been pleased had he seen you! I, a noisy and active child, insisting that guests listen to me recite poetry, now heed you in everything. I have neither your will nor your character, and so when people who knew us as children meet us now, they exclaim: It's as if they've traded places! The cuckoo that burst out of our clock every hour tossed us into an alien nest, and that altered us profoundly. We should put that clock in a stable where it would be flogged to the complete annihilation of time. "The cuckoo isn't to blame," you'd say. "No, it's not to blame." Then who is? Father isn't to blame for their not getting along, Mama can hardly be considered guilty of anything, nor can the cuckoo; the Rostov Clock Factory required it to proclaim every hour of time lived, and it didn't teach the cuckoo to turn back time—so who, in the end, is to blame, who? There seem to be a lot of innocent people these days. You and I each accepted Father's desertion differently—I in small doses, gradually. I gathered up incontrovertible evidence, which I am now prepared to list: the strange, unsigned notes warning Mama;

the chance meeting in Riga, where our entire class had gone on an excursion (Father and Natasha walking along the street eating from one bag of popcorn, to which I, in my bewilderment, helped myself; their faces, when I called out to them and went up to greet them). Grandmother came into our room at night more and more often to sit by your bed like a white ghost and cry; grown-ups little by little stopped paying attention to us; Father, who had taught us moderation in bestowing gifts, suddenly began to spoil us with chocolates, hoping to sweeten his departure. Like going up steps, I climbed higher and higher toward insight, until the abyss opened up before my eyes. But you understood everything immediately, instantly, in one day: the day our father went away forever. A light flashed in your mind when you came home after school, a light flashed in your mind, and you saw everything in heartrending detail, the naked truth, all the nooks and crannies where misfortune had been hiding from you until that moment were illuminated with a brilliant light; a wind suddenly blew up out of all the cracks and carried off to the devil your schoolbag and dolls—the sharp scent of misfortune hung in the air of that house. You wandered past tied-up bundles of books, not letting Father, who was muttering something, take you in his arms; you broke Grandmother's glasses so that she would never look for them again; with your weak little hands you tried to untie the knots on the bundles in the hallway, knots that had been tightened by adults. Finally you made an incredible gesture, which Father, if he has any memory at all and it awakens one day from lethargy, will recall at the Last Judgment: You dragged your Mercedes from the nursery and tied it with string to Papa's suitcase, and then you left us forever, to this day we don't know you. . . . I remember vividly how you slammed the door of our room behind you as I again began to persuade Father to stay with us. Our mama had gone out somewhere for the entire day; the car Father had ordered was already waiting in the courtyard. Father insisted that he would always be our father and Grandmother, needless to say, would remain our grandmother. And then you came stumbling out of your room once again, suddenly your eyes rolled back and you fell on the bundles in the hallway. The mystery of your fainting spell was solved in our room— an empty packet of sleeping pills that Mama occasionally took by the half-tablet, which you had thought were strong-acting poison. Father, realizing everything, didn't lose his wits; he dragged you into the bathroom, brought you to your senses and made you drink warm water; you drank and drank, and with every swallow I stepped further and further away from him until the grief of parting came up against a solid and eternal wall of contempt: He was not frightened for your health, sister, he was afraid of a bigger scandal! Mortal fear was written on his face, and he kept babbling, "We have to clean out her stomach, we have to clean out her stomach," while Grandmother cried, "An ambulance!"

"No, no," he whispered, "it's nothing serious, come on, Mama, get me a bucket!"

That's when you and I changed radically. It was probably easier that way; at the time you were a despondent little girl with a constant sniffle, while Father thought I, on the contrary, was clever; he believed that I would amount to something one day and bring honor to our name. Now I have a different last name, as do you, and whether or not we have amounted to anything is not for us to say. And so you never did learn to sing, even though you had perfect pitch. Instead, your voice went into your hands, into the keyboard, as water seeps into the earth to nourish a bush, but our parents dreamed that you and I would sing duets, and that's the goal they had in mind when they bought the piano. So you see, no matter how you and I twist and turn our memories, we are inevitably brought back to the center and focus of our childhood—the piano.

On that Sunday in 1957 Mama didn't hurry out of her room. She sat in the armchair, holding her head in her hands, listening to songs on the radio; one after the other her daughters came in to say good morning. But as soon as the door had closed behind the children, Mama unexpectedly changed. We would have been amazed by her face, had it been accessible to our spiritual gaze, which can penetrate walls as well as smiles, but in those days our spiritual vision had not yet matured, and so we believed Mama's grimaces and the tapping of her shoes against each other. But Mama, when she was alone, turned a thoughtful gaze into the otherworldly wilderness that she detected at times in her soul, and studied the feasibility of mastering it with an expression of profound peace, humility, and solitude. Such moods sometimes came over her, and you and I, like our father, considered her younger than any of us and didn't suspect Mama's strength and courage.

Meanwhile someone rang the doorbell, and by the timid trill of the bell we knew that the graduate student Gosha had arrived. He came in sideways, obediently, fawning upon us girls, leaving himself open to Grandmother's barbs, who mocked him by referring to the classics, scornfully assuming that Father's guests were not conversant in them. Grandmother, a smart soul, knew the value of Gosha's obedience.

"Gelya, you have such a lovely doll," poor Gosha said, and Grandmother, affectionately squinting her eyes, agreed quietly, almost inaudibly, "Your spitz is a lovely spitz."*

The gleam in Gosha's eyes didn't go out, but for the time being it shone dully, promising that in the future he would give a haughty dry nod toward the children of his former teacher, trip up the teacher himself, and refuse to acknowledge the teacher's mother, who had tormented him so. But for now Gosha kept the flame low, wrote his dissertation, courted Professor Stratonov like a girl, and stubbornly refused to marry Tsilda. Stratonov tested his dissertation on Gosha, Gosha tried on Stratonov's job, Tsilda tried on Gosha like a ring, and roses and diamonds flew out of her pink mouth, paving the way for future vipers and toads, while Natasha . . .

But then the cuckoo popped out once again and emitted a fierce squawk. Its cry was answered by the doorbell: It was she, the graduate student Natasha, a girl with a face eroded by nature's too frequent use, a face that was impossible to remember; it wasn't unattractive, but there was nothing of herself in it—no expression, no thoughts, no gleam in the eye—the kind of face fate should have?! Natasha made herself useful to everyone: Her fellow students and girlfriends thought of her when they needed someone to babysit, visit a sick person on behalf of the work collective, go to Riga for a couple of days, or take care of a dog, who contemptuously pulled its snout away from Natasha's timid, caressing hand. Only Father said that he had great respect for her, and since he had an aversion to lies, it meant that he was telling the truth and only the truth. Natasha conscientiously did the work that Marina didn't want to do, since Marina was a rather vibrant, emotional person and couldn't sit still for long. Natasha handled Father's correspondence with scholars with whom Alexander Nikolaevich was writing papers or conducting scientific surveys for scholarly journals; she helped him set up his program, prepared chemical solutions, carried out series of experiments, and read over Father's abstracts; with him she ran the branch of the All-Union Chemical Society that Father had founded in our city; together with him she fought for equipment for the laboratory, displaying a certain flair; she typed his scientific papers and secretly studied German. By cramming up to twenty German words a day into her head, Natasha was preparing the subversion of her teacher; she correctly sensed that this man,

---

*A line from the play *Woe from Wit,* by Alexander Griboyedov, 1833. —Trans.

who was indifferent to flirtation, to beauty in general, and inaccessible to the most attractive women students, was the one man who might someday need her. The time would come and they would speak the same language, one that Marina didn't understand. It didn't occur to anyone, of course, that the little turtlelike steps that Natasha was making in the field of chemistry and in the German language were nothing other than the quiet, indiscernible advances of the pawn on the queen. Our grandmother was not at all cruel toward Natasha; she was simply an implacable enemy of any mediocre person who was for some reason mysteriously drawn to her son and clung to him, while interesting and vibrant people such as Albert disappeared from his orbit.

And in fact, to everyone's surprise, Albert had left Father; he had applied for a transfer to the Department of Organic Chemistry at the Polytechnical Institute, and, most importantly, we found out about it only later and completely by chance. For an entire month Father was in a terribly bleak and depressed state; Mama attributed it to the failure of a series of laboratory experiments he had conducted and didn't question him about it. But one day she ran into Albert on the street. To her utter amazement, when he saw her he lowered his head and tried to slip past. But when she stopped him all the same, she was struck by the expression of confusion and despair on his face. She opened her mouth to ask if he were ill when suddenly Albert, dismissing her with a wave of his hand, cried, "No, no—don't ask me anything!" and ran off. Mama came home bewildered and told Father about her encounter. And suddenly Father frowned and informed her that Albert had left him for another adviser. That said, he fell silent. "What does this mean, Sasha?" Mama asked. Father looked at the floor and grinned wryly. Then he shot her an uncertain glance—of a kind she had never seen before—and, waving his hand exactly as Albert had, disappeared into his study. Mama rushed to Grandmother. Grandmother didn't know what was going on either; she went to Father, leaving the door slightly ajar behind her. Mama pressed up close to it. "Did you insult him in some way?" Grandmother persisted. "Alexander, what happened?" Father didn't answer. He sat at his desk, covering his face with his hands, upset and weak. Grandmother walked away without an explanation. "He probably insulted Albert," she told Mama. "But how? When?"

But how, when? Mama kept asking herself that question and couldn't come up with an answer. She knew Father well: When someone got on his nerves he broke off relations explosively, publicly, drawing a wide circle of people into it. But a conspiracy of silence surrounded this incident. No one knew anything. No one could explain anything. Mama went to see Albert at his home. She returned even more upset and confused. Albert refused to explain anything, and when Mama began to insist, he uttered, quietly but firmly and deathly pale, "I beg you, don't ask the impossible of me. I can't tell you anything." Where did the truth lie, then? Both Mama and Grandmother didn't doubt for a minute that Father was to blame and not Albert. They began to list the various possibilities. Had Albert caught Father plagiarizing? Impossible. Had Father proposed some shady deal to Albert? Nonsense. Then what was it—what? The poor women—they were looking in entirely the wrong place. It didn't occur to any of us to tie up in one knot of cause and effect Albert's departure, Father's embarrassment when someone brought up the subject of Albert, and a certain grand but guilty serenity that had recently appeared in Natasha. Mama, and especially Grandmother, thought that Natasha was such a nonentity, such a total zero and cipher, that even if one of them had caught her and Father in a discussion of their already existing relationship, as Albert apparently had, they wouldn't have believed their ears. You could expect anything from Father but adultery—he always spoke with such feeling about the moral foundation of the family; but it was adultery and it was Natasha, and all of us, including Grandmother, who later sided with Father, paid for our gullibility and condescending irony toward quiet Natasha—whom Grandmother, pretending confusion, called Sonya for a while in a reference to one of Tolstoy's heroines. But Natasha wouldn't have dared to correct Grandmother. At that time, none of us, except you, suspected that Natasha was keeping an exact tally of the insults she had suffered in our home, that she had her own bookkeeping system for the caustic comments and criticism she had to swallow, that she wasn't at all the nonentity we imagined her to be. But you had perfect pitch, you sensed something in her voice, you saw something in the soul of that Rusalka whom everyone else considered as clear and transparent as the day is long; your gaze was directed at something else, far different from what was implied by her words or the way she timidly stirred the sugar in her tea, afraid the spoon would clatter against the sides of the glass. You refused the tea she poured as if you could see the drops of colorless and tasteless poison in it. Your intent gaze sent her from the table; Father saw you frightening Natasha and felt even more estranged from you. You got up from the table and went into our room to spin your top, and Father drank the ill-fated drink to console Natasha. Afterward he didn't keel over, poisoned—because he had a healthy stomach and farsighted eyes.

"Have some jam," Father said. "It's delicious."

.

"It is delicious," Natasha agreed, and tried a little.

Marina was having fun scaring Gosha with her compliments, and Grandmother, Serafima Georgievna, questioned Tsilda about what she planned to do with her life, since she couldn't be a laboratory assistant forever. Tsilda, a strapping, broad-shouldered girl who spoke with a lovely accent, admitted that she couldn't be one forever, of course, and that she planned to become the wife of a promising student and nothing more—such was her wit. In general she didn't put up with much from Serafima Georgievna. Gelya, the older daugher of Alexander Nikolaevich, hung on her father's every word and was pleased that he was so kind to the pitiful Natasha. And it was in just this mise-en-scène, with these characters in these poses, which the director of a future play might use in exactly the same way and with exactly the same expression, that the words "grand piano" were first uttered.

Gosha, wisely addressing the space between the professor and his mama, said, "So you want to buy the girls a piano?"

Serafima Georgievna corrected him, "A grand piano. It's not the same thing, you know."

"A grand piano is big," Natasha quietly explained to Gosha. "And an upright piano is smaller."

"Of course, of course," Tsilda said, smiling complacently. "But they delivered only uprights to the store, two of them. My neighbors asked: uprights, not grand pianos."

"The fact of the matter is," Grandmother said, feeling Marina's eyes on her, "that at first we actually decided to get an upright. But yesterday Sasha happened to notice an advertisement for a grand piano. Today we're going to have a look at the intended, as it were."

Marina paled. It made no difference to her, of course, if it were a grand piano or a drum, but from what was said she caught one thing: He had confided in his mother and not in her.

"A grand piano will take up too much room," she said in a trembling voice.

The guests held their breath. They could see that the jousting had begun: The two horsemen, visors lowered and spears atilt, were moving across the kitchen table, hurling cups to the floor as they headed straight at each other. Marina's mother-in-law grinned slightly, knowing that she was in complete control of herself and that everything was fine, while her rival was about to reveal all her weakness and lack of self-control.

"A grand piano will take up a lot of room," Marina repeated.

In response her mother-in-law noted in a genial tone that some people, unfortunately, choose practicality over beauty. Of course, she added, a grand piano is a cumbersome thing, but if you regard an instrument as furniture, then it would be best to buy a balalaika (Father burst out laughing, Gosha let out a hoarse chortle), since it, the balalaika, would take up little space and all it needed was a nail in the closet. Alexander Nikolaevich patted his wife on the cheek: A grand piano and only a grand piano, he said, can impart to the girls the sense of responsibility that is essential for so important an undertaking as music. A grand piano is an entire realm, an autonomous republic of music in the home, and not a piece of furniture against the wall; it's also good that this particular instrument apparently has its own history, and personally I believe in things that have a history and an individuality—I can't bear the slightest hint of mass production!

It was strange to hear that admission coming from the lips of a man who couldn't tolerate lies. Like the changing of the seasons or the law of conservation of energy, the serial nature of people and actions was a condition of his own existence, which wasn't as independent as we were led to believe; any kind of individuality or unpredictability in a human specimen was anathema to him. An awkward pause was the response to this admission. Natasha cautiously stole a glance at Serafima Georgievna, expecting to see a subtle smirk on her lips—but she wasn't looking in Natasha's direction. Serafima Georgievna, leaning back in her chair, gazed contentedly at the expression of unbending will on her son's face. Marina crumbled a pastry in her fingers.

"Let's ask the girls themselves," Father said.

"I want a grand piano!" the older one cried, pounding her fist on the table.

"Where's Taya?" Father asked.

"You punished her!" Marina cried, running out of the room and slamming the door.

Father scowled. With tactful expressions the guests quickly began to take their leave. Serafima Georgievna ironically tried to convince them to stay a while longer. Natasha looked at Alexander Nikolaevich with compassion, sighed deeply, and tiptoed away.

"Don't be angry with her," Serafima Georgievna said to her son. "You know how high-strung she is. Don't spoil the children's Sunday."

Alexander Nikolaevich drummed his fingers on the table a moment and, without answering his mother, went to his wife.

In our room we fearfully listened to the voices of our parents on the other side of the wall. You shut your eyes tight. We thought they sounded tired.

We didn't know which was better: when they screamed and wept or when they spoke in tired voices. Grandmother came in and whispered, "Girls, get dressed!"

We put on our plush coats with hoods, you in red and I in blue; we looked like two pages attending our majestic grandmother. Father's coat, hanging from the rack, seemed like an utterly harmless creature. Grandmother took us by the hand and we went outside.

"Don't worry, girls," Grandmother said affectionately. "Mama and Papa will have a talk and then come out."

But we were suffocating from a strong sense of foreboding. We silently sank to the bottom—I behind you—and disappeared in the depths of our grief, where no one could console us, since we had already glimpsed the truth even if we couldn't yet express it in words.

But then Father and Mother came out of the entrance with completely ordinary expressions on their faces.

"By majority vote the grand piano wins," Father said. "If it's in good condition we'll take it."

Mama made a face, and we laughed, coming back to the surface of that marvelous April Sunday in 1957.

It was a splendid, sunny day, with the smell of melting snow fermenting in the air; the sun shone through a tangle of naked, shining branches; the music of those times burst out of the windows; the trams clanged, the reflection of a cloud floated across the surface of deep blue puddles.

We pulled Father by the hand to the bus stop; we wanted to get as quickly as possible to the place where the piano was waiting for us. Father displayed rare understanding; after standing at the bus stop for several minutes, he remarked that he would never be late the way the bus was. Although you tugged at Grandmother's sleeve, she expressed the view that in the splendid air and expanse of morning it wouldn't be bad to walk through the park. Father asked what the comrade children thought of that idea and the comrade children said ecstatically that they thought it would be fun, and we set off through the park, hardly able to keep up with him. Mama, and we, too, soon began to lag behind him, but Grandmother tried to keep pace. He walked with his head stubbornly bent forward, giving him a double chin; the wind hit his clear forehead and bounced off. "What air!" he said and suddenly realized that no one could hear him but the trees—Grandmother had fallen behind, and we had fallen behind. He waited for us to catch up, fiddling with a piece of bark, breathing in the familiar scent of spring: "What air, eh?" "Mar-

velous, marvelous," Grandmother said. After crossing the park, we came
out on the streets in the part of town that lay along the Daugava River.

Acquaintances on the street greeted the Stratonovs with pleasure. Alexander Nikolaevich took off his felt hat somewhat hastily and nodded several
times with a cordial smile, and the girls stopped and curtsied, as was the
custom in this Baltic town. Sometimes Alexander Nikolaevich lingered at an
intersection, having snatched an acqaintance out of the crowd; people flowed
around them, the acquaintance shyly answered in Russian while Stratonov,
pleased that he had mastered a foreign language so easily, spoke in Latvian.
Alexander Nikolaevich was in fact held in great esteem.

They turned onto an utterly quiet street. Here there was a row of old
mansions with turrets, balconies, circular windows, and magnificent entrances. Lindens stood like doormen at the entrances; they had nowhere to
escape from these once luxurious homes that had outlived their time. Two
years before, when the Stratovnovs had just moved to the city, Alexander
Nikolaevich had been offered an apartment in one of these houses, but he
flatly refused because these mansions had hardly any amenities—no central
heating or gas, and the plumbing was hopelessly antiquated, not to mention
that the area was on the outskirts of town, and Stratonov didn't want to be
dependent on anything.

The Stratonovs went up a wooden staircase with wide, slippery banisters
to the second floor, breathing in the sad smell of old wood, neglect, and dis-
repair. Father knocked on the massive door with a sure hand. It seemed that
steps immediately rang out from every side of the house, from every corner, shadows took wing, the door opened, and then something strange happened—the air suddenly hardened, covered with an amalgam: The door had
opened onto a mirror.

The Stratonovs stood in the doorway, forming a group of four women:
Grandmother and Mother embraced the girls from either side, Father had
stepped back toward the wall to make way for his family. Across the threshold, in the dark recess of the hallway, stood identical women, identical girls.
An old woman with luxuriant gray hair on that side gazed fixedly at the majestic, silver-browed old woman on this side; two little, curly-haired women
stared at each other in amazement; the girls across from Gelya and Taya
stood with fingers linked in the same way. All of them wore dark dresses, in
contrast to the brightly attired Stratonovs. Then a ripple seemed to pass

over the smooth surface of the mirror: Alexander Nikolaevich stepped forward without noticing anything strange except the dark dresses of mourning, the meaning of which he instantly surmised. But Marina's heart contracted.

"Please come in," said the woman whom she resembled. "Come in. Come in, girls."

"*Paldies,*"* Gelya and Taya said in unison. The old woman raised an eyebrow, looked at them, turned, and moved down the hall, switching on lights as she went and illuminating a tunnel narrowed by the grief encroaching from all sides.

Alexander Nikolaevich stole a doubtful look at the loosely nailed, crooked coat rack and signaled for the rest to leave their coats on. The old woman glided forward smoothly, accompanied by the girls, while the woman, seeing Alexander Nikolaevich bend down to untie his shoes, began waving her hands. The Stratonovs, quickly wiping their feet, walked past bicycles leaning against the wall, past children's sleds, an iron bathtub, and a potbellied chest of drawers.

"In here, please," the old woman said, standing in the doorway of one of the rooms. "Here's the instrument."

It looked like a sunken ship; you remember, that very comparison came into our heads as soon as we saw it and before we discovered such details as the yellowed keys and the scratched music stand—and we could clearly sense the smell of abandoned lodgings, the orphaned smell of a box out of which music and life had fled long ago, so long ago that if you put your hand on the keys the piano wouldn't believe it and would chop off your hand at the wrist. Its strings were already accustomed to a lethargic sleep. We saw that only one thing had settled on the smooth surface of the piano, which had once been cluttered with music, lined paper, and opera scores—it was a reproduction of a portrait of the tender genius of harmony; a photograph of his tombstone hung on the wall. A lamp with a handmade bugle-bead fixture dangled down from the high molded ceiling to the keyboard; an armchair expressively arched its legs as if it were planning to run away if anyone dared lower himself into it. We sensed that the grand piano ruled this room, and everything from the ceiling to the parquet floor was subordinate to it. To us it seemed that the instrument was rooted to the floor and would be impossible to rip out, but we already wanted it and only it, no matter what—not some white-toothed upright with mirrored sides.

"In here, please," the woman said, beckoning to the Stratonovs.

*"How do you do?" in Latvian. —TRANS.

Father's lips quivered; he glanced at his wife and in his glance she read: Where else would you find such a fossil? In what tomb, in whose sarcophagus had it stood guard for a thousand years?

"The instrument is truly very old," the old woman said. "My son purchased it many years ago."

"Don't your girls study music?" Marina asked.

The old woman sat down on a chair by the door and began to smooth the creases in her black dress.

"My son died tragically a month ago," she said.

"Mama," the woman whispered reproachfully.

"My son died tragically," the old woman repeated, her eyes flashing at her daughter-in-law. "Since that day we haven't opened the instrument."

Grandmother, who was about to touch the keys, pulled her hands away.

"No, please," the old woman continued somewhat loftily. "You must try it, of course."

"Perhaps you need money," Father said sympathetically. "Could I help you in some way? . . ."

"We certainly need money," the old woman firmly replied, "but there's nothing you can do to help us."

"Mama!" the woman exclaimed.

"Be quite, Anna. Lelde," the old woman said to one of the girls, "please wipe off the dust. Gelya, bring the stool closer."

"What a coincidence!" Mama prattled. "Our older girl is also called Gelya."

"You're Latvian?" the woman asked.

"No, her name is Russian—Angelina, Gelya."

"Ours is Gelena. Her father was half-Polish and I am—"

"Anna, these people aren't interested in those details," the old woman said, stopping her.

Serafima Georgievna hit the keys, and a brilliant Chopin mazurka sparkled under her still-beautiful hands.

"Mother, these people are in mourning—play something more sedate," Father said in German, but the old woman grinned dryly, understanding exactly what he said.

Grandmother broke off the mazurka and played scales up and down the keyboard.

"How much does the instrument cost?" Father asked.

The old woman named a price.

The Stratonovs didn't have that kind of money. But Father was already overcome with compassion.

■

"It's a splendid instrument," Grandmother confirmed. "The G key in the second register sticks a bit, but that's nothing."

"For that," the old woman said, "we'll call in a repairman. Don't worry, we'll only sell the instrument in good condition."

Grandmother ran her fingers over the keyboard again and began to play a Chopin fantasie. Marina looked at the old woman and nearly cried out: She stood there absolutely pale, clenching her teeth as if she were being tortured. The woman who looked like Marina swayed and, clutching her hand to her breast, ran from the room.

"Pull yourself together, Anna," the old woman called after her weakly.

Taya's eyes filled with tears and she reached out to pat the younger of the girls on the head. The girl looked at her in amazement, transferred her gaze to her grandmother, and moved away.

"It's decided," Father said. "Tomorrow morning I'll make arrangements with the movers."

"Perhaps you might still change your mind about selling the instrument," Grandmother said. "Your girls are growing. . . ."

The old woman looked at her with a long, tired gaze.

"God forbid you lose your son in your old age," she said.

Serafima Georgievna lowered the lid of the piano and Marina shuddered— it seemed to her that they should all walk past and toss a handful of dirt on that black box. The grand piano, like a Trojan horse with funeral music hidden inside, would be brought into her sunny home—no, no!

"We share your grief with all our hearts," Father said sincerely.

"Thank you," the old woman replied. "Gelya, show the people out, please."

"Good-bye," Gelya whispered to the girls.

"Good-bye," they answered amiably.

Not for anything, Marina thought, not for anything will I let them buy that thing with its traces of other people's sorrow. They won't get my approval. And without my approval they can't bring that thing into my home, where . . .

. . . The cuckoo popped out of its hole and furiously cuckooed. The hours ticked by, but time howled like a beast with a belly wound and cast out of its opened veins the live blood of the living and the ashes of the dead, objects and works of art, petty considerations and great ideas, mammoths and moths, grand pianos and ladies' compacts, while the spring wind puffed out its cheeks over the city and chased Empire-style clouds across the sky.

The Russian language is extraordinarily sensitive to insincerity; it has been created in such a way that heart and mind must be in complete accord with its breadth and directness in order for creativity to take place; but if heart and mind are deceitful, the language instantly identifies cavities and pockmarks invisible even to an eye equipped with the most sophisticated lens; it will set itself against solid walls that can't be penetrated—nothing reveals the character of the creator more than his language. My dears, you ask: How can we distinguish the true from the false? I can't come up with an answer that would be worthy of the question. So I won't give an answer, I'll give advice: Read, develop your ear, mind, and heart, and you will never say that black is white. The cipher and code of poetic language is accessible to the dedicated; work on yourselves, yes, and that work will be one of the most important goals in life. And then, whenever you open a book of hack verses, you won't be deceived by a glib volley of rhymes, your ear will timorously shun the howl of a heavily weighted load of participles and adjectives, and you won't confuse the beam of a flashlight with sunlight. Russian poetry is enriched by music; through its tactful prompting love is linked with blood. In the poetic line we come across laws inherent to harmony: Any chord gravitates toward the dominant triad—that's rhyme. Even Pushkin couldn't battle that gravitation, so he resorted to irony in anticipation of our own: "The reader awaits the rhyme for 'rose.'" . . . Yes, rose, glows, snows—each word unleashes a flock of images; road, load, abode—can you sense it? None of these words can do without the others; alchemists often exploit this, and quite successfully, too, for in the end they produce the expected gold. But sesame will not open for them no matter how much they knock or pound their fists against the door or pack dynamite under it: That ethereal door will open only for those who know the Word. Learn from Pushkin, Lermontov, Nekrasov. Servitors to the Russian Language have stood above us like stars all down the long road of our history and life, from the authors of folk epics to the modern muse. Russian classical poetry, which has withstood time, is unconditional; it is given to us like sails for plying the waters. Contemporary poetry, if you read today's criticism, is a shifting clump of names—just try to find the truth in it. In one hundred years, when the battle of opinions is over and covered with ashes, poetry will remain and nothing will be able to shake it; whom will we then call a genius? Don't ask what genius is. Here we have to shrug our shoulders or raise a smoke screen of approximate words—in the dictionary that word should be followed by a blank space, an ellipsis leading beyond the limits of understanding for even the most enlightened minds. Oh, there's the bell. . . . Class, unfortunately we must break off our discussion. The weeping civic muse of Nekrasov will be the subject of our next exploration. . . .

"Write down the assignment," Mama said. "The lyric poetry of Nekrasov, pages 147 to 156 in your textbook, and read 'The Poet and the Citizen' and 'The Muse' in your anthology."

The lecture hall emptied. The night school held its classes in the building of a branch of the Petrochemical Institute. It was not a cozy place: fluorescent lights, chairs and tables in tired colors, and a blackboard covered with formulas left by a physics class. The students, too, were often tired, with faces blank from fatigue—you can't overlook the fact that they had just stood through a shift at the factory or sat one out in some shop. During the lesson Klimentev dozed again, hiding behind Batishcheva's back just like a schoolboy, and Batishcheva looked out the window vacantly; the poor thing— she was divorced and her son was often ill. Nikitina was doing everything in her power to flirt with Gevorkian, a married man; Kiktenko, the star student, was sick for the second week—class was boring without him.

The chemistry teacher, a downcast expression on her rather simple face, entered the lecture hall carrying a tote bag full of food; she had come in to complain. While she related how her old mother didn't want to move in with her, which might mean the loss of her apartment, Mama agonized over the most tactful way to remind the chemist about the fifteen rubles that she had borrowed a month ago. The chemist went on and on, with a trace of tears in her voice, with passion and commitment, quite unlike her teaching manner, because chemistry and her students were the farthest things from her mind, whereas increasing her housing space was crucial: Her apartment was crowded, she and her grown daughters bickered and fought. Each person has his own life, and no matter how it fills your thoughts to overflowing, it still doesn't truly affect anyone else, the chemist continued resentfully, having noticed that Mama was barely paying attention. And it's true—everyone has his own life, lives are tightly pressed up against one another, each in its own cell, the tongues of others' misfortunes and joys envelop your cramped, lonely existence like a flame; you get scorched around the edges but you no longer burst into flame as is expected of you. Not anymore. "Excuse me, Vera Maksimovna," Mama thought, rehearsing her speech in the meantime. "You wouldn't happen to have the fifteen rubles you owe me?" Or perhaps:

"You know, Vera dear, I'm a little strapped for money right now, would you be so kind as to . . ."

". . . After all, I'm not thinking of myself, but of my daughters. They're grown girls, the oldest is about to get married—and where are they going to live? But Mama won't budge. You understand, I don't have any ulterior motives, let her live, God grant her health, but if something should suddenly happen to her—we'll simply lose her room. It would be a shame!"

Of course, of course, Mama nodded, and the chemist went on reproachfully. The reproach was directed at Mama, who had a three-room apartment so large you could play soccer in it, whereas she had only two little adjacent rooms, and her girls were grown up.

Maybe I'd better spend the whole fifteen rubles on apples for the girls, Mama thought. Let them eat their fill. New sneakers for Gelya and maybe a pretty slip—she's so neat, she takes care of her clothes, not like Taya. A purse for Taya, yes, a purse. I promised. A shoulder bag.

"Mama's stubborn, God knows, she won't let go of her little room—she just won't budge!"

I'll be the same, Mama thought, I'll get old, as weak as a child, and I won't be able to understand the girls' concerns—and they'll complain behind my back the same way. . . . No, no, my girls are good; no, mine are different. The hell with them, the fifteen rubles, Mama finally decided and felt relieved. I'll just try not to lend any more money.

Getting used to the girls growing up was impossible. Mama recalled her own life with difficulty, like a book read in childhood: The paths of her past were shrouded in mist, and suddenly the mist released to the light of day a picture rendered in the most minute detail—and the girls were in the center. . . . Holding a book in one hand (ah, Dumas's *Vicomte de Bragelonne!*), she was pushing her younger daughter in a stroller around the grounds of a deserted kindergarten after six o'clock one long ago summer that has disappeared forever along with a throng of other summer evenings; a little neighbor girl was quietly swinging on the swings, dangling a tanned, scratched leg (a kitten!); she was wearing a bright dress and had thick black tresses. Mama picked a flower and brought it to her daughter, who clasped the flower tightly in her little fist; Raoul, sent by his Highness, galloped interminably to England, the ghost of Mademoiselle de Montalais, the embodiment of intrigue, slipped into the windows of Versailles, duels and duennas and duels and duets, each more dashing than the last—suddenly Mama went stiff with horror, but not because Louise had fled to Chaillot: her four-year-old daughter was riding a two-wheel bicycle on the roof of the high veranda. Louise fell into a deep faint, Mama waited for the stratified air to coalesce before her eyes, then gently called to Gelya. The little girl climbed off the bicycle. Now Mama looked at the crowd of kids who stood under the veranda craning their necks to see her daughter. Yes, quite a few years had passed since those spirited times. Now Gelya is a quiet young woman who never asks at the market, "How much for the currants?" but always, "Excuse me, could you please tell me the price of your currants?" and she doesn't buy from the person selling the best or the cheapest, but from some old grandma for whom she feels the sorriest. To Mama's great distress, she constantly discovers Gelya's girlfriends wearing her things; Gelya can't say no to anyone. Her girlfriends are three times richer, but they don't have Gelya's sense of style, so they covet her accessories, her scarves and ribbons. Gelya gives everything away; she doesn't mind giving anything away and she doesn't feel sorry for herself. Yes, they keep growing and growing, moving away from her in different directions, each with her own set of values, her own problems, her own memories. You think you're walking in step with them; after all, you spend the evenings in the kitchen with them, talking about all their problems, about Kolya Sazonov—What does Gelya see in him? It's a mystery!—about Taya's friends. You talk about just everything. But it's only a hundredth of it, not everything. When they were tiny you could know everything, but now each of them lets you no closer than her mood allows. Taya asked to go away for a weekend—that was two years ago—saying she was going to visit a friend's grandmother in the country. Two days later she returned—tan, fit, with tales about the village, about a cow. She demonstrated how her friend's grandmother milked the cow and described how flies tormented the cow and what a sweet little piglet stood by the trough— "such a tiny little thing, no bigger than this." Mama was touched and called Olya's parents, whom she didn't know, to thank them for Taya's weekend in the village. But over the phone blew the icy wind of truth: It was all a lie, there was no cow and no grandmother. Olya's grandmother had died two years ago and the house in the village had been sold. Mama's first thought was: When she gets home from school I'll thrash her. Taya came home, but Mama didn't have the strength to raise a hand to her and she couldn't cry. She asked: Why did you lie? Taya's lively, shining eyes dulled, she stood with her arms at her sides and looked at the floor. Her pose lied: She wasn't the slightest bit afraid of her mother. Where had she been? She sighed, stared out the window dreamily: on a ship. On what ship? She gloomily corrected herself: a steamer. Picking at the tablecloth with her finger, she added that the steamer was called the *Academician Kurchatov*. She had taken it to Syzrana and come back on a different one, the *Alexander Nevsky*. With what? That is, what money did you use? Without money. What do you mean, without money? I asked permission. From whom? She dismissed the question with a wave of her hand. She thought a moment, and her eyes shone again: There really was a piglet—more than one—a lot of them; they were brought there to be sold, tiny little things. Why did you lie? Fearfully: I didn't lie, I didn't want to upset you—would you have let me go on a ship? It was terrifying to imagine this fifth-grader sailing on some ship God knows where. The main thing was that she lied like an adult, with the same fervor and convincing details. What was her true nature—was it in this act or in another? Not long ago at the market we had bought a lot of watermelons, tempted by the cheap price—but how could we carry home such a heavy load? Taya said, "Just a second," and ran over to a two-story house nearby. She came back accompanied by two boys her age, who snarled and spit on the pavement, but they went along and like sweethearts hauled the watermelons all the way home. What's more useful for life—Gelya's inability to say no, her delicacy, or Taya's impudence? One lets everyone have his way, the other is learning how to take the lead, but which is better, wiser, the first or the second? On the one hand, both girls are open, exposed: Everything blows on them through that hole in space that their father fell through. When the conversation touches on him, the older one says dryly, "Father," and the younger one sarcastically calls him "Daddy." Ahead of them lies as much of life as I have behind me, Mama thought, but who can advise whom, who can teach whom how to live, when no one pays attention to losers, to those who have suffered a fiasco in their lives, but heeds only the winners? Then again, have I been defeated?

While trustful Mama was discussing the lyric poetry of Nekrasov, excitedly, touching her fingers to her weary neck, at home a magical tablecloth was being spread. Fixing her hair, Gelya rushed back and forth through the apartment—the candles were lit, the needle was lowered on a record of Vitali's chaconnes, the music welled up, in Mama's cache there was a bottle of grain alcohol that she had gotten through connections at an analytical chemistry laboratory; the alcohol was on the table and diluted, lemons were sliced on a plate; a cabbage pie was being taken out of the oven by Gelya's friend Alla, who muttered, "Oh—hot!"; the hour hand was approaching seven;

both girls flopped into armchairs and lit cigarettes. Just then, as if on cue, the doorbell rang. The girls jumped up, looked at each other, and Gelya, as the hostess, went to open the door for the marvelous Kolya Sazonov, who had thinning blond hair and a winning, smiling face. We said "thinning" hair—in novels such a description obliges the author to portray a negative character; if he's bald or has a nasal voice, he can't be the hero of a novel or a short story, although in real life he very well might be. So Kolya's prematurely thinning hair did not mean that he was a bad person who was going to lay a trap for us, but referred only to his hair and to that alone. Kolya the wit entered wearing a starched white shirt and black bell-bottoms (his brother had just gotten out of the navy); in his hands he was holding one pickle. "Ha-ha-ha!" the girls laughed. "Heh-heh," responded Kolya, pleased that his joke had come off. Gelya's mother didn't like him much because of his gentle, merciless eyes, his budding success with women, and his flirtatiousness. Ah, Gelya was aware of these things herself, but Mama saw Kolya only in the light that he himself, poor dear, considered to his greatest advantage: as the youthful seducer. But he was nothing of the kind. For example, sweet Kolya loved children and wasn't squeamish about squatting down in front of a kid and wiping his nose with his fingers—not even he suspected how good he was at that moment. We often don't notice when we are good, and present ourselves in the light we think most flattering, but in actual fact we are good in a different light, especially when we don't understand that we are. Kolya still hadn't decided which of the girls to court, Allochka or Gelya. Each was fine in her own way: Alla was more mature, modern and lively, but Gelya was sweet and domestic. Besides, he didn't want to destroy the girls' illusions about him; he was delighted that they were both head over heels in love with him and nurturing hopes. And so he drank the diluted grain alcohol with bravado, became flushed, flashed his eyes first at one and then at the other, and cracked jokes. While Gelya went to get a fork he patted Alla on the shoulder; when Alla was in the kitchen he looked at the romantic Gelya with a meaningful and sad expression on his face. For him as for the girls, a long life lay ahead, and he didn't want to start it for real yet, he didn't want responsibility, he wanted to hold out, sow his wild oats until someone nabbed him and married him; he wanted to hone his charms on two equally inexperienced hearts.

While trustful Mama was telling her students the story of Nekrasov's muse, her younger daughter, Taya, was not doing her homework as Mama thought, but was standing in the rain outside the music school, waiting for her best friend, Olya. Olya's parents didn't permit their daughter to be friends with Taya, believing that Taya was a bad influence on her, but how could you keep an eye on them? Olya's and Taya's piano teacher, Anna Tarasovna, was in on all of this like a confidant. Taya's lesson began at 4:45. She gave a lackluster rendition of a Clementi sonatina and Schubert's "Musical Moment," and both she and Anna Tarasovna were bored, but at 5:30 the leatherette-covered schoolroom door opened and in walked the brilliant Olya. "Hello, Anna Tarasovna. Hi, Taya," Olya said and looked at her friend. Taya, more adept at pretending, gave her an indifferent glance, nodded, got up from the stool, and walked away from the piano. "No, no, they don't meet at all," Anna Tarasovna later reported to Olya's mother over the telephone. Anna Tarasovna was a myopic, lonely woman for whom only music was important. Olya sat at the instrument, distractedly ran her fingers through the required B-flat major scale, arpeggios, and triads—distractedly, because she was preoccupied with Taya's cold glance. It was her fault, of course; given to compromise, she couldn't just say to her parents: Leave Taya and me alone; only the two of us, she and I, can judge people and morals correctly, and you are Philistines interested in nothing but your own lousy well-being. "Lousy" was Taya's expression, for which Olya's father had slapped her across the face, mortally, irreparably wounding her pride. "Olya, pull yourself together," Anna Tarasovna said. "That's enough of your scales. Warm up on the Ganone." She knew that once Olya had played a few exercises, true creative feeling would break through. Olya was amazingly, fantastically musical, but no one fully understood it yet—not her parents, not the director of the music school—no one except Anna Tarasovna. Olya was her pride; she had nothing left to show the girl, nothing else to teach her. And in fact, Olya's shoulders and spine had loosened up, she could start now. "The Pathétique, please. Olya played only the third movement. Anna Tarasovna knew that in the next hall, where the fourth grade was taking a solfeggio class, everyone had given up writing the dictation and had pressed their ears to the wall: "That's Olya playing." And beneath the window Taya was also listening to Olya play—envy, happiness, and ecstatic love filled her every time she heard Olya's Pathétique. It was half past six, she should have gone home long ago, but Anna Tarasovna had specially scheduled Olya last so that no diligent student could encroach on their lesson. Seven o'clock, quarter past, Tchaikovsky's "Barcarole.". . . Where did that little girl get such adult feeling and understanding—her every note was precise and hit the mark, making you want to cry and recall that you didn't have what it took to be a performer:

Here you sit in a music school in the boondocks, where the one reward for your unrealized dream is your student Olya. And Taya patiently waited to walk Olya home, tormented by the slap in the face that Olya got because of her, and prepared to stand in the rain and wait forever.

Remember, Taya, how much we missed at first the Baltic town where we spent our troubled childhood and how long we disliked this city on the Volga, although the great Russian river was in no way inferior to the Daugava? We couldn't get used to the local customs. At first, when we visited the homes of our new friends, we kept forgetting to take off our shoes in the foyer; our friends' parents irritably had to remind us. Where we lived before, people didn't take off their shoes when they came to visit, but here we were lucky if we were given someone else's slippers to wear. In school we automatically curtsied when we saw our teacher as we had done in our old school, and our new schoolmates giggled and teased us to death. When we were praised or given something to eat, we thanked them out of habit in Latvian: *"Paldies."* But little by little we forgot Latvian.

In our new home Mother arranged the furniture exactly as it had been in our old apartment, and sometimes when we woke up we thought, out of habit, that we could hear the voices of Stasik and Vita outside the window and that the red flag with the white stripe would be fluttering on the corner of August 5 Street, and that Laina had gone into the courtyard with her new bicycle. But when we looked out the window we would see Vova ringing the bell on his bicycle and little Tonya in the sandbox—it was a different courtyard, but the arrangement and atmosphere in the house were the same.

. . . And if you approach the open doors of the study, stand in the doorway and look long at the room, in the dim light of half-forgotten childhood fear you'll see Father's awesome head bent over his papers. I run my fingers over my eyes, adjusting the focus to the objects in the study; I squint, and Father's leather armchair begins to beckon to me from an empty corner; in the weak glow an inkstand appears on the desk, the desk raises itself up on its four paws over the current little desk, the chairs around it suddenly scatter helter-skelter: one behind the couch, another behind the desk. Now the piano stands here although it wasn't here before, but nevertheless I see Father, his eyes tightly shut in satisfaction, listening to our duet. Our playing was off, false, and Mama shook her head in torment, as if trying to shake out the wrong notes like water from her ears, but Father didn't notice a thing. He took in the overall picture: his daughters sitting at the piano and amiably playing a piece for four hands. We played, and I won't tire of repeating that we played wretchedly, but to make up for it we sang beautifully, which Father didn't suspect. We divided up the parts like this: You were the mezzo and I was the soprano, and we crooned in our childish voices: "Evening's come, the clouds' edges have dimmed . . ."

Yes, Gelya, it all happened as you say. I'd only add that you developed a voice of marvelous beauty, a soprano as high as the heavens. My little voice was a duenna to yours; it accompanied you to the gates of the temple, followed from afar your dizzying affairs, followed your velvet skirt, was the reverse side of the cloth embroidered with lilies. You stood at the piano, and your hands touched the hands of the woman drowning in its pure depths; light bouncing off the lake's smooth surface beamed on your chin and bathed your thrown-back face. Your voice opened like a flower, and out of its very heart flew a golden bumblebee. The most vivid and significant aspect in the spectrum of your voice was an eternal sense of guilt—the theme of repentance—but your voice was so bright that everything around it in our house began to cast blue, snowy shadows. In the boundless expanse of your voice, every note was as distinct and fresh as a single grape. It was hard to imagine that you could sing like that—and no one knew it except me, because you had learned to overcome your shyness in front of me alone. Father never learned about your marvelous gift, or he would have taken you to the conservatory, and you might now be singing Gilda in the Bolshoi Theater.

Music preceded the appearance of the couch: We always sat on it before putting a record on the record player. No, Father's habit of singing along with the record didn't strike me as idiotic as it did you; it was touching, since he had no ear whatsoever. Remember how he would break into song in the bathroom? To this day I hear Cavaradossi's aria and the Demon's Song through pouring water, don't you? And whenever I put things in their old places, some little detail calls to me: oh, the bookshelves. At the very top, like the expanded bellows of an accordion, stood the collected works of Balzac; lower stood Dickens, and lower still was Kuprin; they had their own hierarchy. Remember how he clipped together several pages of Pushkin that we were still too young to read? On Tuesdays you would narrate the plots of books to him: *Uncle Tom's Cabin,* for example, or *The Land of Salt Cliffs,* while you had already gotten through all of Zola bit by bit and didn't understand a thing in *The Magic Mountain.*

He relentlessly preached to all of his acquaintances: Don't smoke, drop that pernicious habit, take a cold water sponge bath in the morning—and I even suspect that our guests really did sponge themselves down in the morning. What can be said about you and me, when adults who were in no way dependent on him were a little afraid of him? Everyone recoiled from him; he lived in an aurora borealis of solitude. Even when he was in a good mood, there was no guarantee that there wasn't something invisible to the eye that would skim away his fine disposition like foam off cocoa and expose burning lava. Speaking of foam on cocoa, you once stuck your finger in a cup to scoop it up—oh, it's terrifying to recall how his lovely blue eyes darkened, how horror welled up in your gut.

He was good at nabbing hooligans on the street and I don't remember any of them ever putting up a fight. His polite iron hand and unflinching gaze made a big, unshaven man bend down to pick up a cigarette butt he had thrown on the ground. Under Father's gaze, and holding the butt by the end like a slippery fish, the man seemed to tiptoe over to a trash can and throw it in with a hapless grin. Father was so majestic in his righteous indignation that not a single bell would dare to tinkle on the fool's cap of his entourage. His good deeds subjected people to no less trepidation than his anger. Alexander Nikolaevich's enfeebled old nanny suffered from his yearly raids on her quiet home outside Kaluga. He would appear—a gloomy do-gooder with meek eyes, inquire about her health, and give her money with a generous hand. His nanny would sniffle, recall her ward's short little shirt and naked, helpless legs, and call him Sashenka, but deep in her heart she couldn't believe that that quiet, patient child could have grown into this daunting person.

When he went for walks in the park, the wind fanned his massive brow deferentially and he sucked in the generous world with a half-moan of "good Lord." He sat on the grass, but even in a relaxed pose his untapped strength could be sensed all the same. One imagined the shining lance of an archangel next to him, at his right hand, and it seemed to us, his unworthy daughters, that we were only the stunted shoots born in his ray of light while his true children had dissolved in the shimmering ether—twelve fine sons and twelve bright-eyed daughters.

Incidentally, Father loved nature. Don't you wish you could find other epithets for the verb denoting the action of the heart besides that clichéd team of horses without which the word seems incomplete or denuded? But alas, no more precise words exist, so we'll have to make do with these torch song lyrics: He loved nature tenderly and madly. And living nature idolized our father, sensing a gardener and protector in him. When he left the house in the morning at seven o'clock sharp and set off for the institute, a pack of stray dogs would already be sitting in front of the door waiting for his departure. It can't be said that he bought off the animals with bones (as he did not buy off people), although, of course, as he was leaving the house Grandmother would give him some kind of treat wrapped in newspaper for the dogs, and he wasn't averse to going out with leftovers and feeding them. The strays greeted him with delight (unlike people), and as he walked along the street, the shepherd of an obedient flock, the dogs ran ahead of him, yelping with joy. Along the way Father would talk with them, chuckling to himself: "Well, now, my sweethearts, Alexander Nikolaevich is going to work, he leads a dog's life—only work and more work." As they drew closer to the town square where his institute was located, the dogs slowed their pace, began to lag behind and run off, and only the most devoted and impassive little mutt walked him all the way to the door. Mama Marina told us how astounded she was at first by Father's love of nature; she suspected him of a tendency for posturing, although it was impossible to imagine a person less inclined to showy displays than Alexander Nikolaevich. Once—at the earliest and most splendid time in their relationship—they went into a delicate October forest. Mama tried to keep up with Father's pace and was telling him some girlish, naive, dreamlike story when she suddenly noticed that not only was he not listening to her but he was muttering something to himself under his breath. As she listened, Mama was able to make out something like this: "Oh, Lord, how marvelous, how wonderful, ah, what is this all for. . . ." Mama got frightened. With hurried steps, trying to fill his gaze, having forgotten about her, he walked farther and farther away, and with horror she saw Father gently lean over a branch of a hazelnut tree, and touch his lips to a crimson leaf as if it were a woman's hand. Mama recoiled and took to her heels. A few hours later she lay on the sofa in her room with a compress on her head, overcome by inexplicable fears, when he suddenly appeared: happy, noticing neither the compress nor her tearstained eyes—blind, completely blind. "Oh, my dear, you know, I was in the woods, it was so marvelous there, and the whole time I was thinking about you and our happiness!" When Mama related the scene to Serafima Georgievna, trying to cast it in a humorous light, Serafima Georgievna replied seriously, "Marina, get used to such things, it happens to him. Since childhood he has been mad about nature, and on a fine day among the trees he loses his senses completely. His father was the same way. Nature overwhelms Alexander on the spot." We should clarify that nature was the only thing that overwhelmed him. This man, before whom many people trembled, toward whom not a single saleslady had ever been insolent, at whom not one bureaucrat had raised his voice, a man who could make us burst into tears at a glance— we saw this man squatting down and weeping over the downy head of clover blossom. . . .

And here our dialogue is joined by a third voice, our mother's voice, and there's no way we can slam the door in her face, although we don't want her to encroach upon the image of Father we have created. But Mama is insistent, she appeals to our sense of justice, and, dropping what she's doing, with grated carrots clinging to her hands, she comes into our room: Oh, girls, it's not like that, it's not true! What isn't true? That he prostrated himself before a flower? No, that part's true. I recognize him in your stories and see him before my eyes, but it's not true that everyone was afraid of him. It's just that people sensed his intelligence and strength, and he treated shopkeepers and bureaucrats with deliberate respect, immediately assuming that each of them was a thoroughly decent person and a master of his trade. His speech was classically correct; he spoke slowly and felt responsible for every word he uttered. He had a pleasant voice and an old-fashioned manner of conversing with people. He would bow slightly to his interlocutor and ask questions with sympathetic attention. . . . Stop, Mama, don't get upset. We are in fact testifying in his favor, didn't you realize that? We were talking about his love of nature, we'd just dipped our brushes in soft pastel shades; in a word, we were talking about nature, and we won't quarrel with you over whether people were afraid of him or not. Let's bring that picture before our eyes once again: He was bending over a flower. . . .

The fragility and gentleness of a simple flower utterly exhausted him, and a mortal yearning for life constricted his heart when, with a strange look in his eyes, he followed the clouds. You drink and drink and it's still not enough, you still can't drink your fill, and you still don't know what you can do to drink your fill, to fill your lungs, and the clear day is disappearing, and we have only this one life. . . . Perhaps that was his train of thought. Sometimes he would take us to a park on the outskirts of the city, to a marvelous botanical garden. The black iron fence would have had the lock on our memory if it weren't for the roses—roses with names as wonderful as those of the constellations; we liked to try out the sound of them. Papa Meiyan—purple, velvet, with hard-boiled petals and an enormous heat at its very heart, a scorching, almost black vortex. Tatyana's Bush supported burning crimson flowers covered with dust like the wings of butterflies; they grew at a respectful distance from one another, so that the beauty of each individual bloom was indisputable, and so that there was indeed a good amount of air between them. The crumbly, provocatively large Baron E. de Rothschild, decorative as a sponge cake; the Peer Gynt—yellow with red splashes; the fateful queen of hearts, Lily Marlene, on its low-growing bush; the joyless, pale lilac blooms of Mainser Fasonacht, monsters among roses, reminiscent of the powdered Giselle in the second act; the luxuriant pink Suspense; and finally, the heavenly Dolce Vita, so classical it rendered us speechless. And once again a hungry gaze from the shadowy side of the park to see the roses all at once, en masse, in a splendid throng, a kingdom of extravagant beauty, a world of paradisiacal fecundity. Music surely resounded in Father's ears.

We often accompanied him on walks and were delighted when, little by little, in a grove of trees or by a pond, he would stop paying attention to us. He became distracted. He sat on the grass and a sweet ladybug crawled back and forth on the palm of his big, calm hand. But when the ladybug flew away, Father stood and walked straight through the bushes, through the darkening woods; he walked and walked, and it seemed that his walk had been this straight and rapt since the moment of his birth—the heavy tread of a commander. And I didn't wave to him or walk with him farther, but when he called to me from the depths of the park, I dashed headlong in the opposite direction. When I returned home and entered our empty apartment, one thing on the wall suddenly stunned me: Mama's portrait, which Father always took with him. Mama's portrait was hanging on the wall.

In that photograph our mother is sitting on a fallen tree in her lilac crepe de chine dress, illuminated by a sun so generous that its rays extend beyond the frame and fill the entire room with the ecstatic light of the past. Her head is thrown back slightly, her hair shines in that day's summer air. Father photographed Mama in a pine forest; can't you smell the scent of the needles in the study? The brightest spot in the photo is Mama's neck, which the sun also caresses. Mama is blissfully nibbling on a blade of grass, thinking about giving birth to a son. This blade of grass was the last thing that the fairy godmother gave to Cinderella as she sent her off to the ball, and Mama's face reaches out to it and she drinks in the air through it. . . . Don't you want to extend every pine beyond the frame, roll out the clearing where Mama was being photographed to its full expanse, extend the July air to the sky, and thus restore her whole devastated life? . . .

We remember her weary and broken, like a bird drawing its wing out from under the rubble of a house in ruins. Her shadow incessantly wandered through the rooms and moved the shadows of objects from place to place. Our things, from the furniture to a statuette of a muse holding a lyre, had no permanent place. No sooner had dust settled on the base of the clock on the sideboard than the clock was moved to the refrigerator in the kitchen; the three-sided mirror migrated from corner to corner like a New Year's tree; the house sucked up small objects—irretrievably: mittens, a slide rule, scissors—it was impossible to find anything, everything slipped away from your hands and hid. Mama was constantly looking for something or other. "How could that be, I precisely recall putting those bonds in this vase. Gelya, you cleaned up last. . . . "I didn't see anything. You tuck things away someplace and then you torment us." "Have I gone mad or something? Right here in this vase!" She defiantly clattered dishes in the kitchen, electrical sparks flew across the floor when she started to turn the desk drawers inside out, pain radiated from her in shimmering circles throughout the apartment as she raced about, her voice penetrated all the nooks and crannies, and her steps began to evoke in us the same dull fear as Father's heavy tread. For a long time Gelya's piano scales competed with Mama's growing irritation, until Gelya couldn't stand it anymore; she tore away from the piano stool and threw herself into the search, less believing in the possibility of finding the bonds than simply adapting herself to the course of the hurricane. But there were no bonds, and there was no peace. The furies tore through the rooms, glasses were dropped, the pile of the rug on the sofa stood on end, doors were slammed: "No, I'm not mixing anything up. I remember thinking, Why don't I put them right in this vase, and I even made a special point of remembering. . . ." In that draft of air we wanted to remove ourselves from life somehow, if only by the simplest method of deductive reasoning: to melt away in the myriad possible means of melting away, to separate our ancestors, to make a deal with fate, so that our grandfather and grandmother lived in different cities and our other grandfather and grandmother never played a scene from *Othello* in a summer production; to throw a mountain range between our parents and then have unpassable forests arise and seas overflow along their path to each other; to subtract love from love, to pull time apart, to destroy even the hope of our appearance. . . . But we never fought with Mama, not over the slide rule, not over the bonds, even though it wasn't our fault that they disappeared; we didn't even argue with her, we didn't attempt to resist her, because we knew that we still had unused reserves of life— remember, sister?

But Gelya was silent, Gelya had gone into hiding. At night she would sit on the balcony, hugging her knees, and look into the darkness, into the deep August night. Faceted blue stars followed their familiar path through a fine layer of clouds; the new moon rose and seemed to pause, transfixed, above the balcony. Her sister, bare feet slapping, came out and sat next to her.
  "Geliko-san, why aren't you sleeping?"
  "I'm not sleeping because I'm not sleeping," Gelya replied curtly.
  "Did something happen?" Taya quickly asked.
  "Happen. Happenstance. A happy happenstance."
  "How come stars twinkle?"
  "You have to study your lessons, then you'll know why."
  "I am studying, Geliko-san, but we haven't gotten to that yet. So why do they?"
  "Because the wind blows on them," Gelya answered angrily.
  In two weeks he'll go back to Moscow, to the physics institute. He's so smart, he got in on his own, without any tutoring. You can't charm him, Gelya thought absently, but it's impossible not to be charmed by him. Oh, why does he insist on being friends with her, why does he take off his jacket when it's raining—she doesn't take her raincoat on purpose—after all, it would be so nice to walk under one jacket with him—but no, he courteously throws it over Gelya's shoulders—he's a friend, a comrade, a buddy. He chats with her about such nonsense—good Lord, who cares about the Taganka Theater or the Archangelskoe estate anyway? And who's Marcel Proust to her? But if she were to say that to him—Who's Marcel Proust to me?—he'd be disappointed to find out that she's no different from any of the others, with whom he has nothing to talk about. . . . But just two years ago he was an unremarkable classmate, a boring, ordinary boy with pale blond hair and eyebrows, and when he jumped over the horse in gym class, everyone giggled. Go ahead and giggle now, his sweet and haughty face says. And Mama, by old habit, seeing Gelya lost in thought, still laughs and says, "Kolya Sazonov." What Kolya? Kolya had dimmed, faded, dissolved into the

crowd on the street, nobody-Kolya, a Don Juan of local import. But about *him* Mama says: Gelya's admirer. Oh, Mama, if only he were my admirer! Alas, he's only a friend, a buddy from summer days, and you can't complain to anyone about that kind of friendship—they were friends for a month and a half, just friends, she didn't so much as dare to touch his hand, but her friend Alla walked up to them on the street, said something banal—and his eyes lit up and became warmer. The three of them walked on—and no Proust, no Taganka—the conversation was silly, giggly: She took him away. She'll always take them away.

. . . In mentioning Kolya Sazonov, Mama is behind the times—alas, she can't keep up with the changing of the seasons in Gelya's maturing heart—then it was shy spring, now it is summer, a storm is gathering, clouds are swirling, hanging lower, the scent of flowers in their beds is heartrending: August.

. . . But in Taya's thousand times cursed and unworthy life a certain vitamin finally appeared, under whose influence her life recuperated and pulsed with strength and youth, and this vitamin was called—with Valka's light touch—walking the razor's edge.

Valka was Taya's classmate. In the ninth grade she'd had a bold affair with an athlete, and in the beginning of the tenth she had another with a mama's boy, a terrible wimp, who was willing to wash Valka's stockings but didn't dare bring her home to meet his parents, and Valka threw him over in splendid style, cuckolding him with one of his own buddies. What would happen after graduation, God only knew. Valka didn't even try to guess—she couldn't have cared less—she was a reckless girl. This Valka began to drag Taya along with her to parties; to be sure, those people didn't suit Taya and Taya didn't suit them, because as midnight drew near she tried to slip away like Cinderella. We only live once and Valka had fun; she wasn't afraid of anything and didn't regret anything, she wasn't too stingy to give Taya her best earrings. She lived in a communal apartment in the center of town with her mother, who was still young and had the same lively dark eyes as Valka. Valka spoke endearingly of her mother's suitors: my 101st or, God help me recall, 102nd Papa. (The papas, incidentally, already coveted Valka herself, causing minor scandals at home.) Valka flirted for all she was worth wherever she was. When she was around, the atmosphere became alarmingly giddy, filled with the expectation of wonderful things; men began to be witty and scintillating—what jerks, Valka used to say, planting her hands on her broad hips. The jerks were thrilled and enthralled, presented themselves as bachelors, and ran out to get wine and chocolate, looking askance at Taya—who was this strange bird? The bird herself didn't know what kind of bird she was, but in these matters Valka was a wise old owl. A whirlwind blew up, a tiny whirlwind, and it whisked away the student allowance that had been scrupulously saved up for a tape recorder; music wailed, parents' china was taken out while the parents worked the night shift, the floor shook, candles shook, glasses were broken, Valka made the whole group form a chain and forced the boys to dance the letkajenkka.* . . . Meanwhile, Taya sat on the sidelines; boys came up to her uncertainly and even unwillingly—they couldn't stay away from Valka, although she dispensed sonorous slaps right and left with a generous hand, muttering: I'm a serious girl and a wise old owl. At one of these parties Taya saw one of her mother's students. He recognized her, his face changed, he walked up to her, took her firmly by the ear, and led her out the door: "Now get out of here." Taya got scared and slipped away.

There were many other kinds of capers: They hitchhiked, stopping trucks and taking off with the driver God knows where, howling with laughter at Valka's jokes, their eyes shining. The driver would trustfully stop the truck and dash into a store—the girls, giggling, would disappear. There were some dubious birthday parties, poems of dubious quality read by a supposedly well-known poet who said his work had been published, though he was probably lying; there was a fellow named Dima who hinted he had been in prison so much he was a top dog there. There was a New Year's party in some dormitory, a window was broken, but they hid from the militia. There was much, much more. And there was nothing but emptiness, and by spring everything was a bore. Happy-go-lucky Valka was a bore, and walking the razor's edge was a bore. The same boredom, the same indefiniteness, the same thoughts—what next, what are we living for?

. . . Now I have something to confess to you, Mama, even though one's not considered a thief until caught. But there's nothing to hide here, and I'm prepared to justify my actions.

Love for one's mother is the most awkward feeling on earth, and for a long time there was nothing I could say to you that would help us understand each other. Once you've heard my confession, you'll say, "Gelya, how hu-

---

*A dance resembling the bunny hop. —TRANS.

miliating. You've demeaned yourself," but I'll reply by saying: I care more for the truth, however base. I wanted to know the truth, no matter how much I suspected that it was utterly impossible. Truth is portioned out here and there, and it can't be crystallized out of a mass of circumstances and causes, but I wanted to get my own solid piece of the truth, and that's why I secretly read your letters and old papers. But I couldn't change anything—what had to happen, happened. It was too late to gather up those letters—yours and Father's—and, carefully putting them in chronological order, send them off to general delivery one by one, into the past, before the darkest of days, before the very seed of our existence, send them off starting with the last cruel telegrams and ending with Father's first note: "Marina—come to Staroye Boulevard after the lecture!" And dream as I was doing it that Mama, the way she used to be, a lively beauty, would receive the note, snort, tear it into pieces, go off to meet someone else, and not give me life.

A cake box in the depths of a closet held the old letters, an archive, a chronicle of our family, a saga about us, a book in which everything was written down—I read it with grim satisfaction, with horror and sorrow; I studied its pages like a homework assignment, to the detriment of my other assignments. I read it and reread it, days passed, months, years—but I still couldn't tear myself away from it. How random is the accumulation of one thing or another that later comes to be thought of as the very embodiment. . . . Father returned from a business trip and shouted from the doorway, "Guess what Papa brought for his girls?" "What, what?" We began jumping up and down. This is what he brought. This. This cake. Every last crumb of it had to be eaten. "My dear, my dear, I'm going mad, I'm going to shoot myself if you don't come! Drop everything, I beg you, I can't go on another day without you!" And then there's a leap across time and life and people: "Marina! I've put four hundred rubles in the girls' name in savings account number . . ." I'd rather return to the time when he wrote ". . . and I'm a child, a complete child before you, before Woman, before this miracle of love." "Sasha, Sasha, we shouldn't do this, it's worse than murder, but why don't you hear me, why doesn't your shout reach its mark, what's going on? Why are we moving away from each other, why? Come back, we'll go to that city, we'll stand on that bridge, and we'll come to an understanding. I believe people should come to an understanding when their hearts have been cleansed by suffering. I believe in it!" No, she didn't believe in it, and the letter wasn't sent.

What was written begins to dissolve on the paper—time is such a powerful catalyst, more powerful than anything that could ever exist in chemistry—and it seems as if you're reading on the bottom of a river. Barely distinguishable, skeletons of shipwrecks lie in the depths with the dead still on board. The letters must be handled chastely, like dried flowers, they are so fragile; but suddenly, in the amber twilight of the past, among the yellow petals, a lock of hair is discovered—it's so alive and shiny, as if it had just been cut from Mama's head. Alive and whole, like a gem brought up to the light from the bottom of a river. The voices sound so tremulous and warm-blooded: After all, our two lives depended on the outcome of their arguments; voices severed from the living so many years ago, but just as real and unexpected as that strand of hair. Living voices, drowned in pieces of paper as delicate as autumn leaves, as the treasures of a herbarium. Like bubbles of air they rise up from the roiled depths, they burst, and out of them escapes a cry: Oh, Mama, Mama, Father! What have you done!

As I bend over the table, having covered the lamp with a brick-colored apron that casts a bloody reflection on your letters, I can reconstruct our entire frenzied drama by playing these old notes: People die, clouds blow over, letters disappear from the alphabet, rivers run dry. In today's novels there are no gloves dropped on purpose, but there is the same passion, the same deafness and madness, the same immortal sobriquets that we give the ones we love. . . .

And then there's this:

Once upon a time there lived an old couple, our neighbors, and they were well off—they had a breakfront, a sofa, a table, chairs, the old lady's childlike bed, and a photograph. The old folks died one after the other, their younger daughter moved to another city, their granddaughter got married, the breakfront, sofa, and bed were simply taken out into the courtyard, but what was to be done with the photograph? It was of a dark-haired young man with gentle eyes and a barely discernible smile on his young face. One looked at that face and immediately realized that the youth was long gone from this world. He was killed during the war. For some time the photograph hung on the wall, but one day we visited our new neighbors, who had just moved in, and the empty place on the wall seemed to cry out. The bare expanse with its walleye looked reproachful and terrible, so terrible and reproachful that they put up a false eye, Kramskoy's painting *The Unknown Woman,* in its place, but the eyes of the old couple's son, who had died in the war, shone through the reproduction all the same.

And I think: Whose hand will take down our photograph, exiling it first to a drawer in a desk, then simply to a box where letters wind up, when everything that had been saved from the past will have sunk to the bottom of the river—this time forever?

Here it is—the last letter Mama Marina wrote to her mother, dating to the very beginning of the tragedy that took place in our house so long ago. Between this letter and Father's first letters lie years, a bridge that is crossed at the risk of one's life; how steep, hunchbacked, and slippery is this bridge leading to the wilderness, how rich in evil omens, solar eclipses, broken mirrors, empty pails, and spilled salt; listen, isn't it better to pay Charon and be done with this journey, shortening it by a third? And to know that in so doing you are breaking the chain of heartache and countless hardships? To fall asleep . . . and dream?

Mama didn't reply. The day around her shone, filled with the distinct, divine scent of pine needles; there was a twittering and chirring and bustling in the grass, birds looked down from the branches. Let it be a son, she thought, positioning herself in a sunbeam so that there would be a lot of light while the photograph was being taken. The light wandered over the grass and set afire the blade of grass she held in her teeth.

1984

Translated from the Russian by Michele A. Berdy

THE OVERLOOK

LYUDMILA PETRUSHEVSKAYA

He stroked his girlfriends' hair, and, taking off his cap, asked them to stroke his hair, too. This usually took place on the overlook in the Lenin Hills in front of Moscow University. Down below, on the other side of the river, stretched the panorama of Luzhniki Park, and beyond that the panorama of Moscow with its towering buildings. He did the same thing with every one of his girlfriends, literally every single one: Either our hero didn't know where else to perch other than on the overlook, or he really did experience spiritual exaltation and craved for space, wind, and majestic panoramas every time, with every new love. It is also possible to imagine that a certain provincial admiration for the capital had not yet faded in him, a truly thrilling feeling, a feeling of victory over the huge city that lay at his feet and securely stood guard at his back in the form of the university's massive wall.

An integral part of this feeling of victory over the city was the feeling of numerous minor victories over its inhabitants—men and women alike—or, in any case, it should have been. We can't expect to understand anything at this point, even if we were to add to the aforesaid that these victories were to a certain extent undesired and that the victor himself, apparently, yearned in the depths of his soul to be vanquished. And yet, he was the one to vanquish every time. What exactly happened every time, what happened to him and to those he vanquished—women, old ladies, old men, coworkers, supervisors, fellow travelers—why they all so willingly agreed to be vanquished, why they didn't resist, but submitted every time with an apparent feeling of total surrender and defeat, and whether they felt that all this was a temporary, one-time-only defeat, requiring but a wave of the hand for ordinary life to resume without all these horrors, it is difficult to say and difficult to fathom. One thing is certain: He himself yearned to be vanquished and he himself was setting the scene for his own defeat; to all appearances this was what he was doing, insofar as he acted carelessly, worked crudely, built everything, all his constructions, shoddily. Everyone saw straight through it all, but he advanced openly, as if there were no obstacles before him, as if what was of primary importance to him was not the matter to which he devoted his energy at any given, particular stage but some thought that he mulled over from all angles as if to determine: Now what if I do it this way? And what if I ask this question and call so-and-so and talk this way or that way (as if he were always thinking not of the matter at hand, but of some problem apparent to him alone).

This, apparently, was the source of his constant appearance of preoccupation not with that which occupied him at a given moment, as though he were occupied not with that, but with something else and were anxious about something else, too, something of primary importance, although it might even appear that there was nothing behind all this that warranted being anxious about. But the anxiety was there; he seemed to rush events in the present so that they might pass by as quickly as possible to make way for something else. But what?

And so he went, from one victory to another, from one phone call to another, and all this in a rush, pell-mell, never forgetting his primary problem, whatever it was. But on the surface it all looked as if, you might think, for example, that he was a cunning victor, taking one position after another. And so he took his newest girlfriend to the university.

Well, come to think of it, where else, in fact, could this Andrei take his latest chosen one, if his soul, to all appearances, demanded something deeply individual, something of its very own, and was on the threshold of supreme happiness? Not to a restaurant, after all, which so often serves as payment, a bribe, compensation for imminent physical pleasure, so that some girls refuse to go to restaurants with men they don't know very well, aware that money spent is not spent for nothing, and, needless to say, presupposes a response and repayment, and if they don't respond and don't repay, then it'll be seen as petty thievery: Drink a little, eat a little, enjoy the music, have a look around, be looked at yourself, eat and drink some more without objection, without complaint, and with apparent enjoyment, and then clear out without paying? The girl herself is aware of that certain mood that develops when petty concessions in the form of pecks and smooches in the back of a cab come across as an even greater deception, an even greater villainy—tantamount to drinking and eating even more, for an even greater amount of money. That's what adults, wise with experience, think about all this, and Andrei was an adult and he might have been familiar with such a point of view, but, apparently, he had abandoned it at some earlier stage of his development.

This option of using restaurants as a lure assumed, needless to say, that without the restaurant things might not work out. And Andrei, as we've already said, always forged straight ahead. And even if he did take his girl-friends to the overlook, he did so purely for his own sake, for the sake of tender feeling, for the sake of the soul's lofty flight; or else he'd already developed a certain tradition that was dear to his heart, a once-attained happiness had acquired a permanent form. Well, and come to think of it, it is quiet on the overlook, there's a soft breeze, snow flies gently over the black ice, and the lights in the city below glow so cordially as they wink at you. Indeed, it's quiet, there's no one around, you're not likely to find other admirers of precisely this kind of nocturnal urban landscape; some might even say that an overpowering, colossal architectural idea, a superhuman surge of desires, comes into its own here, compared to which even the Cheops pyramid, as it is usually imagined by those who have never seen it, looks homey and harmless, just your basic upward-sloping symmetrical hill.

So there's no one else on the overlook, the city lies at your feet, winking peacefully, all of it at your disposal, you're a welcome guest everywhere, everything is open to the conqueror, and he, no longer marauding, can start loading up the city by the carful—and take it in, take it *all* in; that's how it appears on the surface. Take a look, it's not so much the city that gradually disappears into him; no, it is Andrei who spreads himself further and further out over the city, the absorption takes place all by itself, while the mind is free and the striving for happiness is no longer satisfied by the mere act of devouring ever new streets and alleys, the tasty morsels around Kropotkin Street.* This striving ascends one step higher; it requires not only living here and vanquishing one thing after another, vanquishing opponents, rivals, blatherers, wrongdoers, bigwigs, underlings, and brothers, and friends, and

*A street in the heart of Moscow containing many fine examples of eighteenth- and nineteenth-century private mansions once inhabited by rich merchants as well as various famous writers and artists. The street is therefore associated with the flowering of nineteenth-century Russian culture. —TRANS.

girls, and mature women whose breasts surpass, for example, all possible bounds and quiver, and everything in you quivers at the thought that this mature matron—a mother and a wife, she who drives her own car, she who goes to diplomatic receptions and is surrounded by a whole world of comforts and is constantly fussing over these comforts—that she humbly goes where she isn't even asked and suddenly unbuttons her fur coat and . . . oh my God! But again all of this is purely external—everything that has been ascribed above to Andrei as purportedly his very own oblique-sounding monologue—insofar as he himself would never even have thought of delivering such a monologue, he himself thought quite differently, ever having in mind that main idea of his, and it merely appeared that he acted in such and such a way, which made everyone think that that's just what Andrei must be thinking since he acted in such and such a way. If I do this, then this will be the result, everyone around Andrei had him thinking. But what he himself was thinking, we don't know.

Returning to the oblique monologue delivered in Andrei's name, let us continue the thought: Yes, striving for happiness is not limited to this. The matron with her indescribably voluminous breasts, her fear and craving, her naive awareness of the value of her breasts, which she thereby devalues completely, this matron floats into and is absorbed by Andrei along with her five-room apartment; her husband, an inveterate motorist and member of the auto club; her children, among whom the youngest daughter in particular, a virtual Lolita at five, falls in love with their guest Andrei and immediately crawls into his arms and onto his lap, to everyone's laughter: "Andrei—the lady-killer!"—while the girl sits there staunchly and looks around vacantly. And she, this amazing little girl, is also absorbed and floats into him, this house is already flickering somewhere inside him, its welcoming windows glow faintly, its broad armchairs are there, it is warm and cozy, the food is delicious, perhaps just the hostess sits a little too straight and walks and bends with too straight a back, again, keeping within her field of vision that bust, her bulwark, her enduring treasure. But the matron is no longer a matron, her name is Sonya, she now comes to light as an unloved wife, as a wife whose husband has placidly not been living with her for many years. This placid motorist somehow makes other arrangements, and there are suspicions that there's something fishy about these arrangements; he has some junior research assistants, his students, his followers, the followers of this crudely jolly sap who lives quietly, idiotically full of his own car and cooperative garage. O Lord, why is the world constructed in such a way that it contains nothing of literature, nothing requiring but a single reading, a single point of view? Why can everything have deeper and deeper meaning, why can ever greater abysses open up? Plunging into these abysses, searching for the very bottom, for truth itself, people lose a great deal along the way, paying no attention to truths no worse than the one that awaits them at the bottom. But people want to know everything through and through, and then they laugh and say (as does Andrei in our case), that the world is full of such-and-such people, and women are all either such-and-such or old maids. "But what about Sonya?" the typists to whom Andrei was delivering his speech asked him, and Sonya was indeed a matron, we'll recall, but Andrei cunningly gave no answer.

By the way, how much real bile there was in Andrei's voice when he pronounced this cynical maxim of his, beginning with the words, "the world is full of," so it follows that Andrei was still not entirely engrossed in thoughts only about himself, he was not stewing and worrying solely and exclusively about his own inner theme since he was presenting these bitter grudges against the world to the world, in which everything has become mixed up and there is no honor, but on the other hand there is no genuineness either, and manifestations of masculinity and femininity are rare and provoke general curiosity bordering on indignation, and where can a poor man hide? Really, either a eunuch, or something on that order, which sounded so offensive to the ears of the typists (we will note that the poor typists, onto whose heads Andrei's speech had fallen, were trying to make Andrei understand with their hint about Sonya that something else does exist, but Andrei, after all, cunningly remained silent).

So it follows that everything in the world is suppressed and Andrei himself, an absolutely normal person without any deviations (else why all these accusatory speeches against every form of deviation, why this desire to castigate and abuse, this whole gamut of feelings—from laughter and contempt to the stupefaction of a betrayed soul to sadness and sorrow), so Andrei, a man in a million, constantly walks around as if poisoned by his reputation, when rumor precedes his appearance and women go weak, incapable of resisting the fate in store for them for the coming week, insofar as Andrei can't tolerate all of this for more than a week and impatiently breaks it off. And because of all of this, even the very beginning, the whole ritual of the overlook and standing above the city loses something of its grandeur and tenderness.

And yet, at first Andrei can't help himself; a new attachment makes him softer and kinder, instills in him a hope for God knows what. But this bright period cannot be trusted, insofar as it very quickly turns into a period of boredom, and is then replaced by exhaustion and ennui. Our Andrei, however, when taking off his cap and seriously saying "stroke my hair," would bravely disregard what was bound to befall him after the hair-stroking, after only one week, and most of the time not even a week would go by and the unpleasantness would start immediately. Immediately, that is, after a lady's visit to him, after Andrei had asked, "Are you going home or staying?"

This unpleasantness included the inevitable comment that he was too businesslike in fulfilling his masculine obligations; but what does businesslike mean? God only knows. A whole range of interpretations is possible, right up to the one that Andrei might have perceived his actions as a pure waste of time, a waste of energy, a disgraceful act of charity, as a wasting of himself on someone—while (let's imagine this possibility, too) his main problem was standing still and not moving, not developing, everything in general had come to a halt, nothing was happening, as if life had been forcibly stopped— and Andrei might have suspected his partner of sheer greed and the desire to take a ride at someone else's expense, to use someone else's energy for personal, mercenary goals. This, apparently, was the source of that economy and absence of spiritual animation, of that restraint, which became a generally known fact and is the evidentiary backbone of this story, but the ladies interpreted that economy as haste and a businesslike approach.

After all, he himself grieved (this, too, is an established fact) that he wasn't able to grab the bird of happiness by the tail, wasn't able to let himself go, couldn't get into the spirit of it, as they say. He himself admitted his defeat every time and would say in such instances, "You can consider me a heel, but we won't be seeing each other again."

Yet each time, everything was supposed to happen in the best possible way; Tanya, for example ("Are you going home or staying?"—that same Tanya who was to hear this cruel question), Tanya was so unattainably delightful and sweet, off the wall, adored by men, childishly innocent, not yet subject to any categorization (she was subject to it, of course, but as yet only vaguely, half-consciously), Tanya, who played hard to get, suddenly allowed herself to be gotten, called and said that since he was sick she would be right over with a chicken. There obviously could be no ambiguity here. What an unnatural situation: The chicken was running toward the rooster! Andrei opened the door to Tanya, Tanya was familiarly awkward, acting like an old buddy, but shivering from the cold, so she immediately pounced on the tea and shook over the glass and under the lap rug, and how obvious and clichéd this shaking was and it didn't go away even when Tanya was settled in with her feet on the sofa, cozily listening to music—a fashionable pop-opera, a hundred-ruble record—covered by his lap rug, in his house, to the sound of his record, chewing the walnuts that he had brought in for himself, and, on top of that, breathlessly awaiting pleasures—she was awaiting payment for some service or other she had performed! And he started going through all the necessary motions, went through with them, but he was racked with chills, racked with a high temperature, and he didn't feel like it at all, while Tanya felt like it indeed, and that's how it all went. And the incongruous thing was that Andrei, whose very character sharply negated a sense of duty to anyone at all, still did not fail to perform this duty the very first time—that's how it had to be.

And that's how it all went, we repeat: on the one hand Tanya with her rising fever, on the other Andrei with his rising fever of an altogether different nature.

What did they all want from him? How was he supposed to serve them and the world? What did this world lack if it needed him so badly? Those were the questions that invariably must have arisen every time Andrei refused to put anything more than a businesslike efficiency into the execution of his mission; he clearly refused to put all of himself into it, refused to expend, to waste himself. After all, something still lay ahead for him, something important, a decision of some sort, whence the conclusion that he performed what was demanded of him simply and economically, conscious of the fact that no one but he would perform this task and that he was needed. There was only one thing, I guess, that he could not supply the craving world—emotions. Insofar as the only emotions, you might think, that truly inflamed him—nothing else comes to mind—were the emotions he experienced in the gentle whistling of the wind on the overlook, at the sight of the lighted city lying below, with the huge bulk of the university towering over it all. And indeed, on balance, only here would the possession of a woman have any sense or sanctity for Andrei, on the one condition, however (if we may add an observation of our own), that he grow to gigantic size so as not to look puny next to the railing of the overlook, but tower over it all and fill everything up with his own person. And then, what would really be appropriate here would be not a woman but the whole body of the city, its whole gigantic organism, its wholly independent soul, and the secret little alleyways of Kropotkin Street with its lordly mansions, embassy town houses, with its girls walking their dogs, with its stores and its unimaginably gentle and grand old ladies, who walk in their tea-rose-colored lace, in their drooping skirts and slightly twisted stockings, carrying ephemeral net bags with a roll and a bit of cheese for tea, and what things these old ladies have at home, what Gardner plates* on the table, what linen in napkin rings, what silver tongs and sugar bowls—and what a life!

What a life indeed, a measured, empty life, half a portion of cheese for dinner, half a portion of cheese for breakfast the next day, and once a month a visit from a niece and her husband and some Alexandra whom nobody knows, including us, and on the wall a portrait of the lady of the house by Serov . . .† What else: her late brother's doll collection, Nesterov water-colors,‡ furniture—reupholstered by her mother in 1904.

Oh! All of this could have been appropriated, the old lady could have been appropriated and absorbed in such a way that she couldn't have lived a day without a phone call from us; her niece and the unknown Alexandra could have been absorbed without any particular trouble; finally, the furniture could have been absorbed and appropriated; something, however, pre-vented us from doing this, insofar as an appropriated old lady would have become a single, isolated old lady requiring this and that, medicine and chats, and the silver sugar bowl, relocated to our table, would have meant immeasurably less than it had before it was appropriated, before it lost pride of place on the old lady's table for the monthly teas when the unknown Alex-andra would visit, when the niece, a plain, plump individual with a silver brooch and a tear in her eye, would visit and eat the pastry she herself had brought. This niece has a slew of the most amazing qualities, among which we can name an incomprehensible, punctual loyalty to the old lady, as dem-onstrated by the monthly visits, the uncomplaining, loveless, decent, and honorable staying power at the table, and the equally necessary things she does for numerous other aunties and uncles. And the apotheosis of all this is the niece's own birthday, when the whole gang gathers once a year and takes stock of its ranks, and presents the most precious of gifts, namely, gems, precious stones, earrings (a sapphire in a bow, platinum encrusted

*Francis Gardner, an Englishman who settled in Russia around 1746, started one of the most notable private porcelain factories near Moscow in 1756. The factory's high-quality porcelain items continued to be produced successfully by his descen-dants until 1891. In the latter part of the nineteenth century, the Gardner mass-produced tea services, painted with roses in white medallions on dark blue, red, or green backgrounds, were very popular. —TRANS.
†Valentin Serov (1865–1911), a Russian painter, was considered the best portraitist of his generation. From 1897 on, he was the official portraitist of the court and the Russian aristocracy. —TRANS.
‡Mikhail Nesterov (1862–1942), Russian painter. —TRANS.

with diamonds). The main thing is that the niece gives the same kind of gifts to her own nieces and godchildren on their birthdays and weddings and that she visits the old lady not for the sake of profit and not out of love and not in the hope of getting all that antiquarian junk and the Serov—the niece herself has plenty of the same junk, where would she ever put it? This is why knowledgeable scroungers are amazed when they happen upon Biedermeier armchairs and Empire furniture of Emperor Paul's reign* and similar valuables in cheap secondhand stores on X Square, mindlessly brought there as to a junkyard or dump; such things, after all, are just what other people hunt for, they keep their eyes peeled for just this kind of furniture, they keep their eyes peeled for years on end, waiting for a sale, a death, or an owner's rainy day, they keep their eyes peeled, breathless with the anticipation of bringing the object home, skinning it, restoring it, covering it with Edelwax paste, and then what? Then, once again there's the hitch: possession, seeing as how a single precious object heaped together with other precious objects at best constitutes a collection of furniture, but who collects it in our times? Who's going to start collecting it for show, complete with conducted tours and a pointer? And without conducted tours and pointers you can't get many people together; in any case no furniture is going to ensure tedious tea parties on a regular basis, nor will it ensure the loyalty and devotion guaranteed on both sides by the observance of traditions.

At best you will be guaranteed a single visit and a single expression of admiration. By the way, there are known instances when fully furnished, equipped, and prepared apartments have succeeded only in shocking the guest. And then, of course, no traditions have evolved around furniture, whereas the old, prefurniture traditions have remained: old squabbles with relatives, the reluctance to put up out-of-town guests, the necessary traditions of going to the laundry and making preserves for the winter, and it must be said that Andrei himself, while remaining an affable and obedient observer of Sunday teas, was himself painfully devoid of traditions. He shunned traditions, he didn't take his dirty linen to the laundry on a set day but slept on it until it won out, and he couldn't stand visits from relatives, never breathed a word about his mother—his mother was a village woman— and to imagine that traditional teas with napkins and sugar tongs in a pot-bellied, medallion-covered sugar bowl could be arranged with such relatives, to imagine this was impossible. Such relatives, rather, required a barrel of pickles and a fold-out bed.

*Paul I, son of Catherine the Great, was Tsar of Russia from 1796 to 1801. —Trans.

■

True, Andrei did have attachments—both the already-mentioned majestic overlook, and another attachment, to a certain family where he had a so-called mama, as Andrei would say, "My friend's mama and my adopted mama and my adopted father." Andrei sometimes called them long-distance; apparently they had the same kind of tradition-filled life as the old ladies from Shchukin Street,* and one can imagine what order, warmth, and coziness reigned there, one can even imagine theater tickets propped up in plain sight behind the glass of the bookcase as a reminder, and one can also imagine a multitude of guests, even guests from the country, whom no one shuns and for whom a fold-out bed is always held in reserve, but then how jolly the family table can be, laden with aspic, preserves, mushrooms, suet, and smoked ham! And the man of the house is so considerate of everyone; he irons his white shirts on the dinner table on Tuesdays, let's say, not trusting this manly task to his wife! Needless to say, anyone would enjoy such a home, and the home described above was once enjoyed by the author, whence the knowledge of just this kind of setting, in which what is most amazing is the bunch of theater tickets standing in wait behind the glass. But this home no longer exists, the man of the house now cooks for himself, the mistress runs her household for herself and her son and treats endless bouts of eczema, and the daughter has fled to a cooperative apartment and apparently leads a nomadic solitary life without even a hint of theater tickets, insofar as theater tickets require a great deal of effort, too much attention to oneself, and love, whereas the soul seeks peace above all.

We have strayed somewhat from our main theme, but this digression will be useful to us in the part of our story involving the tall, beautiful, young Artemis, the daughter of a professor-mother and an associate professor–stepfather, a daughter growing up in solitude and neglect in a three-room apartment where (let's imagine) her mother locks herself in one room, her stepfather reads galleys in another, and Artemis sews herself a dress (cut out by her mother, who understands these things—she is a professor in all respects), so Artemis must be sewing in the third room, and she finds it uncomfortable because it's the common room, the living room, where the television set is, and everyone barges in, the pests—another pleasant, sweet, funny picture of someone else's home, an integral part of which is the word "pests"—just as one of the attractions of the pleasant home described earlier includes the fact that the daughter there also used various pet words.

*A street not far from Kropotkin Street. —TRANS.

We know how that case turned out in the end, and later we'll see how events were to unfold in this second home dear to Andrei, and they will unfold rather strangely and piteously. But that's later. In the meantime, in connection with what we have yet to hear about Artemis and her home we'll just mention that it will also concern Andrei's patriarchal aspirations, his attraction to traditions, his longing for decency—that's right, decency and loyalty to duty; his longing for everything that isn't created deliberately, that doesn't spring up on the spur of the moment, but seems simply to live, acquiring stability over the years, that continues on without dying, lives its own life, like the external appearance of a city that we come upon ready-made, and the earlier it was created the more we believe in it, just so long as it was not created in front of our eyes, and that city is the one we will absorb, we will inhale all of its beauty, which seems untouched by human hands, and we will absolutely refuse to absorb and inhale anything that has only just been put together intentionally. And in the young Artemis one sensed good blood, a mixture of her parents' long, stable love; in other words, all in all one felt a certain stability, which was always the object of Andrei's desire, and in this, apparently, his inner Theme asserted itself, craving contact (and battle) with another inner Theme, or so we may surmise.

And when we do get around to talking about the young Artemis—one of Andrei's failures—that's when we'll discuss his attraction to someone else's patriarchy, but in the meantime our subject will be the agile, light, gentle, homely, slender, thin-haired Lidka; Lidka, always flying, like a sailboat, that is, stomach first; Lidka, ardent and concerned, meek and forgiving . . . Lidka, who had so many admirers and a red-faced husband, to whom she was faithful, although she argued with him in her good-natured voice whenever he announced to her that he had to marry someone or other because there was going to be a child, and Lidka had two children of her own.

Depriving a person of his pride—something that Andrei would not tolerate with regard to the affectionate old lady from Shchukin Street, something that could have been accomplished easily but brought nothing except additional pains—this was precisely what Andrei would not tolerate, to all appearances, in any of his relationships with women, girls, or the young Artemis, who was kind of special, swore readily, dressed with indescribable elegance, wearing only what she had sewn herself—the only thing she didn't sew was boots—and was involved with an artist-millionaire so as not to be dependent on her careless professor-mother, whose money flowed like water and went primarily to her two other married daughters. As far as the young Artemis was concerned, she didn't need much, and her artist gave her only objects of great value, and also loved her and called her at the office and picked her up after work in his dark blue Mercedes.

Andrei, therefore, couldn't stand objects deprived of inherent value, whereas he tried to make objects that possessed this quality his own. But in making them his own, apparently, he could not keep himself within bounds and the objects would break. For example, he damaged all the furniture (by placing a teakettle on each piece) in the apartment of his coworker who had gone to Africa for two years and had left, first and foremost, his flowers, Alpine violets, in Andrei's care. The flowers, being dependent and weak creations, were abandoned by Andrei during his first business trip and only the aloe, a hundred-year-old plant, proved capable of weathering all the storms of living with Andrei, all the floods during his invasions and all the periods of drought, which would last up to a month and a half at a stretch. During such periods the aloe seemed to draw in its claws; it shrank, curled up its leaves, and began to soften, which was a sign of demise in its case, Andrei would return, however, and douse the plant with a kettleful of water from the tap, which (the water) had long since become, in spite of its tox- icity, the aloe's natural means of existence, its native environment, so that the plant became a chlorinated aloe and an anticorrosive aloe, never again susceptible to rusting, like a water pipe. That the lady of the house used to let tap water sit for several days had already been forgotten by the hapless aloe, which now grew only in length and stuck out of the pot like an aspen stake. To a certain extent the aloe demonstrated what a being could turn into when it was dependent on Andrei but durable in and of itself, that is, forced to endure for a long time, in this case at least a hundred years. The aloe, you might say, lived as if standing, but standing on its knees, and spent water with the stinginess of the elderly, as, apparently, Andrei's mother spent her retirement pension in the country, living on potatoes, cabbage, and mushrooms.

In concluding this extented introduction to the story about Lidka, we still cannot refrain from adding that people of Andrei's ilk could not hang on to anything—not a cat or a dog or a parent's grave, not to mention Alpine violets, which need tender loving care, and on a regular basis at that. Conse- quently, the owner of the apartment, arriving for a vacation after a year, was grievously shocked at the sight of the wallpaper, the dry flowerpots, the furniture, the aloe, which looked like some kind of symbol, and the floor in the front hall. Consequently, Andrei shrugged his shoulders and found him- self other accommodations, while the owner of the apartment spent three

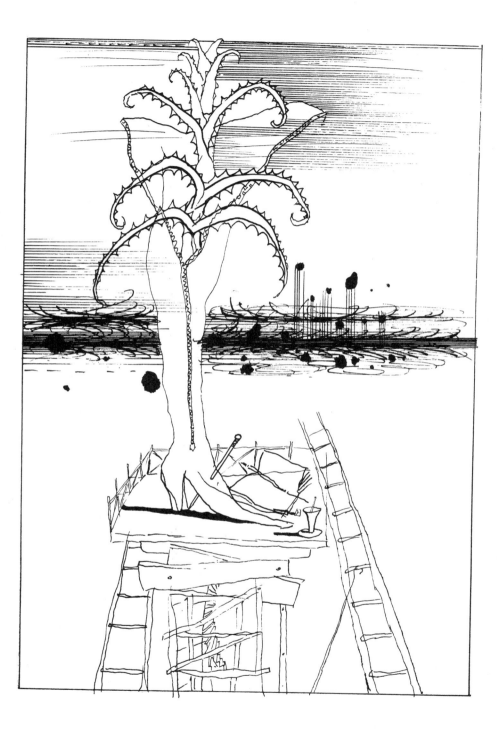

days clearing out the dirt and had to answer to his returning spouse for the peeled finish on the furniture and the circles covering everything.

Andrei, it must be said, was a man without an apartment; he was registered in a dormitory, but living there was inherently unacceptable to him. He could have married dozens of times and acquired ready-made living quarters or bought into a cooperative, but he didn't want that, he didn't marry, seeing as how—I guess—he considered the sacrifice on his part much too great, he couldn't lose his freedom, he couldn't take anything without immediately spoiling and ruining it, and he was a man of comfort who loved conveniences. He loved, as we've already said, to get plenty of sleep and to put the kettle wherever he felt like it. And let us recall the aloe, transformed from a slender shrub into a gnarled symbol with only a faint hint of leaves, and let us imagine how difficult it is for a man to feel at all times his destructive, fatal influence. Who fancies being a despot, who wants to listen to justified reproaches of amorality?—well, then, bug off and don't provoke my amorality, I'll make it on my own and will go on, there's something out there waiting for me, after all. This—or something like this—is what Andrei might have thought at the sight of that gnarled stake growing in his flowerpot, and time and again he blindly believed in happiness, just like the first and only time he got married; the next morning, however, he left his wife and never saw her again, although word reached him that she still loved him and was waiting for him faithfully, like a mother.

But we've digressed from the theme that we rather awkwardly designated as "depriving a person of his pride," although, as it turns out, we've merely developed it, but using different examples, whereas we began with Lidka, a creature so soft, quick on her toes, and light as a feather, that her coworkers liked to grab her and lift her up in their arms, and she would get angry and say "son of a bitch," seeing as how she was a serious woman.

She was once an ice racer. Sports leave their mark primarily on how a person moves: Gymnasts all walk with precision and springiness, like a clicking pendulum, while Lidka, a long-distance racer, moved like a pointer on a map, elusively covering distances and seeming to touch earth only at certain points. In Lidka's case, even a comparison with a ballerina won't do, insofar as a ballerina's walk is anything but aerial, and what can compare with the lightness, the flutter of the end of a pointer?

So Lidka flitted about, doing everything terribly quickly and deftly; her home sparkled, and her neighbors in the communal apartment would give up their rooms to Lidka's guests, so that her children could sleep peacefully in their own beds. And so on festive occasions the neighbors, who simply adored Lidka in spite of a difference in age, were saddled with her guests. It's true, Lidka's husband had a constant chip on his shoulder because of his wife's popularity and got back at her with endless affairs, not even hesitating to bring his lady loves home, which upset Lidka, of course, but somehow only slightly. "Ah!" she would say, shrugging her shoulders, which were, by the way, sorely overburdened, the shoulders of a housewife and mother. "Ah! He can go to hell!"

But her husband's parents would visit from Lithuania and he would get down on his knees (morally speaking) and during one of these visits Lidka picked herself up and went off on a two-week vacation, and for some reason she left quickly, secretly, and hurriedly, saying only, "Andrei is a strange person." Apparently, that already-mentioned circumstance came into play here: the impossibility of determining what was occupying Andrei's thoughts while he was performing one action or another, which he accomplished hastily, as though in passing, as though he had in mind some other, more important business, something in the future, something that had yet to occur. This was the reason for Lidka's description: a strange person. As for me, I can add that even the behavior of a cat or a dog can appear strange; it may be incomprehensible what a dog running down the street has in mind, why it happens to run into a yard and just as hurriedly run out or to what purpose it sits in the middle of the street, but that it has a purpose is indisputable, seeing as how it looks precisely as if it had sat down for a moment, awaiting something important, something unknown to anyone, something strange.

There was also a certain Edik, a coworker in the same department, who constantly worried about Lidka and about the other girls in the department who had been afflicted with Andrei. So there was this Edik, almost a girl himself, one of those guys who notice when someone's slip is showing or stocking has a run in it, and this Edik, loving Lidka like a dear girlfriend, was the one who jealously waited for Andrei to get Lidka into his clutches. And, unfortunately, wouldn't you know that it was to none other than Edik, as to a dear girlfriend, that Lidka kept repeating, while hurriedly putting her business affairs in order before her vacation, "Andrei is a strange person, Andrei is a strange person."

And Andrei—here's a coincidence—was at that very moment going on a business trip in the same direction, and Lidka—now this is strange—didn't even buy a ticket for the trip to her nature preserve. "Did you buy a ticket?" asked the dear girlfriend Edik. "I didn't buy one, it was bought for me," Lidka, a generally secretive and reticent person, answered mysteriously. "Lidka," Edik entreated, "who bought you your ticket?" "A certain strange person," Lidka answered pensively, quickly gathering up some papers and fastening them together with a paper clip.

Now begins that part of our story that does not resemble the preceding, insofar as what follows is an enumeration of Andrei's actual, real actions, his service record, if one may put it that way. And if in the first part of our story much space was devoted to conjecture, speculation, and attempts to draw conclusions, then it is now high time to look truth in the eye, to see how Andrei actually lived and how his life was seen from the outside by his coworkers. In the second part, therefore, various episodic characters will appear who will bear close attention, insofar as, as we all know, man is a product of his environment and everything that will happen to Andrei in the end can be attributed to the influence of his environment.

Well, so, consequently, they left—Lidka and Andrei, that is—and Edik was the first to decide not to pay any attention to how they looked upon their return: tanned, well fed, both simply gorgeous, like twins whose lips were sealed with an identical stamp. Lidka, loved by everyone, looked even more enigmatic than usual; her stern husband met her after work a couple of times and was obviously depressed, seeing as how he had once again announced his intention to marry, and had even made the announcement this time in the presence of his parents. It's difficult to say what happened after that; Lidka kept a humble silence, while Edik, walking on thin ice, raged on about how Andrei had played another dirty trick. "Where were you, Andryusha?" Edik asked. "You're so tan." "Oh, among the pines, among the pines in the great virgin forest," Andryusha replied, showing his hand for some unknown reason. (Speaking of which, you might recall Andrei's propensity, mentioned in the first part, to walk on thin ice in every situation, as if tempting fate.)

What happened next was that in response to Andryusha's demand as supervisor (although a minor one) to write a report immediately, Edik histrionically said that he was tired of slaving away for everyone. "I'm tired of slaving away, too, and I haven't had a vacation this year," Andryusha replied, itching for battle, and he got his battle, and in battle he was an incomparable opponent, a powerful, logical machine, except that he plunged in without particular desire, as if entering the fray under pressure, reluctantly, dragging his feet.

Speaking of which, the story (again we're digressing slightly) about how he got his small promotion is of interest, and it was no simple matter.

The former supervisor, Borya, asked for a vacation without pay, and everyone knew that he was going off to play a scuba diver in a film and would make lots of money. The boss, B.D., in his laxity, was ready to sign the required form, but Andryusha, who would have had to cover for his scuba diver that month, went on strike secretly and furiously. Andryusha accurately judged the temptation clouding Borya's mind (the filming was supposed to take place in Bulgaria), and the fact that Borya wouldn't be hired anywhere without a recommendation from his place of work.

Andryusha had influence over B.D., who, moreover, had no fondness for any sort of lordly airs or scuba diving, and the ground had already been heated to volcanic temperatures, seeing as how Borya had a record of inappropriate trips to scuba-diving competitions, rallies, gatherings, and filmings. B.D. curtly told Borya: Write a request for a transfer to senior engineer. Borya, pinned to the wall, wrote it and left. Andryusha became supervisor himself and received, as a kind of gift, the neurotic Edik, whose disturbed eyes followed all his former colleague's manifestations of will and power. By the way, throughout all of this, that headlong striving somewhere into the distance, in a different direction, was again noticeable in Andryusha, in light of which any episode, even this acquisition of power, looked accidental, unnecessary, whereas what was necessary and not accidental was something that was still taking shape somewhere in the future.

The next move in the course of events was bound to be the firing of Edik, and let's see how it happened. Well then . . .

"I'm tired, too, and haven't had a vacation this year," Andryusha said provocatively, although without particular fervor.

"You haven't," Edik said, dumbfounded.

"No, I haven't," Andryusha said, egging Edik on.

"Then who just went to the nature preserve?" asked Edik, losing his head from rage. "Who sat in the sun with whom?" forgetting about Lidka, about poor Lidka, whose husband was just lying in wait to get some facts for his duel with his parents.

"You'll pay for this slander," Andryusha said, and the next day the whole group, gathered together by B.D., discussed this emergency in their intimate family circle, discussed this case of slander and moral downfall, and Edik's tardiness as well. B.D. was particularly livid; he didn't like Edik because of his tardiness, because of his friendship with the lady guard, who didn't record Edik's tardiness but warned him not to get caught in the next shift, where the guard was not really mean but begrudged Edik his friendship with the first shift.

Under such complicated circumstances Edik apologized to Andryusha in front of everyone (he didn't have to apologize to Lidka—they all decided not even to bring up Lidka's name—the issue here was Andryusha, and all the paperwork from his business trip was in perfect order), and it was clear that B.D. was furious most of all, apparently, because of feelings he didn't understand, out of a sense that he had been coerced, forced into being a pawn in a game, and the unexpected finale of it was that Edik was asked to submit his resignation. "Either me or him, but I'll take him to court for slander," Andryusha allegedly said, knowing full well that the fussy Edik would never utter Lidka's sacred name. "Clear out, Edik," B.D. said, and Edik spent the rest of the day writing his letter of resignation and was afraid to look at Lidka, who put on an enigmatic air and typed away with one finger.

And Edik disappeared, vanished into the haze, and Edik had a wife and son, and a mother, and this was the second job Edik had lost.

And Lidka, unfathomable woman, didn't give in to Andrei, oh joy! And she maintained a secretive air, although everyone knew that her husband had gone back to her—his parents had reconciled them.

At first glance it may seem that the incident with Lidka represented a model of that long-dreamed-of union with an independent woman who didn't lose her pride. It all came to naught, however, seeing as how Lidka didn't plan to leave her husband and Andryusha didn't plan to take her who knows where with her two children, that much was clear. Andryusha's path, apparently, lay elsewhere, after all, and something hadn't worked here since it all ended as it did: not in shame, suffering, and death—it just came to an end. The absurdity of their union did not intensify their feelings or kindle them into a mutual flame, they did not flail and they did not cry about having no future, and they were even in a strange way satisfied, these deceivers of a red-faced husband. To make a long story short, it all fizzled out, if you don't count Edik, who was the sole victim. He kept calling Lidka and kept cursing, vilifying, and slinging mud at Andryusha. The poor, ill-informed creature, he did it all in vain, seeing as how it was already a moot point. Now there's another funny situation for you.

However, the unconquered, unbroken, quick, gentle, ardent, commonsensical Lidka is being kept in reserve and will appear at the very end of our story, and we will also bid farewell to Edik before we're through. He left, and it's a good thing he did, seeing as how Lidka wasn't his only girlfriend; he had two adored girlfriends in the laboratory—Lidka and Artemis, the young professor's daughter, such a young, lissom, and fresh being, such a weeping willow, and at the same time a rare rascal, and at the same time a skilled and spunky girl, who once went through almost an entire day with a nail in her boot and consequently walked around covered in blood, seeing as how she had nothing else to wear and the nail refused to be pounded down; well, so this Artemis, who was always late and ran into the office with a sleepy pink little face, and ate only one little sandwich for lunch, this Artemis worked in the lab as a typist, but everyone knew that she simply hadn't gone to the university after her English school and that her salary was only mad money, and that her mother and the millionaire-artist stood around their Artemis like a thick wall, not letting a speck of dust fall on her. Her mother cut out all her things for her, the millionaire drove her around in his car, and she ate little; so solve the simple puzzle: How much did she spend on clothes? Everyone loved Artemis like a daughter; only one of her contemporaries, a girl who worked in the same department, couldn't stand her, insofar as she knew better than the others Artemis's place in the new era, in the new generation, and she always chuckled when Andryusha started up a conversation and listened with interest to what Artemis had to say. And this poor contemporary of hers, a splendid working girl from a family of simple intellectuals, took her friendship with Andryusha seriously and had no ulterior motives. You have to think that he didn't have any either, seeing as how he would often bypass all the other ladies and start bugging Artemis. "Humph!" said her contemporary, grinning. "Who do you think you're talking to? You might as well talk to that empty oak chest over there."

It was beginning to feel crowded and stuffy in the laboratory because of these two, Artemis and Andrei, especially when he went up to her typewriter to dictate—his voice would break—it's a documented fact. She was no whiz at typing to begin with and now in Andrei's presence her quiet "Oh, damn" could be heard constantly, as well as her eraser scratching the paper.

And suddenly she stopped talking to her artist on the phone. And she brushed past his Mercedes after work. And, being a rather fat fellow, he couldn't run off and leave his car open, but by the time he locked it, she was already in the metro. . . .

Finally the moment came when the artist called and asked for Andryusha. Andryusha spoke with the inflamed artist long and tediously, and for some reason through his nose, about how everyone in the lab only wanted what was best for Artemis, seeing as how she was young and had her whole life ahead of her, and they didn't want her to be dragged through the mud. Leave, Andryusha said, and Artemis left the room. I didn't mean you, Andrei said into the receiver, and nasally, devilishly, continued to weave his demagogical web, although without apparent desire, and in conclusion said, thinking that he was alone: Well, all right, I'm an outsider, just an impartial observer, so go ahead and take her, but treasure her, she deserves it. And with reckless abandon the artist muttered that he would marry her, he would, although how could he marry her, having a living wife and children and also a certain Olya? But he would marry her, he would, and having agreed upon that, Andrei replaced the receiver. And sitting behind the cabinet, not hiding, just sitting at her desk, was Alya—that same contemporary, Andrei's sincere friend without ulterior motives—and she came out in a fury, saying, "What filth, what mud they drag you through! You said all the right things to him," and she left, and there, in the corridor, leaning against the wall, almost like a little girl outside the teacher's room where a teachers' meeting is being held, stood the young Artemis. Alya walked right by her without saying a word. And a few minutes later Andryusha walked out carrying his briefcase, insofar as it was the end of the workday and they were locking up the institute, and the two of them, he and Artemis, took off somewhere, and their witches' Sabbath began to spin; the fat artist loomed on the horizon several times, surrounded by his students, but in vain.

At this point, by the way, it's perfectly appropriate to bid a fond farewell to the artist-millionaire, who was, in fact, not an artist but simply a great master of organization as well as a great host who loved getting people together and drinking and who did the job with relish and fed not only five students but a wife with two children, and Artemis, and also his unforgettable love—a certain graduate student—and others as well from time to time, and he did all this unhurriedly, pensively, colorlessly looking out from behind his gold glasses, never going out of bounds, except perhaps when he was pushed out of these bounds by Andryusha, who succeeded in taking Artemis away from him, but couldn't or didn't want to take care of her properly; in short, Artemis ate but one sandwich for lunch as before and still swore quietly at the typewriter, but never again did she lay her eyes on fancy dress balls, or the Mercedes, or Italian suits. Artemis, a secretive individual, lived silently and never complained—only Lidka saw the blood in her boot, and that was in the ladies' room, where Artemis was examining her losses in the form of a blood-soaked stocking (a gift from the millionaire, fifteen rubles cash). The blood resulted from the fact that Artemis would not allow herself to limp and just walked around in a sort of funk, with an iron spike lodged in her flesh, until Lidka ran and got a piece of cardboard, but there are far greater torments than this!

Indeed there are greater torments, and later on we'll find out what nails pierced Artemis's tender flesh besides those that everyone could see.

And the nails everyone could see appeared immediately after the May 1 holiday. That year the weather was just gorgeous and people first had a number of days off for May Day and then three days for the Day of Victory, and there were only a few weekdays left in between, and those who were well connected arranged a vacation for themselves for these eleven days and headed for the shore, either to the south or to the west, and there was a hubbub around the Aeroflot offices.

Andrei, too, went off somewhere—he had some time off, he always had a lot of time off, seeing as how he, as an unmarried and unattached person, was sent vegetable picking on Saturdays, or potato harvesting in the fall, or haying in July.*

(People have their own individual ways of arranging vacations—if we may digress from the plot once more: One woman gives blood twelve times a year, that is, every blessed month, free of charge, but in exchange for time off, and, to the helpless fury of her superiors, spends every spring in Dombay on skis, which is to say on her own blood, and she gets away with murder both there and here, while someone has to sweat and slave those twelve days for her, work doesn't stand still, after all!)

But Artemis, who was cunning in a blind, childlike way, managed simply not to show up for work those several interim days, and, coming back and appearing at work on the same day as Andrei, just as tanned and fresh as he, she began quietly to lie that she had been in Kiev and that it had been impossible to get a plane ticket for the fourth, fifth, or sixth. She just stuck to this guileless version of hers all the time they dragged her from one department to another, and Andrei stayed out of it, and everyone once again decided to keep silent, not wanting to entwine Andryusha into Artemis's disgraceful crown of thorns. Finally B.D., secretly sympathetic to Artemis's cause, got fed up with it all and merely gave her a reprimand for being late for work, but Andrei, it should be made very clear, did not apply the slightest effort of his own to this kindhearted and charitable act. He followed the course of events aloofly and somehow even wearily. From the very beginning he did not exactly welcome having Artemis along on the trip and he resigned himself to it, as to the fact that it would have been dishonorable to put her off his plane, unbecoming and impolite (let's recall that characteristic feature of Andrei's, that, all right, he allowed himself to be taken advantage of, but only the first time, as if he wanted to see what would happen).

Besides, Andrei didn't entirely support Artemis's certainty that they

*Soviet urban workers are often recruited to do farm work during peak seasons because of the shortage of agricultural labor. In compensation they get extra time off from their regular job. —TRANS.

would easily forgive her four days of truancy. The delicacy of the situation was further compounded by the fact that Andryusha was Artemis's immediate superior and that he was the one who drafted the order to place the reprimand on record and he was the one who authorized Artemis's application, fabricated after the fact, for four days' vacation without pay. One could see how repulsive and undignified the whole thing seemed to him, all this falsification and the general knowledge that he was the one who was obliged to take care of it for some reason. But he, as always, went through with all the requisite manipulations, and Artemis continued her quiet, restrained existence at the typewriter by the window, an existence interrupted only by a feline hiss, a quiet "Oh, damn," and the aforementioned scratch of eraser on paper.

By the way, those four days of Artemis's truancy had to be made up at her typewriter by Alya, who hated inequality in any form, especially the type of inequality in which she herself was not equal to Artemis, whose professorial heredity had been hatched in the course of a single generation, whereas Alya herself was a fifth-generation member of the intelligentsia, at least. And there were no more neatly typed pages in the world, and there was no ocean in the world that could be compared in volume to the ocean of quiet contempt in Alya's eyes.

Now we are close to the finale, to that moment when the quiet and triumphant contempt that filled Alya's entire being to overflowing was suddenly replaced by a sharp and unreserved, somehow even frightened disgust for, cringing from, and horror of Artemis, who continued to sit at the typewriter by the window with her back to the light and her face to the laboratory, and only the bulge of the "rhinemetal"—the gray iron bulge of the typewriter—could screen any part whatever of Artemis's being. One could not say that Artemis looked crushed, she just sat there in a funk, and speaking of which, we will recall the nail in her boot, the blood, and how at that time Artemis walked around in a funk, but not limping, oh no!

The whole matter involving Artemis was cleared up with unexpected simplicity. Alya, being not bad-looking, met a certain fellow who was of the same generation as she and Artemis, more precisely, he was born in the same year as they and was, as it turns out, at one time a classmate of Artemis's. Anyway, this fellow simply announced that Artemis was not a professor's daughter at all, but the daughter of a typist, and that she had graduated not from an English school where typing and stenography were taught, but from an ordinary, everyday school, and yes, they had been given an apartment at one time, but a two-roomer, not a three-roomer, and the second, walk-through room was occupied by a married sister and her family, so there.

So there, that's how shamefully it all turned out, how ridiculously, and Andryusha would sometimes even throw his head back and shake it, as if not comprehending the world he lived in, and Artemis just hid behind her defensive rampart, her little rampart, behind the tiny breastwork, barely defended, defenseless against all nails and bullets, but what could you do with her, with this fibber! She had punished herself, whipped herself like a slave, and just look how long she had been spinning all those tales, making things up, how she ate her pathetic little sandwich, allegedly so small because her stomach had shrunk in childhood, had shrunk and shrunk, and her famous mother didn't know what in the world to do with her skinny daughter, while in fact this whole sandwich business was the result of budgetary considerations!

And the situation in which she found herself was in fact so ridiculous and stupid that there couldn't even be any room left in anyone's heart for pity— what was there to pity here? one may ask. Here there could only be laughter and bewilderment and that's all, and a shaking of the head, as in Andryusha's case.

However, pity goes its own inscrutable way, as does love, and to pity someone—to pity desperately and with all your heart—is, as it turns out, a random and illogical affair.

And quite unexpectedly, Andryusha was forced to leave his job and get away from this incident—not exactly the incident involving Artemis, which his austere soul could not endure—but simply from the strange incident that transpired between him and B.D. Something happened to B.D., who until then had always considered Andrei the sole hope of science and had related to him like an obstinate father, helpless in the face of his love. And what could have forced Andrei to leave his job? It wasn't, after all, the presence of the sinful Artemis right there next to him? No, something happened, and apparently, a situation suddenly developed in the department that put an end to all of Andrei's prospects at once, seeing as how B.D. kept trying to look right past Andrei's head, and Edik kept calling Lidka frantically, and she answered him in monosyllables, and it was apparent that Edik knew what was going on and was even more deeply wounded and that it was none other than Lidka who enlightened him about the whole scope of events in such a way that Edik started fuming.

But suddenly B.D., moved by who knows what, began to rail at Artemis during a meeting, telling her that she had no intention of entering college, and was wasting time who the hell knows on what, on clothes.

Artemis, not at all pleased, went on leave to take the entrance exams for a college that was recommended to her by B.D., a college where they remembered him and where he had some pull. And only Lidka knew that Artemis didn't take any exams, but went to stay in a hospital and returned three days later wary and in a funk, telling everyone that she had flunked.

Andryusha was somewhere beyond the horizon by then, in a spiffy new institute, and beginning a new life filled with hopes for advancement, an apartment, and so forth, and that's how it all turned out.

And so our story ends in total victory for the hero.

Some will say that a victor is fine, but who was there to vanquish here—old men, women, and neurotics? But then again, that's just what we all are.

But then there's something else: What *are* victories over us? And shouldn't we support the idea already expressed at the beginning of our story, that all victories are only temporary phenomena, that the nature of life is such that it is constantly bobbing and weaving, constantly getting up after a blow, constantly growing and expanding?

To be specific, one fine workday a frightened Lidka, if we may return to her, called Edik and informed him that she had seen Andryusha in town and that Andryusha had presumably said that he would soon promulgate her (Lidka, that is), Lidka said, he would probably tell her husband everything, but why? In response to which the already remote Edik automatically gasped, but without his former enthusiasm, as though he were thinking something to himself, as though at that moment something was distracting him, some bitter thoughts.

But a week later Lidka again called Edik and now said that everything was okay, she had found out that Andryusha had simply decided to become a writer and depict her, Lidka.

And at that Edik started laughing long and joyfully, the way he used to, as though all his strength had returned and he had again become young and healthy.

But a joke's a joke, as one unmarried librarian is in the habit of saying, a joke's a joke, but the heart still aches, it still bleeds, it still wants revenge. What for? one might ask. After all, the grass keeps on growing and life is indestructible, right? But it is destructible, it is, and that's just the point. . . .

1982

Translated from the Russian by Dobrochna Dyrcz-Freeman

INFIRMARY AT THE STATION

BY INNA GOFF

They were waiting for their middle daughter, Lida. The telegram informing them of her arrival lay on the television set. It was a rather old set. "The first television in the city," they said proudly. They said the same thing about their refrigerator. When they bought it, it was also the first in the city. They were attached to old things, maybe because they were already old themselves, in their "inclining years," as Sergeyevna, who came on Thursdays to wash the floors, put it. They both really liked her calling their age "inclining." They thought that it was a more precise description of the state of old age and brought them closer to nature, like an ancient tree that is already bent over and about to topple.

Sergeyevna washed the painted floors and shook out the carpet runners. Then she dragged over a huge pumpkin from her garden—Lida loved pumpkin porridge. You could have made Cinderella's carriage out of that pumpkin—neither the old doctor, who had suffered two heart attacks, nor his gray-haired wife could budge it at all. And even Sergeyevna, a hefty and strong woman, admitted that her son, a metalworker at the station, had helped her drag it in. Through their joint efforts the pumpkin was installed on a kitchen stool, where it also had to wait for Lida.

But the doctor put on his railwayman's overcoat with its two rows of metal buttons, four on each side and one on each lapel, and his railwayman's cap, and set off for the station to meet the train.

"Vera dear, don't fuss with a pie," he said as he was going out. "You'll get tired. We have a lovely cake and pear jam."

"Go on, go on," she said. "Call me from the station."

They had lived in the city for thirty years. As the doctor walked to the bus he often raised his hand to his cap—everyone he passed greeted him. He walked along the wide country road, which was dusty because there had been no rain for a long time. It was just that, a country road, and it seemed particularly wide owing to the squat, whitewashed little houses trimmed in blue and engulfed by gardens.

All the bus routes here led to the station. The station and the railroad junction were the most important things here, and the reason why one day this big village around the station had been termed a city.

The bus driver waited patiently as the doctor climbed the steps of the front platform. They said hello. The bus was jam-packed, but someone shouted, "Sit down, Grandpa!"

The doctor shook his head and remained standing—he was only going one stop. He smiled joyfully and meekly and nodded—it was too crowded to raise his hand to his cap. He liked seeing these ruddy, healthy faces leaning closely over him. He didn't recognize them, and that's why, afraid of being impolite, he smiled at them all like old friends, just in case.

An entire hour remained until the train arrived. The trip to the station was the one pleasure that he could still allow himself. Sometimes he would simply come here, without any reason, to breathe the air, in which the scent of the steppes mingled with the scent of warm railroad ties and axle grease, and to watch the trains—cargo, passenger, diesel, and the special express train. After his second heart attack he had been forbidden to take any trips at all, even to the sea, which was only three hours away by diesel. So trains evoked a slight sorrow in him. But the infirmary, where he always dropped in for old time's sake, restored his self-assurance. And now, passing by the cool waiting room decorated with potted palms and the hot deserted platform overhung with rustling old acacias, their drooping black pods resembling unrolled film, he hurried toward the infirmary. He really hurried—he had to stop along the way to catch his breath. There was a telephone in the infirmary.

"Vera dear," he said, "Everything's fine. I'm already here."

She said something to him, a great deal and quickly. He knew that she always told him the same thing—not to lift anything heavy, to look where he was going, not to sit in the sun. He knew it all by heart, and so, not listening, not paying attention to the sense of her words, he agreed.

"Of course, dear. Don't worry. I promise you . . . yes, yes, yes!"

The aide at the infirmary, old Dasha, looked at him with admiration. She found him amazing, this man she remembered when he was young and quick. He had managed the railway hospital, worked in the ambulance service, in the X-ray department, in the infirmary at the station. She wasn't amazed that he used to run around like a rooster and now his legs could barely support him—she herself had changed from a freckled young girl to a young widow and was now even a grandmother. . . . Instead, she was amazed that the old doctor always spoke quietly and always smiled. And life had dealt him some hard blows! He had also been widowed, before the war, and he hadn't been left alone but with three children—what choice did he have? And then they found him that little fool, Vera Lekseyevna. Would a smart woman take on three children? Well, there was a war on. The doctor was at a frontline hospital and she, that fool, had her hands full behind the lines with three young children who weren't her own. She must have torn her hair out, but what could you do with the kids? Well, what choice did she have? Or course, he sent them his ration voucher, when he could. . . . They survived, they raised the children, and now they're living alone. So it just goes to show you—Lekseyevna might have seemed like a fool, but she was smart enough to marry a man like that. Listen to the way he talks to her, "Don't worry, dear." Dear! Not just anyone!

The doctor put down the receiver and looked around.

"Well, there, Dasha. How're things?"

"How're you?"

"I've come to meet my daughter." He smiled joyfully and meekly. "The middle one. She should be coming in on the Forty-seven. Ninth car."

"The one who's up north?"

"Yes. In Syktyvkar."

"Good Lord, what a name for a city! How did you learn to say it?"

"Practice."

"Peter Piper picked a peck of pickled peppers," Dasha said and laughed. But she stopped right away—the new lady doctor walked in.

The new lady doctor didn't care much for the doctor. Especially after the time he once saw her green, fashionably made-up eyelids and thought she had a sty. She had followed her husband, a Party worker, here and cursed fate for landing her in this spot. She didn't like anything here, and the doctor, who liked everything here, infuriated her even more. But he didn't notice and smiled at her as joyfully and meekly as he did at everyone else.

"How are things, colleague?" he asked.

■

"Hanging together."

"What was that?" The doctor didn't understand. He didn't know that it was now the fad to answer that way to the question "How are things?"

The lady doctor was silently filling out a form, and he didn't ask again. Beyond the windows a freight train slowly pulled out. In the glass cabinet the supply of sterilizers, surgical scissors, clasps, and syringes of various sizes glistened. On a separate shelf stood bottles of ether, alcohol, and camphor. A closed lower section held medicine that lost potency in the light. The infirmary consisted of two rooms—a dispensary and a surgical unit that even had an operating table, although it was more often used for bandaging people. It was a model infirmary, his baby, and he was proud of it. His last place of employment.

"I've come to meet my daughter," he said—this time to the lady doctor. "She should be coming in on the Forty-seven, ninth car. . . ."

"Please have a seat," the lady doctor said, giving him permission, and walked out. She thought that he was apologizing for his presence in the infirmary. It flattered her.

But he wanted to share his joy—his daughter was visiting! Their children didn't lavish them with too much attention: Once a year one or another would look in on them for a day or two. They were also lazy about writing. When things were going well for them, they were silent, but when things were bad—they'd show up fast enough. And now he was worried that Lida was coming. To be sure, the telegram said that she was just stopping over. Perhaps she was going on a vacation. She was the unluckiest of their children. She had been a sickly child and hadn't gotten married. Then she'd fallen in love with a married man. . . .

"Well, Dasha, it's time," the doctor said. There were another ten minutes or so before the train was due but he couldn't sit still. "If she has a lot of things, you'll help us to the bus. . . ."

"I'll walk you there, I'll walk you. . . . Get a move on."

Sometimes she spoke formally to him, sometimes informally. She was formal with the doctor she had known before, and informal with this meek old man in a black railwayman's overcoat. She, Dasha, was curious to get a look at their Lida. She remembered her as a puny little girl with thin braids— and one ribbon always untied. Then as a girl who'd come to see her folks on her school vacations—she was nothing to look at then, either. And then a rumor went around that this Lida, mousy Lida, was after another woman's husband.

The doctor walked along the platform nervously. He loved Lida more than his other children—his younger son and older daughter. Maybe because Lida took after her late mother and the other two looked like him. They were as ruddy, dark-eyed, quick. . . .

The Forty-seven Special had a lovely name—The Black Sea. The train had already come into sight in the distance and the blue cars flashed by—Blacksea, Blacksea, Blacksea. . . . They swam before the doctor's eyes.

"Right across from the infirmary," he heard Dasha say.

But Lida already stood in the door of the ninth car, a gray-eyed woman with a weary face. The suitcase she held was not big at all. A suitcase and a traveling case.

When the doctor and Lida had finished hugging each other, Dasha wanted to take the suitcase, but Lida wouldn't let her.

"Thank you, Dasha." She turned to her father. "Papa, I'm not alone."

And at that moment the old doctor and Dasha realized that the person in the blue shirt who was standing nearby wringing his cap wasn't on his own: He was with Lida.

"Let me introduce you," she said. "This is my husband, Seva."

"Seva," said the person in the blue shirt and put out his hand to the doctor. "Seva," he repeated and shook Dasha's hand.

The doctor looked up at him and smiled meekly. He looked even smaller next to the burly Seva.

"This is your Lida's husband!" Dasha exclaimed. She thought the old man hadn't understood anything.

But the doctor was too agitated to speak.

"I'll go call Mama," he said. "I better let her know."

The door of the infirmary on the platform was open. There was no one in the dispensary. He took the receiver and said in a voice strained from excitement, "Vera dear, it's me. . . ."

She immediately started telling him that the pie wasn't turning out well. And that she'd cut her finger when she was cleaning the fish, and there was no more iodine in the house. . . . He waited patiently. And finally she asked, "So, did you meet her?"

"She's brought her husband," he said. "She came with her husband!"

They were put up in the middle room. The dining room table stood in the center under an orange lamp shade. The table had been bought a long time ago with a big family in mind. And now Lida sat at her place, with her back to the television and face to the window. The uninitiated Seva took the old doctor's seat, but was immediately expelled from it and seated next to Lida on a stool. He was amazed by that—two chairs were still empty.

"My sister, Katya, sits here and my brother, Tolya, here," Lida explained. "They sit at this table once in a thousand years, but no one can touch their places. And from now on your stool belongs to you alone—no one would dare usurp it."

With sad tenderness she looked at her parents, who had aged so much in the past year, as they fussed over her and Seva, whom they immediately liked. Her mother had said as much aloud, looking at him almost ecstatically.

"How big he is!" she said, studying Seva as if he were an inanimate object. "A man should be big and kind. . . . Are you kind, Seva? He's kind, I know it! Tomorrow I'll tell you the story of our family. . . . Lida can't tell it right, she was only six years old. . . . Ivas, do you like Seva? Why aren't you saying anything? He's always like that—he smiles and doesn't say a word. You know, Seva dear, what Lida said when she was six years old? 'Our papa isn't fool enough to marry you!' She was such an adorable little thing. Isn't that true, Ivas? Look at what musical fingers Seva has. . . . An electrician? That's wonderful. Our iron is broken. Can you fix an iron? . . . No, no, tomorrow, of course! Now you're going to relax. . . . Have some more fish, Seva dear! It's fish from our South—you don't have fish like that where you come from. And we don't either. A patient got it for us. One of Papa's patients, Lida. Yes, a former patient, of course. He found out that you were coming. Our Ivan Petrovich is a famous person here. The entire city says hello to him as we walk along—it's even embarrassing, like walking with some famous movie star. I'm not bragging at all! There are stars among doctors, too. In my opinion, a star is any person who does his job well. Don't you agree with me? Seva, get that dictionary off the shelf there. Your father and I, when we fight, we always check the dictionary. . . ."

Seva listened to the old woman's chatter with a good-natured, tolerant smile, preferring, in his heart, the reticent doctor. He had already decided for himself that Lida's parents were harmless senile old folks and was prepared to play to the hilt the role of the good and strong giant. Especially since he had to put up with their company for only one day—the next evening he and Lida would travel on to the South, to their trade union's sanatorium.

There was plenty of food on the table, what there wasn't enough of was drink—only one bottle of sweet wine for the whole group. The old folks, however, merely clinked their glasses, Lida drank, but only a little—she was inhibited. Back in Syktyvkar, she could almost keep up with him drinking stronger stuff. On a cold sober head nothing might have happened. A sober head is terribly sensible. And, if you thought about it sensibly, she was five years older than he, the head of a laboratory. Her girlfriends tried to talk her out of it, and his buddies tried to talk to him. . . . But they decided to get married anyway. They put in the preliminary papers and time would tell. Of course, her facade had slipped. What do you want—she was forty years old! But with a little fattening up and baking in the sun, you can bet she'd get back into shape in no time!

A clock in a carved wooden setting melodiously struck ten times. Her father had been given that clock when he retired. It was placed up high, on a bookshelf, and struck every half hour, chiming at noon and midnight. It had to be wound once a month—fifty turns of the key. Lida happened to be there for that. Her father carefully took the clock off the bookshelf, her mother dusted it with a flannel rag. Her father sat down, her mother stood by him, and the sacred ritual began. Her father turned the key and her mother said, "One." Her father turned it again, and her mother said, "Two." Up to fifty.

Lida tried to convince them that one person could do it, but they rejected the idea indignantly. Over thirty-five years, they had gotten too accustomed to doing everything together. Outwardly they seemed different: Her father was shy, reticent, her mother bustled around and chattered, but they were alike, because they looked at the world the same way, with trusting, childlike joy, expecting only gifts from life. They even regarded Seva as a gift. And after all, Lida had in fact brought him for her parents' judgment, because she herself still hadn't made up her mind. Once, about five years before, when her father was taking her to the station—she had stayed with them after deciding to break up with Vadim—he had said something to her that she couldn't forget: "My girl! Besides love there's also *putting your life in order.*"

Recalling those words at home up north, she thought about her father. When he, a widower, married this tiny, funny woman with shining black eyes and a lively, homely face, did he love her? After all, her real mother, with her gray eyes and ash-blond braid, had been so pretty, and if she hadn't died giving birth to her third child, she would have been living with Lida's father to that day.

No, it wasn't a marriage of love. When he was widowed, her father put his life in order and seemed to advise Lida to do the same.

They went to bed early, the old couple in their room, and Lida and Seva on the big couch in the middle room. Seva fell asleep right away, but Lida tossed and turned for a long time. The old couple didn't sleep either. Her father carefully rustled the pages of the newspaper and heard the whisper: "Ivas—want a piece of candy?" The clock struck the hour, the refrigerator growled as it turned on, and something cracked—either the wallpaper peeling off the wall or the floorboards.

Oh, how sweetly she used to sleep on that wide couch in her parents' home! As a student she would come here after her exams and finals, eat well, and catch up on her sleep. Later she came here to cry her heart out—when she understood that she had to break off with Vadim.

And now she had come with her husband. Actually, not her husband yet. She could still change her mind.

He would come to the laboratory to adjust and check the instruments, sometimes several at a time—they had a lot of equipment. And then he'd go. Later he began to drop by for no reason at the end of the day. She would stay behind, and the two of them would remain in the empty laboratory alone. She was pleased that he liked her. Her, and not the young lab assistants, whom he didn't even notice. It was flattering that a handsome young fellow preferred her, but she never dreamed it would get serious. And she wouldn't let him take her out—she made up a husband for herself, a jealous husband, with enormous fists. . . . She knew that Seva had graduated from an institute correspondence course without taking time off from work. Twice he had tried to marry divorced women with children, but for some reason it hadn't worked out. He lived in a dormitory. And that was all she knew about him. But he knew even less about her. He knew only one thing for sure—that she was hoodwinking him about the husband. And it hurt him because he didn't understand why she had to do that. It must be that she holds a high opinion of herself, he decided. That aroused him and infurated him at the same time. And the next time she refused to spend her day off with him, he stood up resolutely and said as he left: "Say hello to your husband for me!"

And he didn't show up anymore. She began to miss him. She was even delighted when there was a breakage: The thermoregulator went on the blink and she called the repairman.

But someone else was on duty that day.

They saw each other again only in March, a month later. There was a party at the factory. She, who had never gone to a club before, went in the hope of meeting him. And she did. He had already parted with his buddies someplace and was also looking for her—he was sure she'd come.

"What a nice surprise!" he said casually, out of embarrassment.

There was a snack bar where men were treating women to pastries and champagne.

"I drink to your husband!" he said, using the informal form of address for the first time. And added. "Your future husband!"

That night he walked her home and stayed until morning. After that he just stayed there.

The next morning it was pouring rain, which no one could have predicted the night before. Low gray clouds had crept in from somewhere, the trees outside the window swayed, dropping purple plums like heavy drops of ink.

For breakfast they ate the leftovers from dinner at the family table, where Seva already had his own stool. Her mother kept thinking that Seva was hungry. She would jump up and bustle around, pushing glass jars in front of him: bilberries with pears, pickled tomatoes. Seva obediently kept his jaws working and praised everything. He asked if they had pickled the tomatoes themselves or bought them. And her mother beamed from his praise and interest.

"How could you ask such a thing, Seva? Do you think you can buy them like this! Our Katya sent them to us. Someone was passing through here going south and she sent them with him. She spoils us every year! She's such a good cook! I can't cook at all, and Lida took after me. . . . Don't get angry, Lida. You can't get mad at the truth."

The doctor listened to his wife, smiling silently. Just as silently he poured some medicine into a glass and handed it to her. And two pills from a box. She swallowed them as usual, without water. Then the doctor took some pills himself, from a different box.

The rain continued to pour outside the window, rattling the old plums. The plums and the rain reminded Lida of school. Her mother had saved everything, including their notebooks—the neat ones with the blotters tied on with pink ribbons were Katya's, hers were marked with inkspots and Tolya's with Fs. They used to laugh at their mother for keeping everything, like the director of a house that had been turned into a museum, where there was only one trifling thing missing—the great person who had grown up within these walls, surrounded by these objects. Now, on their rare trips home, they loved to go into the old storeroom, where perfect order reigned, and go through those long-forgotten things. Homemade sleds, oilcloth schoolbags, Young Pioneer ties, tree ornaments, school diplomas, old letters—three packets tied with braid, the smallest of which was the packet of letters from Katya. Photographs were also kept here, divided into separate envelopes, each with an inscription in her mother's hand: "Tolya," "Katya and her first family," "Katya and her second family," "Lida," "Tolya and his wife," and again "Lida," but here with the label "grown up."

And now her mother got out those envelopes and spread them on a clean oilcloth. All except one: "Lida grown up." Because in that envelope, next to the adult Lida was her Vadim. The man she had loved. It had dragged on for twelve years. And it might have dragged on forever. In the photographs he looked willful, slightly stern. In life he was spineless and soft.

Her mother seemed to have inadvertently left the envelope with the photos of Vadim on the shelf in the storeroom, and Lida thought that this would never have crossed her father's mind; a woman's diplomacy was needed in such matters.

"They were such tiny things! Eight, six, and four years old! I brought them sweets. They pounced on everything like little beasts. They would run in, grab a handful of candy from the table and run out . . . then hide in a corner and eat it there. They didn't like to wash, and they would even bite. Lida was the most difficult. Huge gray eyes—enormous—'Our papa isn't fool enough to marry you!' . . . I would cry at night, thinking, 'I'll leave, I can't stand it!' Katya was the first to accept me. 'Aunt Vera! Aunt Vera!' Tolya was next—'Aunt Vera!' But you still looked at me like a savage. In the evening when I would start to tell a fairy tale, Katya and Tolya would listen, but you would run out of the room on purpose, and then quietly, on tiptoe, steal back and stand behind the door. I would start to lower my voice on purpose so you'd have to open the door to hear. I would speak more softly still and you would come in. You'd come in, and I'd pretend I didn't notice you. You would come closer and closer. . . . That's the way I tamed you, little by little. And imagine, Seva, one day I came home from the store—bread, milk, a heavy sack—and they were sitting in a row at the table, quiet, washed, solemn, and Katya announced, 'We've decided to call you Mama!'"

Seva listened with polite attention. He was the only new listener here, but he wasn't as interested as Lida and the old doctor, who had heard it all a hundred times. For Seva it was a stranger's life, and strangers looked back at him from amateur and professional photographs. A young guy with an impudent gaze wearing a beret with the words "Black Sea Fleet" on it. A pretty woman with dark eyebrows that looked painted. The woman was smiling a slightly mysterious smile, like an actress on a postcard. Seva turned the photo over; on the back was an inscription in large handwriting, "To Mama and Papa from their daugher Katya." Seva liked Katya, so he was interested in hearing the stories about her. How she had been in medical school but got married in her third year and left her studies. Then she left her husband and married another man. Both of them were here, in the photographs. The first was a young fellow with a slender neck. The second was older and balding. Seva studied them and measured himself against them: Would Katya have liked him?

Lida also looked at Katya—would Vadim have liked her? And if that had happened, she wasn't Lida. She would have taken him away from his wife and two children. Katya was ruthless and kind at the same time, everyone liked her and forgave her sins as mere pranks. . . . And Katya forgave herself for everything, didn't blame herself for anything. An enviable character trait!

When her mother found out that Katya was leaving her husband, she wrote her a letter—twenty-eight notebook pages. Katya read it, laughed a bit, cried a bit, but proceeded to do just as she pleased. On a visit to her parents, Lida read a copy—her mother kept the drafts of her letters to the children—thought about it, and broke off with Vadim.

It was still pouring outside. The old doctor turned on the light over the table, and the orange lamp shade, like the setting sun, brought the still-distant evening closer. The doctor had grown weary of all the talk and sat in his armchair by the window. It was his favorite chair, made of canvas and aluminum, with a stand for a book—a gift from a former patient. When the doctor had a heart attack, various people called him and every one of them asked if there was anything they could do to help. They were all people he had treated. They didn't give their names. He had saved many people. Often, when he couldn't sleep, he would recall his failures. Because there were so few of them, he remembered them well. He recalled his youth. The North, Arkhangelsk, serving in the Arctic air force, the U-2 flights beyond the Arctic Circle. That case of mass food poisoning . . . Sabotage was suspected, but he proved it was botulism, a microbe that got into some canned goods. And Vaska! How old was Vaska now?

He had been working in the ambulance service at the time. One night during a blizzard he got a call—a woman was giving birth somewhere on the edge of town, in a shed. . . . The blizzard was terrible: It was pelting down and you couldn't see more than two yards ahead. Who called, from where—he had no idea! Maybe someone was pulling his leg? A false alarm? But he had to go. The driver was experienced. They drove carefully, afraid of getting stuck. The car was plastered with snow. Finally they found the shed. It wasn't really a shed, but an abandoned structure that even had a little stove. They went in, lighting the way with a flashlight—a woman groaned. She was lying on a bench, ready to give birth. They never did find out how she had ended up there. They quickly stoked the fire, melted some snow, and boiled the water. He and the driver delivered a boy, but he wasn't breathing. The doctor shook him and then tugged at him. The newborn didn't want to live. But when he gave him a good slap and shouted, "Vaska, scream!" the boy gave his first cry. About three years later the doctor was walking along the street when he met a woman with a little boy, a young woman, very pleasant. "Hello! Don't you recognize us? This is Vaska. Your godson. You named him yourself!"

A book of his reminiscences could be written, but who would do it? Vera wrote well, but she forgot everything. He remembered everything but he didn't like to write, and he was too lazy to relate it all to someone; besides, it was exhausting. . . . What's Vera getting so worked up about? Talking about Tolya! He was her favorite. She felt miserable about ruining his life. That letter, thirty-four pages . . . Why did she have to interfere? It was a casual relationship, the woman was experienced, much older than he, and there wasn't any love. . . . Of course, there was the child. But there is such a thing as financial support. . . . And there was a girl his age here, tender feelings, joy. Now Vera felt miserable—her Tolya had begun to drink. A victim of morality on thirty-four pages, an obedient son! . . .

Seva was holding a photograph of Tolya. On the back was the inscription "My slogan: Don't say everything you know, but know what you say." A clever fellow! He could turn a girl's head, that was for sure. It wasn't like him to drink. And now as soon as he got his wages or an advance, he'd buy a bottle.

Seva stood up and stretched. He placed his hands on his hips, like a weight lifter before picking up a barbell.

"Well, where's your iron? Let me take a look at it—we've got to go soon."

"The iron? Yes, of course, right away. Where is it? We haven't used it in a long time. We bought a new one. Maybe the next time?"

She was sorry her story had been interrupted. It seemed she still had something very important to say. She had to finish what she was saying! But she had already lost her train of thought and everything was a muddle in her head, like the photographs from the different envelopes on the oilcloth.

The iron was found and Seva started working on it, whistling.

"Hey, there—do you have a screwdriver in the house?"

He had big hands with broad, pink nails. It was even strange that they could take hold of a fine wire or turn a screw so deftly. He was a master of his trade, and it was a pleasure to watch him. That's the way he was when he fixed the instruments in the laboratory. Indispensable Proshin—that was his nickname at the factory. Because he could do in one try what others struggled over for a long time.

Lida slipped the photographs back in their envelopes and put them back in the storeroom. The envelope marked "Lida grown up" lay there by itself. She took out the photographs of Vadim—there were three of them, all for identification cards. She stole a glance at them and put them away, thinking, "Just like a schoolgirl."

In the end they never did get to the South together. How they had dreamed about it. . . . They thought they would stop by here on the way— Vadim wanted to see her folks, whom he knew without having seen them— he even sent them greetings in her letters. Now it would never happen. Never!

Her mother forgot to make lunch. They scrounged up lunch out of left-overs from breakfast. And then her mother remembered the pumpkin.

"Lida, child! This is for you in your honor!" she wailed. "Pumpkin por-ridge, your favorite! And no one reminded me! Ivas, it's your fault! Why didn't you remind me?"

"Vera, don't get upset," the doctor said, "It's bad for you to get upset. . . ."

He poured some drops of medicine into a glass for her, and she drank it in one gulp, followed by two pills. The doctor took his pills too—from an-other box.

It was getting lighter outside. The rain had stopped and it was only drip-ping from the trees. Big blue plums lay on the ground, and Lida wanted to run out into the garden and pick them as she used to do in childhood after a rain. But her mother began to talk again, this time about the war. About the winter Lida came down with the measles and was delirious, and she had to get some milk. So she took a liter container from the landlady of the apart-ment—Ivan Petrovich was in a frontline hospital and she was with the three children in the Urals—and went to look for milk. Finally she found a milk-maid, but the woman didn't want to sell her any milk. She said she'd only trade it for bread and kerosene. Lida's mother took the ring from her fin-ger—a gold one with a small stone that Ivan Petrovich had given her—and held it out to the milkmaid. "Please, take it. I don't have anything else." And the milkmaid began to cross herself and started to cry. "What are you doing? God forbid! I'll give you as much milk as you want!"

Seva listened with effort, no longer hiding his boredom. And Lida was embarrassed for her mother, who didn't notice, and for Seva, who couldn't hide it, and for her father, who kept smiling the kind, rapturous smile of a man who is certain that everything on earth is just splendid.

It was impossible to understand whether he liked Seva for himself or was just happy that Lida had accepted his formula—besides love, there's also putting your life in order—and she had put her life in order.

Behind the clouds an orange sun was setting. It was time to go to the station, especially since her father had volunteered to see them off. In the Russian tradition, they sat down for a moment before setting off.

"Seva dear, lean down so I can kiss you," her mother said. "How big you are! You'll come back to see us, won't you? I have so much to tell you. We've had so little time to talk! Such a long, hard life . . . I can see it all before my eyes, but to tell someone new . . . You aren't offended that I called you 'Seva dear'? We liked you right away. Right, Ivas? We're never wrong about such things. You're a good man. I'm happy that Lida has been lucky. . . ."

Small, gray, like a half-blown dandelion, she waved to them from the window. The air was fresh after the rain, and it smelled of the sea—that's where the clouds had come from, from the sea.

Seva walked along, whistling, carrying two suitcases as if they were nothing. He jumped over puddles and stopped, waiting for Lida and her father, who trudged along behind. The stopping irritated him, but the old man couldn't walk any faster—he was out of breath. He was wearing his railwayman's overcoat with its metal buttons and often raised his hand to his cap, responding to greetings. Good grief—he thinks he's a bigwig, Seva thought, He salutes like a marshal! The old man's not bad, but he won't last long.

The bus brought them to the station. Washed by the rain, illuminated by the evening sun, the station looked festive. Music blared out of loudspeakers in the nearby park where old chestnuts grew.

"Let's sit in the infirmary," the doctor said.

The benches on the platform were damp after the rain. Lida looked at Seva.

"Go on. I'll stay here and have a smoke," he said.

The dispensary was empty, and quiet voices drifted out of the surgical unit.

"Sit down," the doctor said. He felt like the host here. "I have to call Mama."

Lida watched her father as he squinted at the telephone, myopically leaning over the dial to pick out the numbers, and her heart contracted from pity and love, and from the premonition of an imminent parting—not this parting, in half an hour, but the eternal one that inevitably lay ahead.

"Vera, we're here." Her father spoke in a cheerful, somewhat thin voice. "Everything's fine. I'll wait for the train. Of course, dear. Yes, yes, yes!"

The new lady doctor came out of the surgical unit and greeted them perfunctorily. She was preoccupied with something.

"What are you worried about, colleague?" the doctor asked. "If I can be of service . . ."

"A man was taken off the Thirty-nine. They thought he'd had a heart attack, but it was hypoglycemia. Now he's back to normal and wants to take the Forty-seven."

"Give him an escort and let him go."

"I already thought of that, but there's no one to send with him." She glanced at Lida. "Is your daughter taking the Forty-seven? She's not a doctor by any chance? It would come in very handy. Half the hospital is out harvesting, and there's absolutely no one available."

"You go with him, and I'll fill in," the doctor said. And his eyes shone so that Lida thought: He's not kidding.

"Oh really now," the lady doctor said angrily and left.

They sat across from each other, Lida and the old doctor, and were silent. The doctor smiled joyfully and meekly. Everything was said in that silence. Everything that could be expressed without words. And they both seemed to forget about the man who was then smoking on the platform, spitting in the direction of the flower beds flattened by the rain, and glancing at the jumping hand of the station clock. They rested from him, as he, perhaps, rested from them.

"Take care of yourself," said the doctor. "Do you promise me?"

In response, the gray-eyed woman with the weary face nodded at him in agreement.

"You must remember that your mother and I love you very much."

Lida nodded once again. How else could he, old and feeble, protect her from life's storms, except for those few words? And wasn't that why the three of them came here, to hear those words?

"You're our infirmary," Lida said. "Infirmary at the station. You and Mama."

The Forty-seven Special came into the station right on time, as always. And once again the blue cars flashed by, Blacksea, Blacksea, Blacksea. They swam before the doctor's eyes.

The metal had heated up over the day and made the train stuffy. The last stop was three hours away, and the passengers talked quietly and lazily, like people who have already said all there is to say. Many spoke with a familiar northern intonation—they were also going south on a trade union vacation.

"Lidia Ivanovna," Seva called, "They're bringing around tea."

She got angry when he called her by her patronymic, as if emphasizing that he was five years younger than she. And now she didn't answer. But not because of that.

Outside the windows, swallowed up by speed and darkness, the autumn landscape of her childhood whisked by. White, blue-trimmed stucco houses, cores of pumpkins, and cornstalks without their ears, like disarmed troops. For some reason, in childhood that landscape always reminded her of pages from *War and Peace.*

"Lidia Ivanovna, should I order tea for you?"

Everything had somehow been decided of its own accord. She knew that there was no turning back. But there was no sorrow. On the contrary, she felt a kind of relief.

And she already thought about him in the past tense: "He wasn't bad, a great guy, that indispensable Proshin. . . ."

1977

Translated from the Russian by Michele A. Berdy

Parade of the Planets

Larisa Vaneeva

Saveleva, E. P., actually sang to herself as she returned home that night. At long last she had started humming again, just as she used to before her marriage to that creep who had driven her to her wits' end, and the fact that she once again could sing further improved her mood. They'd let her into the metro, although the escalators had already stopped working. It's a good thing they still let me into the metro, thought Saveleva with joy, rippling with the laughter of a bemused mermaid as she stood on the motionless escalator steps.

It's possible she fell asleep on those steps and awoke only the next morning, sometime between five and six o'clock, and returned home on the commuter train. Where else could those three or four hours have gone? Saveleva later recalled the escapades of that night and her encounter in the empty metro car on the long span between the Komsomolskaya and Kurskaya stations, with them, the redheads, all four of them absolutely carrot-topped, three men and a girl, so modestly dressed you'd never notice them in a crowd were it not for that fiery red hair and those slanted eyes, deep green with truly abysmal sorrow. . . .

Saveleva guessed immediately. As soon as she flew through the slamming doors—overjoyed by yet one more stroke of luck, because it was entirely possible that this was the last train for the night and now she wouldn't have to waste money on a taxi—she immediately understood it all. And they too immediately understood that she had guessed. All of us at once immediately understood everything, including the fact that the realization wouldn't do any of us any good. They probably didn't see me coming and didn't have enough time to turn me away. It's quite simple. All they had to do was put me in another metro car. But by this time I had already gotten on. I repeat, I was overjoyed at my string of good luck, because, for example, they don't let my seventeen-year-old daughter into the metro anymore, but they let me in. Even though it was already past 1:00 A.M. And the escalators weren't running. And there was not a soul around. Plus, there I was singing to myself out of this wonderful feeling of innocence and purity. I had just begun to sense something, a new Exit, a positive platform . . . you know what I'm getting at . . . when I ran head-on into them. The main thing was that I still hadn't managed to figure out what was going on. Where that sense of purity had come from. An infant's innocence. In principle, I should have hanged myself. But it all turned out just the reverse.

We stared at each other. And instantaneously understood it all. And I understood that for them this understanding was hardly desirable. They hadn't planned on making contact. It's possible that now I was supposed to be exterminated . . . my mind sterilized . . . but I remember everything. . . . Except for three or four hours . . . Perhaps at some point earlier they had wanted to make contact, but not anymore. Now they were getting ready to fly off without having accomplished a thing. We're hopeless, you see. Even though they'd come to us with good intentions. They'd doubtless been all for us back home. But now they were bitter and they were pulling out any way they could. Their encounter with me made them absolutely nauseous. They almost puked when they saw me. But what could they do? They sat me down across the aisle and twisted my head around so that at least I wouldn't watch. I rode the whole way with my head turned around—the pain was awful. It still hurts. But by the time I was supposed to get off, they were gone. It's hypnosis, you see. . . . And Saveleva hasn't been the same since. Since then. Because even though contact hadn't actually been made, there had been contact. There had!

Saveleva, E. P., took a deep drag, fanned the smoke, narrowed her watering eyes, and tossed the cigarette into the spittoon. Naturally, she missed.

"Let's go," she said to the stranger with the sallow triangular face as she took him firmly by the arm. They entered the metro and were swept up by the human stream. Her legs had been aching since morning, and it was difficult to stand on the swaying floor. Her legs would have to be amputated, the doctors had predicted, if Saveleva continued to abuse nicotine. At times her legs would give out entirely. Saveleva would fall, most often in the metro. For that reason she held on firmly to the stranger's sleeve. In fact, she even draped herself on the stranger, hiding a bit behind his back out of fear that they might not let her in after all. Every morning on her way to work she was afraid of being stopped at the turnstile, and she heaved a sigh of relief each time she managed to pass through. Otherwise, it meant being late for work. You see, they don't let her seventeen-year-old daughter in anymore, and a lot of the time the kid wouldn't get home until dawn, days—sometimes even a week or two—later. It's a long and difficult trek over crisscrossed urban terrain.

And that's exactly how Saveleva, E. P., found herself somewhere beyond the city limits at an unfamiliar summerhouse that cold and windy Monday morning. The stranger walked ahead and she followed in his tracks, tripping and falling into snowdrifts. She just couldn't be late for work, there was a staff meeting at 10:00 A.M., and the night before she had dragged herself all the way home despite the late hour just so she could get some sleep and regain her senses in her own bed. The stranger's powerful attraction convinced her to alter her normal route. You have to be able to set priorities in life. In the given situation, the stranger needed her badly—he'd almost knocked her feet out from under her at the newspaper stand when he announced that she was a biospheric entity and that she alone could help him. That meant she had to help, right? Saveleva was known for her sympathetic kindness, and, after all, work, well . . . work wasn't going to run away. . . . God knows she put out. . . . You're always using me to fill in all the gaps. The slightest thing happens and Saveleva gets sent on assignment, let Saveleva write the features on those damned "Starry Towns" and "Camp Lightnings." On the last trip, one of the scout leaders in Adler had almost wasted her with a signal pistol. . . . Saveleva was wearing winter boots, rayon tights, a suede miniskirt, and a short sheepskin coat. Her frozen kneecaps glistened like a teenage girl's. All her clothes were from back then. Ah, mini-youth . . . Despite the fact that her daughter was only seventeen, they looked like sisters, and Saveleva, after all, wasn't even thirty-five. . . . True, when her daughter goes on a binge and comes home beaten up—she's already had a lung and a kidney punched out—Saveleva looks even younger.

Shh. . . . Saveleva looked around in alarm. The garage under the building where he'd taken her looked more like a laboratory: the streamlined dull-black surfaces of some sort of lab apparatus, the fluttering needles on what seemed to be meters—that's a vacuum chamber, I can get the temperature in here up to thousands of degrees—drills, gas masks, retorts. . . . So where's the car? Saveleva thought in disappointment. There were only heaps of black cable lining the cement walls and floor of the garage. Blue compression tanks the size of human beings. I'm a clean-air advocate, and wheels are a luxury, don't you agree? What can I say, said Saveleva. Say it as it is, said the stranger. Protective plating, a welding table . . . Careful! Saveleva got tangled in a bundle of wire and lost her balance. Just don't touch anything. Without changing his pace, the stranger yanked at a lever and connected the circuit. A blinding arc shot through the air, followed by a flourish of plasmic sparks. . . . She edged back. . . . He grabbed her by the coat: One more step and you'll make a giant fireworks display out of the place. . . . He let go. Saveleva felt another jolt. Stop! An exposed fuse panel on the wall with copper-wire terminals. She smiled helplessly. Among the yellowish, smoke-darkened cutters one stood out as conspicuously white. Memories of yet another scout leader. This time from Barnaul. A Siberian bear . . . Shh . . . the stranger put his finger to his lips. Saveleva listened with him. The clatter of a train grew in the distance, the concrete walls began to shake, resonating with the clicking on the rails, dust floated down from the ceiling, and the lamp over the table began to swing. . . .

"I managed to generate a biofield," the stranger muttered, his face deadpan, without moving his lips. "If I hadn't succeeded in generating a biofield, I would have blown up the train line."

"How could you . . . how can . . ." Blotches appeared on Saveleva's face. Insulted to the point of tears, she accidentally twisted her sore neck while trying to focus on the ruler that hung from the ceiling. The ruler markings were blurred and got no sharper, no matter how hard she focused. The stranger beat out a taunting sort of rhythm with his leather boot. The dimly lit metro car rocked evenly back and forth, the drivers were not announcing the stops, were not saying, "Watch the closing doors," there was no one else on the train but them, and this was when Saveleva, E. P., pain shooting from her neck to her shoulder blade, saw the reflection of the redheads in the window. . . .

Once again before her eyes appeared the picture of her innocent late-night good fortune. The snow-covered boulevard was frozen in a mysterious chorus line. Only her unevenly winding footprints disturbed the sparkling white shroud. She felt the urge to dance, jump up and down, and sing like a young girl on her way home from a first date, like an innocent, fresh-faced child rejoicing at the sun. The amazing thing was, though, that by now she was completely sober. Damp slabs came loose from the rooftops, whistled as they fell, and crashed with a heavy bang on the sidewalk, exposing a deep metallic carmine around the lampposts that looked like heavily painted women's lips.

The moss-covered, smoke-stained skeleton of a tower floated past in the moonlight and disappeared, just like an old raven, behind a contemporary high-rise. It couldn't be she'd gotten off that easy. Her blissful mood made her uneasy. Could it mean she wasn't going to have to settle the score with herself for this one? She sang to herself. The doctors had warned Saveleva not to stay in her apartment alone. Especially at dawn and dusk, "between the dog and the wolf. . . ." As a result of alcohol and nicotine abuse your condition is borderline. Saveleva had told them she lived with her daughter. But Saveleva failed to add that her daughter frequently disappeared for months at a time. In the past Saveleva had kept a permanent lover, but recently she'd sent them all packing. . . . People are like mold in the crevices of the planet, where the more densely settled plains resemble mossy trails of jet exhaust. The pathetic mold of life. The thin mold of life. So thin and fragile, caught in the chaos of inorganic matter. Ultraviolet, a clouded pane of glass.

Entering the stairwell, Saveleva somehow made out in the dark corner near the radiator her daughter's thin shoulder illuminated by a ray of light from the broken window. A hairy paw held back the shoulder, and a syringe jutted from the bluish forearm skin near the elbow. Saveleva went and hid in the bathroom and for a long time kept banging her head against the wall, plugging her ears so as not to hear her own screams. Then she sat down at the table and spent the rest of the night writing an essay on Young Pioneer Scouts. She didn't beat her daughter this time, although in the past she would beat her mercilessly with whatever was at hand. Once she had broken her daughter's arm with a boot brush. Since then she had stopped beating her. Now whenever her daughter shows up, there's a bath and supper, clean pajamas and iodine waiting for her. Then they crawl into bed together and sleep in each other's embrace, like two sisters. Everyone says they look a lot alike, only her daughter is taller, broader, and older. The next morning Saveleva takes the bed linens to the laundry to be sterilized and carefully washes down the bathtub with disinfectant, even though she doesn't believe in casually transmitted syphilis. At the editorial offices Saveleva doesn't talk much about her daughter. Everyone thinks the girl's a journalism student in Sverdlovsk. And it's hard to get in there, if not as hard as Moscow. It takes good connections and the lowest form of pulling strings. The university's been turned into a kind of privileged kindergarten. A regular Institute for Young Women of the Nobility . . .

"No," Saveleva sniffled. "Don't . . ."

The stranger jumped up and stretched.

"Should we keep moving?"

He opened a door in the wall. A metal staircase wound upward through a narrow shaft. Saveleva went first, conscious of the faint wafting of her perfume and the gracefulness of her movements. . . . Removing her hat, she fixed her hair quickly and with a sort of casual abandon. A small head with a little bun pinned at the nape, a couple of stray wisps winding down her long neck. A neck like that was meant for kisses and axes. Saveleva's husband had made several attempts at strangling her. Saveleva turned around coquettishly. She knew she made a good impression, even when she was trembling slightly from a hangover. Saveleva periodically plucked out gray hairs because she considered dyed hair vulgar. When she was younger, her husband had insisted that she was born for lovemaking. Saveleva called her husband Nikola. She had been absolutely sure of herself and of his faithfulness to her until she caught them in bed. Not that Saveleva herself was without sin. She still remembered that assignment at Artek. Blue waves and hot sand certainly make you weak, don't they? Though, come to think of it, the beach was pebbled. Except for Urek, you won't find decent sand anywhere along the whole stretch of the Black Sea coast, unlike the Baltic, where the sand is fine and white as salt. She had always preferred northern scout leaders. What irked her most was that the bitch had rearranged all the dishes in the kitchen. Saveleva always stacked the plates one on top of the other, cups inside cups, rationally, to save space, but that bitch had lined up all the cups on saucers, as if they were on parade. At that point she and her husband had been living together for about ten years, and once over the initial shock Saveleva soberly rationalized that after all the tempests they'd weathered, this shouldn't bother her. She put all the cups and saucers back in their places. That was when she developed her almost satanic powers of observation. Over the next five years she would return from assignments to observe the cups and saucers in the most unusual places and in the most varied combinations. But her patience exploded when she found wine goblets in the bedroom, turned upside down, cloudy with condensation, stuck to the paint on the windowsill. The windowsill was damaged beyond repair. Ever try to remodel in the middle of winter? Now you've done it, she said to Nikola and tried everything possible to make him leave. She essentially threw him out, though over the phone she carped at him for heartlessly running off and abandoning her and her daughter. She called everyone she knew and everyone she knew called her, and she informed them all that that pig Nikola had finally abandoned her and her daughter, and to punctuate her words she systematically threw the cups, saucers, goblets, plates, and all the rest of the chinaware at the wall until the rug was blanketed with white shards. Before hanging up, having worked her way through their wedding china, she finished it off with the bottle she'd just sucked dry, then fell asleep in the armchair, hugging the telephone.

"Would you really agree to live side by side with creatures like those?" There were containers swarming with spiders—large and small, fat and paper-thin.

"Poor creatures! Poor, unfortunate, dear creatures! Why don't you let them out?" Saveleva shouted.

Roused by the light, the spiders scurried about anxiously. They tried to make their spindly little legs stick to the cellophane wrapped around the front panel of the container, but they would lose their grip, roll up into a ball, and fall.

"Let's let them out! Let's let them out so they can crawl all around us, over the walls and the books, and weave a huge web that you and I can get caught in!"

. . . Spiders are the dearest creatures around, and they've done a great deal for science. It all started when I had to milk the gossamer out of the spiders and suspend bits of straw on the strands. . . . It took a lot of effort before I got the hang of it! But now I can complete the whole procedure in five minutes. . . .

The sealed retort in front of Saveleva contained a piece of straw suspended on an invisible strand.

Try staring at it. Without taking your eyes off it!

Look! Notice how it started to move. . . . And now it's moving . . . moving in a circle . . . counterclockwise . . . always counterclockwise, around the axis. . . . That's the direction of the force of your gaze . . . water swirls in the same direction in a funnel . . . your hair's twisted in the same direction on the nape of your neck . . . and lotus flowers turn the same way in your chakras. . . .

Concentrating, the stranger guided her from behind, kissing the back of her neck. Saveleva brushed against his aroused flesh with her spine, and that's probably what made the straw in the retort spin faster and faster.

What are you doing, exclaimed the stranger in astonishment. No, what are you doing!!!

Still spinning, the straw began swinging jerkily back and forth.

I was just narrowing and relaxing my eye muscles. . . .

■

I get it, an overlay of telekinesis, the stranger said, calming down. But please, leave the muscles for later. You can't imagine how important this is to me. . . . A whole stage of work completed. . . . See, there's a lot of interference here—the heat, static. . . . But the idea itself . . . the idea was correct. . . . That's why I love my spiders so much.

It was the spiders who gave me the idea of creating an artificial biofield, although there's no form of energy more organic, more natural and vital. . . . Has it ever occurred to you that the key to human existence lies precisely in the transmutation of this energy into a higher psychic power, into spirit . . . into the divine . . . into the cosmos, toward those redheads of yours, if you will? Aren't we more than just milking cows— He stopped short, pondering for a minute. In order to manifest the unmanifest chaos contained in each of us, to metamorphose it creatively, uniting the material world with the spiritual . . .

"I read something like that somewhere," Saveleva said, absentmindedly describing circles with her wrist while continuing to amuse herself with the straw.

But the times nowadays . . . the times are near overflowing . . . do you hear . . . an ocean of will could wipe out all the dams, turning the flow of thought into chaos . . . if only it's not too late . . . is it a panacea I've created or . . . do you hear me. . . ?

Gossamer strands, straws, vacuums, retorts . . . how simple . . . how very simple, there are no surprises left in the world . . . not because you've forgotten how to be surprised . . . look at the way you're swinging my straw around, destroying the experiment, just as people who haven't seen the light do. . . . You can be surprised from a distance, by words, but when you see it for yourself, you understand that's the way it's supposed to be. . . . Bonpo . . . What's really real, what's vital, is that there are four redheads sitting in front of you, three men and a girl, only not one of them is a man or a woman, they're just forms, and in the glass, it turns out, you can see that they're holding what looks to be a map of Moscow on their knees, and if Saveleva, E. P., were a bit younger (she sagged like a leather wine pouch) and lighter on her feet, she certainly would have flown off with them. Suddenly the girl lifts her head. Even in the shuddering glass, in the interweavings of merging cables, you can see how her hair shines, like a fiery helmet. Saveleva's afraid. Now one of the men raises his slanted green eyes. Saveleva's frightened. Then the rest tear themselves away from the map. But Saveleva has neither the strength nor the courage to face them. . . .

"I'll tell you frankly, I got fed up with all this a long time ago. . . . Maybe I ought to go someplace like Madagascar. Or visit the walruses in Alaska."

"Be a little more patient."

Patient? Sure, why shouldn't I be patient? . . . The sounds flowed, collecting under the ceiling. . . . All she did was be patient. Business as usual. The usual, I tell you, business. You, of course, will save us. But I don't buy it. She's patient because she doesn't want to get mixed up in causes. All her friends and acquaintances, too, keep as far as possible from causes and are patient. . . . And when somebody gets close to overstepping the mark, he gets told in no uncertain terms that he's either a fool or a provocateur. . . .

It happens sometimes that Saveleva, E. P., oversteps the mark. Out of stupidity. Like right now. What devil had got her by the tongue?

Never, moreover, on real issues. No, it would be one thing if it were . . . a conscious act. . . . Once Saveleva ripped the newspapers off a public display stand. The result: ten rubles and a whole hour wasted placating the militia officer. A whole bottle of cognac!

Another time, you see, her conscience got worked up at the local trade union committee. That time it was a bit more complicated. She spent a whole week trembling, but what were the consequences? You've shown your true colors more than once. Without so much as an explanation they refused to grant her a tour pass abroad, even to Bulgaria! . . . So her rightful turn at that family resort landed in someone else's pocket, so what else is new? At that point her daughter had just started clawing at the door after midnight. Two weeks of sea breezes would have allowed her and her husband to make up for the gaps in their daughter's upbringing. . . . What a joke. . . . Of course, they practically never saw the girl, working year-round, and with her at camp in the summer. Two weeks' vacation together in a different setting with the tension off might have brought them a bit closer, all three of them. . . . She really let the trade union committee have it! Though she knew damn well you couldn't squeeze those fat asses for anything. They'd get together for a little chat and go their separate ways. Still, there was some satisfaction to be had in seeing their faces swell up. The chairwoman had a diarrhea attack. Saveleva shouted so loud you could hear her all the way down the corridor. She was on a roll. She managed to weave into her story the entire overfed million-strong elite and something about the Chinese—how all the revolts in China had started with peasant uprisings but then the next peasant leader set up a new dynasty. . . . Are you suggesting an analogy? Do you have any idea what you're saying? . . . The hell

■

with analogies. The hell with you all! shouted Saveleva. How long do you think you can continue to make fools of us!

Well, it wasn't her best performance. . . . But it put a stick in their spokes. Her boss was a real sweetie. A brother by the bottle. Her boss was in his cups when he called her on the carpet, so he used the familiar form of address with her. . . . Listen, my dear, there's no need for me to prove to you that you're not a camel, you know the score, but you forget that you work in ideology! On the ideological front lines! Gradually raising his voice to a thunderous pitch, his fists clenched, he slowly and imposingly rose from behind his mammoth table, then, losing his balance, he keeled back and sank into his armchair. "Get out of here," he said, waving her off weakly. "Talking to you is like . . . And watch your tongue in your pieces! Everything gets back to me! Everything! Keep your opinions to yourself, if you're going to work at a job like this! Adieu!"

"Is it all right if I take off my boots?" Saveleva suddenly asked.

"You can take everything off."

Saveleva undid the zippers, moaned, and carefully extracted her swollen, battered feet. She stretched out her short, still outwardly strong legs, shiny from the elastic. She'd had a complex about her legs until someone convinced her that plumpness and a slight crookedness added a special charm, a wild hypersexuality. Long-legged women are cold. Still, she wasn't entirely rid of it. That sensation of having two halves: the most exquisite Chardinesque bust and the Tatar-Mongolian bottom half of a stone maiden. As if a magician had cut her in half and set her in a gaping cast-iron mold. If she keeps smoking at that rate, two packs a day, she'll be able to forget about her complex entirely. . . . There were times when by the end of the day Saveleva could barely crawl and would curse her high heels, but yesterday, she remembered, she'd had no trouble walking. . . . How strange that she had been so pure, so happy the night before. The snow swept away her tracks, and only gentle indentations, like shadows on the face of an aging woman, reminded her that she was surrounded not by a white desert or the shroud of the unmanifest chaos of inorganic matter, but by human habitation. On the way to the metro she didn't meet a single soul. . . . Or was it that she had finally been expelled from the ventilation pipe of passion and that's why it was so heavenly walking through the snow blanketing the earth, along the undisturbed path in the garden, seeing the unfrozen patches of water in the river, the foggy thickness that hid the city. . . . The snowy shroud was untouched. Angels—illuminated lampposts, if you looked closely—rose above the purity-dusted city, their wings of light dissolving into the starry sky. . . .

At dusk and at dawn E. P. Saveleva would see a rope extending from the heavens. From a fluffy cloud hung a long, long tether with a noose at the end. All you had to do was walk up and stick your head in. And up above they'd try to yank in such a way as to pull you neatly above the cloud. It was like the children's game of fisherman, in which a magnet on the end of a thread is used to catch fish.

Then there are the dreams she keeps having, in which she can barely, and with incredible difficulty, move her legs, while in her arms is a three-year-old child, her eternal burden, a boy who has to be saved, come what may. But in the end he betrays her, going over to the side of her tormentors. I'll draw you four pictures of Beria, shouts the boy, her eternal burden, in order to be saved. And he gets taken away. Saveleva also gets taken away, to the executioner's block, and then her numbed extremities are chopped off—wham! Saveleva's leg flies off the ax. Wham!—the other leg. She sees the stumps of her own steaming flesh. Flesh and blood. The executioner wipes the sweat from his brow. And always, you know, on Thursday nights . . .*

Before her eyes arose once again the picture of the nighttime metro. For the first time she began to have doubts about it, the redheads and all. . . . Perhaps she'd just had too much to drink and babbled whatever came into her head. What had she managed to concoct? A dozen men sleeping and dreaming of marrying her. Every last one of them wanting to screw her. The next morning the mistress of the apartment where they had been drinking announced to Saveleva that she couldn't feel anything, that what she had needed was spiritual contact. You think I felt anything? Absolutely nothing . . . my soul aches, it's begging, why can't you understand that? . . . That may be, but I also know perfectly well—Saveleva was indignant now—that in a month you'll swear to everyone that he was a total zero. . . .

Because of the hostess's soul, Saveleva spent the whole night running around the apartment, unable to fall asleep, her bare body wrapped only in a robe. The guy she'd been set up with, the worthless heap, had long ago crashed in the kitchen. At first they'd agreed to do it all together. They got rid of the extra guests. But then the hostess began to have doubts. Instead of offering any support, Saveleva's partner just yawned. The hostess began

---

*An old superstition holds that the dreams one has on Thursday nights come true.

to have more serious misgivings and refused. They broke up into pairs, one in the kitchen, the other in the main room. They drew lots. Saveleva and her partner got the mattress in the kitchen. Without giving it a second thought, he fell asleep. She grabbed a bottle and went wandering through the apartment. The hostess's john called her over. Saveleva, bottle in hand, arranged herself at their feet, and she and the john started working on the hostess so that the three of them could sleep together. The john had gotten a suntan someplace during the winter. He was a poet. All poets sleep with two women, one on each side. Leo Tolstoy slept with two Gypsy women. But the hostess wouldn't budge. She threatened to leave. She chased them out. She asked them to wait until morning. Wait for ten hours, and then do what you want. Why ten? That's absurd. . . . A quarantine. I'm asking you, I'm begging you, leave. . . .

The hostess had just been released from the hospital a few days before. She'd almost croaked right there in the hospital ward. Now she watched her john lovingly, never taking her eyes off him, just the way they do in operettas. Saveleva sat back down with her bottle on the edge of the couch. The john was all worked up and kept sticking his leg out onto the floor, and the sheet kept slipping off him. The hostess would cover him up securely, as if he were an infant who'd kicked off his blanket in the heat. The two of them in chorus attempted to convince the hostess not to be so egotistical. Not to let personal feelings get in the way. To forget about her own ego once and for all . . . Besides, he's an absolute zero as a personality, Saveleva argued, a jerk, a lousy little poet. I'm an absolute zero as a personality, the john echoed pleadingly. The main thing was, were they planning on abandoning her? No, of course not, they wouldn't do that. If she wasn't going to do it, they wouldn't. Without you we're not interested. . . . Of course, they could lock themselves in the bathroom, but afterward she would surely kick them out into the cold in the middle of the night. And besides, they were friends. That's the main thing. They couldn't possibly lay an insulting blow like that on a woman who'd just gotten out of the hospital. The john kept turning on and off, now rubbing the back of his neck on the pillow, now scooping the hostess up in an embrace and kissing her hard on the lips. With his free hand he simultaneously groped under Saveleva's robe. He did this as he stroked the hostess. Saveleva was horrified to find his hand everywhere, as if he were stroking her not with one but with three hands. He managed to get under her robe, grab her breast, and pinch her buttocks exactly as if he were a multiarmed Siva. Saveleva well remembers how she couldn't get hold of his hand. In the meantime the hostess kept shoving her away. Saveleva barely extracted herself from this orgy of extremities. In the end they had to make do with cognac and cigarettes. She and the john drank from the same side of the glass and smoked a single cigarette, and Saveleva withdrew. In the kitchen she found a half-bottle of vodka in the refrigerator, and stepping on her sleeping partner, she gulped it down without anything to eat.

It's possible that Saveleva had simply had too much to drink in an attempt to drown her sorrows and that was why she had imagined seeing those four redheaded aliens from the UFO, what people used to call angels. After all, drunks often see double. In point of fact the glass reflected not four, but two or maybe only one.

The staircase once again changed its shape. The climb became more difficult, the stairs narrow, slanting at the corner. You had to put your foot down sideways. Saveleva's legs were like weights and refused to mount the high duralumin steps. By the time she got to the top she had banged up her toes. Panting, she plopped herself down on the soft green floor. Saveleva, E. P., wiped her face, sighed deeply several times, and looked around. They were in the attic under the roof, but the roof was glass. Snow lay in a solid mass clearly visible through the glass. Snowflakes descended slowly from an open square just overhead. It was warm, dimly lit, and the thick layer of snow pressing against the glass made the space seem closed in. But it wasn't stuffy. On the contrary, Saveleva suddenly found she could breathe as easily and soundlessly as if she were in an alpine meadow.

"Have you figured it out? You're in a pyramid. Look!"

Saveleva remembered how she had barely crawled to the kitchen that morning. More precisely, at 3:00 A.M. They had stuck a glass in her hand. I like that Western way of life: You haven't even managed to wake up yet and you stick out your hand and there's a cognac . . . said the impoverished poet. Why can't you understand—we're in love, explained the hostess. Nevertheless the john, who sat across the table from Saveleva, was squeezing her knee between both of his as he polished off his hot dogs. He had an amazing appetite. The hostess kept flinging him food from the refrigerator. He fished olives out of a jar with his fingers. Sit around for a bit, don't go, coaxed the john. It's terrible, but it seems she loves me. Saveleva felt nauseated, the shuddering passed, but she still mapped out the shortest route to the bathroom in her mind. Which is it, the second door? Saveleva kept asking anxiously. Let's drink. Let's drink in a circle, like a peace pipe. Once again they loved each other. Friends. Saveleva even exchanged a tender word with her partner. Although he really wasn't up to it. He was trying to figure out what condition he was better off showing up at home in: Should he

get even more drunk or would that be doubly suspicious? They started argu-
ing about the origins of the Slavs . . . who were the Russians really, and did
any such nation even exist. . . . People always argue about origins the
morning after. As for Saveleva, she felt that her Tatar-Mongolian bottom
half was giving out. . . . As for the Byelorussians, now there's a pure
race. . . . Each praised his own. . . . Thank God there aren't any kikes
among us. . . . Or are there? . . . If I were a Jew and not a Byelorussian,
said the poet, a full-blooded Jew, such a show I'd put on for you now!

"Now . . . now, now . . ."

The green floor began to move beneath Saveleva. There was the heady
aroma of grass and damp earth. The grass rose in a springy, swelling wave
to its full rustling height. . . .

Parade of the planets, said the hostess's john, by the year 2000 all the
major planets will be lined up in a row. When the Sun and the Moon and
Tranquillity and Jupiter move together, then the white age of Satya will return. . . . Oh, my life, my ragged and difficult . . .

John Lennon, just murdered halfway around the globe, started singing
that old tune by the incomparable Beatles, the music of Saveleva's marble
university, cool vestibules, overheated classrooms, a song that evoked
simple happiness, the joys of family life around the hearth, of hard work, in a
voice that cracked slightly in the upper register, a song to which . . . well,
how could you help but love one another, when May and June and July were
fine, and the daisy field outside the window opened out beyond the concrete
wall to a world of birds, lions, antelopes, and monkeys, a heavenly design
created so that all might achieve harmony and beauty, gradations of an image expressed in matter and illuminated from within by the light of an idea
. . . everything about it inclined you to unity, to a common cause that filled
the air, to forget the individual, to meld egos, and to wallow in the nirvana of
love, of fresh river air and water, of a place where there was no need for
wine. . . .

Saveleva's legs suddenly weakened, she lost all sensation in them, then
they warmed up and seemed transparent. . . . The pyramid was flooded
with light, and the stranger, sitting under the slanted wall like Atlas under
the snowy weight cast upon his shoulders, slapped himself on the right
cheek and his coal-black left eye pierced right through her. . . .

Had the grass lifted Saveleva or had she floated up under her own power
on an invisible cushion of air? . . . Saveleva gave him a spirited wink.

Placing her feet wide apart and performing a series of frenzied body
movements that invited him to dance, Saveleva started to vibrate from the

powerful stream of energy running through her spine, then went into a sequence of stunning ballet steps, just as she had once done in her youth, across the thundering parquet boards, her hair sweeping along the floor, and her partner tossing her into the air and spinning her in a *salto*.

No, she would yet dance in this life! She'd still do a mean shake, twist, and Charleston, disco style. She'd turn on the heat, light up the lights.

Saveleva knew that a high like this required a lot of energy. The air around seemed to resound and vibrate with a muted roar. Saveleva did a wild shake, discharging the energy that streamed over her as if from a bottle of champagne. Brut! She was already starting to gag on the energy, but wanted more and more. . . . This was real, unadulterated delight. . . . What a high, came the voice of her daughter. Through transparent walls, trees, buildings she saw the little ragamuffin slouched against the dirty wall of an underground pedestrian crosswalk. The girl wanted to go inside the metro to warm up. But they wouldn't let her in. Saveleva's daughter had always despised her, as all drug addicts despise alcoholics. Alcoholics are crude, uncultivated creatures who don't understand or know how to achieve a pure high, her daughter thought. But still, when she wasn't on the needle and when there wasn't any money, vodka would do, and that was when the girl would turn into a dirty stinkpot, wandering from bar to bar. Interesting, what would she say if only for a moment she could taste the high Saveleva was experiencing right now!

Saveleva's body movements became more and more constrained, more labored. She fell into the tall, waving grass as if into a stack of hay and pulled the stranger in with her. The love vine began to wrap them in a cocoon, then blossomed in bright color, emitting an aroma as if from an atomizer. It blossomed, ripened, pollinated, grew heavy with fruit, withered, and sprouted anew. . . . Through the mound of grass, from beyond the glass of the pyramid, the redheads watched her. . . . The redheads watched her from beyond the glass of the metro. . . . The grass grew into her hair so that she couldn't lift her head, then it started to grow into her spine. They looked at each other in the glass like animals from separate cages, and maybe it was she who looked at them the way an animal in a cage at the zoo looks at visitors, volunteer protectors of flora and fauna, friends of nature, who have gotten it into their heads to destroy all the zoos and release the animals into the wild, into their natural habitat, and the beast, indifferent and lazy from too much food and too much sorrow, suddenly understands. . . .

Suddenly understands the desire, the call, the kinship.

But the cage . . . the steel bars. The locks.

■

Along the tree-spine with roots of hair slithered a lissome snake, whispering truths. Approaching the end, Saveleva decided that this truth was the most wonderful thing in the world. Beyond all doubt, it was the most wonderful thing in the world. Strange that in other moments of peace she forgot about this.

Oh, it's the most wonderful thing in the world!

But Elena Petrovna Saveleva never did find out why she was so happy that winter evening as she hummed a simple little song on the motionless steps of the escalator. Perhaps she had fallen asleep, otherwise where else could those three or four hours have gone?

1981; first published in 1990.

Translated from the Russian by Diane Nemec Ignashev

Sisyphus and the Woman

Vytautė Žilinskaitė

Afterward Sisyphus couldn't decide whether to curse or bless the moment when, wearily swinging his leaden, throbbing arms, his head empty of thoughts and his heart even emptier, he set off down the hill after the tumbling rock and suddenly felt a light tap, as if a passing insect had collided with his bare shoulder. Looking around, he spied a wild daisy on the well-worn path. A living flower in the realm of the dead? He bent down, picked it up, and twirled it in his fingers pensively. Unable to believe his eyes, he sniffed it, even licked it, and then he heard a strange sound: Someone was clearly trying to stifle a giggle. What was going on? Again he looked around, but not a living soul was to be seen. A mere trick by one of his guards? Yet he held on to the flower all the same. He splashed some water into a clay pot and, plunging the daisy into it, left it by the cave that he called home. Then he returned to his rock and began to push it uphill. As usual, when it was nearly at the top it struck against an invisible wall, tore out of his hands, and rumbled back down. And then something unexpected occurred for the second time: The sound of quiet weeping reached his ears.

"Who's there?" Sisyphus called out.

Nobody answered, but the weeping ceased. There was no time to seek out its source, but that would have been pointless anyway: Tears and teeth-gnashing abounded in the Kingdom of Hades. Sisyphus went back to his insurmountable task, but the next time the rock rolled downward, the crash-

.

333

ing that accompanied its fall was pierced by a loud sob. The sound was coming from behind the craggy ridge where flowed the dead waters of the river Styx.

"All right, who's there?" Sisyphus cried out in exasperation.

Suddenly, a woman appeared from behind the cliff. Her russet hair, caught up in a golden band, was gathered into a large, heavy knot at the nape of her neck. The folds of a diaphanous tunic rustled at her knees, her firm bosom heaved convulsively, and her cheeks and chin were wet with tears. Sisyphus couldn't remember when he had last seen a live woman, and he stood there as if struck by a thunderbolt.

"I know everything, down to the last detail," the newcomer chattered without a word of introduction. "I've been watching you for the longest time, and today I just couldn't hold back, my heart is breaking from the injustice of it all. It shouldn't be like this, it's not right! Crueler than cruel . . ." And again she began to sob.

"Where are you from? Who do you belong to?" asked Sisyphus, finally returning to his senses.

"I am Idona, Charon's granddaughter. You know the ferryman Charon? Tell me, tell me how I can help you! When I saw how lovingly you picked up the flower and hid it, I realized that your heart has not gone cold, like this hard stone—that it is yearning. . . . But wait!" she interrupted herself, straining to hear something. "They're already looking for me. Ciao, Sisyphus, we'll meet again soon!"

The soles of her light sandals flashed briefly, the folds of her tunic rustled, and she was gone. When Sisyphus again found himself alone with his rock, he had something to think about. He continued to see lips swollen with grief, his ears were filled with stifled sighs, his nostrils still caught the scent of lavender that emanated from Idona's hair. How tenderly, how compassionately she had looked upon his rough and calloused palms, all scratched by the rock! Idona . . . He could almost stretch out his hand to touch her shoulder. But no, better not to dream, better to put it right out of his head, otherwise he might start hoping for something and end up suffering. . . . No, no more hollow dreams!

But Sisyphus's whole being burned with impatience, despite his best intentions. For the first time he realized what it meant to drag and push his rock in expectation, to come down the hill in expectation, to go to bed . . . His neck began to hurt because his head was always turned toward the cliffs at the riverside, whence the flower had come, the flower that was now wilted but retained an acrid aroma. Idona . . . If she let down her luxuriant hair, it would envelop her body right down to her knees. . . . Sisyphus, mighty Sisyphus, you now know all too well what loneliness in the realm of the lonely is like, when there's no one beside you, only you and your heavy rock. But she had promised, saying, "Ciao, Sisyphus, we'll meet again soon!" For the accursed, expectations are a second curse. It would be better not to believe, not to hope, and simply say to hell with it all!

"Sis-y-phus!"

He was practically paralyzed: His hands dropped from the rock and fell limply to his sides. Idona was standing not far off, the golden band twining around her head like a ray of sun. Sisyphus was unable to greet her properly or even to smile at her. "You oaf!" he reproached himself as he followed the rock down the hill. Idona came to meet him. And when, without a word, he began to roll his rock up the hill, she didn't leave his side but climbed with him, laying her hand on the rock from time to time. How sweetly the bracelets jingled on her wrist! Sisyphus avidly stole glances at her slender pink fingers, her round, dimpled elbow, her plump little shoulder, her . . . Oh, my gods!

"You have nothing to say, you don't feel like talking? And to think I climbed over the cliffs to see you!" Idona let fall a mild reproof.

"Well, I, uh . . ." Sisyphus began to defend himself, but stammered to a halt in confusion. After so many centuries of solitude, he had lost the knack of expressing his thoughts aloud.

"I'm not good enough for you, then? Well, it's not surprising. After all, there are legends about you: You're a martyr, and of royal blood at that! You should have a goddess, or maybe a titaness, not the granddaughter of a poor ferryman. . . . And here was I, silly fool, climbing across the cliffs . . ." she said again, and turned away in a fit of pique.

"It's not true," said Sisyphus.

"Really?" Idona brightened and, gaily shouting "Evoe!" ran down the hill, outstripping the rolling boulder. Sisyphus, who was accustomed to descending slowly, nearly tumbled down head over heels after her. After galloping about the valley, Idona ran back to the rock and hugged it so tightly that when he started to push it up again, Sisyphus had to encircle her, too, with his arms.

"Why don't you smile for a change? Don't be such a sourpuss, come on, Sisyphus!" Suddenly she was serious. "Myself, I don't need anything, all I want is for things to be better for you. For you, understand? If only a little bit . . . The cup of sorrow shouldn't be bottomless, you know. As I watched you from behind the cliff, I thought I would die of grief."

"I heard you," replied Sisyphus, daring to look directly into her eyes for the first time.

Idona held out her arms, and they embraced. His rough hands, coarsened by the jagged edges of the huge rock, stroked her smooth feminine skin so cautiously they barely touched it: He was afraid he might hurt her with an inadvertent gesture.

"From here on in, everything is going to be different," she said, walking up the hill with him behind the rock. "From now on we'll always be together. Always!"

"But what about your grandfather Charon?"

"He's lost his head over a certain maenad," said Idona, laughing.

"And my guards?"

"I gave them a few obols," she reassured him. "Trust in the wiles of women, Sisyphus!"

"I'm afraid this will all turn out to be a dream," moaned Sisyphus, unable to believe the good fortune that had so suddenly befallen him. "Before, I had nothing to fear, but now I'll be living in eternal fear of losing you."

"What do you have to fear when my love is stronger than yours, when it was I who came to you first, approached you first? And what is this?" Feigning sternness, she poked a finger into the clay pot standing at the entrance to the cave.

"It's . . ." Sisyphus, as though caught at the scene of a crime, lost command of his tongue.

"I saw you, I saw how you picked up the flower I'd thrown down, how you looked at it and licked it—I bet you wanted to swallow it whole!"

Sisyphus smiled.

"Evoe!" Idona cried, clapping her hands. "This must be your first smile in Tartarus! And it was reserved for me, Idona! Sisyphus, it's driving me crazy, I love you so much it's choking me. . . . Oh, my master, at last you've smiled!" And she sank to her knees at his feet.

"Stand up, love—what are you doing?"

"Do my ears deceive me? Did you say 'love'? Who would have thought I'd hear that word in the kingdom of Hades?" Tears of amazement and joy spilled from her eyes.

Again he drank ambrosia from her lips, until the warning trumpet of the guard split the air.

"Grandfather must have missed me," said Idona, extricating herself from his embrace. "Ciao, Sisyphus, I'll be back again soon—but next time, for good!"

•

And she kept her word. Toward evening of the following day she appeared with her few belongings and settled into his cave.

"You know what your movements remind me of?" she whispered, winding her warm arms around him. "A tiger! Especially when you're coming down the hill—you're so powerful, implacable, forbidding. But you remind me even more of Hercules descending from Olympus. . . . From the first moment I saw that in you, I knew it was the Moirai themselves who had brought me to your hill, and that our fates would be entwined from then on." Laughing softly, she drew the golden band from her hair and tied it around his wrist.

The cave where only the deepest of silences had reigned for centuries was now filled with the sweetest of sounds. They intoxicated Sisyphus more thoroughly than a bottle of hundred-year-old wine.

"Do you know what drew me to you most of all? Your determination. Even though there's not the slightest hope you can drag the rock to the top of the hill, you throw yourself at it like a hungry beast at its prey, like a hawk at a chick. I have never seen anything more beautiful or more grand!" Idona laid her head on his chest and clung to him fiercely, as if afraid they might be parted. "My darling, I even love the smell of your sweat."

"O gods, if you dragged me down here so I could meet Idona, I forgive you everything!" He repeated the words to Idona, but she was already lost in sweet slumber.

She awoke at dawn with Sisyphus and accompanied him to the rock. Then she sat in the valley, humming and combing her long hair, and whenever Sisyphus arrived at the bottom of the hill, she ran up to embrace him. As time went on, however, Idona stayed more often in the cave, snoozing on soft animal skins.

"I hear the crashing of the rock less in here," she said defensively. "Loud noises disturb me."

Sisyphus, who had never paid much attention to the sound made by the rock, now anxiously held it back so that it rumbled less while rolling down. But Idona's antipathy to the rock continued to grow.

"It's the cause of all your troubles," she would whisper at night when, in bed, they would talk their fill after the long day. "If you could get rid of it, you'd be free of your curse, and then we could go away from here. You could take me to Corinth, and we'd live happier than the gods. You're sinking like a drowned man, with a rock around your neck: Tear it off and swim up to the surface, to freedom!"

"It's impossible," said Sisyphus, sighing.

"But I looked very carefully today, and you know what I saw? At the top of the hill, the rock comes up against an invisible wall. . . . There are only a couple more inches to go . . ."

"But . . ."

"I'm telling you, just have faith in my feminine wisdom, and we'll both be free! If you could do it—no, just listen!—if you could break through the wall and roll your rock right to the top, the curse of the gods would lose its hold over you forever."

"I've already tried many times, but . . ."

"But has it ever occurred to you to storm the unseen wall in the name of love?" She grinned guilefully in the darkness. "Confess!"

"No!"

"There, you see? Yet there are no obstacles, no boundaries, where love is concerned. Remember Orpheus and Eurydice! If miracles do exist, it can only be love that creates them. Someday, people will make our love into a legend, too."

"Oh, if only it were true!" Sisyphus sighed.

"It will be! You'll see, you'll conquer the heights. The most important thing is the final burst of energy," explained Idona in the darkness. "And now you have to build up your strength. Go to sleep!"

In the morning, Idona walked resolutely up the hill, stood at the very top, and fixed her burning eyes on Sisyphus. He strained like a buffalo preparing for a death-defying leap: The extraordinary exertion sent his bulging muscles rolling under his skin, and his eyes gleamed with passion and hope. He was off up the hill in a shot and put all his superhuman force into a final burst, the last step, exactly as planned. So powerful was the blow that a hundred-year-old oak wouldn't have withstood it—but the cursed wall knocked back the rock as if it were only a pea.

"I heard it crack—it actually cracked, I heard it with my own ears!" gaily cried Idona to Sisyphus, whose preternatural effort had knocked him to the ground. "It's all right, don't worry, you'll have a second shot at it, and a third. . . . Only, please, Sisyphus, put everything you've got into the final thrust—make the sparks fly!"

Sisyphus staggered downhill, took a deep breath, and gathered his strength in preparation for a second assault. He hit the wall so hard that sparks flew not only from the rock but from his eyes, too. Foam formed on his lips, his pores exuded not sweat, but hot steam, like a boiling kettle. But the heights remained unconquered. The same thing happened on the third and fourth tries. Idona returned sadly to the cave. When, at the end of the

working day, Sisyphus came in—or to put it more accurately, crawled in—
he found the woman in tears.

"I believed in you, I had so much faith in you," she wailed plaintively, and
when he tried to caress her, she curled up into a ball and growled in irritation, "Go to sleep, Sisyphus, you've had enough exertion for one day."

"O gods—let me be victorious, I beg of you." Sisyphus' prayer throbbed
against the dark vault of the cave. "Not for myself—when I was alone, I
never asked you for anything. For Idona—you see how she's suffering. And
why? She hasn't done anything wrong. Please, o gods—for the sake of our
love . . ."

In the morning Idona stayed behind, sitting at the entrance to the cave.
Her eyes no longer sparkled with yesterday's confidence: She slumped,
hunching her shoulders despondently. Sisyphus took one look at her pale,
sad little face, and such a powerful wave of love and strength rose up in him
that he knew there and then he would either smash through the wall or bash
his head into a million pieces. He became a steel battering ram before which
a wall was no longer a wall. Idona must have sensed the transformation, for
she stood up and joyfully exclaimed, "You're going to do it, Sisyphus!"

The whole place shuddered with the crash: Nearby cliffs crumbled, new
chasms gaped, and as he fell, Sisyphus just had time to think: It's done! He
wanted to shout, to cry, to see the miracle of his victory, but green bolts of
lightning were flashing before his eyes and his ears were ringing. His heart
was nearly jumping out of his chest—it had turned into a stone itself and
was rolling downward. . . . Yes, he clearly heard his heart thundering
downward. . . . Opening his eyes at last, he saw the rock back in its usual
place—in the middle of the valley. He didn't remember how he managed to
stand up and stagger down. Passing Idona, he kept his eyes on the ground
so as not to meet her disappointed gaze.

"I did all I could, and more," he whispered guiltily.

"More?!" She pounced on him. "So that's what your love is like—that's
how little it can do! A man who really loved a woman would either succeed or
fall down dead. But here you come shuffling in after losing the battle, and
still you have the nerve to brag! Don't you have any pride? And don't you
dare come near me!" She jumped aside when Sisyphus tried to stroke her
shoulder to calm her down. "Don't you dare touch me until you've proved
your love!"

He spent the night in the open air, and in the morning resumed his single
combat with the wall, but his former strength was lacking now. And every
time he came back down the hill, he met the glance of his beloved, full of

frustration and disappointment. He didn't know which was worse: pushing the stone up the hill for another fruitless encounter with the wall, or going back down to the valley to be met by Idona's contempt and disgust. She had stopped combing her hair and rubbing it with aromatic oils—it wasn't worth putting herself out, she said, for a man who was not to be a man at all. As disheveled as a Fury, she sat by the cave in a dirty tunic, her legs unbecomingly spread wide, thinking up "loving" phrases to bestow upon Sisyphus when he came back down the hill: "Wimp . . . Weakling . . . Nonentity . . . ."

"O gods, you led me to hope for the heavens from this woman's lips, and all I got was another hell in Hades!" groaned Sisyphus to himself—he didn't dare utter a peep or even wince in response to her poisonous gibes for, if given half a chance, she'd eat him alive! How carefree, almost happy, his recent solitude seemed to him now. How comfortable he had been with his rock, how pleasant the evenings when, wiping off the bitter sweat after a day's honest labors, he would go off to sleep the sleep of the righteous. No one reproached him for anything—on the contrary, he was almost on a par with the gods! Ah, those were golden days . . . not at all like his present, rotten life!

One night he mustered the courage to enter the cave.

"You said yourself that you loved me because of my fruitless task . . . that you yearned to share the burden of my curse with me . . . that you felt sorry for me. . . ."

But she was as cold and unyielding as the invisible wall.

"Yes, I was sorry for you, but now I'm sorry for myself! Have you given me the tiniest speck of consideration? You do your best to make sure I have nothing and never see anything but that cursed hill and my slave of a man—ha!"

"But what about our love?" Her body's proximity excited Sisyphus and he drew closer to the woman.

"Go away! You stink of sweat—slave's sweat!" Idona pushed him away disdainfully. "I told you once before: Don't come back until you've done it."

He crawled out of the cave like a dog that's been whipped. What a comedown—kicked out of his own allotted quarters!

In the morning Sisyphus began to roll the rock without the slightest enthusiam. Each of his movements exuded apathy and indifference.

"Just look at him—thinks he can thumb his nose at me!" Idona's shrill voice rang out. "The dirty dog! This is how he repays me for my sacrifices. . . . My life is ruined thanks to him, and there he stands, playing with a rock."

She grabbed the earthen pot and hurled it in a rage at the rock, which was then rolling by her. Clay shards rained everywhere, and the rock crushed the dried daisy, leaving it flat as a pancake.

"How unfair this is, o gods. You condemned me to drag one rock around, but now you've saddled me with two! I'll never ask for anything again if only you take back this witch."

Sisyphus gritted his teeth—what else could he do?—and resolved to be as silent as the earth, as a rock. His cheeks were sunken and his eyes gleamed sullenly from beneath his lowering brow, as from a black abyss. Nowadays he followed the rock without raising his eyes from the beaten path, and when he finished work he dug in like a lizard behind that same rock, stuffed his ears with strands of tow, and sat there quiet as a mouse. The woman's reproaches, demands, and threats reached him as from another world—from the other side of the Styx. It seemed that this arrangement had become permanent and would never change. But then he began to notice that the stream of insults and abuse was diminishing—sometimes in the valley there reigned a quiet that was noticeable even to stopped-up ears. Once, when this blessed silence lasted from morning till night, he couldn't resist the temptation to glance up from his rock and look quickly around. Idona was nowhere to be seen. Was she sick? He stole toward the cave, as timid as a scared rabbit, ready to recoil at any moment. Idona was not there either, but her things were, so she hadn't gone back to her grandfather. Where could she be? Overcome with curiosity, Sisyphus hurried to the pass where the road that ran through the valley led. Floundering in the sands, tearing his way through the thornbushes, he suddenly heard a familiar laugh. Shivers ran up and down his spine as he cautiously peeked out from behind a cliff. Beyond it lightly rippled the waves of a cove, in the middle of which sat Tantalus. The unfortunate sufferer first stretched his parched lips toward the water, then tried to reach the bunch of grapes hanging over his head, but the curse of the gods prevented him from tasting either of them.

"My poor dear," sweetly chirped Idona. "My heart is breaking from the injustice of it all. . . . Crueler than cruel . . ." She began to sob piteously.

Tantalus looked at the woman as if he'd been hypnotized: Had she been sent from Olympus to ease his sufferings? The powerful neck of the man condemned to eternal torment rotated his head in her direction, like a sunflower on its stem, and his muscular arms were already reaching for something other than the bunch of grapes. . . .

"Tell me, tell me how I can help you. . . . Your efforts, all in vain . . . your valiant determination . . . The Titans would have reason to envy you.

■

Wait, I'll just take off my sandals and come into the water. Soon we'll be together. . . ."

Sisyphus sighed deep down inside, as if a whole mountain had been lifted from his shoulders. "Tantalus, old pal"—he smiled in commiseration—"if only you knew, if only you could see what you're in for. You wouldn't be heading for the bank, but diving under as deep as you could!"

Coming home, he sprang across the bushes, whistling without a care in the world, and even struck up a gay little ditty for the first time since arriving in the kingdom of Hades. Let's leave him that way: singing, leaping, drunk on his freedom in bondage, and offering prayers of thanksgiving to the gods. Of course, just like the unfortunate Tantalus, he has no idea what's in store for him. He doesn't see that jealousy, desire, anger, longing, and emptiness will soon creep up on him. He doesn't know that he will curse the gods with all his might for having taken Idona from him, that he will beg them on bended knee to bring her back—no matter how malicious, insulting, and scornful, just as long as she's back, back by his side again!

That's why we'll leave him in mid-leap, skipping like a little boy toward his rock. It will be better that way for him, for us, and for the gods, who don't like it one little bit when someone guesses their intentions.

1983

Translated from the Russian by Debra Irving

Biographical Notes

ZOYA BOGUSLAVSKAYA was born in Moscow. Her father was a university professor and her mother a doctor. She graduated from the State Institute of Dramatic Art and went on to receive a graduate degree in history of art from the Academy of Sciences of the U.S.S.R. A member of the Soviet Writers Union since 1961, she began her career as a film, theater, and literary critic, turning to fiction in 1975. Since her first short story, ". . . and Tomorrow," appeared in the literary journal *Znamya,* she has published novellas (including "700 Rubles in New Currency," "In Transit," and "The Race"), novels (*The Defense, Close Connections*), plays (*Contact, The Promise*), and essays (such as "Brigitte Bardot in Her Own Eyes and in the Eyes of the Mass Media," "Collage of Paris," and "Nathalie Sarraute: Years Later"). Two collections of her works have been published, *Bus Stop* and *Close Connections.*

When her essay, "What Are Women Made Of?" appeared in the weekly newspaper *Literaturnaya gazeta* in 1987, its candid appraisal of the position of women in contemporary Soviet society caused quite a stir. Her most recent book is *Women in the Modern World* (1989), published by Progress Publishers.

Boguslavskaya heads the Soviet Writers Union's Council of Women Writers on International Contacts. She is married to the distinguished poet Andrei Voznesensky and has one son, a computer analyst.

Born into a physician's family in St. Petersburg in 1909, NATALIA BARANSKAYA studied literature but never intended to become a writer. For many years she worked in the Pushkin Memorial Museum in Moscow, mounting its first exhibition and eventually becoming its assistant director. She retired in 1964 after the birth of her grandson and only then began to write. Her first stories were published in the prestigious literary journal *Novy mir* in 1968. When her novella "A Week Like Any Other" appeared in the same journal the following year, it drew the censure of contemporary critics and closed the doors of Moscow publishing houses to her for a time.

Baranskaya began to publish her works in other parts of the Soviet Union. Her remarkable novella "The Color of Dark Honey" about Natalia Pushkin's first year as a widow appeared in an anthology entitled *Siberia*. Then *Portrait Given to a Friend,* a collection of literary works devoted to Pushkin, was published in Leningrad. The first collection of her works, *Negative Giselle,* was published by Molodaya Gvardia, and *The Woman with the Umbrella,* a collection of short stories and novellas, was published by Sovremennik in 1981.

In her writing Baranskaya addresses issues that are understandable and close to everyone, such as the plight of women, postwar loneliness, fidelity, and relationships among various generations within a family. Her works have been translated into twelve European languages and she is best known to American readers for her novella "A Week Like Any Other."

LIDIA GINZBURG: "I was born in Odessa in 1902. In 1922 I moved to Leningrad, where I studied at the State Institute of Art History. My teachers were the remarkable literary theorists Boris Eikhenbaum, Yuri Tynyanov, Boris Tomashevsky, and Viktor Zhirmunsky. Their influence determined my choice of profession.

"As a literary historian, I have published studies of Pushkin, Lermontov, Tolstoy, Herzen, Blok, Mandelstam, and a number of other nineteenth- and twentieth-century Russian writers. The books I wrote during the 1960s and 1970s—on lyric poetry, psychological prose, the hero in literature—deal primarily with issues of a theoretical nature.

"In addition to literary studies, I have written essays, memoirs, and narrative prose throughout my life, but I began publishing them only in the 1970s. These writings appear in my two most recent books, *About the Old and the New* (1982) and *Literature in Search of Reality* (1987).

"During the war and the siege I never left Leningrad, where I worked in the literature section of the Leningrad Radio Committee. In the spring of 1942, when life under siege conditions eased slightly, I began to gather material for a future book that was as yet unclear even to me; I recorded impressions, facts, conversations, and various traits of human behavior. Only twenty years later, at the beginning of the 1960s, did I assemble these preliminary notes into a documentary novella with a composite, fictional hero. It was first published in the journal *Neva* and later appeared in *Literature in Search of Reality*. Excerpts from this novella appear in this collection." EDITOR'S NOTE: Lidia Ginzburg died in 1990.

INNA GOFF: "I was born in 1928 in Kharkov, the Ukraine. My mother was a French teacher and my father a doctor. I wasn't a literary child, although I began to write stories at a very early age. I know this from an entry in my mother's diary. No one in my family foresaw that I would become a writer. And during my school years, although I continued to write, I would always get angry when my classmates and teachers predicted a future as a writer for me. Writers, it seemed to me then, only described other people's exciting lives. I dreamed of becoming so many things—a sea captain, an astronomer, a film director—anything but a writer.

"In our home books were loved, but we didn't collect them or store them away in bookcases. Books lived with us and lay about everywhere. My first impressions of childhood are associated with the Ukraine. The war, which took away my native land, gave me my second homeland—Siberia. In the city of Tomsk, while I was still in high school, I worked as an aide at a military hospital and then in a factory. Writing about these experiences was the only way I knew to preserve them, to claim what had been lost. And so I wrote, without giving a thought to becoming a professional writer.

"I entered the A. M. Gorky Literary Institute in Moscow on the basis of my poetry, but then I began to write prose. At first I wrote novellas, but later became intrigued by the genre of the short story. Eventually, however, the parameters of the short story began to seem too confining, and so the 'short story/essay' as well as the 'short story/investigation' developed. The main topic of my 'investigations' was the element of the unknown in the relationship between Chekhov and the writer Lidia Alekseyevna Avilova.

"In my stories I write about faithfulness to the ideals of one's youth, about love, about the complexity of human relationships, the feeling of responsibility to oneself and one's era.

"Readers in the Soviet Union are quite familiar with my books: *I am the Taiga, Heartbeat, Later You May Not Be Here . . . , Northern Dream, The Telephone Rings at Night, Don't Trust Mirrors, Singers at the Table, A Youth with a Glove,* and *The Transformation.* A good number of them have been translated into many languages."

I. GREKOVA is the pseudonym of Elena Sergeyevna Ventsel. She was born in 1907 and is both a writer and a professor of applied mathematics. She received her doctorate in the technical sciences in 1954 and is the author of a number of books on the theory of probability, game theory, and operations research. Her fiction includes the novellas "Ladies Hairdresser" (1964), "On Probation" (1967), "The Hotel Manager" (1976), "The Faculty" (1978), "Widow's Ship" (1981), "The Pheasant" (1985), "No Smiles" (1986), and "Turning Point" (1987); a book of poems for young children, *Seryozhka at the Window* (1976); a novella for preschoolers, "Anya and Manya" (1978); and the novel *Rapids*.

NATALIA ILINA: "I was born in Petersburg in 1914, not far from the famed Tauride Garden. In 1918 my father took me to the Far East (at that time we were living on my grandmother's estate near Saratov). In 1920 we found ourselves in Harbin, China, where I attended the American School for Russian Emigrés. After graduating in 1936 I left for Shanghai and immediately took a job as a satirist for a newspaper (simply to keep from starving), never suspecting that I had any talent for this line of work. I was twenty-two years old. Three years later I changed my profession and even became a shareholder in an advertisement circular.

"In 1948 I returned to my homeland and worked in Kazan for a year before enrolling in the Literary Institute. I've written a novel, *The Return* (1957–65), and two volumes of reminiscences, *Human Fates: From Past Meetings* (1980) and *Roads* (1983). In my autobiographical prose I've written about Anna Akhmatova, Kornei Chukovsky, Alexander Vertinsky, the linguist Alexander Reformatsky (my husband), Yuri Trifonov, and others. I've never stopped writing satirical pieces; my collections of these works include *Careful: Danger!* (1960), *No Ovations Necessary* (1964), *Something's Not Right Here* (1963), and *Shining Tableaux* (1974). I've also worked as a translator.

"A new chapter of my autobiography was recently published in the literary journal *Oktyabr*. I want to return to satire, but, then again, I've never abandoned it."

NINA KATERLI was born in Leningrad in 1934 and lives there to this day. She graduated from the Lensoviet Technological Institute and worked as an engineer. Her first story was published in 1973 in the journal *Kostyor*. She is the author of four collections of stories, including *The Window* (1981) and *Colored Postcards* (1986). Her works have been translated into German, Bulgarian, Hungarian, Polish, English, and other languages.

GALINA KORNILOVA was born in Moscow in 1928 into a family of physicians. She graduated from the Pedagogical Institute and went to work at the journal *Kultura i Zhizn*, then at the newspaper *Literaturnaya gazeta*, where she contributed essays and short stories. After that she worked for the journal *Oktyabr* and, from the end of the 1960s to the beginning of the 1980s, she headed the poetry division of the journal *Znamya*.

The collections of her works include *Big Houses* (1966), *Walks at Midnight* (1970), *Music in Skatertny Lane* (1980), *In the Direction of the Sadovoye Ring* (1986), and *Childhood Friends* (1987).

Kornilova is a doctoral candidate in philology and specializes in the literature of the French Resistance. She is also a permanent contributing editor to the journal *Oktyabr*.

TATYANA NABATNIKOVA: "I was born in the Altai Mountains and lived there until I was eighteen. I graduated from the Electrotechnical Institute in Novosibirsk and was a bicycle racer during my student years. For seven years I worked as a building engineer, while completing a correspondence course in literature from the Gorky Literary Institute in Moscow. Then I worked as an editor for a book publisher for two years and ever since I have been writing professionally. Three collections of my works have been published (in 1982, 1984, and 1987). Nineteen eighty-seven turned out to be a bumper-crop year for me. My novel *Every Hunter* was serialized in three issues of the journal *Sibirskie ogni,* and three stories appeared in the journals *Yunost* and *Ural* and the weekly newspaper *Literaturnaya Rossiya.* The critics had noticed me before, but that year they began to take me seriously. To my mind, it is because of the method I use, a method that has proved productive. It is based on energetics: I build my works on an alternation of energetic thickenings and thinnings, as a result of which something akin to music takes shape, music that works independently of the meaning, along with the meaning, and in addition to it—just as songs have both words and melody. But it is not the rhythm, not the meter of a line (rhythm and meter—style—are important to me of their own accord); rather, it is precisely the energetics of word and phrase: their speed, intensity, tension. Those who are affected by this hidden "music" like my work (although they don't understand why). Those who aren't affected by it find my work irritating. There being a good number of the former and the latter, I consider myself a lucky author.

"I now live in Chelyabinsk, a city of metallurgists in the Ural Mountains, with my two daughters."

LYUDMILA PETRUSHEVSKAYA: "I was born in Moscow in 1938, a child of war, destruction, and arrests. My generation witnessed a lot: hunger, cold, life without light and warm clothing. The children's home was our salvation.

"Then normal life began, if you can call a mattress on the floor normal life—one mattress for my mother and me. Then came rehabilitation; we were given a room, I graduated from Moscow University, worked as a radio reporter and a television editor, and gave birth to three children.

"I began writing late, when I was around thirty years old and all of my literarily talented peers were already well-known authors. My first two short stories were published in 1972. By the end of 1986 a total of seven of my stories had appeared in print, but during the first six months of 1987 alone, another seven were published (the result of *perestroika*).

"Not all of my plays have yet been staged, nor all of my stories published, so there is much to look forward to in the future.

"Some of my stories have been published and some of my plays have been staged in Sweden, Finland, Switzerland, the United States, Eastern Europe, and other countries. My major publications include the stories 'Clarissa's Story,' 'The Storyteller' (1972), 'The Violin' (1973), 'Nets and Traps' (1974), 'The Thunderclap,' 'A Nice Woman,' 'Youth,' 'Elegy,' 'Uncle Grisha,' 'Dark Fate,' and 'Weak Bones' (1987) and the plays *Love* (1975), *Cinzano, Smirnova's Birthday* (1977), *A Suitcase of Nonsense* (1978), *Music Lessons* (1979), *Moscow Chorus, Two Windows, Glass of Water, The Staircase* (1974), *Golden Goddess, Andante, Columbine's Apartment* (1981), and *Three Girls in Blue* (1980).

■

"I coauthored the script of the animated film *Fairy Tale of Fairy Tales,* directed by Yuri Norstein. The film won nine international awards, including the Association of Film Critics award, the prize for the best animated film 'of all times and nations' (Los Angeles, 1980), and the Grand Prix in Lille."

IRINA POLYANSKAYA was born in the Ural Mountains in 1952. She graduated from the drama department of the Academy of Arts in Rostov-on-the-Don and from the Gorky Literary Institute in Moscow. Her stories have appeared in the literary journal *Avrora.*

MARI SAAT, an Estonian writer, was born in Tallinn in 1947 into a scholar's family. She graduated from the economics department of the Tallinn Polytechnical Institute and went on to receive a candidate's degree (equivalent of a doctorate in the United States) in economics. She works in the Economics Institute of the Academy of Sciences of the Estonian Republic.

Saat made her literary debut with the story "Catastrophe" (1973), which was awarded the prestigious Tuglas prize the following year. A collection of stories, *Rhododendron Buds,* was published in 1975; the novella "What to Do with Mother," in 1978; a novel, *The Hazel Grouse,* in 1980; and a collection, *The Apple in Light and Shadow,* in 1985. In her works she deals primarily with the moral issues and searchings of today's youth, students, and the young scientific community. She was awarded the title Laureate of the All-Union Literary Competition of the Communist Party of the Soviet Union, the Komsomol, and the State Committee for Publishing for the best first book by a young author.

VIKTORIA TOKAREVA, an author of short stories and screenplays, was born in 1937 in Leningrad and graduated from the All-Union State Institute of Cinematography in 1967. She began her literary career in 1964. Her first book of short stories, *About What Wasn't,* was published in 1969. The heroes of her works are our contemporaries—the most ordinary sorts of people. But for all their ordinariness, they are drawn so vividly that they seem unique and inimitable. Gentle humor pervades Tokareva's writing and imparts a singular coloring to the funny, and at times sad, circumstances in which her characters find themselves.

Her collections of short stories and novellas include *When It Turned a Little Warmer* (1972), *Flying Swings* (1978), and *Nothing Special* (1983). Among her screenplays, some of the most notable are *Gentlemen of Success, Literature Lessons, Mimino, The Dog Walked across the Piano, Between Heaven and Earth,* and *The Hat.* Many of her works have been translated into other languages both within the Soviet Union and abroad.

TATYANA TOLSTAYA was born in Leningrad in 1951. She graduated from Leningrad State University with a degree in philology. In 1974 she moved to Moscow and worked for a time as an editor in the Eastern literature division of the publishing house Nauka. Her first short story, "On the Golden Porch," was published in the journal *Avrora* in 1983. Her first collection of stories, also entitled *On the Golden Porch,* was published in 1987. It has been translated into many languages all over the world, including Greek, English, Bulgarian, and Italian, and has been received with great critical acclaim.

Tatyana Tolstaya descends from a long line of writers. As she once explained in an interview, "My grandfather on my father's side was Aleksei Nikolayevich Tolstoy. My grandmother was Natalia Vasilievna Krandievskaya-Tolstaya, a poetess. Their mothers were also writers. My grandfather on my mother's side was Mikhail Leonidovich Lozinsky, the translator of the *Divine Comedy.* Only my father was a physicist. When he was applying for entrance into the physics department, he forgot to put commas in his essay, so he placed a whole string of them at the end as a protest against literary subtleties: Put them where you wish. . . ."

LARISA VANEEVA: "I was born in Siberia in 1953 into a family of teachers. Raised during the ongoing debate 'between physicists and lyricists,' I was given a decidedly humanities-oriented upbringing. I first tested my writing skills as a journalist; right out of school I was asked to join the staff of a youth newspaper in Novosibirsk. But the age-old conflict—to write not what is, but as you're told—turned me away from a career in journalism.

"Creative freedom, which was still possible to find in the Literary Institute, where I studied with Yuri Trifonov and Alexander Rekemchuk, met with iron-clad resistance from publishing houses. Of all that I had written, only one 'harmless' short story, 'Two and One More' (1980), was published by a western Siberian publisher. Literary life, however, went on beyond the printed page: There were readings in friends' apartments, serious discussions, the circulations of typewritten manuscripts.

"But times change, and the story presented in this collection, 'Parade of the Planets,' is one of the stories included in my book *Out of the Cube,* which was published by Sovetsky Pisatel in 1990."

VYTAUTĖ ŽILINSKAITĖ was born into a railwayman's family in Kaunas, Lithuania, in 1930. Since 1940 she has lived in Vilnius. She graduated from Vilnius State University with a degree in journalism and worked for a number of years as an editor for a youth magazine.

Žilinskaitė writes in a variety of genres. Her first book was a collection of poetry (1961). Then there were children's books—tales and stories—and a nonfiction work about an underground youth organization that was active in Lithuania during World War II. But it is satire and humor that predominate in her work. Several collections of her humorous sketches, satirical pieces, and parodies have been published in Lithuanian and some have been translated into Russian, including *An Angel over the City,*

Paradoxes, Variations on a Theme, and *My Poor Neuron.* Her humorous works have also been translated into German, Polish, and Slovak.

Žilinskaitė's work is enormously popular in Lithuania and throughout the Soviet Union. Her humorous pieces are often heard on Soviet radio. She was awarded the State Prize of the Lithuanian Republic twice (1972, 1979) and has received many other literary prizes from such organizations as the Lithuanian Journalists Union, the magazine *Krokodil,* and the weekly newspaper *Literaturnaya gazeta.*

FIRST PUBLICATION
INFORMATION

All stories published after 1973 have been copyrighted in the original language in the Soviet Union.

Zoya Boguslavskaya, "Kakie my, zhenshchiny?" *Literaturnaya gazeta,* 8 August 1987.

Lidia Ginzburg, "Zapiski blokadnogo cheloveka" (excerpts), in *Literatura v poiskakh real'nosti* (Leningrad: Sovetskii Pisatel', 1987).

Tatyana Tolstaya, "Somnambula v tumane," *Novy mir,* No. 7, 1988.

I. Grekova, "Khozyaeva zhizni," *Oktyabr',* No. 9, 1988.

Nina Katerli, "Chudovishche," in *Tsvetnye otkrytki* (Leningrad: Sovetskii Pisatel', 1987).

Tatyana Nabatnikova, "Na pamyat'," in *Domashnee vospitanie* (Moscow: Sovremennik, 1984).

Galina Kornilova, "Ostrabramskie vorota," in *Druz'ya i podrugi* (Moscow: Sovetskii Pisatel', 1987).

Natalia Ilina, "My remontiruem avtomobil'," in *Svetyashchiesya tablo* (Moscow: Sovetskii Pisatel', 1974).

Viktoria Tokareva, "Pyat' figur na postamente," *Oktyabr',* No. 9, 1987.

Natalia Baranskaya, "Dom Laine," in *Zhenshchina s zontikom* (Moscow: Sovetskii Pisatel', 1981).

Mari Saat, "Koobas," *Looming,* No. 9, 1972.

Irina Polyanskaya, "Predlagaemye obstoyatel'stva," *Literaturnaya ucheba,* No. 2, 1984.

Lyudmila Petrushevskaya, "Smotrovaya ploshchadka," *Druzhba narodov,* No. 1, 1982.

Inna Goff, "Medpunkt na vokzale," *Novy mir,* No. 7, 1977.

Larisa Vaneeva, "Parad planet," in *Iz kuba* (Moscow: Sovetskii Pisatel', 1990).

Vytautė Žilinskaitė, "Sizif i zhenshchina," translated into Russian from the Lithuanian, in *Variatsii na temu* (Moscow: Sovetskii Pisatel', 1983).

■